Modern Hindu Personalism

Modern Hindu Personalism

The History, Life, and Thought of Bhaktisiddhānta Sarasvatī

FERDINANDO SARDELLA

OXFORD
UNIVERSITY PRESS

OXFORD
UNIVERSITY PRESS

Oxford University Press is a department of the University of Oxford.
It furthers the University's objective of excellence in research, scholarship,
and education by publishing worldwide.

Oxford New York
Auckland Cape Town Dar es Salaam Hong Kong Karachi
Kuala Lumpur Madrid Melbourne Mexico City Nairobi
New Delhi Shanghai Taipei Toronto

With offices in
Argentina Austria Brazil Chile Czech Republic France Greece
Guatemala Hungary Italy Japan Poland Portugal Singapore
South Korea Switzerland Thailand Turkey Ukraine Vietnam

Oxford is a registered trademark of Oxford University Press
in the UK and certain other countries.

Published in the United States of America by
Oxford University Press
198 Madison Avenue, New York, NY 10016

Library of Congress Cataloging-in-Publication Data
Sardella, Ferdinando.
Modern Hindu personalism : the history, life, and thought of Bhaktisiddhanta Sarasvati /
Ferdinando Sardella.
p. cm.
Includes bibliographical references and index.
ISBN 978-0-19-986590-1 (pbk.: alk. paper) — ISBN 978-0-19-986591-8 (alk. paper)
1. Bhakti Siddhanta Saraswati, 1874–1936. I. Title.
BL1175.B437S375 2013
294.5′512092—dc23
[B]
2012018344

ISBN 978-0-19-986590-1
ISBN 978-0-19-986591-8

1 3 5 7 9 8 6 4 2
Printed in the United States of America
on acid-free paper

For all seekers of a more personal world

Contents

Foreword

THE PERIOD IN which the subject of this important work, the Bengali Bimal Prasad Datta (1874–1937), later known as Bhaktisiddhānta Sarasvatī, was active both in India and also in Europe, was of seminal importance for Indian and global history. In India, the stage was set for a modernist reconstruction of what we tend to call Hinduism; in Europe, the prospect of a particularly dark and destructive conflict was looming. Many key figures of Indian and European history had become or were about to become active, and their influence was to have global consequences in one way or another in due course. One such figure was Bhaktisiddhānta Sarasvatī.

In the Indian context, his name does not tend to ring bells, as the name of Bankim Chatterji or Gandhi would. Yet Bhaktisiddhānta played a vital role through his work in articulating the theology and role of a movement that was to have a palpable and familiar impact on the Western stage. Toward the end of chapter 5, Dr. Sardella describes it as follows: "Some thirty years [after Bhaktisiddhānta passed away] a watershed event would propel his movement to surprising heights and rapidly spread his perspective on the teachings of Caitanya throughout the world.... On August 13, 1965, one of Bhaktisiddhānta's disciples, A. C. Bhaktivedānta Swami (1896–1977), set out by steamship for New York City to fulfill Bhaktisiddhānta's instruction to carry 'the message of Caitanya' to the English-speaking world." Thus was born the Hare Krishna movement, which continues to exert its leavening spiritual effect on our consumerist Western societies.

Dr. Sardella's work illuminatingly reveals the intellectual and spiritual background of this movement, hitherto almost lost to the dim recesses of history, but in the process he also casts welcome light on a range of topics for the reader interested in the social, religious, and political climate of nineteenth- and early twentieth-century Bengal: issues concerning cultural hybridity between India and the West, the hegemony of nondualist theology among the Bengali elite of the time (to which Dr. Sardella opposes the personal monotheism of Bhaktisiddānta), the possibility of affirming a universalist dimension to Gauḍīya Vaishnava bhakti, or religious devotionalism, in the face of caste in India and non-Hindu culture in Europe, and somewhat more controversially among other matters, the need (or otherwise) for a religious leader to be involved in topical political concerns. There is also a discussion about the visit of some of Bhaktisiddānta's disciples to Britain and Nazi Germany, and an analysis of how Bhaktisiddhānta's Gauḍīya thinking was opposed to Nazi ideology.

There is a great deal the thoughtful reader can gain from this carefully researched book, not only with respect to the considerable legacy of Bhaktisiddhānta's own thought and life, but also in connection with the formative concerns of the age. We are indebted indeed to Dr. Sardella for a landmark work.

Julius Lipner
Fellow of the British Academy
Professor of Hinduism and the Comparative Study of Religion
University of Cambridge
November 2011

Acknowledgments

I MUST FIRST thank Åke Sander at the University of Gothenburg's Department of Literature, History of Ideas and Religion for his extensive and thoughtful comments. Then there are William Deadwyler (Ravindra Svarūpa dāsa), who, during an informal conversation in India, suggested that I make Bhaktisiddhānta's life and thought a major theme of my research, and Graham Schweig, who helped throughout this long and at times tortuous venture with his acute advice.

At the University of Oxford, where I conducted part of my research, there are Shaunaka Rishi Das, Polly O'Hanlon, Judith Brown, and Elizabeth De Michelis, all of whom gave many valuable suggestions, specifically with regard to modern Hinduism and the social and cultural history of India, as well as Gavin Flood, who offered his profound knowledge of Indic religions and phenomenology. Imra Banga at the Faculty of Oriental Studies reviewed and discussed my Bengali translations, as did Sanjukta Gupta Gombrich, who also shared her vast knowledge of late-colonial Bengal. This book is a contribution to the research project "Bengali Vaishnavism in the Modern Period," based at the Oxford Centre for Hindu Studies.

Among those who gave me access to unpublished writings about the Gaudiya Math and Vaishnavism in Bengal I would like to thank Måns Broo at the Åbo Akademi University, Finn Madsen at the University of Copenhagen, and the late Joseph O'Connell at the University of Toronto. There is also Kid Samuelsson, who provided access to the writings of Ernst Georg Schulze, one of the few Western disciples of Bhaktisiddhānta.

In West Bengal and Kolkata a number of persons provided invaluable assistance, ideas, and access to materials. Among them are Ramakanta Chakravarti, who at the time was the Asiatic Society's general secretary, Gautama Bhadra at the Center for Studies in Social Sciences, Swapna

Bhattacharyya at the University of Calcutta, and above all Ruby Sain at the Department of Sociology at Jadavpur University, Hena Basu and Bharati Roy. Then there is Swami Yati Bhakti Prajñāta, the head of Mayapur's Śrī Caitanya Math, Bhakti Sundar Sanyasi Maharaj of the Gaudiya Mission in Kolkata, and Nitāi dāsa Roy, who provided me with a firsthand account of Bhaktisiddhānta's life. I must also especially mention Swami Bhakti Bibudha Bodhayan of the Gopinātha Gaudiya Math, who gave me access to his extensive library in Mayapur. Then there is the Ramakrishna Institute of Culture in Kolkata, which also allowed me the use of its general Indic library.

Among the members of the International Society for Krishna Consciousness (ISKCON) who either directly or indirectly contributed to this work, special mention should be made of Jayapatāka Swami and Rādhānāth Swami. Bhakti Vikāsa Swami and Chaitanyacaran Das took the time to comment on the entire manuscript.

I must also extend a note of thanks to Abhishek Ghosh at the University of Chicago, a close friend, research assistent, and colleague who provided me with valuable academic discourse regarding my subject. It was his family who provided me with lodging, direction, and warm conversation during my various research trips to India.

There are a number of libraries that were essential to my research, and I would like to mention them here in thanks for their cooperation: the Central Library at Gothenburg University, the Bodleian and Indian Institute Library in Oxford, the South Asian Library in Cambridge, the British Library in London, and, in Kolkata, the National Library, the Caitanya Institute, the Asiatic Society, and the Bhaktivedanta Research Centre. In terms of the funding for this work, the following institutions and foundations provided needed moneys: the Adlerbertska foundations at the University of Gothenburg, the Knut and Wallenberg Foundation, the Paul and Marie Berghaus Foundation, and the Royal Society of Arts and Sciences in Gothenburg. There was also a grant from STINT (Swedish Foundation for International Cooperation in Research and Higher Education) that allowed me to spend four fruitful months at the University of Oxford and one from the Swedish Research Council that contributed to the final stages of this work.

Måns Broo, Rahul Peter Das, Thibaut d'Hubert, Gavin Flood, Hans Harder, Brian Hatcher, Folke Josephson, Julius Lipner, Tony Stewart, and the late William Smith and Joseph O'Connell made invaluable comments on various chapters of this work, and in some cases on the work as a whole;

I thank them for their efforts in this regard. Cecilia Wejryd, Eva Hellman, Mattias Gardell, and my colleagues at the Faculty of Theology at Uppsala University provided the best possible environment for the completion of this work. Cynthia Read, Sasha Grossman, and others were of excellent assistance during the production of this book at Oxford University Press.

Finally, I wish to extend my thanks to English editor Allan Anderson, whose close involvement in helping to structure, present, and articulate the material, and whose editing of the text, have contributed to the final development of this work. His suggestions and precision of thought have helped to make this a more coherent, rich, and eloquent book. It has been a great pleasure as well as a learning experience to work with him.

On a more personal note, I want to extend a heartfelt thanks to my wife Katja for her spiritual and marital devotion. Her loving support has given me the required stability and strength to see this project through to the end, despite its many challenges and demands. She and my son Robin also patiently tolerated long periods of absence during my stays in India.

Without the contributions and support of all involved parties, this book would never have been written. This notwithstanding, I take full responsibility for any and all faults that may be found herein.

Uppsala, June 2012

Phonetic Guide

A BRIEF GUIDELINE for Sanskrit words:

Vowel pronunciation approximates Italian—that is, short **a** is pronounced like the **u** in b**u**t, long **ā** is pronounced like **a** in f**a**r (and held twice as long as the short **a**), **e** is pronounced like the **a** in ev**a**de, and long **ī** is pronounced like the **i** in p**i**que. The vowel **ṛ** is pronounced like the **ri** in Krishna, and **c** is pronounced like the **ch** in **ch**air. The consonants **ch**, **jh**, and **dh** are pronounced like staun**ch-h**eart, hed**ge-h**og and re**d-h**ot, and the palatal **ś** is pronounced like **sh**ine, with the tip of the tongue pressed against the inside of the upper teeth. The retroflex **ṣ** and the retroflex consonants **ṭ**, **ṭh**, **ḍ**, **ḍh**, **ṇ** are pronounced with the tip of the tongue turned up and drawn back against the dome of the palate. The *anusvāra* (**ṃ**) is a nasal sound, pronounced like the French word bo**n**. The visarga (**ḥ**) is a strong aspirate. The pronunciation of the remaining consonants approximates English.

The Bengali pronunciation of Sanskrit and Bengali script is somewhat different; a brief guideline is as follows: short **a** is pronounced like an open **o**, **ai** is pronounced like the **oy** in b**oy**, and the final **a** is most often silent. The **v** is pronounced like **b**. The sibilants **s**, **ś**, and **ṣ** are all pronounced like **sh**ine.

Modern Hindu Personalism

Introduction

SWAMI ŚRĪLA BHAKTISIDDHĀNTA SARASVATĪ,[1] the subject of this book, was born in Calcutta 109 years after the British East India Company took possession of Bengal, 16 years from the time that the British Raj officially took over India's rule, and 73 years before Indian independence was finally achieved. The year was 1874, a time in which a vast and ancient civilization was ruled by the inhabitants of a small North Atlantic island that had managed to project its culture, its religion—and its economic interests—to every corner of the globe. It was a time, in other words, when India was the "jewel" in the crown of the British Empire and Calcutta had been transformed into a Eurasian metropolis that was second only to London itself. Bhaktisiddhānta was a Vaishnava guru and preceptor of the school of Sri Krishna Caitanya Mahāprabhu (1486–1534).[2] The period in which he lived traversed two centuries and witnessed both the apex and the final setting of Britain's imperial sun. Before his departure from this world in 1937, he had managed to build a unique and powerful religious institution that responded to the social, political, and religious circumstances of India's late-colonial period.

The year 1874 arrived at a time of transition in India, when events that began more than a century earlier had started to produce novel patterns of change. In 1757 the battle of Plassey paved the way for single domination, as Britain won over French influences in the East. By 1772 the Mughal emperor Shah Alaam II (1728–1806) had ceded Bengal, Orissa, and Bihar to the East India Company, Bengal had become the first region of India to experience British rule, and Calcutta had been named the capital of British India (remaining so until 1911). Subsequent years witnessed the unfolding of colonial culture, as well as indigenous reactions for and against it. The period between 1815 and 1914 came to be regarded as Britain's "Imperial

1. Hereinafter referred to as Bhaktisiddhānta.

2. Hereinafter referred to as Caitanya. The name "Caitanya" is pronounced "Chaitanya."

Century" and the period between 1837 and 1901 as the "Victorian Era." The Sepoy rebellion of 1857 marked the end of the East India Company's autocratic rule and the beginning of control by the British government itself. In 1876 Queen Victoria was named Empress of India, and in 1920 Gandhi was elected leader of the Congress Party. By 1922 the British Empire included one-quarter of the world's population (ca. 458 million people) and encompassed one-quarter of its land area as well (ca. 33,670,000 square kilometers). Throughout this period, Britain's political, linguistic, and cultural influence in South Asia profoundly linked India to the rest of the world until colonial rule ended in 1947.

In the West, the period between 1874 and 1937—the years spanning Bhaktisiddhānta's life—witnessed a series of watershed events that permanently transformed the cultural, geopolitical, technological, and scientific face of the earth. Just prior to this period, Karl Marx and Friedrich Engels had published *The Communist Manifesto* (1848), Charles Darwin had released *On the Origin of Species* (1859), and Alfred Nobel had invented dynamite (1867). And within this period, Alexander Graham Bell patented the telephone (1876), Paris hosted the first international electrical exhibition (1881), Karl Benz produced the first automobile (1885), Sigmund Freud published the *Interpretation of Dreams* (1900), the Wright brothers flew the first motorized airplane at Kitty Hawk (1903), and Albert Einstein published his groundbreaking theory of special relativity (1905). Then World War I (1914–1918) cast a veil of senseless darkness over the world, and its aftermath witnessed the rise of communism, fascism, and Nazism. India itself was influenced by these global events on several levels, but nowhere more visibly than in Calcutta, which around the turn of the twentieth century had become one of the major crossroads of the world.

By the time of Bhaktisiddhānta's birth, Calcutta had risen from rural anonymity to become the "second city" of the British Empire: larger and more magnificent than either Edinburgh or Glasgow and the equivalent in beauty, magnificence, and population to famed London and Paris. But like all metropolises, Calcutta also had a darker side. Rudyard Kipling described Calcutta as "a city of dreadful night, filled with poverty, famine, riot and disease, where the cholera, the cyclone, the crow come and go ... by the sewerage rendered fetid, by the sewer made impure, by the Sunderbunds unwholesome, by the swamp moist and damp."[3]

---

3. Rudyard Kipling, *Departmental Ditties, Barrack-Room Ballads and Other Verses* (New York: United States Book Co., 1890), p. 234.

To convey a sense of this city's unique mingling of two starkly contrasting milieus as they converged at the end of the nineteenth century, I herewith include the following brief, if somewhat tangential, description, freely adapted from two Western memoirs of that time: Zebina Flavius Griffith's *India and Daily Life in Bengal* (1896) and Anna Harriet Leonowens's *Life and Travel in India* (1884):

Calcutta near the turn of the century contains a population of approximately one million people, and is organized in such a way that British and native districts are kept carefully apart. The British sector extends five miles along the Hoogly River and includes a nobly appointed and much-frequented esplanade that separates the town from Fort William. Along one side of this esplanade are the government house, town hall, Treasury, and High Court, and on the opposite side is Fort William, with the fine steeple of the Baptist cathedral rising just beyond. From there, after passing under a triumphal archway, one emerges onto a spacious grassy area famously known as the Maidan. Here, all principal roads converge, and one is surrounded on all sides by an elegant display of stately architecture. This is the fashionable suburb known as Chowringee, which in every respect makes Calcutta worthy of the appellation "City of Palaces." All the houses are of European style, three or four stories in height, and most of them are connected by handsome terraces or open sunny balconies. The more opulent ones have shady verandas or high carriage-porches supported by Romanesque pillars, while some are rendered even more attractive by lush flower gardens with fine fruit trees.

Yet even this more regal and Westernized section of town abounds with contrasts and contradictions. Beautiful carriages containing personages of the highest social rank travel down the boulevard alongside rickety old streetcars, oxcarts, rickshaw wallahs, and the like. On the avenue, the most magnificent European stores can be found located within a few meters of poor Bengali natives peddling their wares from small, meagerly appointed shops. And right next door to the Eden gardens—with their electric lights, fountains, and exquisite music—are the shanties of native candy vendors, who can be seen leaning over pots of boiling oil making their sweets. On any given day within the same vicinity, one can see mingled together English bureaucrats running about at breakneck pace, Chinamen arrayed in red and greens silks, Zamindars adorned in spotless white clothes with jeweled chains of heavy gold wrapped around their necks, Parsees walking tall and proud in peculiar stovepipe hats, Burmese wearing red silk handkerchiefs wrapped tight around their heads, zenana missionaries, Catholic padres, and many more. Scattered all through this diverse crowd of people are the watermen, with leather bags of water on their hips, sprinkling the streets to keep down the dust.

In stark contrast to the grandeur of the British district stands the native portion known as "Black Town," the residence of more than three-quarters of Calcutta's entire population. The severe transition between these two opposites is made even more extreme by the architectural pretensions of the one and the crude mud or bamboo habitations of the other. And yet within this relatively impoverished section of the city, with streets all narrow, unpaved, and teeming with excessive population, there can be found no less than twenty bazaars, well stocked with commodities, goods, and articles from all corners of the world: rare and valuable products of the Indian loom; shawls and paintings from Cashmere; kincobs from Benares; teas and silks from China; spices, pearls, and precious stones from Ceylon; rupees from Pegii; coffee from Java and Arabia; nutmeg from Singapore. The list goes on and on. Here the air is filled with the fragrances of vanilla, saffron, cardamom, and sandalwood, all mingled with the scent of hot, newly prepared Bengali sweets, rich with cream and ghee; and here can be heard at all times the principal cry of the market: "Come please, Memsahib, I've got it!"

Walking among these relatively few and scattered "memsahibs" are the throng of Hindus: graceful nut-brown maidens tripping gracefully with rows of water-jars nicely balanced on their heads; dark-hued young men—clean, washed, and robed in pure white cotton—laughing, talking, or loitering about; Westernized babus sauntering along, dressed in handsome Oriental costumes, but with European stockings and shoes. Then there are the common street women, the brilliantly attired dancing-girls, the Brahmins, the sepoys, the fakirs, and the swamis, all bedecked in various costumes, all conversing in manifold tongues and dialects. And above all, there are the strolling jugglers, snake charmers, and fortune-tellers, all plying their curious arts and completing the picture of an Oriental bazaar. And it appears as if this teeming flow of humanity has been passing and gurgling through the streets of these native bazaars for all the centuries of foreign rule, unchanged in type, character, feeling, religion, and occupation. Side by side with the churches of the Brahmo Samaj, and the eloquence and sharp intellect of the educated Bengalis and other cultivated natives of Bengal, there are the temples of the goddess Kālī and the large festivals in honor of Jagannātha. Remarkably enough, among the majority of the native population of Calcutta, as well as the rest of India, the European influence is hardly felt at all.

The above vivid depiction by Griffith and Leonowens makes plain the stark sociocultural and religious divide that existed between Calcutta's British and Indian populations, accurately represented by the names "white town" and "black town." It is important to note as well, that this condition had a long history of negotiation. The gradual development of colonial administration and trade created an early need for a new indigenous middle class—a class that became known as the *bhadralok*. The *bhadralok* was comprised of Bengali Hindus rather than Muslims, and although it initially included only wealthy landlords, it eventually incorporated clerical personnel, journalists, teachers, and lawyers who were recruited from the peasant gentry. These individuals worked as brokers to British traders, interpreters, and mediators in matters of justice and revenue, and assistants in matters of economic and political administration. They also became respectfully known as *babus*, a title given to those that acquired fluency in English. The defining traits of the *bhadralok* were an inclination for secular and liberal views and a strong commitment to education, which was the basis of their success. Also characteristic of this class was the tendency to emulate the British in habit, culture, and taste. Although, under the circumstances, this sort of reaction can be considered fairly standard, it resulted to some degree from the fact that both Christian missionaries and British educators successfully conveyed the notion that Bengalis could progress, culturally and morally, only by ridding themselves of native habits and religious practices.

Throughout the nineteenth century young upper-class Bengalis filled the ranks of the *bhadralok*. Eager for employment in civil and professional services, they were carefully selected for admission to a handful of English medium schools on the basis of rigorous examinations. Such institutions were designed to create an educated class that could serve British interests with loyalty and expertise, and professionally function in a secular environment. Protestant missionary schools also became popular among the *bhadralok* because of the quality of their English education. Beyond this, however, these schools had a twofold agenda: on the one hand, they aimed to convince indigenous students that "Hindoo" beliefs and practices were irrational, idolatrous, insensitive to human suffering, and neglectful of the rights of women; on the other hand, they were intent upon promoting the superiority of Western Christian culture by exposing students to monotheism, rationalism, humanitarianism, and European literature and thought. Through these various educational institutions a new generation of Bengalis were trained to look at their own culture—and reality itself—in a way that Indians had never done before. But the success of such efforts remained largely incomplete. While Western ideas eventually came to influence the thinking and attitudes of the *bhadralok*, these notions did not cause most to entirely reject their own Indic traditions as valueless. Nonetheless, as the nineteenth century drew nearer to its close, the admixture of European and Indic cultural and religious ideals created a powerful group of intellectuals whose thinking inaugurated what has come to be known as the "Bengal Renaissance." These individuals, the most significant of whom went on to become major historical figures in the development of modern India, tended to promote nondualism as *the* fundamental expression of Indic thought or to champion social and religious reform in accordance with their unique understanding of modern ideals. Of these, Rammohun Roy (1772–1833), Bankim Chandra Chatterjee (1838–1894), Bipin Chandra Pal (1858–1932), Keshub Chandra Sen (1838–1884), and Swami Vivekānanda (1863–1902) will be briefly introduced below. Some of these individuals will be further discussed throughout this work.

Rammohun Roy is considered by most historians to have been the inaugurator of the Bengal Renaissance. He published various works on nondualistic Vedanta, which he later came to view as a viable alternative to the gospel of the Protestant missionaries. He planted the seed of a bourgeois Vedanta that was specifically inclusive of householders and eventually became the prototype of the "spiritual seeker" among the Hindu middle class—that is, individuals who lived in the world while pursuing spiritual ideals.[4] Throughout his career, Roy vigorously campaigned for social, political, and religious reform, achieving remarkable results that had a long-term effect on modern Hinduism. This was particularly so in the case of his starkly rational outlook on religion as well as his critical historical reading of religious texts. Although he also fought against the practice of image worship, which he viewed as a corrupted version of the genuine Hindu faith, this effort did not have a long-lasting effect. His reinterpretation of Vedantic nondualism, on the other hand, which he blended with an understanding of God as creator and sustainer, was a precedent to the thinking of various Bengali intellectuals, including Swami Vivekānanda, perhaps the most prominent among all of these. This, in my view, is his most enduring contribution to the development of modern Hindu thought.

---

4. See Brian A. Hatcher, "Bourgeois Vedanta: The Colonial Roots of Middle-Class Hinduism," *Journal of the American Academy of Religion* 75, no. 2 (2007): 298–323.

Bankim Chandra Chatterjee was a *brāhmaṇa* by birth and an accomplished Bengali writer.[5] He was one of the first students to obtain a degree from Calcutta University and make a career as a deputy collector and deputy magistrate. Of particular interest, in terms of this work, is his study *Krishna-Charitra* (1886), in which he went against the aniconic tendencies of his time by promoting the idea that India's Krishna embodied all the sought-after qualities of a national hero. In the process, he treated all descriptions of Krishna that appeared to contradict this view as interpolations. Eventually, Chatterjee rose to become a significant source of inspiration for the nationalist movement, and his poem *Vande mataram* became the national song of India. This song, still sung today, is his most remembered contribution.

Bipin Chandra Pal is widely considered to have been a founding father of the modern Indian state. He studied at Calcutta's Presidency College and then went on to play an important role in nationalist politics, embracing a form of activism that included the boycotting of British-manufactured goods, the burning of British-produced clothes, and the locking out of British-owned businesses. In terms of his own political thought, he developed a form of theological idealism that viewed the progress of society as the unfolding of God's immanent presence in history. He was extremely influential during the early phase of the Indian independence movement, and his place in Indian history is largely connected to this.

Keshub Chandra Sen was arguably the most eclectic personality of the Bengal Renaissance. He developed different systems of religious practice for different categories of individuals, and his experiments with communal living can be regarded as prototypical of the modern-day "lay ashram." Sen believed religious enthusiasm to be the heart of religious life, and thus attempted to revive the Caitanya Vaishnava tradition of publicly chanting the holy names of God. Perhaps inadvertently, this created a new interest in Vaishnavism among the *bhadralok*. Sen's emphasis on internal experience, as opposed to ritualism, organized religion, and priestly mediators, influenced later forms of modern Hinduism. He created a manifold universalism inspired by Hinduism, Christianity, Caitanya Vaishnavism, and Western esotericism—a "New Dispensation" that highlighted the ultimate similarity of all religious traditions. Unfortunately, however, the

---

5. For an introduction to Chatterjee's religious thought, see Hans Harder, *Bankimchandra Chattopadhyay's Śrīmadbhagabadgītā: Translation and Analysis* (New Delhi: Manohar Publishers, 2001).

charismatic movement that he began lacked a structured institutional form and thus did not survive his death.[6]

Among the historically relevant *bhadralok* discussed thus far, Swami Vivekānanda is the one most known to the West. He promoted a new form of Vedanta, inspired by Śaṅkara's original system, which rose in the early twentieth century to become the standard understanding of Hinduism among most Indian and Western intellectuals, remaining so to a large degree even today. Stated in very brief terms, this understanding is as follows: in its highest and most fundamental essence, Hinduism regards the transitory world of individual sense, form, and personality to be ultimately unreal or nonexistent, considering the ultimate absolute to consist of an underlying, all-pervading and formless oneness known as *brahman*; this understanding is in opposition to the more commonplace belief of the general masses in the worship of the deity forms of gods and goddesses. Unlike Rammohun Roy, however, Vivekānanda believed that image worship played an indirect role by helping to prepare the mind for the ultimate realization of *brahman*.[7]

This nondualistic understanding had important practical implications for the spread of humanistic, rationalistic, and egalitarian ideologies because of its emphasis on the equality of all human beings. It is also likely that the embracing of a parallel view by Gandhi and several other prominent leaders of the nationalist movement facilitated the purpose of invalidating the notion of a racial hierarchy and legitimizing resistance to Western domination. In 1893 Vivekānanda was invited to represent Hinduism at the World Parliament of Religions in Chicago. Exceedingly well received, his reading of Vedanta quickly became the West's standard understanding of Hinduism's philosophical base.

One year later, Vivekānanda traveled to New York to found his first Vedanta Society, and after returning to India he founded the Ramakrishna Mission. The primary aim of the former has been spiritual enlightenment, while the primary aim of the latter has been the education and material uplifting of India's masses. And although Vivekānanda's Vedānta Society never became a mass movement in the sense of making large numbers of non-Hindu converts, and today mostly caters to Hindu populations in

6. Elizabeth De Michelis, *A History of Modern Yoga: Patañjali and Western Esotericism* (London: Continuum, 2004), pp. 49–90.

7. Swami Vivekānanda, *Complete Works of Swami Vivekananda* (Kolkata: Advaita Ashrama, 2006), vol. 5, p. 316.

different parts of the world, the Ramakrishna Mission is still immensely popular and influential in Bengal.

During the same general period in which all of the above figures lived and worked, there was another: born a *bhadralok*, powerfully intelligent, well versed in Western thought, but representing a theological perspective that was in many ways out of step with the apparently progressive currents of his time. That individual, still little known despite the fact that his influence has become surprisingly widespread, is Bhaktisiddhānta Sarasvatī.

Bhaktisiddhānta represented a medieval religious tradition that had offered a seminal understanding of "classical" Indic thought.[8] That tradition is known as Caitanya Vaishnavism and that understanding is known as *bhakti*. Here it is important to once again note that among most of his *bhadralok* contemporaries the primary tendencies were toward nondualism, nationalism, humanitarianism, egalitarianism, rationalism, social consciousness, and the use of religion as a conceptual and practical partner in the achievement of these aims. These individuals were in search of new religious and cultural identities that could domesticate the ideas of the West, creating reform movements that were competitive with the more traditional strands of premodern and early-modern Indic thought. Being one of these more traditional strands, and beset with a number of other "unattractive" features, Caitanya Vaishnavism was generally absent from their selection list. Inaugurated in the sixteenth century, it is the tradition of bhakti (or devotion) to Krishna and his consort Rādhā, which arose from the life and teachings of Caitanya and included approximately one-fifth of the Bengali population of the late nineteenth century. Caitanya is regarded by Vaishnavas in Bengal as the most recent divine manifestation of Krishna himself.

Although in its original dress this tradition had a profound philosophical basis, over the years it had divided into three general forms, none of which were very appealing to most of the Bengali intelligentsia: the first was its popularized form, which they considered to be sentimental, morally weak, licentious, and mostly the religion of the ignorant and illiterate lower class; the second was its caste-oriented form, which they considered to be elitist, nepotistic, socially callous, and far too old-fashioned and out of step with modern times; and the third was its mystical-ascetic form, which they considered to be too otherworldly. Given this, one might legitimately

8. "Classical" will in most cases refer to the precolonial period. See also chapter 5.

wonder what it was about this tradition that so attracted Bhaktisiddhānta, who was every bit as savvy as the rest. The answer is that it was largely due to the fact that first his father (perhaps the greatest influence in his life), and then he himself, became acquainted with the original medieval writings of Caitanya's immediate and most significant followers: Rūpa Goswami, Sanātana Goswami, and Jīva Goswami. As a result, he concluded that all three contemporary forms were misrepresentations of what he came to regard as a highly austere, philosophical, moral, disciplined, and egalitarian tradition.

Eventually Bhaktisiddhānta came to embrace what he regarded as the original core of this tradition, and dedicated his adult life to the recovery and propagation of its teachings. He did this primarily through the establishment of a pan-Indian religious institution, the publication of newspapers and journals, the printing and distribution of classical and medieval texts, and the writing of original commentaries. Throughout his life he traveled widely about India, lecturing and initiating disciples, and won the esteem of numerous important Indian and European figures. He was also a controversial figure who spoke out against such things as caste barriers, ordinary gender roles, and those sections of the Vaishnava religious elite that he found to be abusive. He introduced such innovations as the establishment of Vaishnava *saṃnyāsa* and the offering of *brāhmaṇa* initiation on the basis of qualification rather than birth. In pursuit of these aims he employed modern methods of institutional organization and modern forms of communication and transportation that caused a good many indigenous eyebrows to rise. His statements against the modern nondualist Vedantic mainstream as well as his critique of religious involvement in political and humanitarian work made him a maverick even among the *bhadralok*.

The really interesting feature of all this, however, was the content of the teachings that Bhaktisiddhānta propagated, which were based on the theory and practice of a personalist, theistic form of bhakti. It stood in stark contrast to the nondualism that had become so prevalent among most of his contemporaries, and was out of step with the progressive, highly politicized, and philanthropically oriented tendencies of his times. These teachings were deeply theistic, presenting the highest truth or "Supreme Godhead" as personal rather than impersonal, with form rather than formless. In this regard he championed Vaishnavism's iconic practices as well as the ultimate reality of the form, abode, and activities of a Supreme Being. He did so, however, not on the basis of popular sentimentalism and eroticism, but on the basis of a complex philosophical understanding that posed a direct challenge to the nondualistic views of Vivekānanda and others.

Through the work of the Gaudiya Math (the name of the institution he founded), Bhaktisiddhānta's voice gradually gained prominence in India. Nonetheless, after he passed away in 1937 his movement largely disintegrated during a crisis of succession that ended in schism, and it seemed as if his life and work would remain a mere footnote in the annals of religious history. Some thirty years later, however, a watershed event would propel his movement to surprising heights and rapidly spread his perspective on the teachings of Caitanya throughout the world, making tens of thousands of non-Indian followers along the way. The focus of this study, however, is *not* on this watershed event, but rather on the still obscure individual that had given it its original impetus.

Simply put, the question that will be explored in this book is as follows: how did Bhaktisiddhānta attempt to translate, establish, and convey the tradition of Caitanya bhakti in adaptation to the circumstances of modern (colonial) society and culture, and how does this relate to his place and significance in the history of modern Hinduism?

To answer this question, this work will pose five subordinate queries:

1. What was the sociocultural context of Bhaktisiddhānta's time—that is, the mainstream middle-class influences of late nineteenth- and early twentieth-century Bengal that may have played a role in shaping his personal perceptions, sensibilities, and choices?
2. What were the major turning points and influences of his life, and in what manner did these affect the formation of his identity and the development of his religious institution?
3. How did he bridge the divide between East and West to fulfill the aim of carrying the tradition of Caitanya bhakti beyond the borders of India?
4. What was his perspective on Caitanya bhakti in general, and specifically in relation to the religion and society of his time? Within that framework, what were the precise processes of religious change that he envisioned and carried out?
5. What is his place in the history of modern Hinduism, and what is his significance?

These inquires will be addressed one after another in the following chapters.

Chapter 1 briefly provides the historical background as well as the contemporary context of the India in which Bhaktisiddhānta lived and functioned. In doing so, it pursues such topics as colonial culture and sensibilities, the emergence of an educated middle class, the rise of the Bengal Renaissance, several of the major figures associated with that renaissance, the challenge posed by Protestant missionaries, and the views of the British and the *bhadralok* regarding Caitanya Vaishnavism.

Chapter 2 explores Bhaktisiddhānta's childhood, education and major influences, as well as his involvement with Caitanya Vaishnavism and the practice of bhakti. It also examines the development and impact of his institution, as well as his attempt to implement religious change on an individual or micro level (by creating a new religious identity) and on an institutional or meso level (by creating a modern religious institution).

Chapter 3 discusses Bhaktisiddhānta's transnational (or macro) attempt to propagate Caitanya Vaishnavism by sending disciples to London and Berlin. In this regard, it provides a fairly detailed description and analysis of their encounter with imperial Britain and Nazi Germany, as well as the manner in which they carried forth Bhaktisiddhānta's message.

Chapter 4 presents Bhaktisiddhānta's philosophical perspective on religion and society as well as on Caitanya Vaishnavism. It also explores the manner in which he was able to carve a certain core understanding of his own tradition that allowed him to promote dynamic religious change. It will explore the interaction between philosophical and social concerns and show how they formed the basis for the restructuring of his movement in terms of bhakti.

Chapter 5 places Bhaktisiddhānta's life and work within a taxonomy of modern Hinduism and compares the significance of his work to the contributions of major figures such as Swami Vivekānanda. The issue of reform versus revivalism is also addressed herein. Finally, Bhaktisiddhānta's work is linked to the development of a worldwide movement that today involves thousands of American and European practitioners, many of whom have become respected representatives of Caitanya bhakti in India itself.

At the end, appendix A presents my position relative to controversial and difficult-to-define terms such as *Hindu, Hinduism, religion,* and *bhakti,* lays out my major theoretical and methodological tools, describes the manner in which my research has been conducted, and discusses the historical distinction between dualistic and nondualistic Vedanta.

Appendix B contains a collection of rare images. Appendix C presents key historical documents such as the last will of Bhaktisiddhānta.

Appendix D provides a detailed account of a journey to Nazi Germany. Appendix E provides a comprehensive bibliography of Bhaktisiddhānta's writings.

Relative to the Bengali language, there is no universally accepted transcription system, but rather a number of options.[9] Bengali reflects the syncretic and complex history of the Bengali people, and the influence not only of Sanskrit, but of Perso-Arabic and English as well. The English transcription of many Bengali words during the colonial period has added much to the confusion. I have chosen to use a transcription system that follows the standard international system for the transliteration of Sanskrit, a language that is far more known among scholars of South Asia than Bengali. Another reason is that Bhaktisiddhānta frequently used Sanskrit in his writings, and even preferred to use Bengali words in their Sanskritized form. As such, this choice more closely follows the style of the original sources. This notwithstanding, geographical, institutional, and personal names in Bengali are transcribed in the way they are commonly pronounced or used. This also applies to a number of common terms such as *bhadralok*. Personal titles and initiated names that have been derived from Sanskrit are transcribed in their Sanskritized form, with the exception of common titles such as swami, maharaja, or goswami. Standardized English spelling is used for well-known Sanskrit terms and names such as Vedanta, Upanishads, and Krishna.

---

9. One example of a transliteration system closer to the phonetics of the language is the one based on the system for New Indo-Aryan presented by Rahul Peter Das, "Review: Dušan Zbavitel, 'Bengali Literature'" (1984), p. 66 n. 2. A Sanskritized transliteration close to the one used here is found in Hugh B. Urban, *The Economics of Ecstasy: Tantra, Secrecy, and Power in Colonial Bengal* (New York: Oxford University Press, 2001), pp. xv–xvi.

1

Rise of Nondualism in Bengal

THIS CHAPTER PROVIDES a brief sketch of Islamic, Indic, and European currents that, during the nineteenth and twentieth centuries, influenced Bengal's *bhadralok* mainstream to embrace various interpretations of *advaita* Vedanta as *the* main unifying philosophy of modern Hindu India. Because of the complexity of the phenomena under discussion, it is often difficult to separate influences that were strictly European from those that were strictly Indic. Both were closely intertwined and will be treated as such herein.

Religious Pluralism in India

The indigenous rule of India's Hindu kings was first challenged by the Ghaznavid dynasty (977–1186), beginning with Sabuktigīn, a former Turkish slave of the Iranian-Muslim dynasty of the Samanids. The Turks originated from the steppes of central Asia and eventually came to play a significant role in the partial Islamization of South Asia. From his base in Ghazna (present-day Afghanistan), Sabuktigīn expanded his domain as far as the Indian border. His son Mahmud converted the Ghaznavids into a Sunni Islamic and Persianate dynasty and developed a powerful military structure funded by tax revenues and the plunder of war. During his reign (998–1030), he invaded the Sind and parts of western India numerous times, looting wealthy Hindu temples in cities like Mathura and Somnath.[1] Under Mahmud, who was known as "the breaker of idols," Hindu India

1. John L. Esposito, *The Oxford History of Islam* (New York: Oxford University Press, 1999), p. 41; Andre Wink, *Al-Hind: The Making of the Indo-Islamic World*, vol. 2 (Boston: Brill Academic Publishers, 2002), pp. 130, 229–233.

became the target of Turkish iconoclastic fervor and also received its first taste of Sunni Islamic culture.[2]

As the Ghaznavid influence declined, it was replaced by yet another Turkish power, this one originating from the principality of Ghor (western Afghanistan). In 1192 Muhammad of Ghor defeated Prithivi Raj and established the first Muslim kingdom in India. Known as the Delhi Sultanate, this kingdom was ruled by a succession of Muslim dynasties until it was defeated by Babur in 1526 and absorbed into the emerging Mughal empire. The empire was consolidated by Akbar the Great (ruled 1556–1605) and came to encompass almost the entirety of India by the time of his grandson, the emperor Aurangzeb (ruled 1658–1707). Throughout the Turkish period, the Hanafi school was the predominant institution of Sunni jurisprudence and law, which is still the case in India, Pakistan, and Bangladesh. The Mughals themselves were Hanafi Sunni Turks.[3]

Akbar has been described by some chroniclers as a comparatively mild and tolerant ruler who abolished the Hindu poll tax as well as the requirement that Hindus journey to Mecca during the month of Dhu al-Hijja. He is also known to have been the first Muslim ruler to enter into marriage with a number of Hindu princesses, a deed that indirectly encouraged intercommunal marriage among the general Hindu-Muslim population. This more benign trend was eventually reversed by Aurangzeb, whose heavy-handed treatment of non-Muslim subjects was one of the factors that contributed to the outbreak of the Deccan wars and the rise of the Maratha empire, as well as the Sikh and Pashtun rebellions.[4] In the end, his attempts to Islamize the Indian subcontinent failed to unseat Hinduism as the main religion of the indigenous population, and the Mughal empire entered into a period of long decline. Within one hundred years of Aurangzeb's death, the sitting emperor had little authority outside Delhi and was spurned by most Indian princes.

A few years before Babur established the Mughal empire, European traders had begun traveling to India to partake of its fabulous wealth of spices, textiles, and ores. On May 20, 1498, Vasco da Gama landed at

---

2. Wink, *Al-Hind*, p. 321.

3. Aziz Ahmad, *An Intellectual History of Islam in India* (Edinburgh: Edinburgh University Press, 1969), p. 2.

4. A. L. Basham, *The Wonder That Was India: A Survey of the Culture of the Indian Sub-Continent before the Coming of the Muslims* (New York: Grove Press, 1954), p. 480.

Calicut on the Malabar Coast of present-day Kerala, initiating the era of the Portuguese.[5] The Portuguese conquered Goa in 1510, establishing a commercial monopoly in the Arabian Sea through their military and naval superiority. In an attempt to spread Catholicism and counteract the influence of nearby Islamic rulers, the Portuguese dispatched Jesuit missionaries to zealously preach their faith.[6] It would not be long, however, before India began to attract Dutch, French, Danish, and British competition.

The British East India Company was established in the year 1600, creating new trade stations in Surat (1613), Bombay (1661), and Calcutta (1691). Throughout the seventeenth and eighteenth centuries the company seized every opportunity to extend its influence as the Mughal empire crumbled under the weight of both external rebellion and internal conflict.[7] The greatest challenge to the rise of British influence during this period came not from the Muslims, but from the French. The bitter rivalry between these two powers gradually escalated into a violent conflict that began in 1746 and ended in 1763 with victory for the British. During this period, both nations attempted to gain the upper hand through various alliances with Indian rulers, but it was the British that ultimately prevailed, most decisively in the 1757 battle of Plassey in Bengal, considered a turning point in the company's bid to dominate India.

As Britain's fortunes continued to rise, the other European powers were gradually obliged to recede. The Danish East India Company established its first trading post in 1620 at Tranquebar in Tamil Nadu; over the next century and a half it went on to establish commercial outposts on the Malabar Coast (1689) and the Nicobar Islands (1754), as well as in Serampore near Calcutta (1755). In 1656 the Dutch built a factory at Hugli-Chuchura near Calcutta, the site of an old trading post that had been originally established by the Portuguese, and later abandoned it when they

5. William Wilson Hunter, *A History of British India*, vol. 1 (London: Longmans, 1899), p. 88. The Portuguese pioneered large-scale European expansion via the high seas; see John Darwin, *After Tamerlane: The Global History of Empire since 1405* (London: Allen Lane, 2007), pp. 51–52.

6. K. M. Panikkar, *Asia and Western Dominance: A Survey of the Vasco Da Gama Epoch of Asian History, 1498–1945* (London: Allen & Unwin, 1953), p. 382. The Portuguese destroyed the Hindu temples in Goa, and Jesuit missionaries exerted great pressure on the Hindu population to convert to Christianity. This pressure, however, decreased significantly after the end of the Inquisition in 1774. M. N. Pearson, *The Portuguese in India* (Cambridge: Cambridge University Press, 1987), pp. 120–124.

7. Nicholas B. Dirks, *The Scandal of Empire: India and the Creation of Imperial Britain* (Cambridge, Mass.: Belknap Press of Harvard University Press, 2006), pp. 7–8.

were expelled by the Mughal governor. By 1869, however, all Dutch and Danish settlements in South Asia had been relinquished to the British, while French and Portuguese interests had been restricted to locations such as Pondicherry and Goa.[8] In this way, by the middle of the nineteenth century Britain had gained possession of a South Asian empire ranging from the Himalaya Mountains to Sri Lanka. This had been made possible by control of Bengal's revenues, technological and naval superiority, a cohesive leadership, and a detailed knowledge of South Asia's geography, populations, and administration.[9] The battle of Plassey marked the decline of the influence of the Nawabs of Murshidabad, foreshadowing the end of five centuries of Islamic rule. In 1858, following the Sepoy war, the British Crown assumed direct control of the Indian subcontinent, relinquishing it only after India had won independence in 1947. During the more heady years of the Raj, Bengal played a leading role due to the economic and political significance of Calcutta, which remained the administrative capital of the South Asian dependency until December 1911.[10]

Emergence of the Bhadralok

In the earlier phases of the colonial venture, a new privileged class emerged in Bengal to lead the process of indigenous adjustment, cultural assimilation, and religious transformation; it was known as the *bhadralok*, which literally means "gentle or respectable people." Although the term *bhadralok* is often translated as "middle class," this particular rendering can be misleading since the basis of its prosperity was neither trade nor industry, as in the case of the European bourgeois. Because of their preference for occupations that required intelligence and education,[11] the *bhadralok* as a class were distinct from the *chotalok*, the class of "little people" that consisted of servants, cooks, and sweepers, as well as large numbers of immigrants.

8. The French post at Chandernagore (present-day Chandannagar) near Calcutta, established in 1673 by La Compagnie française des Indes orientales (the French East India Company), remained part of French India until 1950.

9. Christopher Alan Bayly, *Empire and Information: Intelligence Gathering and Social Communication in India, 1780–1870* (Cambridge: Cambridge University Press, 1997), pp. 58, 97.

10. The city of "Calcutta" is today known as "Kolkata" (its original Bengali name). However, in keeping with the historical period at hand, it will be herein referred to by its former colonial appellation.

11. See Tithi Bhattacharya, *The Sentinels of Culture: Class, Education, and the Colonial Intellectual in Bengal (1848–85)* (Oxford: Oxford University Press, 2005).

Yet another class consisted of Muslim moneylenders, shopkeepers, artisans, and laborers, who comprised a large segment of Calcutta's black town population. For their part, the *bhadralok* resided in their own select sector of black town, carefully separated from both these classes.[12] The legitimacy of the *bhadralok* as a "middle" class came from the fact that it played a prominent role in mediations between local resources and systems of production on the one hand and British members of the East India Company and their allies on the other. Throughout the colonial period, the identity of the *bhadralok* came not from their ability to conduct business or perform manual labor, but rather from their ability to acquire various forms of education, gain proficiency in new languages, and assist in the colonial administration. It was therefore largely composed of three literate castes and *jātis*, *brāhmaṇas*, *kāyasthas*, and *vaidyas*. Nonetheless, among the members of the *bhadralok* there were a variety of aspirations, harmonized by a common interest in participating in colonial society.[13] While the *bhadralok* were quite a heterogeneous group, their general status as landed elite, their station near the top of caste hierarchy, their access to education and urban employment, and their position of authority under colonial rule tended to alienate them from the rural populations.[14] This was particularly the case with regard to the Muslim majority of eastern Bengal.[15] Bengali Muslims were far less involved in the process of adjustment to colonial rule, and the Muslim elites gradually receded into the background.[16]

Although the East India Company was a generally hegemonic institution, its authority was never intended to be absolute, since its military, administrative, and economic occupation depended upon the cooperation of large numbers of Indians. Above all, it had no control over the unofficial channels of communication whereby information was disseminated throughout India—that is, family relationships as well as informal networks and commerce.[17] Nonetheless, the company strove to reshape indigenous

---

12. Frederic C. Thomas, *Calcutta Poor: Elegies on Urban Poverty* (Armonk, N.Y.: M. E. Sharpe, 1997), pp. 25–32.

13. Sekhara Bandyopadhyaya, *Caste, Culture, and Hegemony: Social Domination in Colonial Bengal* (New Delhi: Sage Publications, 2004), p. 155.

14. Joya Chatterji, *Bengal Divided: Hindu Communalism and Partition, 1932–1947* (Cambridge: Cambridge University Press, 1994), p. 12.

15. Chatterji, *Bengal Divided*, p. 28.

16. Harder, *Bankimchandra Chattopadhyay's Śrīmadbhagabadgītā*, p. 3.

17. Bayly, *Empire and Information*.

Indian society in ways that would accommodate British economic interests. The rise of the *bhadralok* was accelerated by the fact that the British had discarded the old administrative and judicial system of the Mughals, which had privileged the Muslim elite.[18] To speed participation in colonial society the *bhadralok* founded the Hindu College and introduced English education from 1817 onward. Those among the *bhadralok* that later became Hindu reformers and revivalists in the nineteenth and twentieth centuries were primarily lawyers, brokers, judges, landlords, teachers, and employees of the East Indian Company, and later on, of the Raj.[19] These laymen claimed authority through their newly acquired influence, learning, and merit, and the more progressive among them began to challenge ancient religious *habitus* like caste, early marriage, and sati.[20] These ancient customs were newly regarded as evil, and fresh religious ideas, some inspired by Christian and Islamic currents, but most grounded in novel interpretations of ancient Indic texts, became sacralized in their stead. Furthermore, the progressive wing of the *bhadralok* looked down upon the "orthodox *brāhmaṇa* class" as being incapable of providing an adequate response to colonial culture, having distanced themselves from the center of social and political life—a critique that was consistently maintained during the Hindu Renaissance. As a backlash against these progressive currents, conservative elements within the *bhadralok* began to articulate their perspective as well. These elements resisted the "radical assimilation" of Western customs and ideas, regarded as potential threats to what they believed was the perennial core of Hindu rituals, ideas, and practice.

Early Developments: Rammohun Roy

The foundation of what is generally labeled "modern Hinduism" is said to have been laid by Rammohun Roy (1774–1833), a major historical figure credited with having inaugurated the Bengal Renaissance, a movement of reform and revival that extended throughout the nineteenth century and

18. Bayly, *Empire and Information*, pp. 80–81.

19. Indira Chowdhury, *The Frail Hero and Virile History: Gender and the Politics of Culture in Colonial Bengal* (Oxford: Oxford University Press, 1998), p. 6.

20. The term *habitus* was introduced by Max Weber and adopted by French sociologist Pierre Bourdieu. Axel Michaels describes it as "culturally acquired lifestyles and attitudes, habits and predispositions, as well as conscious, deliberate acts or mythological, theological, or philosophical artifacts and mental productions." Axel Michaels, *Hinduism: Past and Present* (Princeton, N.J.: Princeton University Press, 2004), p. 7.

was pivotal in shaping a larger Hindu "awakening."[21] The end of the eighteenth century was a time of great social, cultural, and political turmoil in Bengal as the old system of Islamic polity gave way to British rule, and Muslims, Hindus, and Christians negotiated new roles under the patronage of the East India Company. Sections of the British tended to put emphasis on the "white man's burden"—the so-called duty to improve indigenous society. Christian missionaries took it upon themselves to attack Hindu customs as unethical and particularly repressive of women; in response, *brāhmaṇas* such as Rammohun Roy were determined to show that Hindu culture and society could be made compatible with modern progressive values.[22] Through his publications he introduced a rational, universal monotheism, inspired by the Upanishads, and promoted a brand of theism that was in keeping with Islamic-Christian sensibilities without being their equivalent.[23] His *Vedāntasāra* (1815) presents nondualistic Vedanta as an alternative to Christian thought, and the basis for social, political, and religious egalitarian views.[24] As has been noted earlier, nondualism nullifies the ultimate form and personality of both God and the individual living being, eliminating all distinctions that may be drawn between the two. On the platform of liberation (*mukti*), both are seen as manifestations of the divine all-pervading oneness known as *brahman*. It also views the

---

21. While there are a number of spellings for Rammohun Roy's name (e.g., Rāmamohana Rāya, Rammohan Roy, Ram Mohan Roy), I have decided to use the spelling used in Noel A. Salmond, *Hindu Iconoclasts: Rammohun Roy, Dayananda Sarasvati, and Nineteenth-Century Polemics against Idolatry* (Waterloo, Ont.: Wilfrid Laurier University Press, 2004).

22. Katherine K. Young, "Women in Hinduism," in *Today's Woman in World Religions*, ed. Arvind Sharma (Albany: State University of New York Press, 1994), pp. 79–80.

23. Rammohun regarded the New Testament as primarily representing the moral teachings of Jesus and paid little attention to claims about the truth of his miracles: "I feel persuaded that by separating from the other matters contained in the New Testament the moral precepts found in that book, these will be more likely to produce the desirable effect of improving the hearts and minds of men of different persuasions and degrees of understanding," Rammohun Roy, *The Precepts of Jesus: The Guide to Peace and Happiness, Extracted from the Books of the New Testament Ascribed to the Four Evangelists* (Calcutta: Baptist Mission Press, 1820), pp. iii–iv. He engaged in protracted debates on Christian theology with Marshman, one of the missionaries at Serampore. See Rammohun Roy, *The Precepts of Jesus: The Guide to Peace and Happiness, Extracted from the Books of the New Testament Ascribed to the Four Evangelists. To Which Are Added, the First, Second, and Final Appeal to the Christian Public in Reply to the Observations of Dr. Marshman of Serampore* (London: John Mardon, 1834).

24. See Bruce Carlisle Robertson, *Raja Rammohan Ray: The Father of Modern India* (Oxford: Oxford University Press, 1999), pp. 165–181. I herein accept the theory presented by Robertson that Rammohun Roy was a key to the revival of *advaita* Vedanta in modern India (pp. 165–166).

world as unreal whenever the awareness of *brahman* is absent from the consciousness of the observer.

In his religious orientation, Rammohun Roy firmly rejected the worship of images and the performance of temple rituals, and fought alongside the missionaries against the abuses of caste and sati, but for different reasons.[25] In particular, he concluded that the elimination of Hindu representations of the divine was the key to the unification, modernization, and regeneration of Hindu culture, although he continued to regard God as the creator and sustainer of the world.[26] In this he was opposed by *bhadralok* Vaishnavas, who disagreed with his vision of an uniconic God, as well as by traditional nondualists who considered the worship of images to fulfill an important function relative to the religious imagination of the Hindu masses.[27] He seemingly strove to find a meeting point with European ideas based upon his reading of *advaita* Vedanta and apparently adopted the iconoclastic sensibilities of the Christian and Muslim traditions that were familiar to him.

Rammohun Roy was born in Radhanagar, West Bengal, to a family belonging to the *kulīna brāhmaṇas*, the highest rank in the Bengali caste structure. His father, Ramakanta, was a Vaishnava, while his mother, Tarini Devi, had been raised in a Śākta family. Early in his life Roy was drawn to such foreign innovations as the unique status given to reason

---

25. Rammohun wrote that "the greater part of the Brahmins, as well as other sects of Hindoos, are quite incapable of justifying that idolatry which they continue to practice.... I have forsaken idolatry for the worship of the true and eternal God." Rammohun Roy, *Translation of Several Principal Books, Passages, and Texts of the Veds, and of Some Controversial Works of Brahmunical Theology* (London, 1832), p. 3. His definition of God was derived from *oṃ tat sat*, of which he wrote: "the first of these signifies 'That *Being*, which preserves, destroys, and creates!' The Second implies '*That* only being, which is neither 'male nor female!' The third announces '*The true being*!' These collective terms simply affirm, that ONE, UNKNOWN, TRUE BEING, IS THE CREATOR, PRESERVER, AND DESTROYER OF THE UNIVERSE!!!" Roy, *Translation of Several Principal Books*, p. 22.

26. Roy stated that "[t]he public will, I hope, be assured that nothing but the natural inclination of the ignorant towards the worship of objects resembling their own nature, and to the external forms of rites palpable to their grosser senses, joined to the self-interested motives of their pretended guides, had rendered the generality of the Hindoo community (in defiance of their sacred books) devoted to idol worship;—the source of prejudice and superstition, and of the total destruction of moral principle, as countenancing criminal intercourse, suicide, female murder and human sacrifice." Roy, *Translation of Several Principal Books*, p. 26. See also Salmond, *Hindu Iconoclasts*, p. viii.

27. Dermot Killingley, "Rammohun Roy's Interpretation of the Vedānta," in *Perspectives on Indian Religion: Papers in Honour of Karel Werner*, ed. Karel Werner and Peter Connolly (Delhi: Sri Satguru Publications, 1986), p. 148.

and science in secular European thought and the ethical monotheism propagated by Christians and Muslims alike; and it is thought that the assimilation of such ideas may have significantly contributed to his eventual alienation from the iconic religious practices of his parents. He was educated in Patna, a center of Islamic learning, and then went to Benares to study Sanskrit and Hindu religious literature. His first book, a Persian work entitled *Tuhfat' ul muhwahhidin* (*A Gift to Monotheists*) was written in 1804 with the aim of encouraging monotheism. The book suggested that although individuals are, by nature, rationally inclined to believe in a divine being, they are too often seduced by religious leaders that encourage them to worship idols and accept irrational and intolerant dogmas. In 1815 Roy published *Vedāntasāra*, a major study on Hindu Vedanta that drew an immediate polemical response from more traditional Hindu quarters in the form of the *Vedāntacandrikā*, published in 1817.[28] He read widely and, in addition to his mastery of Hindi and Bengali, was proficient in Sanskrit, Persian, Hebrew, Arabic, Greek, and English. He amassed a fortune through the lending of money, estate management, and investment in East Indian Company bonds, which enabled him to retire at age forty-two to freely pursue his various literary, religious, and societal interests. From that time until his death in 1833, he was exclusively devoted to social, political, and religious reform.

In 1828 he founded the Brahmo Sabha, the first Hindu institution in colonial Bengal, and a precursor of the Brahmo Samaj. Initially just a weekly gathering of Bengali *brāhmaṇas* in a private Calcutta home, the Sabha was eventually constituted by formal deed of trust, consolidated through the construction of a designated building, and managed by a board of trustees.[29]

Rammohun Roy's approach has been described as universalist and rational in orientation.[30] Brian K. Pennington has called it a "rationalist monotheism" and "a program carried forward to this day by the

28. Wilhelm Halbfass, *India and Europe: An Essay in Understanding* (Albany: State University of New York Press, 1988), pp. 210, 221.

29. John Zavos, *The Emergence of Hindu Nationalism in India* (Delhi: Oxford University Press, 2000), p. 44. Zavos also argues that "the state projected a specific image of organization as a cultural language in its attempt to exert discursive dominance in India. Organization was expressed here as a discourse of modernity" (p. 2). The forming of Hindu organizations in Calcutta was a crucial step toward gaining legitimacy and recognition.

30. De Michelis, *History of Modern Yoga*, p. 10.

ascendancy of Hindu nationalism."[31] In reaction to Roy's ideas, as well as those propagated by evangelical Christians and modern secular utilitarians, the traditionalists among the *bhadralok* founded the newspaper *Samācāra Candrikā* (*Moonlight of the News*), which began its publication in Calcutta on March 5, 1822.[32] Its primary aim was not so much to engage in polemical discussions about philosophy, interpretations of sacred texts, and the worship of images as it was to express profound concern over the erosion of customs and ritual practices. Pennington has described this periodical as

> an indigenous voice seeking to shape a deeply popular native opinion in a city recently penetrated by Christian missionaries... a pioneer in Bengali literature, a spearhead in the "Bengal Renaissance," and a persistent champion of the poor. Allied, however, to its many progressive aspirations was an overarching desire to garrison traditional religious ideas and practices and protect them from the corrosive effects of a pervasive reformism—both western and indigenous. Among the many developments it opposed were feverish proselytizing by Christian missionaries, the reforming zeal of Ram Mohan Roy and his Brahmo Samaj, the youthful affronts of a growing student population enamored of such western radicals as Thomas Paine, and the intrusive tendencies of a government learning the fruits of utilitarian policies.[33]

The newspaper came to reflect the transition to colonial society, and raised such questions as the following: Is caste viable in a colonial milieu? What transformations might image worship and ritual practice undergo in an age of rationality and scientific inquiry?[34] It was concerned, in other words, with changes wrought by colonization and urbanization that could potentially unsettle the lives of Indian villagers and constitute a challenge

---

31. Brian K. Pennington, *Was Hinduism Invented? Britons, Indians, and the Colonial Construction of Religion* (Oxford: Oxford University Press, 2005), p. 140.

32. The other three newspapers were the Serampore Christian mission's *Samācāra Darpana* (*Mirror of the News*), the Indian-owned *Bengali Gazette*, and Rammohun Roy's *Saṅ bāda Kaumudī* (*Moonlight of the News*), which was used to promote his political ideas.

33. Pennington, *Was Hinduism Invented?* p. 140.

34. Pennington, *Was Hinduism Invented?* p. 144.

for the *bhadralok*.[35] The existence of such a newspaper indicates that only a few decades after the colonization of Bengal, there was already in place a Hindu intelligentsia that was not only versed in Western civilization, but was able to debate its implications in a vernacular language publication. This fact appears different from what Said interpreted as the silencing of the Oriental culture by colonialist discourse.[36]

The degree to which European and Islamic ideas ultimately influenced Roy's thought is difficult to assess. Although throughout much of his life he embraced many ideas that stemmed from outside his Hindu upbringing, in his later years he appears to have sought inspiration more from within the basket of Indic religions. In the end he adopted a Vedantic nondualistic approach that was blended with theistic notions; but it was mainly upon this *advaitic* framework that the Brahmo Sabha was founded. After Roy's death, however, the Sabha (then known as the Samaj) was transformed into a theistic institution by his successor, Debendranath Tagore, who purged the organization of almost all its Śaṅkara Vedantic elements by 1850.[37] This change of philosophical direction was challenged twenty years later when a branch that had managed to retain its nondualistic orientation decried theism as being overemotional. By then Keshub Chandra Sen had incorporated into the Brahmo Samaj various devotional practices inspired by Caitanyaite Vaishnavism and the dissenting nondualistic section was determined to distance itself from his approach.[38]

Crises of the Bhadralok

Like Rammohun Roy, Bengal's Western-educated indigenous elite made consistent attempts to build bridges and negotiate their role in the novel colonial milieu, first as mediators between the British

---

35. This development was slow, but accelerated with famines and taxation. The initial impact of land reforms in the rural areas has been questioned. Ratnalekha Ray, for example, has suggested that "the Permanent Settlement of 1793, long regarded as the propelling force behind a revolution in Bengali rural society, would appear to have effected a less fundamental change in the agrarian base of society than is usually supposed." Ratnalekha Ray, "Change in Bengal Agrarian Society Ca. 1760–1850. A Study in Selected Districts," Ph.D. diss., Cambridge University, 1973, p. 284.

36. De Michelis, *History of Modern Yoga*, pp. 5–6.

37. David Kopf, *The Brahmo Samaj and the Shaping of the Modern Indian Mind* (Princeton, N.J.: Princeton University Press, 1979), p. 106.

38. Kopf, *Brahmo Samaj*, p. 251.

and the Indian population, and later as subordinate members of the occupier-administration. The *bhadralok* learned English and familiarized themselves with English literature, European philosophy, and Christian theology.[39] Their position was nonetheless ambivalent. The economic and institutional rationalization that colonialism enforced, along with the new demands of urban life, induced the *bhadralok* to alter their collective religious landscape as well as their individual religiosity. Some built unique cultural and religious lenses through which they viewed not only their own indigenous traditions, but also the interpretations of those traditions put forward by members of the Western Indological and/or scholarly community. Many, of course, tended to be loyal to the East Indian Company (and later to the British Raj) so as to maintain good relations with their only source of financial, social, and political advancement. As British attitudes stiffened in the aftermath of the 1857 Sepoy war, and religious involvement increased in the decennia that followed, a tension developed between aspirations within colonial society and an increasing desire for religious and cultural authenticity.[40] This change in societal atmosphere called forth a variety of reactions from among the *bhadralok*. Some welcomed continued Anglicanization, while some remained indifferent; others flatly rejected the West, seeking instead the revival of a bygone "golden age," or merely independence from colonial rule.[41] Most pondered the new and reworked the past according to their own sensibilities, attempting to at least harmonize (if they could not synthesize) them both.[42]

In this way, the search for Hindu identity in Calcutta's modern sociocultural milieu gave rise to a reevaluation of the content of sacred texts and a reassessment of classical centers of authority. It also engendered a need for religious specialists (sadhus, yogis, and gurus), whose prestige as role models of a new ascetic puritanism had substantially increased. This search for religious, social, and cultural identity prompted crucial religious questions: What was dharma? How far should colonial culture

---

39. Regarding the link between the *bhadralok* and education, see Bhattacharya, *The Sentinels of Culture*.

40. Harder, *Bankimchandra Chattopadhyay's Śrīmadbhagabadgītā*, p. 5.

41. Ainslie T. Embree, *The Hindu Tradition* (New York: Random House, 1972), p. 275.

42. Regarding eclecticism and the Hindu Renaissance, see Brian A. Hatcher, *Eclecticism and Modern Hindu Discourse* (New York: Oxford University Press, 1999).

be allowed to transform its foundations? Was there a common religious core that could include all "Hindus"? What was that core, and how much could be changed before it lost itself in the process?

The task of discovering India's spiritual "core" (i.e., pinpointing the *essence* of works like the Vedas, Upanishads and Bhagavad Gītā) and developing a sound religious ethics and praxis was equal to that of identifying a social, cultural, and political periphery in the religious *habitus* that would allow for dynamic change and flexibility. Although this theological and philosophical problem was most meaningful to urban Hindus, it was also meaningful to members of India's Muslim communities, and remains so today. In my view, the general attempt by the *bhadralok* to distinguish a core from a periphery in doctrine and practice, while simultaneously dealing with the challenges posed by colonial influences, can be effectively understood in terms of what can be called a "core versus periphery relation," formulated, among others, by the Swiss Islamic theologian Tariq Ramadan.[43] Put in terms of this perspective, theirs was an attempt to negotiate the borders between a variously conceived core that was both intrinsic and nonnegotiable and a periphery that could be changed or adjusted—that is, to find creative ways to either harmonize these contrasting relations or keep them apart as incommensurable. It was also an effort that held out the possibility of locating philosophical and theological tools that could legitimize, or even promote, processes of religious transformation and change.

As noted earlier, the process of adaptation among the *bhadralok*, and the dynamic creativity that it generated in the nineteenth century, has been called the "Bengal Renaissance." Many among the *bhadralok* searched for ultimate identity within the pool of ancient Indic religions, and these remained established points of reference throughout the colonial period. The historical significance of the Bengal Renaissance in shaping India's religious life has been crucial, and far beyond the relatively small number

---

43. Ramadan writes: "Muslims must differentiate between essential and secondary issues. For example, to pray is more important than to eat *halal* or *haram* food. . . . It is necessary to know what is *sâbit* (immutable) and what is *mutaghayr* (subject to change), what is essential (*asl*) and what is secondary (*far'*). This process is intrinsic to Islam. Things are changing and moving, and Muslims have to deal with this process." Tariq Ramadan, "Europeanization of Islam or Islamization of Europe?" in *Islam, Europe's Second Religion: The New Social, Cultural, and Political Landscape*, ed. Shireen T. Hunter (Westport, Conn.: Praeger, 2002), pp. 212–213. See also Tariq Ramadan, *Western Muslims and the Future of Islam* (New York: Oxford University Press, 2004).

of its more prominent representatives, which constituted a selective elite. These were individuals who searched for a shared universal vision that could synthesize a plurality of indigenous religious views and simultaneously accommodate the scientific, rationalistic, and humanistic concerns of the Christian West. Among the ideas generated by this group, it was Vivekānanda's universalist interpretation of nondualistic Vedanta that ultimately came to influence the religious orientation of most *bhadralok* by the early twentieth century. What follows is an attempt to trace some of the major threads that led to this development, which began with Rammohun Roy's revival of *advaita* Vedanta philosophy and was advantaged by the supporting role of British colonial culture. Because this development served as a key background to Bhaktisiddhānta's life and thought, it is important to understand it in more detail.

Modernization and Westernization

The colonial experience was transformative for Indian society, and Wilhelm Halbfass has aptly described it as an exposure to

> new forms of organization and administration, to unprecedented claims of universality and globalization, to rationalization, technology, and a comprehensive objectification of the world...a new type of objectification of the Indian tradition itself, an unprecedented exposure to theoretical curiosity and historical "understanding," and to interests of research and intellectual mastery.[44]

However, rather than being a systematic plan for the domestication of Bengal, and later India, Britain's colonial rule was born of a number of uneven political strategies. It evolved over nearly two centuries of domination from the blatantly exploitative economic practices of the early East Indian Company to the relatively mild laissez-faire approach of the British Raj after World War I. British attitudes toward Indian subjects underwent a number of transformations as well, most of which were linked to political and cultural developments at home. However, despite the fact that colonial rule was fraught with various inconsistencies, it nonetheless maintained a steady undertone of coercive domination,

44. Halbfass, *India and Europe*, p. 217.

visible in the fact that India, as a British colonial dependency, had far fewer constitutional rights than "white" counterparts such as Australia and Canada.

David Kopf has suggested that the establishment of the Asiatic Society of Bengal in 1784 inaugurated the Bengal Renaissance since it helped Indians to find an indigenous identity in the modern world.[45] The common roots of India and Europe were forged in the theory of the "Aryan invasion," and the racial Indo-European ancestry that both continents were thought to share became an ideological pillar of the colony. Indeed a vestige of that period is still visible today at the University of Oxford's old Indian Institute (its present faculty of History): on a messing plate beneath the foundation stone—laid in 1883 by Queen Victoria's son Albert Edward—the following text can be read:

> This building, dedicated to Eastern sciences, was founded for the use of Aryans (Indians and Englishmen).[46]

The shared lineage of these two cultures was proclaimed in Calcutta in 1786 by William Jones, the founder and first president of the Asiatic Society.[47] However, the benign fascination of leading members of the East India Company with India's history and sacred texts stood in stark contrast to an initial stage of brutal economic exploitation.[48] Even Thomas

---

45. Kopf argues that the early phase of colonialism was receptive to the cultural values of India. It was different from the kind of Orientalism that Said has defined as "the corporate institution dealing with the Orient—dealing with it, making statements about it, authorizing views of it, describing it by teaching it, settling it, ruling over it: in short, Orientalism as a Western style for dominating, restructuring and having authority over the Orient." Quoted in De Michelis, *History of Modern Yoga*, p. 3.

46. The plaque consists of several Sanskrit verses with their English translation below. The above quotation is part of the English translation.

47. See Thomas R. Trautmann, *Aryans and British India* (Berkeley: University of California Press, 1997), p. 28.

48. It must be said that while 190 years of British rule certainly contributed to the improvement of the indigenous population's health, education, and economy, it also directly and/or indirectly contributed to indigenous mass poverty. As noted by Tapan Raychauduri, in 1947, 48 to 53 percent of India's rural population was under the poverty line and could not afford the minimum amount of food needed to sustain the human body. Tapan Raychaudhuri, *Perceptions, Emotions, Sensibilities: Essays on India's Colonial and Post-colonial Experiences* (Oxford: Oxford University Press, 1999), p. 159. For a detailed study of colonial economy, see K. M. Munshi, ed., *British Paramountcy and Indian Renaissance*, vol. 9 of *The History and Culture of the Indian People* (Bombay: Bharatiya Vidya Bhavan, 1963), pp. 1144–1162.

Babington Macaulay (1800–1859), a strong advocate of the superiority of British civilization, openly condemned those early excesses.[49]

In 1770, for example, Bengal was struck by a severe naturally induced famine that was especially devastating in the western and central sections, and that caught the British completely by surprise. As a result, an estimated three million people (or 30 percent of the population) are thought to have died.[50] Two years later, as public opinion at home wearied of British exploitation, Warren Hastings (1732–1818) was elected governor of Bengal, with a mandate to improve the situation. Hastings had arrived in Bengal in 1750, at a time when Fort William, the regional symbol of British power, was still only a trading center. During the years leading to his 1772 governorship, he rose rapidly through the ranks of the dawning colony, managing to accumulate a fabulous fortune along the way. In contrast to many of his predecessors, however, Hastings had a love for the culture, philosophy, and languages of India, and spared no resource in order to build bridges and facilitate British-Indian understanding, primarily through the translation of Hindu law books and the employment of local pandits. He also established an Indian language study program for the East India Company's British employees. Although Hastings was later impeached for suspected crimes and misdemeanors, and returned to Great Britain in public disgrace, he was eventually acquitted of all charges.[51]

49. Looking back on those events, Macaulay laconically commented that "on one side was a band of English functionaries, daring, intelligent, eager to be rich. On the other side was a great native population, helpless, timid, and accustomed to crouch under oppression. To keep the stronger race from preying on the weaker, was an undertaking which tasked to the utmost the talents and energy of Clive.... The only protection which the conquered could find was in the moderation, the clemency, the enlarged policy of the conquerors. That protection, at a later period, they found. But at first English power came among them unaccompanied by English morality," Thomas Babington Macaulay, *Critical, Historical, and Miscellaneous Essays and Poems, Vol. 5–6* (New York: A.C. Armstrong & Son, 1860), vol. 5, p. 9. Commenting on Robert Clive, the first governor of Bengal, he wrote that "when he landed in Calcutta in 1765, Bengal was regarded as a place to which Englishmen were sent only to get rich, by any means, in the shortest possible time." Thomas Babington Macaulay, *Critical and Historical Essays: Contributed to the Edinburgh Review* (London: Longmans Green, 1866), vol. 2, p. 127.

50. Raychaudhuri, *Perceptions, Emotions, Sensibilities*, p. 161. It is difficult to assess the exact amount of famine-related deaths, which may have amounted to less than one-fifth (rather than one-third) of Bengal's total population; see Gordon Johnson and Peter James Marshall, *Bengal: The British Bridgehead. Eastern India, 1740–1828*, vol. 2 of *The New Cambridge History of India* (Cambridge: Cambridge University Press, 1987), p. 18.

51. Accusations against Hastings were lodged by members of Parliament such as Edmund Burke and included allegations that he had breached agreements and employed undue extortion in his dealings with Indian maharajas. See Edmund Burke, *Articles of Charge of High Crimes and Misdemeanors, against Warren Hastings, Esq. Late Governor General of Bengal* (London: J. Debrett, 1786).

Kopf suggests that many of the leading figures among the early British in Bengal were strongly opposed to the Westernization of taste and culture that was later immortalized by Macaulay's famous "Minute on Indian Education," presented in Calcutta to the Supreme Council of India in 1835.[52] In making this suggestion, Kopf raises the legitimate question of whether the processes of modernization and Westernization must always and necessarily go hand in hand.[53] One reading of this more engaging early period is that the British were hoping to transform Indian society from within through knowledge of Indic languages and culture. They appreciated religious pluralism and did not strive to change India on the basis of their own European self-image. They ran schools, contributed to the systematization of languages for comparative and educational purposes, and created presses for publishing newspapers, journals, and books.[54] Richard King, on the other hand, has questioned whether it is possible to draw a fine distinction between Westernization and modernization. King considers modernization to have been a process born of the European Enlightenment and suggests that the early British colonialists always dealt with India on the basis of an ingrained notion of the superiority of European culture.[55] The question of whether modernization and Westernization are necessarily interrelated or wholly

52. Macaulay stated that "a single shelf of a good European library was worth the whole native literature of India and Arabia.... We must at present do our best to form a class who may be interpreters between us and the millions whom we govern; a class of persons, Indian in blood and color, but English in taste, in opinions, in morals and in intellect." Thomas Babington Macaulay, "Minute of Indian Education" (1835), *Macmillan's Magazine*, May–October 1864, 3–6. These statements are quoted in most historical works discussing that period.

53. David Kopf, *British Orientalism and the Bengal Renaissance: The Dynamics of Indian Modernization, 1773–1835* (Berkeley: University of California Press, 1969), pp. 276ff. Kopf concludes that the early Orientalists were opposed to Westernization, and instead promoted a local pattern of modernization, since "nineteenth-century Europe was not so much the source of modernity as it was the setting for modernizing processes that were themselves transforming Western culture." Kopf, *British Orientalism*, p. 277.

54. Kopf, *British Orientalism*, pp. 275–276.

55. While Kopf attempts to defend the sincerity of motive of the East India Company's early British employees, King adopts a more postcolonial perspective, pointing out the dynamics of domination. The fact is that the notable presence of a hegemonic discourse in colonial society tended to obscure the large diversity of formal and informal attitudes, exchanges, and motives among the colonizers and the colonized—a diversity that rendered the colonial project heterogeneous.

independent processes is still a hotly debated topic, and one that will be dealt with in chapter 5.[56]

The British certainly used means that arose from their specific context and generally considered British civilization more enlightened and evolved, but they also lacked a sophisticated understanding of culture, and especially of Indic culture. Although, on one level, they may have desired to replant the European cultural matrix in Indian soil, they simply lacked the resources, interest, and capacity to turn India into a carbon copy of Europe. With the exception of the great metropolitan areas that were replete with European settlers, the British penetration was practically insignificant, and the colonial administration was consistently forced to rely upon numerous indigenous partners. In this regard, first the East India Company and then the Raj came to understand that the maximization of agricultural revenues and cash crops could be best achieved by keeping India rural and "traditional," especially since doing so would pose no threat to industrial centers at home. Furthermore, the territory of South Asia was so vast, and the employees of the East Indian Company so few, that it is difficult to imagine that there was a well-coordinated policy of overall colonial rule; for the most part, British relations with the indigenous population were negotiated according to local needs and circumstances.[57] Regarding Hastings's attempt to establish a program for the learning of Oriental languages at Fort William, it was eventually abandoned not only because of British pressure, but also because educated Hindus such as Rammohun Roy considered English to be more advantageous in British colonial society than either Sanskrit or Persian—although he did promote vernacular languages as well.

Clearly both the processes of Westernization and those of modernization had an impact on Bengal's *bhadralok* community, and prompted a wide range of responses, some of which were broadly in keeping with the nondualistic perspective pioneered by Rammohun Roy. It is nonetheless theoretically important to draw a distinction between modernization

---

56. See S. N. Eisenstadt, "Multiple Modernities," *Daedalus* 129, no. 1 (2000); Studipta Kaviraj, "Modernity and Politics in India," *Daedalus* 129, no. 1 (2000). For a general introduction to contemporary discussions on the historiography of India leading up to 1858, see Robert E. Frykenberg, "India to 1858," in *The Oxford History of the British Empire*, vol. 5, *Historiography*, ed. Robin W. Winks and Alaine M. Low (Oxford: Oxford University Press, 2001). For the period between 1858 and 1930 see Raychaudhuri, *Perceptions, Emotions, Sensibilities*, pp. 172–187.

57. Munshi, *British Paramountcy*, p. 1132.

and Westernization, since in a colonial setting such as India's the two were generally at odds from the point of view of the indigenous population. This is exemplified by the fact that the *bhadralok* often searched for models of modernity that were non-Western and in tune with indigenous values and culture, rather than those that were mere duplicates of one or another Western brand.

At first it was the *bhadralok* more than the Muslim elite that led the way in terms of absorbing European culture. Indeed its more liberal elements responded with great enthusiasm to all things Western and quickly assimilated European ideas such as rationalism and humanism. Perhaps the most radical expression of Western assimilation can be found in the Young Bengal movement inspired by the Eurasian poet and patriot Henry Luis Vivian Derozio (1809–1831). At the age of seventeen Derozio was appointed teacher of English literature and history at Calcutta's Hindu College; there he lectured brilliantly on such topics as the rational principles of the Enlightenment, encouraging students to question orthodox Hindu conventions on the basis of Judeo-Christian rationalism. Derozio promoted free enquiry on religious matters and openly criticized indigenous customs and values, proposing a humanism that exalted the unlimited potential of human progress instead. Although he himself was an atheist, Derozio's encouragement of free enquiry led some students, like Krishnamohan Banerji (1813–1895), to convert to Christianity, and others, like Sib Chandra Deb (1811–1890), to become leaders of the Brahmo Samaj.[58] His challenging rationalism eventually created a backlash at Hindu College and he was asked to resign his post.

Throughout the major portion of the nineteenth century, despite a growing sense of Indian national identity, and several potentially alienating British missteps, the *bhadralok* community remained generally positive toward colonial rule and British cultural influence in Bengal.[59] In the

---

58. Nitish K. Sengupta, *History of the Bengali-Speaking People* (Orpington: Grantha Neer, 2001), pp. 227–228. About this period, Derozio, and his movement, see also Susobhan Chandra Sarkar, *On the Bengal Renaissance* (Calcutta: Papyrus, 1979). Derozio is also discussed in some detail by Sisir Kumar Das, *Early Bengali Prose, Carey to Vidyasagar* (Calcutta: Bookland, 1966).

59. Kopf notes that during the early colonial period, the liberal wing of the *bhadralok* identified so closely with the aspiration of European liberals that "despite the fact that the British had deliberately arrested industrial urbanization in India, had monopolized the administration for their own elite, had denied the principle of legislative and municipal representation for Indians, and had drained India of its wealth to pay for Britain's wars abroad, Bengali liberals identified closely with the modern progressive West, adapting their ideas and programs to the Bengali context," Kopf, *British Orientalism*, pp. 275–276.

latter nineteenth century, however, many in the Bengal Renaissance began to question the legitimacy of colonial culture and Western education, and the relationship between the *bhadralok* and the British became far more challenging, ambivalent, and tense.[60]

Western Search for Origins

Although the Oriental School at Fort William, built to promote the learning of India's languages and history, gradually came to an end during the 1830s, it left one long-lasting impression: the notion that what was to be known as "Hinduism" was synonymous with the early philosophy of the Upanishads, and particularly with nondualism, echoing a view that had already become well established in Europe. As for the numerous iconic elements within various Indic traditions, these were viewed as sectarian degenerations that appeared during the later Puranic period.[61]

The reason for this has partially to do with the cultural climate in Europe. Early on, central and western Europe had shown a keen interest in the historical origins of India. Romanticism had portrayed India as the source of European civilization, traceable to a distant Aryan past. In his book *Über die Sprache und Weisheit der Indier* (1808), Friedrich Schlegel, a prominent German romantic, spoke of his hankering for spiritual guidance from the East at a time when Europe was experiencing a rough transition to modernity. Johann Gottfried Herder (1744–1803) proclaimed ancient India to be the earliest expression of human civilization and the root of Indo-European culture.[62] For these early Indologists, the Vedic texts became the window through which the entire history of the Indic religions could be understood, anticipating the approach of Dayānanda Sarasvatī and the Arya Samaj.

According to Richard King, the influence of romanticism, reinforced by an incipient sense of the evolutionary destiny of mankind, tended to

60. In the book *Towards Universal Man*, Rabindranath Tagore describes the initial enchantment and eventual disillusionment of the *bhadralok* with British liberal values and humanism. Rabindranath Tagore, *Towards Universal Man* (New York: Asia Publishing House, 1961), pp. 353–354.

61. See also Niranjan Dhar, *Vedanta and Bengal Renaissance* (Calcutta: Minerva Associates, 1977), pp. 31–32.

62. Johann Gottfried Herder, *Johann Gottfried Von Herder's Sämmtliche Werke*, ed. Johann von Müller (Stuttgart, 1829), pp. 349–350.

make India a reflection of the childhood of Europe, a living image of what was perceived as the cradle of civilization.[63] This reading of India's antiquity and timeless religion was popularized through early translations of the Upanishads, which were regarded as expressing the core conclusion of the Vedas—that is, the Vedanta.[64]

Because of the focus on early texts such as the Upanishads, which Western Indologists interpreted as conveying an essentially nondualistic perspective, the view emerged that despite their great variety of deities and religious forms, all Indic religions "express the same basic truth" and all Hindu paths lead to the same impersonal goal of *brahman*.[65] This conclusion was later reinforced when the study of the Vedanta (or *Brahma*) *Sūtra* was taken up in earnest and Śaṅkara's *advaita* Vedanta philosophy became more widely known. These occurrences, however, tended to overlook the fact that Vedanta has a number of alternative branches, of which ten are considered prominent.[66]

Despite the later discovery by various Indologists and Christian scholars of profound iconic, dualistic strands, the reduction of Indic philosophy to an impersonal essence has permeated popular Western culture ever since, and has become the dominant understanding in Bengal and other

---

63. Richard King, "Orientalism and the Modern Myth of 'Hinduism' (Western Christian Notions of Indian Religion at the Interface between Post-Colonial Theories of Religions)," *Numen* 46, no. 2 (1999): p. 118.

64. The earliest was the *Oupnek'hat*, a translation into Latin of a Persian rendition of fifty-two Upanishads commissioned in 1657 by Dārā Šokōh, firstborn son of Mughal emperor Shah Jahān, by Abraham Hyacinthe Anquetil-Duperron, *Oupnek'hat (Id Est, Secretum Tegendum): Opus Ipsa in India Rarissimum, Continens Antiquam Et Arcanam Doctrinam, Quatuor Sacris Indorum Libris, Rak Beid, Djedjr Beid, Sam Beid, Athrban Beid, Excerptam*... (Argentorati, 1801–1802). It was translated into German in 1808 and had a large impact in Europe, Abraham Hyacinthe Anquetil-Duperron and Thaddeus Anselm Rixner, *Versuch Einer Neuen Darstellung Der Uralten Indischen All-Eins-Lehre, oder Der Berühmten Sammlung... Erstes Stück Oupnek'hat Tschehandouk Genannt* (Nuremberg: Steinischen Buchhandlung, 1808). The *Oupnek'hat* was particularly inspiring, among others, to Schopenhauer and the German Idealists and was lavishly praised by Jean-Denis Lanjuinais, "Analyse De L'oupnek'hat," *Journal asiatique* no. April (1823). However, it was severely criticized by the Indologist Max Müller, who regarded it as quite unintelligible. Max Müller, *The Upanishads*, Sacred Books of the East (Oxford: Clarendon Press, 1879), pp. lviii–lix. Nonetheless, the *Oupnek'hat* was an important European sourcebook for all early nineteenth-century studies of Indic religions.

65. This understanding was less relevant for German Indological scholarship because it was more focused on the Vedas.

66. Madan Mohan Agrawal, *Six Systems of Indian Philosophy: The Sutras of Six Systems of Indian Philosophy with English Translation, Transliteration, and Indices* (Delhi: Chaukhamba Sanskrit Pratishthan, 2001), p. xxxiii.

parts of India as well. A renowned scholar of Hinduism,
has recently estimated that "three-fourths of modern Hi
subscribe to it."[67] But this anticipates our narrative.

Missionaries and Missions

As noted above, key sections of the *bhadralok* in nineteenth- and early twentieth-century India were inclined to view one or another version of nondualism as the philosophical core of Hinduism and uniconic worship as their natural ritual counterpart. This propensity may have been influenced by yet another important factor: the presence of the Protestant missions, a plurality of institutions that stood for a diversity of approaches and visions. As a point of departure, the nature of this influence will be described below, with particular emphasis on the British side of the equation. This, however, is not meant to imply that a comprehensive understanding of this highly complex phenomenon can be achieved in this way. As mentioned earlier, the *bhadralok* internalized and responded to the influences of these missions in highly personal and independent ways, and this is an important side of the narrative as well.

To properly comprehend the importance of this impact, it is important to remember that the majority of missionaries were not wandering preachers in search of Indian converts, but institution-builders that presided over churches, schools, and hospitals. The encounter with the "Hindoos" occurred most often not in the open air, but in structured institutional settings. The earliest Protestant-Hindu encounters took place in Bengal with English and Scottish missionaries, whose educational backgrounds differed from one another. At the time, England's educational system was far more elitist than that of Scotland's, which had been strongly influenced by the Enlightenment principles of shared opportunities and egalitarianism.[68] As a result, higher education in England was restricted until 1822 to two institutions, Oxford and Cambridge, and available only to those members of the clergy who

67. Arvind Sharma, *Modern Hindu Thought: An Introduction* (Oxford: Oxford University Press, 2005), p. 51.

68. By 1583 Scotland already had four universities: St Andrews, Glasgow, Aberdeen, and Edinburgh. In England, higher education was restricted to Oxford and Cambridge, until the University of Wales, Lampeter was founded as St David's College in 1822, followed by the University of London in 1826.

could afford it. This fact becomes interesting when one considers that the three most prominent British missionaries of the early nineteenth century, William Carey, Joshua Marshman, and William Ward, established a press in Serampore and ventured to publish a large amount of vernacular literature—including early Bengali and Sanskrit translations of the Bible—while possessing only rudimentary formal educations. In this regard, Laird notes that

> the contrast between the educational histories of the English and Scottish missionaries is in fact notable, and helps to illustrate the difference in educational opportunity between the two countries: if Carey, Marshman, and Ward had been Scots they may well have been able to attend a university; and we would not then be marvelling at the example of men who became Oriental scholars without even the benefit of a regular secondary education.[69]

Following the praxis of their time, the early Christian missionaries tended to view Indic traditions through their own religious and cultural lenses. They interpreted Indic religions in terms of such notions as "pantheism" or "polytheism," assuming them to be nondifferent from the religions of Greece, Rome, and the "pagan" civilizations of the Old Testament.[70] They viewed the worship of iconic representations as mere "idol worship" and condemned incomprehensible Hindu customs as immoral on the basis of their own Protestant ethics. Although these first Protestant missionaries lacked classical training in Indian philosophy and thought, they nonetheless ventured on their own to acquire a superb proficiency in Sanskrit and other vernacular languages with the help of hired pandits. These

---

69. M. A. Laird, *Missionaries and Education in Bengal, 1793–1837* (Oxford: Oxford University Press, 1972), p. 192.

70. William Ward compared Hindu theology with Greek philosophy and found that "the agreement betwixt these opinions and those of the Greek philosophers is very remarkable." William Ward, *A View of the History, Literature, and Religion of the Hindoos; Including Translations from Their Principal Works*, 2 vols. (London: Committee of the Baptist Missionary Society, 1817), pp. i–ii (cited hereafter as "*View* (1817). The word "pantheism" was coined by the English writer John Toland (1670–1722). Charles Hartshone, "Pantheism and Panentheism," in *The Encyclopedia of Religion*, ed. Mircea Eliade and Charles J. Adams (New York: Macmillan, 1987), p. 169. The identification of Vedantic *advaita* with pantheism was still prevalent in the early twentieth century; see the Scottish missionary Urquhart's work on pantheism and Indian philosophy, W. S. Urquhart, *Pantheism and the Value of Life, with Special Reference to Indian Philosophy* (London: Epworth Press, 1919).

individuals, however, gave them a highly *brāhmaṇic* and Sanskritized image of Indic religions. Furthermore, Carey (who arrived in Bengal in 1793), Ward, and the couple Joshua and Hannah Marshman taught Western science and Christian theology alongside Hindu astronomy, geography, and philosophy with the expressed aim of training their students to challenge Hindu pandits on their own grounds, rather than developing a sympathetic understanding of the heart of Indic religions. Hannah Marshman established an Anglo-Indian boarding school in Serampore, and Carey dedicated himself to translation work and the teaching of languages to East India Company personnel at Fort William College. After approximately twenty years of teaching in Calcutta, he went on to establish a Baptist college in the Danish enclave.[71] For his part, Ward authored an extremely influential study of the Hindu world entitled *View of the history, literature and religion of the Hindoos: including a minute description of their manners and customs.*[72] In the third edition of this work, printed in London in 1817, he suggested that *brahman*—which he called the Divine Spirit—was at the core of the theology of the Hindus:

> The whole system of Hindoo theology is founded upon the doctrine that the Divine Spirit, as the soul of the universe, becomes, in all human beings, united to matter; that spirit is insulated or individuated by particular portions of matter, which it is continuously quitting, and joining itself to new portions of matter; that the human soul is, in other words, God himself.[73]

---

71. A. Christopher Smith, "The Legacy of William Ward and Joshua and Hannah Marshman," *International Bulletin of Missionary Research* 23, no. 3 (1999): pp. 120–122.

72. The first edition of this work appeared in four volumes and was simply entitled *Account of the Writings, Religion, and Manners of the Hindoos* (1811). Subsequent editions consisted of one to four volumes that had been reworked with different prefaces. The editions also varied in content. Those printed in Serampore were more anthropological and of significant historical value, providing a wealth of information on Hindu customs, life, and religion. They were also more neutral in tone, praising India and Hindu traditions for their advances in science, philosophy, and logic. See William Ward, *A View of the History, Literature and Mythology of the Hindoos: Including a Minute Description of Their Manners and Customs, and Translations from Their Principal Works*, 2 vols. (Serampore: Mission Press, 1818). The editions that were printed in England, however, were more apologetic, attacking Hindu religions as idolatrous, immoral, and misogynistic; see Ward, *View* (1817). The British editions were geared toward the collection of funds for the mission, and thus tended to overstate India's need of salvation.

73. Ward, *View* (1817), vol. 1, p. i and following.

While acknowledging the pervasiveness of Vaishnavism in Eastern India, Ward lamented the tradition's alleged ethical shortcomings:

> Nearly one half of the Hindoo population of Bengal are Voishnāvās, composed principally of the lower orders: great numbers are religious mendicants. Almost all Hindus in Orissa are Voishnāvās... the distinguishing vice of this sect is impurity, as might be expected... from the obscene nature of the festivals held.[74]

He also characterized Vaishnavism in purely homogenous terms, with neither nuance nor reference to the fact that Vaishnava bhakti in Bengal has both a nondualistic and a dualistic tradition, as well as an orthodox mainstream and an erotic-tantric orientation.[75] It was this sort of partial understanding that served to shape nineteenth-century Protestant perceptions of Indic religious life.

Education

Despite their rather small numerical strength, the early missionaries had a profound influence on the *bhadralok*, primarily through the

74. Ward, *View* (1817), vol. 1, p. 219.

75. Rahul Peter Das divides Caitanya Vaishnavas into two distinct groups: the Gauḍīyas and the Sahajiyās. Rahul Peter Das, *Essays on Vaisnavism in Bengal* (Calcutta: Firma KLM, 1997), p. 30. This distinction highlights the fact that Caitanya Vaishnavism is represented by both a textual-*brāhmaṇic* and an illiterate-popular tier, with the latter of these being heavily influenced by Śakta tantrism and other such traditions. Each of these communities counts millions of adherents. The Gauḍīyas follow the authority of the six Goswamis of Vrindavan and consist of both laypersons and ascetic mendicants (*vairāgīs*). In 1896 Jogendra Nath Bhattacharya published a description of Caitanya Vaishnavism in Bengal from the vantage point of orthodox *brāhmaṇic* society. This account is viewed as being particularly reliable since Bhattacharya was not only a trained jurist, but also the president of both the Brāhmaṇa Sabhā of Bengal and the College of Pundits in the district of Nadiya, where Nabadwip and Mayapur are located. Jogendra Nath Bhattacharya, *Hindu Castes and Sects: An Exposition of the Origin of the Hindu Caste System and the Bearing of the Sects Towards Each Other and Towards Other Religious Systems* (1896; Calcutta: Editions Indian, 1973), pp. 370–380. For an overview of Caitanya Vaishnavism in the 1920s see Tanika Sarkar, *Rebels, Wives, Saints: Designing Selves and Nations in Colonial Times* (Ranikhet: Permanent Black, 2009), pp. 69–120. Accounts of folk religion are found in Ajit Das, *Jātavaiṣṇava Kathā* (Kolkata: Charuvaka, 1993), pp. 7–9, 40–49. See also Joseph O'Connell, "Jati Vaiṣṇavas of Bengal: 'Subcaste' (Jati) without 'Caste' (Varna)," *Journal of Asian and African Studies* 17, nos. 3–4 (1981). For a discussion about the divide between orthodox-literate and popular traditions, see also Sudhir Chakrabarty, *Gabhīra Nirjana Pathe* (Kolkata: Ananda Publishers, 1989), pp. 150–157, 225–237.

establishment of an educational system designed to favor Protestant religion and culture. Scottish missionaries such as Alexander Duff (1806–1878), for example, were responsible for training a generation of *bhadralok* Bengalis, equipping them with the ability to scrutinize their own religious customs in ways that were more in keeping with European sensibilities.[76] The Christian influence was especially profound within Indian intellectual circles, where it encouraged critical thinking and kindled a desire for ethical reform, the uplifting of women, religious democratization, and the loosening of the grip of the priestly class. Axel Michaels has gone so far as to label the century from 1850 to 1950 "Christian-Hindu syncretism," and although this characterization may be somewhat overstated, there can be no doubt that the influence of Christianity on Hinduism was felt on all levels of Indian society.[77] The exact manner in which this occurred is an important topic that requires further scholarly attention.

Alexander Duff traveled to India from the Highlands of Scotland, and in 1830 founded what later came to be known as the Scottish Church College, an institution that was responsible for the education of thousands of upper-caste Hindu students, several of whom went on to become leading cultural figures—for example, Swami Vivekānanda, A. C. Bhaktivedānta Swami, the founder of the International Society for Krishna Consciousness (ISKCON), and the religious leader and freedom fighter Brahmabandhab Upadhyay (1861–1907).[78] Duff also played a pivotal role in the establishment of the University of Calcutta in 1857.

Unlike his Baptist counterparts in Serampore, whose mission was primarily developed through vernacular language translations of the Bible and indigenous studies that afforded a detailed understanding of the field, Duff was wholly committed to English language education, which he considered important not only because it improved the chances of a good career, but also because it facilitated the advanced study of European religion, literature, and science. In this he reflected the emphases of the Scottish

---

76. Alexander Duff was first a member of the Church of Scotland; then, in 1843, he became a member of the Free Church of Scotland.

77. Michaels, *Hinduism*, p. 45.

78. Subhankar Ghosh Abhik Banerjee, Srabani Pal, and Kalyan Mitra, "Some Distinguished Former Students: Scottish Church College," *Scottish Church College Souvenir* (1999): pp. 1–6. For a biography of Upadhyay, see Julius J. Lipner, *Brahmabandhab Upadhyay: The Life and Thought of a Revolutionary* (Delhi: Oxford University Press, 2001).

educational system that had formed him.[79] Through the careful selection of teachers, the interweaving of both Christian and secular understandings and the employment of advanced pedagogical techniques, Duff created one of the most compelling and popular educational institutions of his time. One of the key elements of the Scottish system that he implemented involved the employment of the Socratic method, a form of classroom inquiry and debate that stimulated rational thinking and illuminated ideas. This interactive method of posing challenging questions and encouraging his students to polemically discuss them in class had a profound effect on their attitudes toward their own indigenous beliefs. The method, of course, was not new, and had already been tested at the Calcutta School Society in the early 1820s, but Duff was particularly successful in applying it.

In general, the number of Bengali converts to Christianity remained relatively small, partially due to the difficulty of forfeiting caste and other well-established family traditions, and partially because of the link in the Indian mind between Christian missions and imperialistic colonial rule.[80] The schools nonetheless succeeded in transmitting the missionaries' sensibilities to generations of students, who began viewing their own literatures, beliefs, and customs through this newly acquired cultural lens. And while this may not have been a determining factor relative to the students' ultimate choice of religious orientation, it often served as a catalyst for the emergence of original indigenous responses to the West—responses that gave rise to various religious, political, and cultural movements in Bengal.[81] The following section provides a more detailed account of those specific sensibilities.

Perceptions and Sensibilities

Despite the fact that between 1739 and 1850 there were a diversity of Christian missions in India, those of the Protestant persuasion shared

79. Laird comments that while Duff "regarded English—the language of a Protestant Christian culture—as the best medium for evangelism in both the partly Roman Catholic Highlands and in non-Christian Bengal, the other missionaries perpetuated a more characteristic Protestant tradition in preferring Bengali; like the German Pietists and the evangelists of eighteenth-century Wales, they used the local vernacular as the medium for preaching, journalism, and education alike, and the result was the general development of the Bengali language no less than of German and Welsh" (*Missionaries and Education*, p. 271).

80. Gerald James Larson, *India's Agony over Religion* (Albany: State University of New York Press, 1995), pp. 125–126.

81. Salmond arrives at this conclusion in his study of the Hindu iconoclasts Rammohun Roy and Dayananda Sarasvati, *Hindu Iconoclasts*, p. 7.

several basic standpoints that informed their negative opinions about "Hinduism," at least as they understood it.[82] Geoffrey A. Oddie has identified three such standpoints: (1) a hatred of so-called idolatry; (2) a contempt for all forms of sexual expression; and, (3) a high regard for science and rationality.[83] These will be briefly discussed below.

Protestant attitudes toward the worship of "statues," "graven images," and the like appear to stem from a strict reading of Old Testament passages that strongly condemn the worship of "imaginary man-made images" rather than the actual "Creator," whose form, if it exists at all, is not to be seen. The assumption appears to have been that this sort of idol worship leads to ritual and moral degradation, exemplified by the apparent link between temple rituals and prostitution. Protestant missionaries, in particular, were vehemently opposed to image worship, and Oddie has argued that this vehemence was connected to the Reformation, and particularly to the struggle against Catholicism's iconic worship of mother Mary and the holy saints.[84] Regardless of whether or not this argument is accurate, the fact remains that Protestant missionaries brought with them to India a strong disregard for image worship, and this adulterated their perception of the iconic religions they encountered.

Regarding Protestant views on human sexuality, these were formed long before the Reformation, when the early fathers of the Catholic Church promoted the importance to Christian devotion of such qualities as celibacy and chastity.[85] Much later, during the nineteenth and twentieth centuries, Anglican Protestants became deeply concerned about the "ever-falling standards" of sexual morality in British society, and, in response, adopted a severe antisexual orientation. It was with this orientation that Protestant missionaries ventured to India to confront the love

---

82. Some of the most influential Protestant missions in India were the Particular Baptist Missionary Society founded in 1792, the London Missionary Society (1795), the Church Missionary Society (1799), the Wesleyan Methodist Missionary Society (1814–1818), the Foreign Mission Committee of the Church of Scotland (1824), and, after the dissolution of the Church of Scotland in 1843, the Foreign Mission Committee of the Free Church of Scotland. Geoffrey A. Oddie, *Imagined Hinduism: British Protestant Missionary Constructions of Hinduism, 1793–1900* (New Delhi: Sage Publications, 2006), p. 17.

83. Oddie, *Imagined Hinduism*, pp. 24–29. The use of the term "idol" is not intended to convey a pejorative sense. In this work, the more neutral term "image" will be used, unless primary sources are reproduced or paraphrased.

84. Oddie, *Imagined Hinduism*, p. 26.

85. Elizabeth Abbott, *A History of Celibacy* (Cambridge: Lutterworth Press, 2001), pp. 53–54.

mysticism found in various Indic traditions. The natural result was strong condemnation throughout the colonial period, especially of the tales of Krishna's nocturnal dance, the religious significance of which lay outside the scope of their theological views.[86]

The high regard of Protestant missionaries for science and rationality was inspired by the Enlightenment and surfaced in India as a critique of the religious emotionalism and "superstition" found in indigenous practices and rites. While the statements of individual missionaries may have had some impact on the indigenous population in this regard, it was largely institutions like the Scottish College that conveyed Protestant rationalism to the *bhadralok* in a systematic way.[87] These educational institutions became prototypes for Indic institutions such as the Hindu College (1818), founded in order to counteract missionary influence. The missionaries nonetheless succeeded in establishing the grounds for what can be described as a Hindu puritanism cloaked in Christian institutional dress.

Protestant missionaries availed themselves of the financial support of wealthy segments of the home population, obtained by means of fund-raising drives, public lecturing, the issuing of regular reports, and the writing of books and articles. Their sensibilities reflected mainstream Anglo religious culture both in the United Kingdom and in India, and generally represented the standard view on the nature of a civilized society. Christian ethics later found their secular equivalent in Victorian puritanism, which was the orientation of the imperial middle and upper class. The missions created a religious environment that esteemed asceticism, chastity, education, and egalitarianism, which, in some respects, went against the grain of a heavily hierarchical colonial society. But they also inspired a marked preference for uniconic religious worship.

The reliance of early missionaries on Hindu pandits, whose preferences most often leaned toward nondualistic perspectives, strongly inclined Christian scholars to embrace Śaṅkara's *advaita* rather than "iconic" and "erotic" Vaishnavism as *the* religion of India. The influential Scottish missionary W. S. Urquhart, principal and professor of philosophy at both the Scottish Church College and the University of Calcutta, researched the

86. An overview is found in David L. Haberman, "Divine Betrayal: Krishna-Gopal of Braj in the Eyes of the Outsiders," *Journal of Vaishnava Studies* 3, no. 1 (1994).

87. Jeffrey Cox, *Imperial Fault Lines: Christianity and Colonial Power in India, 1818–1940* (Stanford: Stanford University Press, 2002), p. 8.

indigenous impact of Rāmānuja's Vaishnava theology as compared to the theology of Śaṅkara. In 1928 he concluded that

> there can be little doubt that the pre-eminence must be assigned to Śaṅkara. So far as counting of heads goes, it has been estimated even by a follower of Rāmānuja that out of the total number of Vedantins 75 per cent. are adherents to Śaṅkara, and only 15 per cent. of Rāmānuja, while the remaining 10 per cent may be distributed among the minor sects also laying claim to the name of Vedantins. And that this popularity is not merely accidental, but is based upon and justified by a considered estimate of the significance of Śaṅkara's teachings, is evidence by the opinion of leading scholars, even down to the present day.[88]

Without questioning Śaṅkara's obvious importance to India's religious life, Uruquart's estimate only pertained to the literate priestly elite, representing what Axel Michaels has termed "Brahmatic-Sanskritic" Hinduism, and did not take into account Vaishnavism's far greater popularity among the middle and lower social classes.[89] Although Protestant missionaries were certainly aware of the devotional (or bhakti) strands within Indic religion, these strands were most often perceived as nondualistic in essence, and thus their distinctive religious significance was rarely sufficiently explored.[90] The impulse of both Protestant and secular culture to characterize Hinduism as a nondualistic Brahminical "religion" only served to heighten criticism of iconic forms worship—a criticism that began during the period of Islamic rule and found fresh expression in the writings of Rammohun Roy and new Hindu advocates of *advaita* Vedanta.

Apart from the influence of the Christian missions, there was another less visible but rather intriguing channel through which ideas born of Christianity made an impact on the sensibilities of the *bhadralok*—that

---

88. W. S. Urquhart, *The Vedānta and Modern Thought* (London: Humphrey Milford, 1928), pp. 64–65.

89. Michaels, *Hinduism*, pp. 21–22.

90. Oddie, *Imagined Hinduism*, pp. 270–271. During the second part of the nineteenth century, however, as their knowledge of India increased and their experiences in the field matured, Protestant missionaries gradually began to doubt the idea that the essence of Hinduism consisted of a kind of *brāhmaṇic* pantheism.

of Western esotericism and occultism.[91] Western esotericism, which was initially based on Christian ideas, spread its influence in India through the medium of the Freemasons, who established the first Masonic lodge in Calcutta in 1730.[92] Open to both the British and the educated indigenous population, Freemasonry introduced the fundamental concepts of esotericism to the Indian intelligentsia. Its teachings were based on faith in an abstract, formless supreme being and a code of conduct that exalted honor, brotherly love, charity, honesty, and openness to men of all religions. These ideas helped to strengthen the *bhadralok* drive toward universalism, tolerance, and an ethics of duty and work, which found its purest expression in the Brahmo Samaj, perhaps the most complete embodiment of the progressive aspirations of the *bhadralok* at the time. From about the 1870s onward Bengal was also introduced to a more secularized form of esotericism that came to be known as occultism as well as to the powerful influence of the Theosophical Society.

---

91. Henrik Bogdan has suggested that "Western culture is sometimes, somewhat simplistically, viewed as resting on two pillars: Greek rationality and Christian faith." To these Bogdan adds a third: Western esotericism, with its emphasis on the attainment of inner enlightenment and a genuine experience of the "true self" and God—the ground of all being. According to Bogdan, "Western esotericism... [was] a form of thought that took a middle position between doctrinal faith and rationality." Henrik Bogdan, *Western Esotericism and Rituals of Initiation* (Albany: State University of New York Press, 2007), pp. 6–7. Antoine Faivre has defined Western esotericism in terms of the following six categories: (1) the presence of concrete and symbolic correspondences between the macrocosm and the microcosm; (2) the living nature, i.e., the universe is hierarchical and plural and permeated by spiritual forces; (3) imagination and mediations, i.e., the use of the "inner eye" for creative imagination and the possibility of mediation between higher and lower worlds; (4) experience of transmutation, i.e., the inner alteration of the subject while traversing one plane of consciousness to the next; (5) the practice of concordance, i.e., the existence of a gnosis (knowledge) that is at the core of all the "exoteric" religious traditions; and (6) transmission, which refers to the passing of knowledge from a master to a disciple through initiation and according to certain set rules. Antoine Faivre, *Access to Western Esotericism* (Albany: State University of New York Press, 1994), pp. 10–15. Wouter Hanagraaff has noted that in addition to these traits, two further influences accounted for the dynamic changes that occurred from the seventeenth century onward: (7) reformation "spiritualism" and (8) Enlightenment and post-Enlightenment thought. With the arrival of the Enlightenment, the notion that a personal God was the source of the natural world was gradually replaced by the view that nature was essentially mechanistic and that natural events were based on the laws of cause and effect, without external intervention, Wouter J. Hanegraaff, *New Age Religion and Western Culture: Esotericism in the Mirror of Secular Thought* (Albany: State University of New York Press, 1998), pp. 403–410. Western esotericism's view of religion as being primarily individual and rational may have provided a further basis for the emergence of modern Vedanta among educated Hindus.

92. See www.masonindia.org/index10.html, accessed on July 15, 2011. The web page provides information about the history and development of Freemasonry in India, and contains a picture of Vivekānanda in Masonic dress (www.masonindia.org/news1.htm).

While Western esotericism (influenced by Christian "spiritualism") was by no means a pivotal force in Indian cultural life, it can be reasonably stated that it contributed to shaping the sensibilities of educated Bengalis such as Vivekānanda, who for some time was a member of the Freemasons. It created, in other words, an environment conducive to the notion of a formless God that was only approachable by means of abstract symbolism, and not by images and form.

Growth of Nondualist Vedanta

The above discussion suggests that the rise of modern nondualist Vedanta was shaped by indigenous reflections on the early history of Indic religions, on the influence of the Islamic period, and on the validity of Hindu customs and rituals; perhaps most importantly, however, it emerged in relation to the encounter with European culture and religious thought. Although the many ramifications of this profound rethinking of Indic culture and religion are often difficult to map and weigh,[93] this much can be said: from the nineteenth century onward, the idea that nondualism was the core of "Hindu religion" gradually took hold, but not without resistance from Vaishnava and other quarters of society. Despite these opposing voices, which indicated that the *bhadralok* was not cohesive in its response to modernization and reform, colonial needs for rational production and political management generated a climate of widespread opposition to theistic precolonial Indic religions, viewed as irrational and superstitious.

Other currents that encouraged that development can be briefly mentioned here. The notion that human reason was vitally linked to human progress was propagated through both Christian and secular educational institutions, as well as through scientific exhibitions and museums. Colonial secular institutions called for the predominance of science over religion, the patronizing role of the imperial state, and a humanism that subordinated religion to civic life and citizenship to the state. As colonial India approached the twentieth century, the cumulative effect of these forces apparently facilitated a further push toward nondualism, in which

93. For a discussion on the major strands of English liberal and conservative thought in relation to India up to 1857, see S. Cromwell Crawford, *Ram Mohan Roy: Social, Political, and Religious Reform in 19th Century India* (New York: Paragon House, 1987), pp. 19–35.

the aspirations of religion and science were made to converge. Of particular significance was the rise of a positivist movement in Bengal, conceived as a synthesis of science and religion.[94] These cultural processes were further reinforced by the need in East Bengal to create a united Hindu religion and identity that could withstand the threat of rising Muslim self-consciousness.

In sum, the reduction of the vast diversity of interpretations of Vedanta to one fundamental understanding served the interests of a Bengali intellectual elite that was searching for a unifying vision of "Hinduism" that harmonized with their own sensibilities and those of the modern Western world. For this and other reasons they moved toward various interpretations of nondualism's vision of God as an "abstract formless singularity." The promotion of *advaita* Vedanta as the most genuine and essential face of Indian religion gradually helped to counteract allegations of "Hindoo" irrationality and idolatry, and also enabled Indians to approach European culture with a sense of Indic dignity and pride.[95] And of all the members of the Bengal Renaissance that were responsible for the nineteenth- and twentieth-century popularization of this vision, both in India and abroad, perhaps no one contributed more than Swami Vivekānanda (1863–1902). Through Vivekānanda, the English-speaking world came to display

> an increasing tendency... not only to identify "Hinduism" with the Vedanta (thus establishing an archaic textual and canonical locus for the Hindu religion) but also a tendency to conflate Vedanta with Advaita Vedanta.... Advaita, with its monistic identification of

94. Gyan Prakash has described this movement in the following terms: "The influence of positivism was palpable... and positive philosophers were often cited to legitimate 'dispositions' that, according to Hindu intellectuals, Hinduism itself contained. These 'dispositions' were defined increasingly, with citations from Herbert Spencer and Thomas Henry Huxley, as the belief in the oneness of all phenomena, and in the existence of one supreme power; just as science had one truth, so did 'essential religion,' not superstition masquerading as religion. Hinduism, as this 'essential religion,' it was argued, did not reside in its symbols and rituals but in the recognition of the laws of nature in which the almighty manifested itself." Gyan Prakash, "Science between the Lines," in *Subaltern Studies 9: Writings on South Asian History and Society*, ed. Shahid Amin and Dipesh Chakrabarty (Delhi: Oxford University Press, 2005), p. 72.

95. *Advaita* Vedanta was often presented in various forms of interpretation and also, at times, combined with subordinate theistic notions.

Atman and Brahman, thereby came to represent the paradigmatic example of the mystical nature of the Hindu religion.[96]

Swami Vivekānanda

Vivekānanda was born on January 12, 1863. His father, Viswanath Datta, was a well-educated, liberal, and rationally minded *bhadralok* who served as an attorney at the Calcutta High Court.[97] His mother, Bhuvaneshwari Devi, was a pious Bengali lady who imbued Vivekānanda with a profound appreciation for religious thought and practice. In his youth he studied at such prestigious schools as the Metropolitan Institution, Scottish Church College, and Presidency College, but failing health forced him to withdraw and continue his studies at the General Assembly Institution.[98] In 1880 Vivekānanda suffered a type of existential crisis that led him to explore a number of religious groups in Calcutta. He frequented both the Bharatvarshiya Brahmo Samaj (founded by Keshub Chandra Sen in 1866) and the Sadharan Brahmo Samaj. On the advice of his father, he also sought to further his career by becoming a member of the Freemasons, where he encountered the ideas of Western esotericism and occultism.[99] His involvement with these various groups provided his first brush with the modern conceptions of social reform and humanitarianism. Vivekānanda's father passed away in 1884, leaving his family in economic difficulties.

In November 1881, Vivekānanda met Ramakrishna, at the time a very popular religious figure among Calcutta's youthful *bhadralok*. The association continued, and after a period of hesitancy, soul-searching, and scrutiny Vivekānanda became his disciple. By the time Ramakrishna passed away in 1886, the young Vivekānanda had become a key member

---

96. Richard King, *Orientalism and Religion: Postcolonial Theory, India, and "The Mystic East"* (New York: Routledge, 1999), p. 128. This "tendency" was nonetheless more prominent in the English-speaking world than in countries like Germany. See, for example, Rudolf Otto's study of Christianity, Śaṅkara and Vaishnavism, where he favorably compares Christianity and Vaishnavism in relation to the theory of grace. Rudolf Otto, *India's Religion of Grace and Christianity Compared and Contrasted* (London: Student Christian Movement Press, 1930).

97. Narashingha P. Sil, *Swami Vivekananda: A Reassessment* (Selinsgrove, Pa.: Susquehanna University Press, 1997), p. 27.

98. The General Assembly Institution would merge in 1908 with Duff College to form the Scottish Churches College, which, in turn, was renamed "Scottish Church College" in 1929 (its present name).

99. Gwilym Beckerlegge, *Swami Vivekananda's Legacy of Service: A Study of the Ramakrishna Math and Mission* (Oxford: Oxford University Press, 2006), p. 140.

of his monastic community, the Ramakrishna Order. In 1887 Vivekānanda took monastic vows, and in 1888 he embarked on an extensive tour of India, traveling to Benares, the Himalayas, and South India. A second tour between 1891 and 1893 brought him face-to-face with the devastating effects of widespread famine and the plight of India's rural population.

Although Vivekānanda based his work on Ramakrishna's teachings, he placed more emphasis on karma yoga than did his predecessor. Ramakrishna considered the path of bhakti to be most suitable for the age of Kali. Thus he concluded that while philanthropic service might be a legitimate outgrowth of genuine God-realization, a true devotee would forfeit even this should it become a hindrance to the attainment of the ultimate goal. In contrast, Vivekānanda believed that while humanitarian *seva* was not the ultimate goal, it was more than just a step on the path to God-realization; it was an important symptom of that realization as well.[100]

Vivekānanda raised the path of humanitarian *seva* to new heights of institutional sophistication, in pace with the changing needs of modern society. From 1894 onward, his call to help the poor intensified with the introduction of the term *daridra Nārāyaṇa*, poor Nārāyaṇa.[101] Apart from its sociopolitical implications, the expression was also a theological statement about the nature of humanity, inspired by a nondualistic understanding of the ultimate oneness of all beings. For Vivekānanda there was no other God beside the *jīva*, an understanding that was foundational for his approach to religion and society. On its basis, *advaita* and "Practical Vedanta" were designated as superior to bhakti, and the ingredients for *pūjā* were designated as food for "the Living God who dwells in the persons of the poor."[102]

Toward the close of the nineteenth century this message rang true with a certain section of Bengal's young *bhadralok*, who saw Vivekānanda's *advaita* teachings as a potential means for the creation of lasting peace, tolerance, and understanding, and thus regarded him as a major influence for the future of modern India. This, they believed, was especially so in comparison to Vaishnavism, which they viewed as placing too great an emphasis on otherworldliness and bhakti, and not enough on action (karma) and knowledge (*jñāna*). Because of this they viewed Vaishnavism as having little relevance to the political and social changes that had been

100. I here accept the view of Gwilym Beckerlegge in *Swami Vivekananda's Legacy*, p. 233.

101. *Nārāyaṇa* is a name generally associated with Vishnu and Vaishnavism.

102. Swami Vivekānanda, *Complete Works*, vol. 4, p. 404.

brought about by India's contact with modernity. Ascetic mysticism and otherworldliness were not viable alternatives in the eyes of the mainstream *bhadralok*, whose hope for a possible synthesis of Hinduism and science (i.e., European culture) led them in a different direction. The Hindu nationalist Subhash Chandra Bose, for example, found Vivekānanda's monistic universalism far more suited to political and social emancipation than what he considered to be Vaishnavism's otherworldliness. He explained in his autobiography that

> My headmaster had roused my aesthetic and moral sense—had given a new impetus to my life—but he had not given me an ideal to which I could give my whole being. That Vivekananda gave me...the religion that he preached—including his conception of yoga—was based on a rational philosophy, on the Vedanta, and his conception of the Vedanta was antagonistic to, but was based on, scientific principles. One of his missions in life was to bring about a reconciliation between science and religion, and this, he held, was possible through the Vedanta.[103]

In 1893, with the aid of funds collected by various followers, Vivekānanda journeyed from India to the United States to present his religious perspective to the World's Parliament of Religions, set to convene in Chicago, Illinois. And while he may have lacked formal training in a classical school of Vedanta, his unique brand of nondualistic universalism was received with great enthusiasm by the audience since it was formulated in nonsectarian and all-inclusive terms. At the meeting he presented *advaita* Vedanta as the core of Hindu thought:

> Perfection is absolute, and the absolute cannot be two or three. It cannot have any qualities. It cannot be individual. And so when a soul becomes perfect and absolute, it must become one with Brahman, and it would only realise the Lord as the perfection, the reality, of its own nature and existence, the existence absolute, knowledge absolute, and bliss absolute.[104]

---

103. Subhas Chandra Bose, Sisir Kumar Bose, and Sugata Bose, *An Indian Pilgrim: An Unfinished Autobiography* (Calcutta: Netaji Research Bureau; Delhi: Oxford University Press, 1997), p. 37. Bose was later also influenced by the writings of Aurobindo.

104. Swami Vivekānanda, *Complete Works*, vol. 1, pp. 13–14. This is a quote from an address delivered on September 11, 1893.

His view was that the formless feature of the Absolute was higher than the personal one (e.g., the form and personality of a supreme deity), which eliminated the distinction between self and God.

Richard King has suggested that in his Chicago presentation as well as his later writings Vivekānanda appropriated other traditions both within and outside Hinduism in at least two ways: (1) by suggesting that *advaita* constitutes the central philosophy of Hinduism; and, (2) by arguing that nondualism represents the "perennial truth" underlying all religious traditions and cultures, despite the superficial appearance of difference. The claim of a nondualistic core that went beyond what was conceived as a sectarian iconic periphery may have served a variety of purposes. By claiming that nondualistic Vedanta was *the* true world religion, and Hinduism's pristine essence, Vivekānanda can be said to have "provided the rhetoric of tolerance necessary to establish the possession of a high ground."[105] The idea that Hinduism was morally superior to other world religions came to prominence during the nineteenth century. The nondualistic universalism that Vivekānanda suggested was largely in keeping with the mood of the Bengal Renaissance, although it had clearly emerged from Śaṅkara's writings. Śaṅkara's impersonalist commentary on the Vedanta, however, contained no reference to humanitarian applications of the theory of oneness—feeding the poor, educating the masses, and so on. Thus, Vivekānanda's universalist interpretation constituted a modern reading that became most appealing to Indian and Western intellectuals.

Vivekānanda's presentation of *advaita* universalism as the main core of Hindu philosophy has been perpetuated throughout the twentieth century by Indian scholars such as Satischandra Chatterjee of Calcutta University and onetime Indian president Sarvepalli Radhakrishnan.[106] In a speech delivered in Calcutta on January 20, 1963, Radhakrishnan described the impact of Vivekānanda's writings as follows:

> When I was a student in one of the classes, in the matriculation class or so, the letters of Swami Vivekānanda used to be circulated in manuscript form among us all. The kind of thrill which we enjoyed, the kind of mesmeric touch that those writings gave us, the kind of

105. King, *Orientalism and Religion*, p. 136.

106. Satischandra Chatterjee and Dhirendramohan Datta published a standard introduction to Indian philosophy that still remains in use at Indian universities, i.e., *An Introduction to Indian Philosophy* (Calcutta: University of Calcutta, 1950).

> reliance on our own culture that was being criticized all around—it is that kind of transformation which his writings effected in the young men in the early years of this century.[107]

He also wrote with rare clarity of an *advaitic* program for pan-Hindu unity:

> The [*advaita*] Vedānta is not a religion, but religion itself in its most universal and deepest significance. Thus the different sects of Hinduism are reconciled with a common standard and are sometimes regarded as the distorted expressions of the one true canon.[108]

Privileging *advaita* implied downplaying, directly or indirectly, popular expressions of devotional practice, and in particular the dualistic bhakti strands of Hinduism that, according to *advaitic* thought, were subordinate to the ultimate nondual experience. Gandhi largely held a nondualistic outlook, although he did attempt to reconcile this with the dualistic perspective. There were also others who attempted to combine dualistic and nondualistic approaches, but most often with an emphasis on the latter.[109] Even Rammohun Roy's nondualism was not entirely one-sided, as he continued to maintain the importance of worshipping God as both sustainer and creator. This and other factors suggest a need for further research into the nondualist views that were extant at the time of the Bengal Renaissance.[110] This notwithstanding, the predominance of nondualistic religious thought in representations of Hinduism persists even today in both Indian intellectual and Western popular cultural circles—and perhaps

---

107. Speech delivered on January 20, 1963, in Calcutta. Sarvepalli Radhakrishnan, *Our Heritage* (Delhi: Hind Pocket Books, 1973), p. 97.

108. Sarvepalli Radhakrishnan, *Hindu View of Life* (Oxford: George Allen and Unwin Ltd, 1927), p. 23. For a general introduction to Radhakrishnan's nondualistic idealism, see Sarvepalli Radhakrishnan, *An Idealist View of Life* (1932; London: G. Allen & Unwin, 1947).

109. Gandhi explains his position in *Hindu Dharma*: "I am an advaitist and yet I support dvaitism (dualism). The world is changing every moment and is therefore unreal, it has no permanent existence. But though it is constantly changing, it has something about it which persists and it is therefore to that extent real." Mahatma Gandhi and Bharatan Kumarappa, *Hindu Dharma* (Ahmedabad: Navajivan Pub. House, 1950), p. 55. Gandhi effortlessly blended Christian theology and ethics as well as Vaishnava theism with *advaita*.

110. I wish to offer special thanks to Brian Hatcher for pointing this out.

nowhere more than in the North Atlantic region. In this regard, Elizabeth De Michelis has noted that the prevalence of what she calls "Neo-Vedānta" has created a confusion

> widespread at both etic and emic levels of discourse East and West, i.e. the confusion between "traditional"...and "modern" forms of Hinduism. Modern understandings of Hinduism, and more specifically Neo-Vedānta, have been made to represent the whole of the Hindu tradition *vis-à-vis* audiences (both East and West) that had little chance to know otherwise.[111]

This confusion has translated into a still lingering dichotomy between so-called nondualistic, progressive, universal, and egalitarian *modern* Hinduism and so-called iconic, regressive, conservative, and hierarchical *traditional* Hinduism. This antithetical characterization has tended to cloud the fact that precolonial forms of image worship also possess a modern history of transformation, as in the case of Vaishnavism, the subject matter of this book. It also has tended to cloud the internal complexity of Hinduism, which counts a variety of classical approaches, including a long history of theistic rationalist thought. This has been represented by later schools of logic (*nyāya*) such as Navyanyāya ("new" *nyāya*)—a specifically Bengali form that Caitanya himself studied in Nabadwip.

Summary

Great Britain's colonial domination of India began in the vicinity of Calcutta during the eighteenth century, actuated by the venturesome trading activities of the East India Company. Thereafter, a variety of Christian missionaries traveled to the region and came face-to-face with what to them was an indecent and largely incomprehensible religio-cultural milieu. The result was the formulation of a rather one-sided interpretation of Indic religions, based, for the most part, on the following three predispositions: (1) a disdain for the worship of "idols" such as Vaishnava images, which the missionaries considered superstitious and deviant; (2) a high regard for rationalism, egalitarianism, and science, which inclined them to dismiss the role of emotions in popular worship; and, (3) a contempt

111. De Michelis, *History of Modern Yoga*, p. 12. Here the term "Neo-Vedānta" simply refers to modern *advaita* Vedanta, and has no pejorative implications.

for sexual expression, which disposed them to view India's traditions of love mysticism as highly immoral. In addressing this critique, Bengal's emerging *bhadralok* creatively sought for answers from within their own Indic and Islamic past. What arose by the end of the nineteenth century was the understanding that nondualism, in all its varieties, was the *core* of Hinduism—a perspective that simultaneously aligned the *advaita* of Śaṅkara, the legacy of Islamic iconoclasticism, Christian sensibilities, and the growing national aspirations of the *bhadralok*. This nondualistic outcome was facilitated by comparative Indo-European research (which included the romantic search for Europe's civilizational roots) as well as the influence of Western esotericism and occultism.

The creation of modern *advaita* Vedanta as the mainstream understanding of the *bhadralok* gradually developed from the early writings of Rammohun Roy to the progressive rationalism of the Brahmo Samaj to the nondualistic universalism of Swami Vivekānanda. It was further consolidated during the twentieth century by the writings of individuals such as Sarvepalli Radhakrishnan and Mahatma Gandhi, and today remains the standard understanding of Hinduism among the vast majority of educated Indians and Westerners. Nonetheless, as should be obvious by now, the general presentation of *advaita* as the essence of Indic religious life provides only a partial view of a diverse theological and philosophical tradition, something that more recent scholarship has attempted to address through the provision of a more nuanced understanding.[112] After exploring the historical context, the following chapter provides an overview of Bhaktisiddhānta's life.

112. See appendix A.

2

Life and Works

FOR CONVENIENCE THIS chapter is divided into three historical periods: early, middle, and late. These periods mark distinct phases of Bhaktisiddhānta's life, highlighting his development from precocious youth to student intellectual to founder of a successful pan-Indian religious movement. The chapter ends with his passing away and the postcharismatic schism that took place within his institution. Rather than simply cover the biographical material in a linear fashion, I intend to highlight aspects of his life that illuminate his character, intentions, and goals, at times with the help of suitable anecdotes. I will also explore the influences that affected his thought and work, as well as the cultural and social climate of his time. The aim is to explore the possibility that Bhaktisiddhānta's contribution to religious history was such that it transcended the cumulative influence of his sociocultural milieu. In general, this biographical account avoids the tendency to portray Indians under colonial rule as passive, particularly in relation to adherents of the devotional strands of bhakti.[1] Bhaktisiddhānta possessed a sharp intellect and an iron will, characteristics that carried him beyond the confines of both mainstream *bhadralok* and orthodox Vaishnava culture, enabling him to forge a countercurrent of his own devising. I will also pursue this study in terms of dual tensions that had an impact on the work of Bhaktisiddhānta—for example, *varnāśrama* versus caste, renunciation versus worldliness, devotional service versus humanitarian work; it is hoped that this approach will help to extract some of the key elements of his thought as they emerged from the context in which he lived.

The section covering his early period, from 1874 to 1900, begins with a brief biographical sketch of his father, Kedarnath Datta Bhaktivinoda,

1. See Pinch Vijay, "Bhakti and the British Empire," *Past and Present* 179, no. 1 (2003): pp. 112–115.

perhaps *the* major influence in Bhaktisiddhānta's life.[2] The chapter continues with an account of Bhaktisiddhānta's childhood and school years, with an emphasis on the surfacing of some of his most defining personal characteristics. It then explores his intellectual development, his interest in astronomy, and his proneness to debate, even at a young age. The section ends with his taking Vaishnava initiation from the ascetic Gaura Kiśora dāsa Bābājī and his subsequent absorption in secluded contemplation.

The section covering his middle period, from 1901 to 1918, explores Bhaktisiddhānta's intense spiritual practice, his study of various Indic religions, and his stand against the caste privileges and exclusivism of some sections of Bengal's orthodox Vaishnava *brāhmaṇas*. The description of this period ends with Bhaktisiddhānta's acceptance of the order of *saṃnyāsa* and his decision to return to Calcutta to establish an institution representing the universal teachings of Caitanya bhakti.

The final section, which covers the period from 1918 to 1937, provides a fairly in-depth look at the development of Bhaktisiddhānta's religious movement. It explores the structure of the Gaudiya Math, its purposes, and the ways in which it gained support from the traditional strata of the *bhadralok*.

The biography continues in chapter 4 with a description of Bhaktisiddhānta's attempt to spread Caitanya bhakti to Britain and Germany in 1933, setting an important precedent for the worldwide expansion that would occur in the mid-1960s (see chapter 5).

1874–1900: Early Period (to Age Twenty-six)

Bhaktisiddhānta was born in his family home at 3:30 PM on Friday, February 6, 1874; it was a spacious dwelling built on Jagannath Puri's main thoroughfare, aptly called the "Grand Road." He was the seventh child of Kedarnath Datta Bhaktivinoda and his wife, Bhagavati Devi.[3] The house

---

2. Hereinafter mostly referred to as Bhaktivinoda.

3. In 1850, as was the custom of upper-class Hindus, Kedarnath Datta was married at age eleven with five-year-old Sayamani. In 1860, Sayamani gave birth to a son named Annada Prasad, but she died shortly thereafter. Bhaktivinoda then married Bhagavati Devi, with whom he produced the following thirteen children: (1) Saudamani, daughter (1864); (2) Kadambani, daughter (1867); (3) son died early, name unknown (1868); (4) Radhika Prasad, son (1870); (5) Kamala Prasad (1872); (6) Bimala Prasad, son (1874); (7) Barada Prasad (1877); (8) Biraja, daughter, (1878); (9) Lalita Prasad, son (1880); (10) Krishna Vinodini, daughter (1884); (11) Shyam Sarojini, daughter (1886); (12) Hari Pramodini, daughter (1888); (13) Shailaja Prasad, son (1891). These events are narrated in Kedarnath Datta Bhaktivinoda, *Svalikhita-Jīvanī* (Calcutta: Lalita Prasada datta, 1916). The list is also provided by Brian D. Marvin, "The Life and Thought of Kedarnath Datta Bhaktivinode: A Hindu Encounter with Modernity," Ph.D. diss., University of Toronto, 1996, p. 332.

was located a few hundred meters from a large temple dedicated to the worship of the images of Jagannātha, Baladeva, and Subhadrā.[4] Jagannath Puri is one of the most sacred cities of South Asian Vaishnavism, and of Hinduism as a whole, and is located in the state of Orissa on the western shore of the Bay of Bengal.[5]

Bhaktivinoda named his son "Bimala Prasad," which indicates the blessings (*prasāda*) of the personified female potency (Vimalā) of Jagannātha.[6] Because of the pivotal role that Bhaktivinoda played in Bhaktisiddhānta's development, the following subsection provides a short profile of his early life, largely based on *Svalikhita Jīvanī* (an autobiographical account); far less is known about Bhaktisiddhānta's mother.[7]

Kedarnath Datta Bhaktivinoda

Kedarnath Datta was born on Sunday, September 2, 1838 in the village of Ula, today better known as Birnagar.[8] At the time, the village was located on the bank of the Bagirathi River on the western course of the mouth of the Ganges, about a hundred kilometers north of Calcutta in the district

---

4. During the last portion of his life, Caitanya resided near the temple of Jagannātha; thus it is an important shrine for followers of the Caitanya tradition. "Jagannātha" means "Lord of the universe." The deity of Jagannātha is worshipped by Caitanya Vaishnavas as a manifestation of Krishna, together with his brother, Balarāma, and his sister, Subhadrā. The house where Bhaktisiddhānta was born was acquired in 1974 by Swami Bhakti Dayita Madhava and is today a Gaudiya Math temple, see Swami Bhakti Vallabha Tīrtha, *Sri Caitanya: His Life & Associates* (San Rafael, Calif.: Mandala Publishing, 2001), p. 232. Bhaktivinoda wrote an article about the Jagannātha temple on September 15, 1871. The article, which was titled "The Temple of Jagannath at Puri," was published in the *Harmonist* 26, no. 2 (July 1928): pp. 25–31. The *Harmonist* was the English periodical of the Gaudiya Math (figure B.5).

5. Unless otherwise mentioned, the following sketch is based on "Ācārya Carita," a biographical article that appeared in *Gauḍīya* 15, nos. 23–24 (January 16, 1937): pp. 9–40. The magazine was the official periodical of the Gaudiya Math. The issue appeared just a few days after Bhaktisiddhānta's demise. An English translation of this and later biographical articles that appeared in the periodical *Gauḍīya* is found in Swami Bhakti Śrīrūpā Bhāgavata, ed., *Advent Centenary Souvenir of Shri Shrila Prabhupad, 1874–1974* (Calcutta: Gaudiya Mission, 1974), pp. 1–37.

6. "Bimala Prasad," "Sarasvatī," and "Bhaktisiddhānta" will hereafter indicate the same person at different stages of his life.

7. Kedarnath Bhaktivinoda, *Svalikhita Jīvanī*, ed. Lalita Prasad Datta (Calcutta: Lalita Prasad Datta, 1916). The text was written in the form of a personal letter to his son Lalita Prasad. The autobiography provides a vivid description of his intellectual and religious development. It is available at the National Library in Calcutta.

8. The title "Bhaktivinoda" is honorific and was bestowed upon Kedarnath Datta in 1886 in recognition of his learning and scholarly accomplishments. Since most of the events described in this brief biographical section occurred before this date, the name "Kedarnath Datta" will instead be used here.

of Nadia.[9] Kedarnath's parents, Ananda Chandra Datta and Jagat Mohini Mitra, were members of the influential *kāyastha* caste, which for generations had worked as scribes and writers in the royal courts of India, and were often landowners as well.[10] His paternal family was known as the Hatkhola Dattas. Dating back to the time of Caitanya, the Dattas had been mostly Vaishnavas, although some had gravitated toward Śaktism instead.

During the precolonial period, a prominent relation, Govindasharan Datta, received a grant of land from the Sultan of Delhi. The land, which bordered the Hoogly River, served as the location for the village Govindapur, founded by Govindasharan and named in his honor.[11] Several years later, this very land was confiscated by the British and became the site for the erection of historic Fort William, the veritable focal point of the emerging town of Calcutta. In exchange the Dattas received Hatkhola, a territory located to the north of the British settlement.[12]

Kedarnath's paternal grandfather was a prominent Śakta named Rajballabh Datta, and his maternal grandfather, Ishvar Chandra Mustauphi, was the son of a wealthy landowner (*zamindar*) named Rameshvar Mitra.[13]

9. The Ganges and its branches often change course in Bengal due to monsoon rains and floods, and thus the river is today located some distance from the village.

10. In 1876, Kedarnath Datta wrote a genealogical work in Sanskrit verse, the *Datta-vaṃśa-mālā*. There he states that he was the twenty-fifth descendant from Puruṣottama Datta, who moved to Bengal upon the invitation of King Ādiśura in the twelfth century. The fifteenth descendant from Puruṣottama Datta, Rāja Kṛṣṇānanda, was the father of the well-known Vaishnava guru and poet Narottama, and was an associate of Caitanya's closest companion, Nityānanda. The *kāyasthas* in Bengal have about one hundred surnames, of which Mitra, Datta, De, and Das are prominent. The Mitras of Bhaktivinoda's maternal family were also included among the original five clusters of families; see Marvin, "Life and Thought," pp. 55–58. A summary of Kedarnath Datta's genealogical line was published by Bhaktisiddhānta in an article in the *Sajjanatoṣaṇī* 18, no. 6 (1917): p. 223. Many Hindu revivalists and reformers like Swami Vivekānanda, as well as nationalists like Subhas Chandra Bose, were born *kāyasthas*. For a general history of Bhaktivinoda's *kāyastha* clan—Dutt or Datta are its alternative spellings—see Thomas J. Hopkins, "The Social and Religious Background for Transmission of Gaudiya Vaisnavism to the West," in *Krishna Consciousness in the West*, ed. David G. Bromley and Larry D. Shinn (Lewisburg, Pa.: Bucknell University Press; London: Associated University Presses, 1989), pp. 35–54.

11. A descendant, Madana Mohan Datta, was a contemporary of Robert Clive and had business relations with American merchants from the Boston area. Marvin, "Life and Thought," p. 59 n. 14.

12. Bhaktivinoda, *Svalikhita Jīvanī*, p. 3.

13. Śaktas generally worship the goddess Durgā. However, in Bengal the black feminine deity of Kālī is more popular. Brian Marvin suggests that in the eighteenth century "there was an upsurge of Shaktism when many prominent *zamindars* adopted this faith. This accounts for the change from Vaishnavism to Shaktism in Kedarnath's paternal line." Marvin, "Life and Thought," p. 59 n. 15.

Due to a financial crisis on his father's side of the family, Kedarnath was raised in the village Ula, the residence of his maternal family. He describes his early life in this village as idyllic, fondly remembering the beauty and peace of the Bengali countryside, the care and affection of his family, and the perennial celebration of various religious holidays. Eventually, however, Kedarnath's father passed away, and both his paternal and maternal family lost their wealth; by the age of eleven he was plunged into financial destitution. In 1852 worsening circumstances forced him to move to the home of his maternal uncle in Calcutta, where he lived until 1858.[14] From there he began to explore the urban world created by the East India Company, in search of education and employment, and entered the ranks of the *bhadralok*.

Shortly after his arrival, Kedarnath became fully immersed in the small, but very productive, intellectual elite of Calcutta, occasionally writing articles for the *Hindu Intelligencer*, a popular periodical edited by his uncle.[15] He studied at the Hindu Charitable Institution, a *bhadralok* project that offered Hindu students an alternative to Christian missionary education. There he met the prominent educator and scholar Ishvar Chandra Vidyasagar (1820–1891), under whose guidance he studied the history of India.[16] In 1856, Kedarnath began attending the Hindu School, where he met and befriended the brothers Satyendranath (1842–1923) and Gajendranath Tagore, as well as Keshub Chandra Sen (1838–1884), the future reformer of the Brahmo Samaj.[17] He had begun studying the English language before coming to Calcutta, and under the tutelage of competent teachers his skills improved each day. In 1857 he published *The Poriade*, an English epic poem about King Porus (d. 317 BCE), who fought the Hydaspes river battle against Alexander the Great (356–323 BCE) as

14. Bhaktivinoda, *Svalikhita Jīvanī*, p. 54. The uncle's name was Kashiprasad Ghosh (1809–1873); he lived on Bidan Street in Calcutta.

15. Regarding the *Hindu Intelligencer*, see Mrinal Kanti Chanda, *History of the English Press in Bengal, 1780 to 1857* (Calcutta: KP Bagchi, 1987), pp. 272ff.

16. Bhaktivinoda, *Svalikhita Jīvanī*, p. 67.

17. Bhaktivinoda, *Svalikhita Jīvanī*, p. 68. Satyendranath went to England for his education and became the first Indian to join the Indian Civil Service. He was the second son of Debendranath Tagore, the grandson of Dwarkanath Tagore, and the elder brother of Rabindranath Tagore, who won the Nobel Prize in Literature in 1913. Satyendranath was an active member of the Brahmo Samaj, which in large measure owed its development to the Tagore family. Gajendranath, Bhaktivinoda's other friend, went on to become the first Indian barrister.

he entered the Punjab region with his Macedonian army. It began with a lamentation over the fate of the Hindus:

> Alas! The days of glory are no more,
> When Hindu fame rung out from shore to shore;
> When Asak's arms encompassed distant lands,
> And Grecia trembled at our martial bands!

In the poem Kedarnath regrets the loss of a glorious time, perhaps an early sign of his appreciation for India's past history and the ancient achievements of Indic religions. But the main section of the poem deals with an existential crisis, possibly reflecting his own musings at this stage of his life. During a hunt Porus kills a hind and, being struck by the spectacle of death, begins to ponder:

> From whom is life? And whence this frame of man?
> What might power has formed this mighty plan?
> Why live we here? And why desire and feel?
> For what we turn with Time's revolving wheel?
> I eat, and live, and sleep, and spend the day
> But never think of these!—my life is gay!

Porus's contemplation leads him to abandon his father's palace in Taxila to wander alone in the forest, while servants search for him in vain.[18]

Kedarnath showed this poem to the Scottish missionary Alexander Duff, who liked it so much that he took the boy under his wing, helping him to study the works of John Milton (1608–1674). During this same period, Kedarnath also made a study of the works of Thomas Babington Macaulay (1800–1859), William Hazlit (1778–1830), and Thomas Carlyle (1795–1881).[19]

In the same year that Kedarnath published his poem a choleric epidemic broke out in Ula, wiping out most of the villagers, including most of his own family; afterward the village was abandoned. Feeling distressed at the loss of both his relatives and his childhood home, he found a close friend in Dwijendranath Tagore (1840–1926). Together they studied not

---

18. Kedarnath Dutt, *The Poriade, or Adventures of Porus* (Calcutta: G. P. Roy, 1857). Only the first part is currently available at the British Library.

19. Bhaktivinoda, *Svalikhita Jīvanī*, p. 71.

only Sanskrit and religion, but also Kant, Goethe, Hegel, Swedenborg, Hume, Voltaire, and Schopenhauer.[20] Kedarnath began frequenting an intercultural forum, the British Indian Society, where he would sometimes hold lectures on the subject of religion. It was around this time that he embarked upon an earnest search for answers to key existential questions. In the home of the Tagores, he was exposed to the rationalism of the Brahmo Samaj, but he gradually came to prefer Christianity, which at the time was more in keeping with his own theistic leanings.[21] He became a member of the congregation of Reverend Charles Dall, a missionary associated with Rammohun Roy who was sent to Calcutta by the American Unitarian Association of Boston to explore the possibility of cooperation with the Brahmo Samaj. Studying the Bible under Dall's direction and reading the works of Christian theologians such as Theodor Parker (1810–1860) and John Henry Newman (1801–1890), Kedarnath gained a strong appreciation for Jesus Christ.[22] Through the association of the Tagores, the encounter with Unitarian universalism, the pursuit of his own readings, and exposure to the rich cosmopolitan atmosphere of imperial Calcutta, Kedarnath Datta's understanding considerably broadened, and he began to reflect upon the role of theism in the modern world.

For seven years beginning in 1859 Kedarnath Datta worked as a teacher in both Orissa and Bengal, but the precariousness of his financial circumstances eventually led him to seek economic stability in the coveted civil service.[23] The sufferings he endured in his early years were one of the factors that led him to seek financially stable employment in the government. In 1866, after passing the required examinations, he began as a deputy magistrate and deputy collector of the seventh grade, inaugurating what would become a laborious ascent to the higher ranks of colonial service. Kedarnath performed diligently and with great personal sacrifice, oftentimes withstanding excessive workloads as well as constant social and mental pressure.[24] He developed cordial relations with British officers

20. Bhaktivinoda, *Svalikhita Jīvanī*, pp. 78–79. Dwijendranath Tagore was a philosopher and a pioneer of Bengali literature.

21. Bhaktivinoda, *Svalikhita Jīvanī*, p. 80.

22. Bhaktivinoda, *Svalikhita Jīvanī*, p. 80.

23. In Orissa he taught in Kendrapara and Bhadrak; in Bengal he taught in Midnapore.

24. Varuni Bhatia, "Devotional Traditions and National Culture: Recovering Gaudiya Vaishnavism in Colonial Bengal," Ph.D. diss., Columbia University, 2008, pp. 187–188.

such as E. Roer, C. D. Linton, and S. J. Hogg, all of whom wrote letters of sincere appreciation for his services and talents. By the time of his retirement in 1894 he had been relocated twenty-five times, finishing his career as a deputy magistrate of second grade, notwithstanding long periods of severe illness. Varuni Bhatia has noted that Bhaktivinoda's autobiography frequently refers to the uneasiness caused by numerous work-related relocations, regular bouts of illness, and both physical and mental exhaustion. She suggests that this can be contextualized in two ways: first—and she here refers to a view expressed by Sumit Sarkar—as the pain of alienation caused by having to submit to salaried service in the colonial government; second, as a motivation to search for a permanent home, which Bhaktivinoda ultimately found in the sacred space of Mayapur.[25]

Kedarnath Datta's first service appointment was in Chapra in present-day Bihar, where he studied Urdu and Pharsi. Because he had been raised in a Śakta family, his exposure to Caitanya literature had been limited, and it was not until around this time at approximately age thirty that his interest began to develop. In his youth Kedarnath had been in contact with the Kartābhajā, a popular Vaishnava group in Bengal, but nothing substantial had come of it.[26] In 1868 he was transferred to Dinajpur, where Caitanya Vaishnavism was well established. He regularly discussed Vaishnava dharma with local acquaintances and ordered copies of both the *Bhāgavata Purāṇa* (or *Śrīmad Bhāgavatam*) and the *Caitanya Caritāmṛta.* Through close study, he gradually became convinced of the importance of Caitanya. This was challenged, however, by lingering misgivings concerning Krishna's character, pastimes, and activities. In this regard, he describes how after a period of intense study and prayer he came to realize that knowledge of Krishna (*Kṛṣṇa tattva*) was far more profound than that which met the ordinary eye. It was at this point that Vaishnava bhakti emerged as the all-encompassing focal point of his life.

---

25. Bhatia, "Devotional Traditions," p. 186.

26. The Kartābhajās represent perhaps the most important extant branch of Vaishnava *sahajiyā* in Bengal. Hugh Urban suggests that "they have a long and controversial reputation because of their supposed engagement in secret, scandalous, and immoral activities," Urban, *The Economics of Ecstasy*, p. 5. The movement was founded by a wandering fakir named Aulcand (d. 1779) and grew in and around Calcutta during the colonial period; some of its members were alleged to practice left-hand Tantra. Bhaktivinoda made acquaintance with the Kartābhajās as a boy, but later condemned their practice of ritual sex. See, for example, Bhaktivinoda, *Śrī Caitanya Śikṣāmṛta* (Mayapur: Śrī Caitanya Maṭha), p. 127. In their writings, both Bhaktivinoda and Bhaktisiddhānta vigorously opposed *sahajiyā* and left-hand tantric groups that were linked in various ways to the Caitanya tradition.

In the years that followed, Kedarnath Datta produced numerous literary works, from poetic devotional compositions to novels to philosophical treatises (figure B.2). While his works were largely written in Bengali, some were in English, and others in Sanskrit, a language that he studied with local pandits later in his life.[27] He was initiated by Bipin Bihari Goswami, who belonged to the line of Nityānanda of Baghnapara, and in 1886 received the title "Bhaktivinoda" in recognition of his learning.[28] He had also become an established Vaishnava in the eyes of the *bhadralok*. Sisir Kumar Ghosh, editor of the English nationalist daily *Amrita Bazar Patrika*, recognized the efforts of Bhaktivinoda in a personal letter dated November 23, 1888, referring to him as "the Seventh Goswami," an honorific title that praised his accomplishments as a philosopher. The title referred to the Six Goswamis of Vrindavan, the authors of the foundational doctrinal literature of the Caitanya tradition.[29] Bankim Chandra Chatterjee also acknowledged Bhaktivinoda's contribution in the introduction to his own commentary on the Bhagavad Gītā:

> Śrī *Bābu* Kedārnatha Datta, a *Vaiṣṇava* and pandit of the highest order, often supplied in his translation the gist of Viśvanātha Cakravartin's commentary.[30]

For five years between 1869 and 1874, Bhaktivinoda resided in Jagannath Puri. While there he represented the British government as deputy collector and deputy magistrate, overseeing law and order in the region, and supervised the arrangements for the many pilgrims that traveled to Puri each year. This atypically long period of service in one location afforded him

27. Bhaktivinoda published approximately one hundred works, including collections of songs, translations, and commentaries. For a full list see Marvin, "Life and Thought," pp. 320–331.

28. Bhaktivinoda, *Svalikhita Jīvanī*, p. 176.

29. The letter is quoted in *Sajjanatoṣaṇī* 19, no. 2 (1917): pp. 68–70. A translation is given by Marvin, "Life and Thought," pp. 130–131.

30. Harder, *Bankimchandra Chattopadhyay's Śrīmadbhagabadgītā*, p. 19. Chatterjee (also rendered as Chattopadhyay) explicitly cited Kedarnath Bhaktivinoda only once in his text (Harder, *Bankimchandra Chattopadhyay's Śrīmadbhagabadgītā*, p. 89). According to Marvin, however, a pandit named Satkari Chattopadhyay reported that "before Bankim Chandra published his *Kṛṣṇa-caritra* he discussed his ideas with Kedarnath, who objected to the elimination of so much of the life of Kṛṣṇa." Brian D. (Shukavak Dasa) Marvin, *Hindu Encounter with Modernity: Kedarnath Datta Bhaktivinoda, Vaishnava Theologian* (Riverside, Calif.: Sanskrit Religions Institute, 1999), p. 89.

the opportunity to make an in-depth study of Vaishnava literature, scrutinizing the original Sanskrit texts with the help of local pandits. He studied the entire *Bhāgavata Purāṇa*, Jīva Goswami's *Ṣaṭ-sandarbha*, the *Vedānta-sūtra* with the commentary of Baladeva, and the *Bhakti-rasāmṛta-sindhu* by Rūpa Goswami. During this time, he composed the *Datta-kaustubha* (1873) in Sanskrit and began the Sanskrit section of the *Kṛṣṇa-saṃhitā*, published in 1879. Realizing that many Vaishnava texts could only be found in temples and private collections, he also began to search for and copy these rare manuscripts. It was during this period of intense study that Bhaktivinoda's interest in Vaishnavism and bhakti bloomed, and Bimala Prasad was born.

Youth and Education

An anecdote often mentioned in the hagiographic literature may be useful in terms of affording some sense of Bhaktisiddhānta's youthful personality.[31] In Vaishnava families, prepared foodstuffs are first offered to an image of Krishna and then eaten in gratitude or "honored" as *prasāda*, the "Lord's mercy." As a youth, Bimala Prasad innocently ate a mango that was meant to be offered to the family Deity. Seeing this, Kedarnath Datta mildly rebuked him, explaining that it was improper to eat foods that had not yet been offered to Krishna. Despite his young age, Bimala Prasad took his father's words to heart. Humbly feeling that he had offended Krishna, he vowed never to eat mango again—a vow that he is said to have kept throughout the rest of his life. Whatever one may think of this tale, the accounts of his later disciples suggest that even after Bhaktisiddhānta had become an important spiritual leader with numerous followers, he would never accept an offering of mango, claiming to have been an offender at the "lotus feet of Krishna." The narrative has been generally viewed as an early indicator of Bhaktisiddhānta's moral character, self-discipline, and deep commitment to Krishna bhakti; it has also been regarded as an indicator of the profound respect that he felt for his father.

---

31. This event is found in Sundarānanda Vidyāvinoda, *Sarasvatī Jayaśrī, Śrī Parva* (unpublished), pp. 77–78, a book based on interviews with Bhaktisiddhānta himself, and took place ca. 1894, when Bhaktisiddhānta was about twenty years of age. The devotional literature, however, generally claims that this event took place during Bhaktisiddhānta's early childhood.

During his childhood, Bimala Prasad composed two Sanskrit poems in an exercise book dedicated to Caitanya. In these he declared that Caitanya's (*Mahāprabhu*) heart was extremely soft because he radiated love for God and felt very sad witnessing the suffering of living beings around the world.[32] The poem told how once Caitanya had placed his "lotus feet" on a stone, which promptly melted due to his burning compassion, leaving behind permanent impressions as proof of the event.[33] Later in his life Bhaktisiddhānta installed replicas of these footprints as religious markers at several locations in India.

Bimala Prasad began his education at an English school in Ranaghat, and in 1881 was transferred to the Oriental Seminary in Calcutta. In 1881, when he was a seventh-grade student, Bhaktivinoda gave young Bimala prayer beads (*japa mālā*) made of a *tulasī* plant from Jagannath Puri. These he would use for purposes of meditation throughout his life. Bhaktivinoda initiated his son in *harināma* (the name of Hari). This "initiation into sacred sound" is generally performed by a family *brāhmaṇa* belonging to a succession of gurus (*paramparā*). Bhaktivinoda was at that time neither a *brāhmaṇa* nor formally initiated in a Vaishnava line, but he wished to encourage his son's early interest in bhakti. In the same year, an image of Kurma, the tortoise *avatāra* of Vishnu, was found at Maniktala Street 181 in Rambagan, a district of Calcutta, where Bhaktivinoda was building a new house, the Bhaktibhavana. Bhaktivinoda entrusted the image to his son, who from that time on began to follow Vaishnava rules for ritual worship. To nurture his religious leanings, Bhaktivinoda took Bimala Prasad on pilgrimage tours, and together they met yogis, gurus, and other religious leaders. He also began to participate in readings of the Caitanya literature with his son to stimulate his emotional, spiritual, and intellectual development.

In 1881, a young Rabindranth Tagore was brought by Dvijendranth to recite a collection of intimate poems about Rādhā and Krishna for Bhaktivinoda.[34] Bimala Prasada wrote that although he himself had little

---

32. "Mahāprabhu" (the great master) is a frequently used epithet for Sri Caitanya.

33. This was told by Bhaktisiddhānta on December 30, 1927, and recorded in *Sarasvatī Jayaśrī, Vaibhava Parva*, edited by Sundarānanda Vidyāvinoda (Calcutta: Śrī Gaudiya Math, 1934), p. 24n. Unless otherwise mentioned, "*Sarasvatī Jayaśrī*" indicates the *Vaibhava Parva*.

34. For a comprehensive introduction to and translation of the songs see Rabindranath Tagore, Tony K. Stewart, and Chase Twichell, *The Lover of God* (Port Townsend, Wash.: Copper Canyon Press, 2003).

interest in popular songs, he nonetheless appreciated Rabindranath's clarity of expression and language.[35]

One of Bhaktivinoda's most important institutional efforts during this period was the *Viśva Vaiṣṇava Rāja Sabhā* (the Royal World Vaishnava Association), which he founded in 1885 in Calcutta.[36] Sisir Kumar Ghosh and Bipin Bihari Goswami, a caste guru from Bhagnapara, were active supporters, and frequently came to the meetings of the association. Young Bimala also attended and, through his father, met many of the leading Vaishnavas in Bengal, as well as other important members of the *bhadralok*. These encounters enabled him to accumulate social and cultural capital that would be of great value later on.

Bhaktivinoda was appointed senior deputy magistrate in Serampore, the ex-Danish colony north of Calcutta, and old seat of the Baptist missionaries. In 1883, he registered Bimala Prasad at the Serampore Union institution, a local Bengali medium school, which had been newly founded by Vidyasagar. Bimala Prasad possessed a sharp, almost photographic, memory, aptly remembering whatever he happened to read. During this period (at approximately age nine), he is said to have committed the entire Bhagavad Gītā to memory (ca. 700 Sanskrit verses). It has also been noted that even at the end of his life he would recall passages from books that he had read in his youth, an ability that earned him the title of "living encyclopaedia."[37] In 1885, Bhaktivinoda founded a research center, the Vaishnava Depository, with a library intended for the preservation of the literature of the Caitanya tradition. The center included a press that was used to publish and propagate the religious perspectives of the *Viśva Vaiṣṇava Rāja Sabhā*. The press was used to publish the *Sajjanatoṣaṇī*, a new Vaishnava periodical that Bhaktivinoda had started one year earlier. The magazine contained news of Bhaktivinoda's missionary activities and was used to disseminate his devotional poetry as well as his writings on Vaishnava history and theology. It also included reviews of contemporary religious works. Although still a young boy, Bimala Prasad was given the task of proofreading the magazine, an experience that is likely to have given him a keen appreciation for the role of the press in propagating religious ideas, particularly among the educated *bhadralok*.

---

35. *Sarasvatī Jayaśrī, Śrī Parva*, p. 52.

36. *Sarasvatī Jayaśrī, Śrī Parva*, p. 61.

37. *Harmonist* 32, no. 1 (August 17, 1937): p. 10.

Bhaktisiddhānta rarely spoke about his early years. In 1935, in a scanty autobiographical letter, he recalled some of the milestones of that period:[38]

> I entered the Serampore Union School as a student in the month of October 1883, the year when the Calcutta exhibition was held. I left the Serampore school in 1887, the jubilee year of Victorian rule, and joined the Calcutta Metropolitan Institution.[39]

The Calcutta Metropolitan Institution had been founded by Vidyasagar in 1864, and provided a solid modern education for the *bhadralok* youth. Besides the obligatory curriculum, Bimala Prasad studied Sanskrit grammar and classical Hindu astronomy (*jyotiṣa*) with local pundits. In his leisure time, he met with fellow students, with whom he discussed issues of culture, religion and society (figure B.1). In 1891, at age seventeen, he founded the Lifelong Bachelor Association (*Cira kumāra sabhā*), also known as the August Assembly, for the moral regeneration of society.[40] Members took a vow of celibacy and met to discuss current events. Bimala Prasad remained a celibate throughout his life, perhaps one of the few that did so among the members of that group.

Apart from his interest in the cultural, political, and religious developments of his time, Bimala Prasad evinced a precocious interest in mathematics and abstract rational thinking. He studied astronomy with pandits Mahesh Chandra Cudamani and Sundara Lala, who in 1889 awarded him the title "Siddhānta Sarasvatī" in honor of his proficiency in this subject.[41] Soon thereafter he began to use this title on the front page of his own articles and books, something that added authority and legitimacy to his

38. The letter is dated April 9, 1935. Although in standard editions of Bhaktisiddhānta's letters the name of the receiver is withheld, Sambidananda Das, who at the time was completing his Ph.D. dissertation at the University of London, acknowledged receipt of the letter as follows: "he has kindly supplied us with a very short account of his early years at our request." This letter is referenced in his dissertation. See Sambidananda Das, "The History and Literature of the Gaudiya Vaisnavas and Their Relation to Other Medieval Vaisnava Schools," Ph.D. diss., University of London, 1935, ch. 13, p. 32.

39. Bhaktisiddhānta Sarasvatī, *Prabhupādera Patrābalī*, vol. 3 (Prayag: Śrī Rupa Gauḍīya Mission, 1999), p. 48.

40. Celibacy in Hindu society is still respected as a sign of moral and religious commitment.

41. Vikāsa, *Śrī Bhaktisiddhānta Vaibhava: The Grandeur and Glory of Śrīla Bhaktisiddhānta Sarasvatī Ṭhākura* (Surat: Bhakti Vikas Trust, 2009), vol. 1, p. 13.

writing. Calcutta was at the time a center of traditional learning. Astronomy, Sanskrit grammar, logic (*nyāya*), and Vedanta philosophy—also known as "Deism" in missionary circles—were taught by independent maths.[42] Sarasvatī studied the Vedas and the grammatical work *Siddhānta-kaumudī* with pandit Pritvishvara Sharma. He also explored the six branches of the Vedas: *śikṣā* (pronunciation), *kalpa* (assessment of time for sacrificial activities), *vyākaraṇa* (grammar), *nirukta* (meaning of words), *chanda* (meter), and *jyotiṣa* (astronomy and astrology).

Sarasvatī passed the demanding entrance examination for the Sanskrit College and, apart from Sanskrit, studied mathematics, Indian philosophy, and ancient history. The Sanskrit College had been founded in 1824 near the renowned Presidency College, and was at the time one of the finest schools for classical Hindu learning. Vidyasagar, a good friend of Bhaktivinoda, had been elected as its principal in 1851. He had reformed it to allow *kāyasthas* like Sarasvatī—considered elite *śudras* in Bengal—to be accepted alongside *brāhmaṇas* and *vaidyas*. Apart from the privilege of studying at the college, however, Sarasvatī was not that enthusiastic about the regular course literature. Instead he indulged in the reading of bhakti literature such as Narottama dāsa's *Prārthanā* and *Prema-bhakti-candrikā*, as well as books on Krishna mysticism such as *Kṛṣṇa-karṇāmṛta* by Bilvamaṅgala Ṭhākura, which he studied in the original Sanskrit.

Meanwhile, Bhaktivinoda applied the managerial skills he had acquired through his civil service to a new institutional venture. In October 1893, he founded the *Navadvīpadhāma Pracāriṇī Sabhā* (Society for Popularization of the Sacred Site of Nabadwip), which promoted the alternative birthplace of Caitanya that he had seen in Mayapur during a

---

42. William Ward provides an 1822 list of Calcutta maths, but makes no mention of a school of Vedanta. William Ward, *A View of the History, Literature, and Religion of the Hindoos and Translations of Their Principal Works* (London: Kingsbury, Parbury, and Allen, 1822), pp. 495–496. David Kopf states that in the early nineteenth century "Bengal had virtually no Vedantic schools and, with the possible exception of Nabakrishna Deb's pandit, Jaganath Tarkapanchan, and one of Rammohun's own pandits, Ram Chandra Vidyabagish, we have little evidence of Vedantists developing in the region's highly scholastic and ritualized cultural atmosphere." Kopf, *British Orientalism*, pp. 58–59. Bruce Carlisle Robertson has shown, however, that Rammohun Roy was aware of maths teaching Vedanta in Calcutta. Robertson, *Raja Rammohan Ray*, pp. 55–59. Traditional learning in Bengal had nonetheless been strained by the Permanent Settlement, which had displaced the landowning class. This, in turn, had deprived *brāhmaṇa* pundits of their traditional patrons, placing them in financial distress. See Sushil Kumar De, *Bengali Literature in the Nineteenth Century, 1757–1857* (Calcutta: Firma K. L. Mukhopadhyay, 1962), p. 27. Bhaktisiddhānta would often lament the lack of sustained support for classical learning in Bengal.

mystical experience.[43] Mayapur was at this time populated by a Muslim settlement of farmers and fishermen. Bhaktivinoda embarked upon pioneering historical, textual, and archaeological studies to prove the legitimacy of Mayapur as the true birthplace of Caitanya, opposing the old (*prācīna*) location in Nabadwip. To that end he published the *Śrī Navadvīpa Dhāma Mahātmya* in 1888 and gained the support of important Nadia landowners such as Nafarchandra Pal Chauduri (1838–1933), and also of the prestigious royal family of Tripura. At the suggestion of another supporter, Sisir Kumar Ghosh, Bhaktivinoda decided to make his theories public, and he arranged a meeting in the A. B. School in Krishnanagar, the administrative center for the Nadia district, where he presented the evidence for his claim. The meeting was well attended and well received, and with support from members of the middle and upper class, Mayapur grew as an alternative pilgrimage site, posing an immediate threat to the *brāhmaṇic* communities of Nabadwip.[44] Despite this promising beginning, Bhaktivinoda's project was firmly opposed by prominent *bhadralok* such as Akhsay Chandra Sarkar, who worked for a Hindu revival through the Bangabasi press and edited three journals, the *Sadharani*, the *Nabajiban*, and *Purnima*. Another opponent was Kanti Chandra Rarhi, who argued against Bhaktivinoda on the basis of historical-empirical evidence.[45]

It was around this time that Sarasvatī discontinued his studies at the Sanskrit College. The reason concerned a dispute in 1895 about the precise location of the equinox, which was traditionally calculated from a fixed point of the zodiac. Despite his youth and his subordinate position as a mere student, Sarasvatī openly opposed the calculations of the headmaster, Mahesh Chandra Nyayaratna, a *kulīna brāhmaṇa*, and one of the

43. *Sajjanatoṣaṇī* 5, no. 11 (1893): pp. 201–207.

44. Ferdinando Sardella, "The Two Birthplaces of Śrī Caitanya Mahāprabhu: Gauḍīya Vaishnava Groups in Navadvīpa and Māyāpura During the Gaura Pūrṇimā Festival 2002," M.A. thesis, University of Gothenburg, 2002.

45. Bhatia, "Devotional Traditions," p. 173. Rarhi published in 1884 the *Navadvīpa Mahimā* (*The Glories of Nabadwip*). Varuni Bhatia deals extensively with the Mayapur controversy; see Bhatia, "Devotional Traditions," pp. 167–232. Her analysis complements an earlier one made by Jason D. Fuller, "Religion, Class, and Power: Bhaktivinoda Thakur and the Transformation of Religious Authority among the Gauḍīya Vaiṣṇavas in Nineteenth-Century Bengal," Ph.D. diss., University of Pennsylvania, 2004, pp. 200–281. Fuller stresses the ability of the *bhadralok* that favored Bhaktivinoda's position to employ modern fund-raising, organizational, and historical-critical methods to establish their point of view. Bhatia, on the other hand, focuses on the role of Bhaktivinoda's mystical experience as a key legitimizing factor in the still ongoing conflict.

finest Sanskrit scholars of India, arguing that they be replaced by his own alternate calibrations.[46] A college-wide conflict ensued, and a great deal of pressure was brought to bear on the youth. In the end, Sarasvatī decided that rather than compromise what he believed to be the correct interpretation of the data, it would be better to simply depart the college.[47]

During this period Sarasvatī was proven to possess a sharp, critical—even brilliant—intellect. Trained by Calcutta pundits, by age fourteen he had mastered a number of complex mathematical calculations. At the age of twenty-two he undertook the task of translating two classical astronomical texts from Sanskrit to Bengali, the *Sūrya-siddhānta* (1896) and the *Siddhānta-śiromaṇi* (1897), which he published with his own notes.[48] In the preface of the *Siddhānta-śiromaṇi* Sarasvatī acknowledged the help and support of the astronomer K. Datta, with whom he cooperated in many of his astronomical publications.[49] In 1891, at the age of seventeen, Sarasvatī introduced his own tutorials in astronomy, and in 1897, after leaving the Sanskrit College, he used his family home to establish the Sarasvata Chatuspathi, a school of astronomy that prepared students for examinations at the Sanskrit College, attracting a respectable number of individuals. Beyond this, he managed to publish two astronomical periodicals, the *Bṛhaspati or the Scientific Indian* and the *Jyotirvida*—the latter coedited with K. Dutt—and he worked with zeal to rekindle Bengali interest in Indic classical astronomy. With this in mind, he published with K. Dutt works such as (1) the *Laghu-jātaka* with annotations by Bhaṭṭotpala

46. Mahesh Chandra Nyayaratna became the principal of the Sanskrit College in 1877 and remained in that position for eighteen years. For a biographical sketch, see Roper Lethbridge, *The Golden Book of India: A Genealogical and Biographical Dictionary of the Ruling Princes, Chiefs, Nobles, and Other Personages, Titled or Decorated of the Indian Empire* (Delhi: Aakar Books, 2005), pp. 299–300.

47. Sambidananda Das, "History and Literature," ch. 13, p. 33. The hagiographic literature generally interprets this episode in a way that implies that Bhaktisiddhānta left college in search of spirituality. This, however, does not appear to be reasonable since it was during this time that he accepted employment at the princely state of Tripura. On the other hand, it may have been the case that Bhaktisiddhānta himself interpreted this episode as a sign that he was not destined to pursue a mundane career.

48. Bengali translation and explanation of Bhāskara's *Siddhānta-śiromaṇi*, first chapter (*Golādhyāya*) and *Grahaganitādhyaya*. The *Siddhānta-śiromaṇi* and the *Sūrya-siddhānta* are regarded as two foundational texts of ancient Hindu astronomy.

49. Bhaktisiddhānta Sarasvatī, Danavir Goswami et al., eds., *The Sūrya-siddhānta and Siddhānta-śiromaṇi* (Kansas City: Rupanuga Vedic College, 2007), p. 179. It is unlikely that the above acknowledgment of "K. Datta" refers to his father Kedarnath Datta, since there is no evidence that Bhaktivinoda took an interest in astronomy.

(Sept. 1897); (2) the *Laghuparāśarīya*, or *Uḍūdaya-pradīpa*, with Bhairava Datta's annotations; (3) the *Bhauma-siddhānta* according to western calculation; (4) the *Ārya-siddhānta* by Āryabhaṭa; and (5) the *Bhaṭa-dīpikā-ṭīkā*, *Dina-kaumudī* and *Camatkāra-cintāmaṇi* by Paramadīśvara.[50]

According to Sarasvatī, although the works of the sixth-century astronomer Āryabhaṭa, the tenth-century commentator Bhaṭṭotpala, and the eleventh-century astronomer Bhāskarācārya were well known to the pandits of India, they were little studied in Bengal. Apart from these writings, Sarasvatī also published the *Bhakti-bhāvana Pañjikā* and the *Śrī Navadvīpa Pañjikā*, two astronomical almanacs that provided dates for religious events, which he calculated according to the rules of the *jyotiṣa śāstra*.[51] *Śrī Navadvīpa Pañjikā* was specifically designed for Vaishnavas, and Sarasvatī employed various names of Vishnu to signify the months, fortnights, and days of the moon calendar.[52]

In 1898, Sarasvatī became embroiled in yet another confrontation, this time with the elderly chair of astronomy at the Sanskrit College, Pañcānana Sāhityācārya. The pandit, who was reputed to be one of the most learned astronomers in Bengal, questioned the astronomical theories that twenty-four-year-old Sarasvatī had been teaching to his students, and which they, in turn, had been putting forward at Sanskrit College examinations. Finally it was agreed that the two would meet in a public debate, with Satish Candra Vidyābhūṣaṇa, the new principal of the college, presiding. Although Sarasvatī's notions ran contrary to the mainstream astronomical theories of his time, by all accounts he acquitted himself admirably in a debate that may have marked the zenith of his academic carrier.[53] Notwithstanding the apparent success of his defense, Sarasvatī's students were ultimately forced to compromise in order to pass their astronomy exams.

---

50. Most of these works as well as issues of the periodicals mentioned above are found at the Bhaktivedanta Research Centre in Kolkata.

51. Swami Bhaktikusum Sraman, *Prabhupāda Srila Sarasvati Thākura* (Sree Mayapur: Sri Caitanya Math, 1983), pp. 56, 180.

52. He produced Gregorian calendars as well; see Bhaktisiddhānta Sarasvatī, *Almanac for the year 1917* (Calcutta: Saraswat Chatuspathi, n.d).

53. Sambidananda Das, "History and Literature," ch. 13, p. 35. Bimal Prasada Datta's apparent victory is reported in insider accounts. However, since there are no independent sources, this outcome can be legitimately questioned. Nonetheless, the fact that the debate took place at all provides some evidence of Bimala Prasad Dattas's growing reputation as an astronomer.

In 1895, some years prior to the above debate, Sarasvatī accepted a position at the royal court of the Maharaja of Tripura. His aim, among others, was to earn funds for the establishment of the home astronomy school mentioned above. The maharaja was a staunch supporter of Bhaktivinoda, even functioning as the president of his *Navadvīpadhama Pracāriṇī Sabhā* from 1894 to 1896. As such he was happy to secure a position for the son.[54] Tripura (or Hill Tippera) is one of India's easternmost provinces, located between eastern Bengal and Assam. In colonial times it bordered the British district of Tippera and was a princely state under the protectorate of the British Crown.[55] It had been ruled for a long time by the maharajas of the Manikya dynasty, who possessed a vast estate as well as a large residence in Agartala, the capital city. Sarasvatī was first employed by Maharaja Bir Chandra Kishor (1838–1896) to edit a history of the royal dynasty. However, after his death in December 1896, the new maharaja, Radha Kishor (1857–1909), requested Sarasvatī to tutor one of his sons, Prince Brajendra Kishor (b. 1880) (in the future, the members of the Manikya dynasty of Tripura would become lifelong patrons of his mission). Sarasvatī's next appointment was to the Agency of the Tripura State in Calcutta, where he had the opportunity to meet the top administrators and politicians of Bengal. With reference to this time, Bhaktisiddhānta wrote:

> In 1895 I accepted a service in the independent state of Tripura, and in 1905 a full pension was granted to me. I accepted it until the year 1908.[56]

The period around the turn of the century also marked a new stage in Sarasvatī's development: one of deep direct involvement with religious study, practice, and experience. It was at this point in his life that he became seriously interested in undertaking a religiously austere life.

54. A brother of Bhaktisiddhānta would later serve as secretary of the maharaja.

55. "Hill Tipperah or Tripura," in *The Encyclopaedia Britannica* (Cambridge: Cambridge University Press, 1911), vol. 13, p. 469. The Raj allowed the existence of scattered princely states in an effort to create political stability, as well as a network of allies that were required since the British possessed neither the strength nor the economic resources to rule India by force alone.

56. Bhaktisiddhānta Sarasvatī, *Prabhupādera Patrāvalī* (Prayag: Śrī Rupa Gauḍīya Mission, 1984), vol. 3, p. 48.

An anecdote from this period informs us that in 1897, at age twenty-three, Sarasvatī began the strict observance of *cāturmāsya*, a difficult yearly vow that continues throughout the four months of India's rainy season (approx. July–October). In compliance with the severe requirements of this vow, Sarasvatī is said to have set up residence in a small hut, where he ate only rice, only once a day, for the full four months; he prepared the rice himself and ate it by leaning down from a sitting posture and ingesting it with only his mouth. He is also said to have slept on the floor without a mattress or pillow, allowing his hair, beard, and nails to grow unattended. The practice of such severe austerities caused Sarasvatī to become emaciated and weak, and it appears that after some time his father asked him to discontinue the vow (in general, Bhaktisiddhānta is reported to have been afflicted with poor health, and to have suffered from various ailments throughout his entire life—ailments that were at times exacerbated by his insistent practice of austerities).[57]

Although Sarasvatī received a modern Western education from public schools, of greater significance is the fact that he was also educated in traditional Indic knowledge, something that set him apart from many of his contemporaries. Few among his peers were eager to cultivate traditional knowledge, since it offered no tangible advantage in terms of securing a professional career. Despite the fact that he was a non-*brāhmaṇa*, Sarasvatī nonetheless acquainted himself with standard fields of *brāhmaṇic* learning (e.g., astronomy, philosophy, and Sanskrit), largely owing to the wealth and encouragement of his father.

In 1899 Sarasvatī began writing articles for the religious section of the *Nivedana* (*Announcements*), a new weekly periodical published by Bhaktivinoda from the Bhaktibhavana in Calcutta. The periodical contained both religious and secular news and was meant to attract a broad audience. In the same year, at the age of twenty-five, Sarasvatī published *Baṅge Sāmājikatā* (*The Making of Society in Bengal*), a booklet that is still in print at the Gaudiya Math (figure B.3).[58] The work marked his first analysis of the relation between religion and society, providing not only an historical account based on indigenous categories of knowledge, but also a critique of Indology and Western historiography. Its content affords researchers a

57. Vikāsa, *Śrī Bhaktisiddhānta Vaibhava*, vol. 1, p. 26.

58. It was out of print for many years, but it is currently available (2012) at the Caitanya Research Institute in Kolkata.

fairly accurate account of Sarasvatī's ideas as they stood at the turn of the century. In his study, Sarasvatī portrayed Hindu society as a community united by a common religious and social foundation, but deeply divided by multiple identities of caste. In the last chapter of the booklet he explored the concept of dharma and summarized its gradual development from ancient Vedic to contemporary schools of thought, ending with a review of over thirty religious currents. The conclusion suggested the possibility of a global community based on a universal principle of devotional service to God and a vision of the spiritual brotherhood of all beings—a brotherhood that was meant to transcend all "temporal" distinctions of body, race, caste, nation, or creed. Through this early work Sarasvatī was implicitly responding to the three major accusations lodged by colonial discourse against Hinduism and, by default, Vaishnavism: (1) that it lacked a sense of history; (2) that it lacked a moral structure; and (3) that it lacked a rational philosophical system.[59] The booklet was ambitious in its claims, and was dedicated to the Maharaja of Tripura, who may have sponsored its publication. A more detailed discussion of its content will appear in chapter 4.

Despite his intellectual and academic interests, and the respectable level of success he had achieved in the areas of scholarship and occupation, Sarasvatī nonetheless felt a strong calling for religious life. As the twentieth century neared, he became ever more inclined to give up the comforts of home, and aspired to receive instruction from a spiritual master (i.e., a guru) that was wholly situated in renunciation. His father, of course, was a prominent guru in his own right, and one whom Sarasvatī revered and loved. However, he was involved in the life of a married householder (*gṛhastha*) with the responsibilities of caring for a very large family, while Sarasvatī was drawn to a more austere life. As it happened, Gaura Kiśora dāsa Bābajī, a highly regarded Vaishnava ascetic and mystic, would sometimes visit the home of Bhaktivinoda to listen to his lectures.[60] These occasions provided Sarasvatī with the opportunity to meet and observe this singular individual, and he was deeply impressed by his humility, simplicity, and spiritual absorption.

---

59. Shamita Basu, *Religious Revivalism as Nationalist Discourse: Swami Vivekananda and New Hinduism in Nineteenth-Century Bengal* (Delhi: Oxford University Press, 2002), p. 45.

60. For a biographical sketch, see June McDaniel, *The Madness of the Saints: Ecstatic Religion in Bengal* (Chicago: University of Chicago Press, 1989), pp. 53–57. A more detailed biographical overview is found in Śrī Haridāsa dāsa, *Śrī Śrī Gauḍīya Vaiṣṇava Jīvana* (Nabadwip: Śrī Haribol Kuṭir, 1975), pp. 39–47.

Gaura Kiśora dāsa Bābājī is said to have been born sometime in the early nineteenth century in the district of Faridpur, on the shore of the Padma River in East Bengal. As was the custom of the time, his mother and father arranged for their son's early marriage, and shortly thereafter he became a broker in the grain business. He remained a *gṛhastha* until the death of his wife, which occurred when he was twenty-nine years of age. Then, following his own spiritual inclinations, he left home to accept initiation as a *bābājī*—a celibate ascetic that renounces all worldly pursuits to live alone and dedicate himself to spiritual meditation, accepting only a simple piece of white cloth (*veṣa*) as his outward garment. Gaura Kiśora's *veṣa* guru was Bhāgavata dāsa Bābā, a disciple of Jagannātha dāsa Bābājī of Vrindavan, a town held sacred and revered by all Caitanya Vaishnavas.

After initiation, Gaura Kiśora is said to have traveled to Vrindavan, where it is believed he remained in seclusion for thirty years, absorbed in esoteric meditation on the "transcendental pastimes" of "Sri Krishna and His Consort." During this period he would sometimes punctuate his meditations by making pilgrimages to various holy places in India, including Nabadwip, the place of Caitanya's early life. It was here that he is said to have resided from March 1894 until the end of his life.

As noted above, Gaura Kiśora was a singular personality whose behavior was often found to be unconventional in the extreme. Illiterate and lacking formal education, he is said to have kept himself entirely aloof from all things—and persons—material, residing, from time to time, on the banks of the Ganges beneath a portable covering for boats (*chai*). For sustenance, he would beg a quantity of raw rice from local families, which he would soak in water and ritually offer before consuming it himself. When there was need of cooking, he is said to have collected discarded wood to build the fire and discarded pots to contain the eatables. Around his neck he wore *japa-mālā*, a necklace of 108 wooden *tulasī* beads that are similar in appearance and function to a rosary, commonly handled with the right hand by most Vaishnavas; this elaborate counter was used to ensure that he fulfilled his vow to chant the sacred names of God (*japa*) a set number of times each day. Often he would be seen sitting in meditation by the roadside latrines, wearing pieces of cloth that had been used to cover the dead before burning.

These and other forms of extreme or eccentric behavior conveyed a bizarre outward profile that would have been disconcerting and incomprehensible to most Western observers. Indeed, from an "outsider" perspective, Gaura Kiśora's conduct certainly would have appeared like madness to many. From an "insider" perspective, however, this was only half the story, and the superficial half at that; in other words, there was more to Gaura Kiśora than met the eye, and method in his apparent madness: his aim was to subdue self-pride and egoism, maintain a humble state, dampen the self-gratifying spirit, and avoid the cheap self-seeking adoration of the worldly, who were dissuaded by his manner from making their approach. In the view of those Vaishnava "insiders" whom he allowed to genuinely know him, Gaura Kiśora was possessed of many praiseworthy personal attributes, as well as an uncanny ability to detect and expose the faintest taint of hypocrisy in others. He was also considered to have achieved an exalted state of mystical closeness to God and a high level of instinctive spiritual understanding, despite his lack of polish and education. It was this deeper side of the picture that drew Sarasvatī's attention, admiration, and respect, and not the fact that Gaura Kiśora housed himself in unconventional places and so forth.

Quoted below is one of Bhaktisiddhānta's rare memories of this unique Vaishnava ascetic, translated into English by Saṃvidānanda dāsa:

> It was by providential dispensation that I was able fully to understand the language and practical side of devotion after I had met the practising master [Gaura Kiśora dāsa].... No education could have prepared me for the good fortune of understanding my master's attitude.... Before I met him my impression was that the writings of the devotional school could not be fully realised in a practical life in this world. My study of my master, and then the study of the books, along with the explanations by Thakura Bhakti Vinoda, gave me ample facility to advance toward true spiritual life. Before I met my master, I had not written anything about real religion. Up to that time, my idea of religion was confined to books and to a strict ethical life, but that sort of life was found imperfect unless I came in touch with the practical side of things.[61]

Bhaktisiddhānta provided further details of his relationship with Gaura Kiśora in two 1917 articles that were published in the *Sajjanatoṣaṇī*; they were titled "*āmāra prabhura kathā*," or "Tales about My Master."[62] In these accounts he confesses that his education, sharp intellect, and social status

61. Sambidananda Das, "History and Literature," ch. 13, p. 41.

62. *Sajjanatoṣaṇī* 19 (1917), pp. 177–84, 220–25.

had made him proud, and that Bhaktivinoda had cleverly directed him to approach Gaura Kiśora, who evinced not the slightest regard for his worldly competence and intellectual achievement. According to Bhaktisiddhānta himself, this utter indifference induced him to take a hard look inside, curing him of his youthful pride. Bhaktisiddhānta recounted that he had met someone who showed him not only how to live in the world but how to develop his character as well. Noting Sarasvatī's honesty and sincerity, Gaura Kiśora suggested that he reside nearby, and Sarasvatī departed Calcutta to make his base in Mayapur.[63]

From Bhaktivinoda, Sarasvatī had acquired social and cultural competence, a sense of societal involvement, and the vision of a Vaishnava society that could impact the modern world. From Gaura Kiśora he obtained something very different. The *bābājī* was not well educated, highly unconventional, and wholly unconcerned with the sociopolitical aspects of life (although he did at some point encourage Sarasvatī to spread the message of the *Ṣaṭ-sandarbha*, the scholastic exposition of bhakti in six volumes by Jīva Goswami).[64] Moreover, he steadfastly avoided public exposure, despite the fact that his spiritual reputation attracted rich and powerful patrons. What he was able to provide, however, was a keen appreciation for the intimate practice of *ragānūga bhakti*, by which one worshipped "Sri Krishna and His Consort" in the mood of separation (*vipralambha*)—a form of devotional service pursued by advanced Vaishnavas in Vrindavan and Nabadwip. Sarasvatī was particularly touched by a song that he heard Gaura Kiśora sing, which expressed Raghunātha dāsa Goswami's intense feelings of separation from Krishna's consort, Rādhā. He memorized those verses and made them the basis of his personal spiritual meditations.[65] During this period he wore green clothing (the color of *vipralambha*), coloured many of his everyday items green, and even used green ink for writing.[66] Gaura Kiśora practiced strict celibacy—as opposed to the erotic tantra that was popular among Bengal's lower-caste Vaishnavas—and this was something that also appealed to Sarasvatī's personal proclivities, as

63. Bhāratī, Bhakti Bhūṣaṇa, ed., *Śrīla Prabhupādera Goloka-vaṇī* (Navadvīpa: Bhakti-kevala Auḍulomi Śrī Kṛṣṇa-Caitanya Sevāśrama, 1997), vol. 2, p. 3. See also Bhaktisiddānta Sarasvatī, *Prabhupādera Harikathāmṛta* (Mayapur: Śrī Caitanya Math, 2002), p. 31.

64. Paramānanda Brahmacārī in *Sarasvatī Jayaśrī*, p. 154.

65. The song is reproduced in the *Gauḍīya* 16, nos. 20–21 (December 25, 1937): p. 361.

66. Kuñjabihārī Vidyābhūṣaṇa in *Sarasvatī Jayaśrī*, p. 135n.

well as his ethical sensibilities. After a period of testing, he was initiated, and received the name Vārṣabhānavī devī daitya dāsa.[67] Sarasvatī acknowledged Gaura Kiśora as his guru on several occasions, such as when he referred to the *bābājī* as "my master" (*mama prabhu*) at the beginning of his commentary on the *Śrīmad Bhāgavatam*.[68] He came to regard both Bhaktivinoda and Gaura Kiśora as key sources of inspiration, considering both of them to be fully realized Vaishnavas. Bhaktivinoda and Gaura Kiśora nonetheless represented two different approaches to the practice of Caitanya Vaishnavism: the path of the layman on the one hand and the path of the ascetic on the other. The acknowledgment of both paths as viable means for achieving the higher levels of devotional practice (*sādhana*) and realization was an important step, since the laity was generally viewed as being incapable of such achievements.

Bhaktivinoda viewed the British, with their global highways of trade and travel, their powerful institutions, their pragmatic efficiency, and, above all, their religious tolerance, as important assets for the revitalization of Caitanya Vaishnavism. And he equally hoped that Vaishnavism would one day become an important asset to the empire. For these reasons, Bhaktivinoda never opposed the British, nor supported the nationalist movement. Even the violent Sepoy war of 1857 did not shake his commitment, and he remained throughout his life a loyal citizen and servant of the Raj. He believed that the British promoted secularism—that is, the neutrality of the state in religious matters—and with that, religious freedom.[69] He objected only to the marginalization of religion in

67. The initiation of Bhaktisiddhānta by Gaura Kiśora dāsa Bābāji has been questioned by various sources. See McDaniel, *Madness of the Saints*, pp. 319–320. Considering Gaura Kiśora dāsa Bābāji's eccentric, solitary lifestyle, it is highly probable that such an initiation would have been a private, and not a public, event—i.e., one with no third party in attendance. Thus, there is no way to positively know whether or not the event took place. What is known, however, is that Bhaktisiddhānta consistently referred to Gaura Kiśora dāsa Bābāji as his guru, and always in very affectionate and reverential terms. Their guru-disciple relation has been discussed at length by Swami B. G. Narasingha, *The Authorized Sri Caitanya-Saraswata Parampara* (Bangalore: Gosai Publishers, 1998), p. 40.

68. Bhaktisiddhānta and Vyāsadeva, *Śrīmad Bhāgavatam* (Calcutta: Śrī Gauḍīya Maṭha, 1995), p. 3.

69. Bhaktisiddhānta's secretary, Ananta Vāsudeva, wrote in *Sarasvatī Jayaśrī* of personally hearing Bhaktivinoda comment on the occasion of King George V's December 30, 1911, reception in Calcutta that he approved of seeing and offering respect to the king. Bhaktivinoda credited British rule with the fact that Vaishnavas were able to hold public religious activities without hindrance. The British were neutral with regard to the practice of religion, and this itself was thought to be very beneficial. Ananta Vāsudeva in *Sarasvatī Jayaśrī*, p. 1

secular society, and to the claim of superiority by the Christian missionaries. In an open letter to the Christian Tract Society of Calcutta in 1899 he wrote: "To do justice to us, Reverend Gentlemen, you are our superiors in all other respects, but in religion only our equals, and so are our Islam brothers."[70]

Bhaktivinoda frequently traveled in connection with his duties, and during these travels had the opportunity to observe the hardships of the peasants, subject to an ownership system that placed them at the mercy of local landlords, and several layers of ruthless brokers and tax collectors. The system, which was based on the so-called Permanent Settlement, forced farmers to grow cash crops rather than food, making them unnecessarily susceptible to famines and shortages in times of crises, due to lack of surplus reserves.[71] Bhaktivinoda refused to work as a tax collector. In addition, while traveling from village to village during work or in his spare time, he developed a network of several "*nāma-haṭṭa*" for the spiritual upliftment of the rural population. Bhaktivinoda also worked to revive Vaishnavism through cooperation with orthodox communities such as the Baghnapada Vaishnavas.[72] The organization of the *nāma-haṭṭa* was "a scheme of preaching conceived after the image of commodities market."[73] His Vaishnava missionaries in the villages were conceived as "shopkeepers of the sacred name" (*nāma*) that established "stores" in huts, shelters, or rooms, where the congregational chanting (*kīrtana*) and/or recitation of the names of God would take place. The idea of marketing religion

70. *The Hindu Idols: An Answer to "Prof. Max Muller on Durga"* (Calcutta: Tract Society, January 1899), p. 25.

71. For a list of the various capacities in which Bhaktivinoda served from February 16, 1866, till November 27, 1893, see Marvin, *Hindu Encounter with Modernity*, pp. 298–299. On October 4, 1894, Bhaktivinoda retired from government service as a deputy magistrate and deputy collector of second grade. During the colonial period, a deputy magistrate was the de facto representative of the Raj in his district of operation, and would be responsible for such matters as revenue collection, civic duties, and the maintenance of law and order.

72. About the Vaishnavas of Baghnapada, see Ramakanta Chakravarti, *Vaiṣṇavism in Bengal, 1486–1900* (Calcutta: Sanskrit Pustak Bhandar, 1985), ch. 16.

73. Marvin, *Hindu Encounter with Modernity*, pp. 309–312. Marvin discusses Bhaktivinoda's *nāma-haṭṭa* program in detail, showing that Bhaktivinoda had established a large network of "shops" that enjoyed the support of many influential *bhadralok*. Bhaktivinoda himself provides a detailed description of the system in *Śrī Godruma Kalpataru* (1891; Mayapur: Sri Sri Hare Krishna Nama Hatta, 1989). Marvin is of the opinion that these initiatives were directed to the *bhadralok* since the reports in the *Sajjanatoṣaṇī* only mention *bhadralok* patrons (see p. 312 n. 9). This, however, does not exclude the possibility that Bhaktivinoda aimed to create a mass movement among other classes as well.

had already been developed by the Kartābhajās, who in the early colonial period called their society "the poor company," as compared to the wealthy East India Company.[74] Bhaktivinoda's target was not only the *bhadralok*, for whom he wrote many of his books, but also the broader Vaishnava community, and for that purpose he wrote poems and songs in simple Bengali.[75] His autobiography ends on June 21, 1886, and most information about his life after that date is collected from reports in the *Sajjanatoṣaṇī*, which contains detailed accounts of his *nāma-haṭṭa* programs.

Bhaktivinoda's dream of a global Vaishnava community under the flag of Caitanya was not fulfilled in his lifetime, and he spent all his years in East India. Nonetheless, he was able to transmit his vision to his son, who later organized a venture to Europe to carry it out.

1901–1918: Middle Period

Bhaktisiddhānta did not have a specific conversion experience, as did his father Bhaktivinoda, nor was he inclined to making subtle shifts in doctrine, as was Dayānanda Sarasvatī.[76] Throughout his life, he remained a Caitanya Vaishnava, steadily situated on the theological platform established by his father's books and teachings. It was his social role and identity that underwent major transformations. Since the days of the Sanskrit College, he had been torn between the options of becoming a successful, well-paid teacher or a full-time *bhakta*. The meeting with Gaura Kiśora turned out to be pivotal; from that point on he firmly identified himself as a Caitanya *bhakta*. It was around this time that Bhaktivinoda placed "*bhakti*" before "*siddhānta*" in his son's title, an award for his proficiency in reading and explaining Vaishnava texts.[77]

Soon after being initiated by Gaura Kiśora, Bhaktisiddhānta abandoned his life as a privileged *bhadralok* and began to live as a celibate student (*brahmacārī*), dressing in simple white or green cloth. His commitment to Caitanya Vaishnavism—which he had absorbed throughout

---

74. Hugh B. Urban, "Songs of Ecstasy: Mystics, Minstrels, and Merchants in Colonial Bengal," *Journal of the American Oriental Society* 123, no. 3 (2003).

75. For a sample list of his *bhadralok* supporters, see *Sajjanatoṣaṇī* 5, no. 11 (1893): p. 201.

76. For Dayānanda's shifts in doctrine see J. T. F. Jordens, *Dayananda Sarasvati: His Life and Ideas* (Delhi: Oxford University Press, 1978), pp. 275–280.

77. Sambidananda Das, "History and Literature," ch. 13, p. 41.

his childhood by close association with his father—led him toward an intense religious practice. With his newfound freedom from social obligations, as well as the encouragement of his employer, the Maharaja of Tripura, Bhaktisiddhānta took the opportunity to visit a number of major religious centers. He wrote:

> In 1901 I was initiated by my guru. . . . I went to Puri. From that time on I developed a strong connection with Puri and I spent a full year there in 1904. From Puri I set out to travel to South India, from the end of 1904 till January 1905. From that point I began to live in Mayapur and I visited Puri from time to time. In Mayapur, from 1905 onward I began to present Caitanya's teachings. In 1906 Rohini Kumara Ghosh became my first initiated disciple.[78]

In Jagannath Puri, Bhaktisiddhānta discussed philosophy and religion with *sādhus* and pandits of various disciplic lines (*sampradāya*). Of particular interest was the study of *advaita* Vedanta, which he explored at the Math that Śaṅkara himself is believed to have established. The head of the Math, Madhusūdana Tīrtha, paid particular attention to him and guided him in his studies.[79] During this early phase of his religious career, he would sometimes loudly criticize those that contradicted Vaishnava principles and practices, a modus operandi that on several occasions placed him at risk of physical retaliation (later in life, he desisted from such personal attacks, and focused his criticism on the ideas of his opponents instead). While traveling, Bhaktisiddhānta went to great lengths to collect materials for a Vaishnava encyclopedia. For him this was a vital project since he believed that many of the words in the Vaishnava lexicon had been misunderstood, especially metaphysical terms such as *adhokṣaja* (a name indicating that the "Personality of Godhead" was beyond the reach of the senses) and *aprākṛta* (meaning otherworldly).[80] In his pursuit of both materials and personal religious experience he traveled to South

78. Bhaktisiddhānta Sarasvatī, *Prabhupādera Patrāvalī*, vol. 3, pp. 48–49.

79. Vikāsa, *Śrī Bhaktisiddhānta Vaibhava*, vol. 1, p. 35.

80. Ananta Vāsudeva in *Sarasvatī Jayaśrī*, pp. 81–82. The word "metaphysical" refers to that which is beyond the world of matter, both gross and subtle. In Hindu philosophies such as Vedanta a distinction is made between material substance (consisting of the physical body, the mind, the reasoning faculty, and the ego) and metaphysical substance (consisting of the eternal, purely spiritual, self or *jīva*/atman).

India and eagerly explored the customs and teachings of other Vaishnava *sampradāyas*, particularly those of Madhva and Rāmānuja. The encyclopedia was eventually published in four volumes under the title *Vaishnava mañjuṣā*, but never reached full completion. It had been funded by the Maharaja of Kasimbazar.

In Puri and Mayapur, Bhaktisiddhānta lived a life of austerity, filling his time with study, writing, and contemplation. His lifestyle during this period, however, was far from sedentary. He assisted in the development of Mayapur, purchased land, managed properties in Jagannath Puri, and oversaw buildings that his father had rented out to tenants.[81] Nonetheless he vowed to chant the names of Krishna and His Consort one billion times, a feat that took approximately ten years to complete.[82] To count his "rounds," he used the beads that he had received from his father, the ones that Bhaktivinoda had used in the execution of a similar vow.[83] For his *bhājana kuṭīra*, or place of worship, he cleared an area near the *yogapīṭhā*—the birthplace of Caitanya that his father had begun to develop—and constructed a hut. He slept on the floor and ate simple food, surrounded only by his books.

A group of educated youths gradually came and visited him, attracted by his life of contemplation and devotion to God. One of them was Rohini Kumara Ghosh, the nephew of Justice Chandra Madhava Ghosh. He became the first initiated disciple of Bhaktisiddhānta, which was unusual, since both Bhaktivinoda and Gaura Kiśora were still alive. In Vaishnava circles no disciple is generally allowed to initiate as long as the guru is present. It is reasonable to assume, though, that he received permission

---

81. See Bhaktisiddhānta Sarasvatī, *Diary, 1904–1936*, years 1905 to 1907. The *Diary* provides a detailed day-by-day account of the travels, budget, and managerial activities of Bhaktisiddhānta during this period. Bhaktivinoda's guru, Bipin Bihari Goswami, is often mentioned as well.

82. Caitanya Vaishnavas interpret the *mahā-mantra*—consisting of Hare, Krisha, and Rāma—differently from other Vaishnava lines, with "Hare" indicating "Śri Rādhā" rather than "Vishnu." In a letter dated October 10, 1928, Bhaktisiddhānta wrote that when the words "Hare Rāma" are pronounced in a mood of reverential service to God, they indicate Sri Rāma, the son of Daśaratha in Ayodhya. However, devotees who worship in the mood of conjugal service understand Krishna, the son of Nanda in Vrindavan, as the lover of the cowherd girls (*gopī-ramaṇa*), and thus as Rāma. When the word "Rāma" indicates service to Krishna, the lover of Rādhā (*Rādhā-ramaṇa*), the term of address or "Harā" (Hare is the vocative form) indicates Rādhā, understood as the metaphysical or internal energy (*parā śakti*) of God. In accordance with this understanding, the names Hare, Krishna and Rāma refer to Rādhā and Krishna alone. See Bhaktisiddhānta, *Prabhupādera Patrāvalī*, vol. 1, p. 57.

83. Paramānanda Brahmacārī in *Sarasvatī Jayaśrī*, p. 177.

to do so considering the fact that both his preceptors were aging and there was a compelling need to expand the mission. He considered the Hare Krishna mantra to be the main hub around which devotional practices should revolve, even above the performance of temple rituals. The pure, unadulterated, and offenseless recitation of the mantra was the key to entering the esoteric realms of Caitanya bhakti and to awakening full realization of the higher metaphysical planes, something he demonstrated by earnestly practicing the chanting himself.[84]

During this period, Bhaktisiddhānta only sporadically visited Calcutta, which had been plunged into terrible turmoil by the clash between the Swadeshi (self-rule) movement and the British Raj. Swadeshi began as a boycott of British goods in protest of the 1905 partition of Bengal orchestrated by Lord Curzon. Powered by leading figures such as Bipin Chandra Pal, confrontations between the *bhadralok* and the Raj lasted till 1912, and involved public demonstrations as well as the perpetration of severe acts of violence by individuals and revolutionary societies.[85] More than ever before, the Bengali elite was torn by the growing ideological tension between indigenous revivalism and European modernity, and was looking for an authentic identity "amid a maze of alternative loyalties."[86]

Brāhmaṇa and Vaishnava

In the rural areas, Bhaktisiddhānta faced a social system that was reluctant to question the authority of the hereditary *brāhmaṇas*. In August 1911, a large meeting was arranged in Balighai Uddhavapur, in the Midnapur district, to discuss two issues: first, whether or not it was permissible for nonhereditary *brāhmaṇas* to worship Vishnu in the form of a sacred stone known as *śālagrāma śilā*; and second, whether or not it was permissible for them to act as gurus and initiate members of other castes. Sītānātha dāsa Bhaktitīrtha, who was helping to organize the event, invited Bhaktivinoda to attend. Being ill at that time, Bhaktivinoda requested Bhaktisiddhānta to represent him and deliver a speech.

---

84. Even a summary review of his letters from 1915 onward shows the importance that he gave to the recitation of the sacred names; see, for example, Bhaktisiddhānta, *Prabhupādera Patrāvalī*, vol. 1, pp. 1–7.

85. Sumit Sarkar, *The Swadeshi Movement in Bengal, 1903–1908* (New Delhi: People's Publishing House, 1973), pp. 465–492.

86. Sarkar, *Swadeshi Movement in Bengal*, p. 494.

On September 6, 1911, Bhaktisiddhānta left Calcutta, accompanied by Sureshcandra Mukhopadhyay. At 4:00 PM they reached Kontai Road Station, and at 10:00 PM Sauri-Prapannashram. Two prominent pandits, Madhusūdana Goswami of the family of Gopālabhaṭṭa of the Rādhāramaṇa temple in Vrindavan, and Viśvambharānanda Deva Goswami of the family of Śyāmānanda in Gopivallabhapur, received them cordially. Together the group left at 3:00 AM and reached Balighai six hours later. After taking his meal, Bhaktisiddhānta inspected the village, its market, and the large *pandal* set up for the meeting, capable of hosting hundreds of people. Pandits from various districts of Bengal had gathered to participate in the three-day conference, which began at 3:00 PM on Friday, September 8, 1911, under the leadership of Viśvambharānanda Goswami. Prior to his arrival, Bhaktisiddhānta had prepared a paper entitled "Brāhmaṇa o Vaiṣṇava," a different section of which he intended to read aloud on each of the event's three days. On the first day, he presented a section concerning "the people of the material world" (*prakṛti jana kāṇḍa*).[87] By perusing the edited version, published in 1934, it is possible to get a sense of the speech. Bhaktisiddhānta began by making numerous references to the *Dharma śāstra*, the Hindu law, and praising the important role that the *brāhmaṇas* had played in the history of Indic religions, which was meant to offer respects to the assembled pandits. His tone began to change, however, as he explored the path of karma, or action. Quoting from the *Viṣṇu yāmala tantra*, he asserted that in the age of Kali (*Kali yuga*) hereditary lines of *brāhmaṇas* were no longer pure, and therefore no better than *śūdras*.[88] He then went on to provide examples from the Mahābhārata and other Vaishnava texts to indicate that in olden times members of all castes were initiated as *brāhmaṇas* after being accepted as such because of their suitable behavior and character.[89] He asserted that the symptoms of a *brāhmaṇa* were not birth but control

87. Bhaktisiddhānta Sarasvatī, *Brāhmaṇa o Vaiṣṇava: tāratamya-viṣayaka siddhānta* (Mayapur: Śrī Caitanya Math, 1934). The following description is taken from the extended version of Bhaktisiddhānta's speech published in the second edition.

88. Bhaktisiddhānta, *Brāhmaṇa o Vaiṣṇava*, p. 38. The reference from the *Viṣṇu yāmala tantra* reads *aśuddhāḥ śūdrakalpa hi brāhmaṇāḥ kalisambhavāḥ*, "Brāhmaṇas born in the age of Kali are impure and equal to *śūdras*." The verse number is not mentioned.

89. Examples and statements quoted in full in the edited version include Mahabharata (*śāntiparva* chs. 189 and 318, *vanaparva* chs. 180, 211, 215, *anuśāsanaparva* ch. 30, ch. 163, verses 5, 8, 26, 46, 48, 51 and 59), *Hari-vaṃśa* (*Harivaṃśaparva* 11.9, 29.7–8, 31.33–35), *Śrīmad Bhāgavatam* or *Bhāgavata Purāṇa* (5.4.13, 7.11.21–25, 35; 9.2.9, 16–17, 19–22; 9.13.1, 12–27; 9.15.1–4, 9.20.1–7; 9.21.19–21, 30, 31, 33), *Vedānta sūtra* (1.3.34–35, 37).

of the mind and senses, austerity, purity, satisfaction, patience, honesty (*ārjava*), knowledge, compassion, truthfulness (*satya*), and surrender unto the infallible (*acyuta* or the "Personality of Godhead").[90] He concluded by stating that Vaishnava texts paid respect both to hereditary *brāhmaṇas* and to those who had become such by initiation, without ever diminishing the latter.[91] After him, Madhusūdana Goswami and Bhaktitīrtha presented supportive arguments for the universal right of all human beings to worship the *śālagrāma śilā*, and to study the Vedas.

On the debate's second day, Bhaktisiddhānta read the section concerning "the people of Hari" (*Hari jana kāṇḍa*), which discussed the qualities of the Vaishnavas, as well as the paths of *jñāna* (knowledge) and bhakti. In this regard he made an important distinction between "*pāñcarātrika*" Vaishnavas who followed the path of temple deity worship and "*bhāgavata*" Vaishnavas who were more inclined toward *kīrtana* and the path of developing divine love (*bhāva mārga*); these he traced back to Madhva and Nimbāditya (or Nimbārka).[92] He moreover suggested that although Caitanya had emphasized the *bhāgavata* path by widely teaching and popularizing the congregational chanting of the names of God, this emphasis had been gradually supplanted in Bengal by an emphasis on temple ritual instead—that is, the *pāñcarātrika* path.[93] Bhaktisiddhānta concluded that despite the fact that both paths were required to maintain a proper balance, the *bhāgavata mārga* was of greater ultimate importance.

On the final day, Bhaktisiddhānta lectured for almost two hours on the subject of "practice," the section of his paper that explored the difference between a *brāhmaṇa* and a Vaishnava (*Vyavahāra kāṇḍa*). Here he once again suggested that the status of *brāhmaṇa* within *varṇāśrama*, the traditional social structure of Hindu society, should be determined in accordance with personal qualification and not hereditary rights.[94] The mundane inclinations of a person may be assessed between the age of eight and twenty-two, but the religious inclination of a person may arise

90. Bhaktisiddhānta, *Brāhmaṇa o Vaiṣṇava*, p. 52. He quoted from *Śrimad Bhāgavatam* 7.11.21.

91. Bhaktisiddhānta, *Brāhmaṇa o Vaiṣṇava*, p. 72.

92. Bhaktisiddhānta, *Brāhmaṇa o Vaiṣṇava*, p. 116.

93. Bhaktisiddhānta, *Brāhmaṇa o Vaiṣṇava*, p. 124.

94. *Varṇāśrāma* refers to four divisions of labor (*varṇa*) and four divisions of civil status (*aśrama*).

at any time, due to various causes—for example, good fortune. Even if fallen, a person who displays the symptoms of bhakti to Vishnu should be called a realized spiritualist. He also proposed an important distinction between godly (*daiva*) *varṇāśrama*, practiced by those that aim at pleasing God, and mundane *varṇāśrama*, practiced by those that are inimical to God, the "ungodly" (*āsura*).[95] While these two *varṇāśramas* exist side by side, a Vaishnava is said to see all living entities as servants of Krishna, and thus naturally promotes *daiva varṇāśrama*.

In his diary, Bhaktisiddhānta commented on the meeting as follows:

> Friday September 8th, 1911. I was reading the Brahmin Chapter of my writing when the Brahmin sections expressed their uneasiness so I stopped at the request of our friends.... Saturday, September 9, 1911. In the afternoon the Sabha began with great enthusiasm. Two police constables and the S.I.P [came]. I harangued the assembly for about an hour about the Vaishnavas...none disturbed the assembly. Sunday, September 10, 1911. In the afternoon the Sabha got its full perfection. I addressed the meeting for about an hour and a half. The audience quite sympathised with our sorrow and showed indignation at the attitude of the hostile men.[96]

His presentation created a stir among sections of the pundits in attendance, not only because of its challenging content, but also because it had been delivered by a *kāyastha*. In his diary, Bhaktisiddhānta mentioned his participation with members of the Kāyastha Sabhā in a 1910 discussion on the right of *kāsthayas* to wear the sacred thread. Thus he was well aware of the controversial nature of such issues.[97] Bhaktisiddhānta's controversial public debut was a defining moment in his life, and marked the beginning of a lifelong confrontation between himself and Nabadwip's hereditary *brāhmaṇas* over the social status, spiritual capacities, and priestly rights of the non-*brāhmaṇic* castes or *jātis*. In later years, when Bhaktisiddhānta became the head of his own religious institution and gave *brāhmaṇic* initiation to members of the

95. Bhaktisiddhānta, *Brāhmaṇa o Vaiṣṇava*, pp. 182–183. See also the account of Paramānanda Brahmacārī, *Sarasvatī Jayaśrī*, pp. 156–157.

96. Bhaktisiddhānta, *Diary, 1904–1936* (1911), pp. 10–11.

97. Bhaktisiddhānta, *Diary, 1904–1936* (January 3, 1909), p. 4.

so-called lower castes, the conflict considerably deepened. Indeed, this and other acts of open defiance caused such bitter resentment among some of his opponents that they are rumored to have conspired to take his life (as will be seen below).

In May 1913, Bhaktisiddhānta obtained permission to establish a typesetting and printing press on a rented property near Kalighat in Calcutta; this he dubbed *bhāgavat yantra*, which may be rendered as "God's machine." With this press he began producing Bengali publications of canonical Vaishnava texts such as Kṛṣṇadāsa Kavirāja's *Caitanya-caritāmṛta*, to which he added the commentary of Bhaktivinoda (the *amṛta-pravāha-bhāṣya*) followed by his own brief purports (the *anubhāṣya*).[98] In the course of his life, Bhaktivinoda had collected numerous rare books and manuscripts that awaited publication, and Bhaktisiddhānta was eager to produce them. In January 1914, when the Kalighat contract expired, he moved the press to Vrajapattan in Mayapur. Bhaktisiddhānta's extensive use of modern printing methods provides a good example of his willingness to employ advanced technology and media in the effort to popularize Caitanya Vaishnavism, and also indicates his ability to actively respond to a new environment—*and* to urbanized life.

In Mayapur on June 23, 1914, Bhaktisiddhānta received an urgent telegram requesting he return to his parents' home in Calcutta. He set off at once with Paramānanda *brahmacārī*, but the monsoon rains had flooded the roads and they missed the first train. Arriving late in the evening, Bhaktisiddhānta was greeted with the news that his father had passed away earlier in the day, and that his family had already cremated the body.[99] On the eleventh day of mourning, Bhaktisiddhānta requested, his relatives conduct a Vaishnava ceremony rather than the traditional Hindu *śrāddha* for the dead practiced by the ritual *smārta brāhmaṇas*. Following his wish, his family gave away copies of the Bhagavad Gītā and fed sweets to Vaishnavas and *brāhmaṇas*. Fifty to sixty Calcutta pandits attended the ceremony, according to the sources.[100]

---

98. He began to write the commentary in Calcutta on June 14, 1913, and ended it in Mayapur at Vrajapattan, on June 14, 1915. See Paramānanda Brahmacārī in *Sarasvatī Jayaśrī*, p. 176.

99. In many Indic religious traditions it is common to use expressions such as "passed away" or "left the body" rather than "died" to indicate that the inner self leaves the external body at death.

100. Paramānanda in *Sarasvatī Jayaśrī*, p. 175.

In a letter written in 1926, Bhaktisiddhānta presented six instructions that he had received from Bhaktivinoda only a few weeks before his passing. The instructions, as indicated in this letter, were as follows:

1. Persons who claim worldly prestige and futile glory fail to attain the true position of nobleness, because they argue that Vaishnavas are born in a low position as a result of [previous] sinful actions, which means that they commit offenses (*aparādha*). You should know that, as a remedy, the practice of *varṇāśrama*, which you have recently taken up, is a genuine Vaishnava service (*sevā*).
2. It is because of lack of promulgation of the pure conclusions of bhakti (*śuddha bhaktisiddhānta*) that... among men and women of the *sahajiyā* groups, Ativāḍī, and other lines (*sampradāya*) devious practices are welcomed as bhakti. You should always critique those views, which are opposed to the conclusions of the sacred texts, by missionary work and sincere practice of the conclusions of bhakti.
3. Arrange to begin a pilgrimage (*parikramā*) in and around Nabadwip as soon as possible. Through this activity alone, anyone in the world may attain Krishna bhakti. Take adequate care so that service in Mayapur continues, and grows brighter day by day. Real *sevā* in Mayapur will be possible by setting up a printing press, distributing bhakti literature (*bhaktigrantha*), and *nāmahaṭṭa* (devotional centers for the recitation of the sacred names of God), not by solitary practice (*bhajana*). You should not hamper *sevā* in Mayapur and the mission (*pracāra*) by indulging in solitary *bhājana*.
4. When I shall not be here anymore... [remember that] *sevā* in Mayapur is a highly revered service. Take special care of it; this is my special instruction to you.
5. I had a sincere desire to draw attention to the significance of pure (*śuddha*) bhakti through books such as *Śrīmad Bhāgavatam*, *Ṣaṭsandarbha*, *Vedāntadarśana*, etc. You should go on and take charge of that task. Mayapur will develop if a center of devotional learning (*vidyāpīṭha*) is created there.
6. Never bother to acquire knowledge or funds for your personal consumption; collect them only for the purpose of serving the divine; avoid bad company for the sake of money or self-interest.[101]

---

101. The hagiographical literature generally claims that these instructions were contained in a letter from Bhaktivinoda to Bhaktisiddhānta. Thus far, however, no such letter has been recovered.

Not long after his father's departure, Bhaktisiddhānta moved the press to nearby Krishnanagar, the administrative center of the district of Nadia. From there he continued publishing Bhaktivinoda's *Sajjanatoṣaṇī*, at the time one of Bengal's most established Vaishnava magazines. In June 1915, he completed the writing of the *Caitanya Caritāmṛta*, and only a few months thereafter, on November 16, 1915, his spiritual master Gaura Kiśora dāsa passed away and was buried the next day.[102] Thus within the span of a little more than a year, Bhaktisiddhānta had lost both his father and guru. Overwhelmed with intense feelings of grief and separation, he retired to his hut in Vrajapattan. Paramānanda *brahmacārī*, who was close to Bhaktisiddhānta during this period, depicted him as being utterly forlorn. On the one hand, both his father and his guru had requested he spread the teachings of Caitanya far and wide, and on the other hand, he was bereft of the means to execute this task: he had neither the money nor the manpower, and felt himself lacking the personal qualifications as well. At the time, he had been working on a commentary to Rūpa Goswami's *Upadeśāmṛta*, composed of eleven hymns. He had written comments on the first eight stanzas, but had set aside his work on the remaining three, leaving the project unfinished. As related by Paramānanda, it took what Bhaktisiddhānta viewed as a profound personal experience to resolve the apparent impasse. One night Bhaktisiddhānta dreamed that from the eastern side of the temple connected to Caitanya's birthplace (the *yogapīṭha*), "Lord Caitanya" and "His" four companions (*pāñcatattva*) emerged with a large group of devotees playing *kīrtana*. There he saw the "Six Goswamis of Vrindavan," Jagannātha das Bābājī, Bhaktivinoda, Gaura Kiśora dāsa, and others, all in subtle metaphysical forms. These various personalities then spoke to Bhaktisiddhānta, informing him that he need not worry because they would be assisting him, supplying wealth, intelligence, and whatever else was needed. They assured him that no worldly obstacles would deter his efforts and that they would always be with him. Bhaktisiddhānta related this dream to Paramānanda the next day, indicating that he considered it a direct answer to all his personal hesitancies. Shortly thereafter he completed the work on the *Upadeśāmṛta* and began planning for new publications.[103]

---

102. Bhaktisiddhānta, *Diary, 1904–1936* (1915), p. 3.

103. Paramānanda in *Sarasvatī Jayaśrī*, p. 188.

In 1915, as confirmed in a *Sajjanatoṣaṇī* article that bore its name, Bhaktisiddhānta founded the "Committee for the Remembrance of Bhaktivinoda Ṭhākura" (*ṭhākurera smṛtisaṃhiti*), the membership of which consisted of Bhaktivinoda's disciples and followers. This relatively promising start of cooperation between him and these personalities, however, became more and more problematic in the years that followed. With the exception of a handful of persons (e.g., Swami Bhakti Pradīpa Tīrtha), none showed much interest in the development of his post-Bhaktivinoda movement.[104] After an initial phase of working together, cooperation also apparently broke down between Bhaktisiddhānta and his brother Lalita Prasad Datta, at the time employed in the government. Ananta Vāsudeva, a disciple of Bhaktisiddhānta who knew the brothers well, wrote in 1934 that the two had conflicting views on Bhaktivinoda and his contribution.[105] For example, while Bhaktisiddhānta had imbibed Bhaktivinoda's vision of a global Vaishnava movement, Lalita Prasad was more drawn to the esoteric practices that his father had personally taught him after initiation. Ultimately the two brothers were unable to reconcile their differences and accommodate these two aspects of Bhaktivinoda's legacy. From that point on, while remaining in touch as family members, they more or less parted ways in terms of their religious undertakings. In the coming years, the various institutional reforms that Bhaktisiddhānta gradually introduced into his movement further alienated Lalita Prasad Datta, who, after retiring from government service, went on to establish a separate movement in Bengal.

The majority of Bhaktivinoda's disciples were married with children and other household responsibilities; thus their ability to participate in Bhaktisiddhānta's outreach missionary movement was severely curtailed by their preoccupation with family. One member of this laity, Kuñjabihārī Vidyābhūṣaṇa (later known as Swami Bhakti Vilāsa Tīrtha), whom Bhaktisiddhānta regarded as the backbone of his movement, suggested that he relocate his small group of loyal followers to Calcutta, since this large metropolis would likely offer far greater opportunities for missionary activities. Inspired by this idea, Bhaktisiddhānta began planning

104. Niśi Kanta Sanyal notes that while Bhaktisiddhānta strove to maintain a connection with the followers of Bhaktivinoda through his mission, few of them appreciated the manner in which he was attempting to fulfill Bhaktivinoda's vision. Niśi Kanta Sanyal, *Sree Krishna Chaitanya* (Kolkata: Gaudiya Mission, 2004), vol. 2, p. xx.

105. Ananta Vāsudeva in *Sarasvatī Jayaśrī*, p. 56.

for a Calcutta Math that would be dedicated to systematic training and propagation work.

Saṃnyāsa

At this juncture, Bhaktisiddhānta made an important decision that would have a major impact on his future, as well as the future of his movement: the decision to enter the renounced order of *saṃnyāsa,* the most prestigious monastic order of Hinduism (figure B.4).[106] The deaths of both his mentors had left Bhaktisiddhānta feeling uncertain about his next move. The decision to "take" *saṃnyāsa* appears to have resolved this dilemma, as it constituted both a way to reshape the legacy of his gurus and an important step forward in his effort to revitalize the Caitanya tradition. Those that aspire to the *saṃnyāsa* order of life generally find an established member of that community and seek initiation from him. Not so Bhaktisiddhānta. In his characteristically singular style, he simply sat down before a picture of Gaura Kiśora dāsa Bābājī and invested that order upon himself. And from that day forward to the end of his life he not only adopted the dress and symbols of a Vaishnava renunciate, but strictly adhered to the vows and personal sacrifices that the life of a *saṃnyāsin* demands. The change of dress from white to saffron was in stark contrast to the customary dress of Vaishnava ascetics such as the *bābājīs*. In Bengal, saffron was mostly identified with the colors of the nondualistic Śaṅkara line, and not with those of the Vaishnavas.[107] In fact, whereas well-established lineages such as Śaṅkara's and the Vaishnavas of South India had a *saṃnyāsa* order, the Caitanya tradition had none. However, in the eyes of Bhaktisiddhānta, times were propitious for such a move. He had already visited the Rāmānuja ashrams in South India to learn more about their triple staff order, *tridaṇḍa saṃnyāsa*.[108] Furthermore, Christian missions had long since shown that

106. Ananta Vāsudeva in *Sarasvatī Jayaśrī*, pp. 10–11.

107. Conversation with Satyanārāyaṇa dāsa at the Jīva Institute in Vrindavan, March 15, 2006.

108. Rāmānuja's *sampradāya* in South India was famous for its Vaishnava *saṃnyāsa* order. This was noted by William Joseph Wilkins, who in 1877 wrote that the name *saṃnyāsin* was used "with a qualifying word Tridandi for a class of Vaishnavas of the Rāmānuja sect, who have passed through the first two stages of the Brāhmanical order, and have entered upon the ascetic life. The word *danda* signifies a staff, and the Tridandi Sanyasis are those who have taken up the three-fold staff; i.e., have exercised a three-fold restraint of speech, body, and mind, or word, deed, and thought." William Joseph Wilkins, *Modern Hinduism: An Account of the Religion and Life of the Hindus in Northern India* (Scribner, Welford, & Co., 1887; rpt. New Delhi: Book Faith India, 1999), pp. 81–82.

institutions that promote celibacy and chastity are highly regarded and extremely effective, even in modern settings.[109] Apart from this, there was at least some precedent in the Caitanya tradition for the adoption of a monastic order. Caitanya himself had entered the order of *saṃnyāsa*, primarily as a means of obtaining respect and legitimacy for his mission—although he never took the step of conferring *saṃnyāsa* upon others. His disciples came to rely upon the socially less prestigious ascetic orders of *gosvami* and *bābājī*. In Bhaktisiddhānta's time, however, these two orders had lost their respectability. The Goswamis had mostly become a hereditary class of married priests and the *bābājīs* were under clouds of suspicion for alleged erotic practices. Despite the fact that many Vaishnavas lived a pious life, the reputation of Vaishnavism in general was in dire need of repair, and Bhaktisiddhānta had lived as a celibate throughout the entirety of his life.[110] For him, this fact in and of itself constituted enough merit to warrant his acceptance of *saṃnyāsa*—a deed that immediately endowed his budding movement not only with a new look, but with a new ethical profile as well. The glowing saffron vestments of a swami, even in the interwar period, signaled to those whom Bhaktisiddhānta encountered that he was a simple, chaste, and upright individual, selflessly involved in the spiritual upliftment of society. Bhaktisiddhānta thus created a new image for the modern Caitanya ascetic. This move was a watershed in his spiritual career, and marked the beginning of his most productive period, which saw the rapid growth of his institution from a humble center in Calcutta to sixty-seven Maths—sixty-four in India, and one each in Burma, Britain, and Germany. Borderlands, in the words of Suzanne M. Michel, are "places where conventional approaches are questioned, stereotypes dissolve and new understandings emerge."[111] Bhaktisiddhānta now trod a path that placed him on a borderland between rural and urban society, tradition and modernity, and various categories of class and social status.

---

109. Gwilym Beckerlegge, "The Hindu Renaissance and Notions of Universal Religion," in *Religion in History: Conflict, Conversion and Coexistence*, ed. John Wolffe (Manchester: Manchester University Press and the Open University, 2001), p. 148.

110. In a will written in 1923, Bhaktisiddhānta mentioned that he had been strictly celibate up to that point (see "Testamentary Suit No. 2 of 1938 in the High Court of Juricature at Fort William in Bengal," doc. nr. 20); this practice would continue for the remainder of his life.

111. Suzanne M. Michel, "Golden Eagles and the Environmental Politics of Care," in *Animal Geographies: Place, Politics, and Identity in the Nature-Culture Borderlands*, ed. J. Wolch and J. Emel (London: Verso, 1998), pp. 162–163.

This allowed him to explore new venues and generate new momentum in his life.

1918–1937: Late Period

The Gaudiya Math and Mission

The social and political turmoil in India that followed World War I demanded strong action, and Bhaktisiddhānta responded with fresh initiatives. He opened a center in Calcutta dedicated to the practice and propagation of bhakti, presented in a way that was intended to be rational and intelligible, particularly to urban audiences. The opening was reported in the *Amrita Bazar Patrika* on December 17, 1918:

> At 1, Ultadinghee Junction Road, Calcutta, Srimat Tridandi Swami Bhakti Siddhanta Saraswati Thakura, successor of Sreemad Bhaktivinode Thakur, the founder of the Sree Mayapur Temple, has recently founded the Calcutta Bhaktivinode Asana. Here ardent seekers after truth are received and listened to and solutions to their questions are advanced from a most reasonable and liberal standpoint of view. The day is divided into distinct periods during which the respective branches of the Shastras, viz. Veda Vedangas, Vedanta, Sreemad Bhagabat, Smriti and standard treatises on Bhakti are cultured by devotees in the constant presence of His Holiness, the Swamiji.[112]

The center was built around the principles of self-discipline, education, and self-directed action for the spiritual upliftment of the public. The initiative offered long-term systematic institutional training in bhakti at a time when Caitanya Vaishnavism had nothing of the kind in Calcutta.

On February 5, 1919, Bhaktisiddhānta took another major step by reviving one of Bhaktivinoda's key projects: the Royal World Vaishnava Association (mentioned earlier). Following along the lines of a traditional Vrindavan *sabhā*, the society was a forum for discussing various aspects of

112. The *Amrita Bazar Patrika* reported the inauguration ceremony on February 10, 1919, and it was quoted in *Sajjanatoṣaṇī* 21, no. 10 (1919): p. 289.

the Caitanya movement as well as for reviewing new literary works. The *sabhā* had been mentioned in the *Bhakti-sandarbha* of Jīva (ca. 1517–1608), one of the "Six Goswamis" of Vrindavan; there he noted the names of its two Goswami leaders:

> Śrī Rūpa and Śrī Sanātana are the respected leaders of the Royal World Vaishnava Association.[113]

The name of the association reflected the early universal vision of the Six Goswamis, who conceived of a religious society that could embrace all the peoples of the world, regardless of sectarian affiliations; this is indicated by the word *viśva* in the association's title.[114] As a historical aside, it is interesting to note that although Vrindavan was close to Delhi, which at the time was the Islamic center of Mughal India, the Goswamis were nonetheless free to develop an Indic Vaishnava community. This was largely due to the fact that in comparison to other Islamic rulers in India, Akbar was relatively liberal-minded and sympathetic toward Hindu religious expression.[115] While there is no evidence of a reciprocal theological relationship between the two traditions, Akbar's goodwill enabled Vrindavan to flourish. Years later Kṛṣṇadāsa Kavirāja dāsa absorbed the *sabhā*'s vision, restating it in his work *Caitanya Caritāmṛta* (1615), a canonical biography of Caitanya, which was a great source of inspiration for Bhaktisiddhānta.[116]

---

113. This is an extract from the following sentence: *Iti kali-yuga-pāvana-sva-bhajana-vibha jana-prayojanāvatāra-śrī-śrī-bhagavat-kṛṣṇa-caitanya-deva-caraṇānucara-viśva-vaiṣṇava-rāja-sabhā-sabhājana-bhājana-śrī-rūpa-sanātanānuśāsana-bhāratīgarbhe.* Jīva Goswami and Satya Narayana das, *Bhakti Sandarbha* (Vrindavan: Vrindavan Research Institute, 2005), p. 1150.

114. The word *viśva* can be translated in a general sense as "all," "whole" "entire," but is often rendered as "universe" or "world" in compound words such as *viśvātman* (the Soul of the universe). See Sharada Sugirtharajah, *Imagining Hinduism: A Postcolonial Perspective* (London: Routledge, 2003), pp. 992–994.

115. Jean Jacques Waardenburg, *Muslim Perceptions of Other Religions: A Historical Survey* (New York: Oxford University Press, 1999), p. 70. Later emperors were less lenient. In his *Diary*, Bhaktisiddhānta quotes a statement from the *Journal of the Asiatic Society of Bengal* 41 (1872): p. 313, regarding an attempt made to culturally assimilate Vrindavan to Islam: "In the times of the Emperors, the Muhamedans made a futile attempt to abolish the ancient name Brindaban, and in its stead substitute that of Mirminabad." Bhaktisiddhānta, *Diary, 1904–1936* (1929), p. 11.

116. The encompassing nature of Caitanya's teachings, as presented in the *Caitanya Caritāmṛta*, will be further discussed in chapter 4.

The vision of a *sabhā*—a community—that transcended religious borders fit well with the cosmopolitan world of Calcutta, where Bengalis lived side by side with British, Scots, Dutch, French, and Chinese. Unitarians and evangelical missionaries both in India and in England had already propagated a universal Christian religion, conceived as a pluralist, multiracial brotherhood. Institutions such as the Freemasons and the Theosophical Society had propagated the ideals of equality, honor, and respect for the entirety of humanity. Rammohun Roy and later the Brahmo Samaj had translated religious universalism into a struggle for justice, emancipation of women, and the rights of the underprivileged.[117] Vivekānanda had expanded this notion in a way that made service to humanity the key to religious practice. Bhaktivinoda had been exposed to this form of universalism, but his inspiration had come more specifically from the Caitanya tradition itself. In his work *Srigouranga Smaranamangala or Chaitanya Mahaprabhu, His life and precepts* (1896)—the book was also published as *Sri Sri Gourangalila Smaranamangal Stotram*—Bhaktivinoda had portrayed Caitanya as a hero of universal brotherhood and intellectual freedom:

> Caitanya preaches equality of men . . . universal fraternity amongst men and special brotherhood amongst *Vaishnavas*, who are according to him, the best pioneers of spiritual improvement. He preaches that human thought should never be allowed to be shackled with sectarian views. . . . The religion preached by Mahaprabhu is universal and not exclusive. The most learned and the most ignorant are both entitled to embrace it. . . . The principle of *kīrtana* invites, as the future church of the world, all classes of men without distinction of caste or clan to the highest cultivation of the spirit.[118]

The above passage indicates that Bhaktivinoda had consciously borrowed popular Christian expressions such as "universal fraternity," "cultivation of the spirit," "preach," and "church," removing them from their original contexts, and differently applying them so as to better communicate the

117. Crawford, *Ram Mohan Roy*.

118. Kedarnath Datta Bhaktivinoda, *Srigouranga Smaranamangala or Chaitanya Mahaprabhu: His Life and Precepts* (Calcutta: K. Dutt, 1896), p. 60.

teachings of Caitanya to the West.[119] In his view, Caitanya had come to establish a religious understanding that transcended all national boundaries and all narrow sectarian views, an understanding that had the potential to encompass the spiritual aspirations of all of humanity:

> This church, it appears, will extend all over the world and take the place of all sectarian churches, which exclude outsiders from the precincts of the mosque, church or the temple.[120]

Although one can certainly view such statements as being sectarian in their own right, since they appear as an attempt to universalize the specific religion of Caitanya, they nonetheless reflect Bhaktivinoda's conviction that Caitanya's teachings were essentially nonsectarian—that is, that pure, genuine love of God (regardless of how conceived) could bring genuine fulfillment to all the peoples of the world. Indeed, one of Bhaktivinoda's important contributions in early writings such as *Śrī Kṛṣṇa Saṃhitā* (1880) had been to define the realized spiritual seeker (*uttamādhikārī*) as a *sāragrāhī*, a universal seeker of essential truth. Such a person was capable of discerning the essential truth no matter where it was found or how it was presented through various practices and doctrines.[121]

Bhaktivinoda had sent copies of *Sri Caitanya, His Life and Precepts* to Western scholars across the British Empire (e.g., the Oxford Sanskritist Monier Monier-Williams).[122] Moreover, in order to create a new space for an all-embracing universal "church," he set his movement apart from the embedded social structures of the local Caitanyaites of Nabadwip. The truth was that Bhaktivinoda's vision of a global movement had found little support among the hereditary Goswamis from whom he had accepted initiation. He had nonetheless received encouragement from the *brāhmaṇas* of Baghnapada, who had awarded him the title "Bhaktivinoda."[123] His

---

119. Gayatri Spivak has called this process "catachresis," which means "to wrest a conceptual category from its proper, assigned meaning, and to secure it by other places, to disturb its claims to an origin"; cited in Debjani Ganguly, *Caste, Colonialism and Counter-Modernity: Notes on a Postcolonial Hermeneutics of Caste* (New York: Routledge, 2005), p. 14.

120. Bhaktivinoda, *Srigouranga Smaranamangala*, p. 60.

121. Kedarnath Datta Bhaktivinoda, *Śrī Kṛṣṇa Saṃhitā* (Calcutta: Īśvaracandra Vasu Company, 1880), *Upakramaṇikā* (introduction), p. 3.

122. This copy is available at the Indian Library, University of Oxford.

123. Bhaktivinoda, *Svalikhita Jivani*, pp. 176–177. Bhaktivinoda thanked the *brāhmaṇas* of Bhagnapada for the title they awarded him by composing a short poem in Sanskrit.

initiating guru, Bipin Bihari Goswami, had supported him as well, but most other caste Goswamis were too entrenched in the social world of Bengal to be interested in realizing a world vision of the sort that Bhaktivinoda had sweepingly spelled out in 1892:

> When in England, France, Russia, Prussia, and America all fortunate persons by taking up *kholas* (drums) and *karatālas* (cymbals) will take the name of Śrī Caitanya Mahāprabhu again and again in their own countries, and raise the waves of *saṅkirtāna*, when will that day come! Oh! When will the day come when the white-skinned British people will speak the glory of Śrī Śacīnandana [another name of Caitanya] on one side and on the other and with this call spread their arms to embrace devotees from other countries in brotherhood, when will that day come! The day when they will say "Oh, Aryan Brothers! We have taken refuge at the feet of Caitanya Deva in an ocean of love, now kindly embrace us," when will that day come![124]

Bhaktivinoda's movement had attracted some attention in the areas of prepartition Bengal, where Caitanya Vaishnavism had a consistent basis among the lower castes, particularly in the rural areas.[125] Up to his time, however, the teachings and practices of Caitanya Vaishnavism had barely become known outside the school's original strongholds in Bengal, Orissa, and Vrindavan; and, after more than 400 years of existence, they had only become well developed in Eastern regions such as Assam, Manipur, and Tripura. The book copies that Bhaktivinoda had sent west received only a few polite letters of appreciation. Nothing substantial appeared to have come of it.

---

124. *Sajjanatoṣaṇi* 4, no. 3 (1892): p. 42.

125. The 1931 census of India indicates, for example, that in greater Bengal the percentage of Vaishnavas among the total number of Hindus was 33 percent in the Dacca division, 7 percent in the Burdwan district near Nabadwip, but only 0.36 percent in Calcutta. These statistics may be misleading since they depended on the willingness of respondents to answer detailed questions about their religious affiliation and did not reveal the percentage of Hindus whose general orientation included both Vaishnavism and Śaktism. Nonetheless, they do provided some indication of the greater popularity of Caitanya Vaishnavism outside of Calcutta in the nineteenth and early twentieth centuries. A. E. Porter, *Census of India 1931: Bengal and Sikkim, Imperial and Provincial Tables*, vol. 5, part 2 (Calcutta: Central Publications Branch, 1932), pp. 220–221.

With the revival of the *Viśva Vaiṣṇava Rāja Sabhā*, Bhaktisiddhānta intended to reestablish his father's "universal church" agenda.[126] In 1920 he published a *Sajjanatoṣaṇī* article that once again presented its aims and made clear the direct link to the original association created shortly after Caitanya's departure in 1534 (mentioned above).[127] It also presented a charter with an institutional outline covering six areas of service (*sevā*) run by six committees (*maṇḍalī*). A summary of that charter, which was designed for global application, is paraphrased below:

1. The honoring committee (*mānada maṇḍalī*) was responsible for image worship and providing assistance to Krishna *bhaktas*.
2. The Sri Krishna Caitanya missionary committee (*śrī kṛṣṇa caitanya pracāra*) was responsible for three basic functions:
   a. spreading of God's sacred names (*nāma*), which involved traveling around the world and performing public chanting (*kīrtana*), teaching the conclusions of the *Bhāgavata Purāṇa* to the masses, and fulfilling the intentions of the movement's preceptors;
   b. dissemination of sacred books (*śāstra pracāra*), which involved the acquisition, preservation, publication, and distribution of Caitanyaite and other Vaishnava texts. This group also researched the history of these books, as well as their authors;
   c. teaching of scriptural instructions (*śāstra śikṣā*), which involved the creation of programs for the systematic study of bhakti literature.[128]
3. The investigative committee (*jijñāsa maṇḍalī*) was responsible for evaluating the character, background, and nature of a candidate before assigning a service in the movement.
4. The festival committee (*utsava maṇḍalī*) was responsible for arranging celebrations on various holy days.
5. The polemicist committee (*pāṣaṇḍadalana maṇḍalī*) was responsible for the rational defense of bhakti against arguments that were opposed to the conclusions of Caitanya Vaishnavism.

---

126. *Sajjanatoṣaṇī* 21, nos. 8–9 (1920): pp. 259–262. "*Rāja*" (king) referred to Sri Caitanya, who Gaudiya Vaishnavas regard as a manifestation of Krishna and the symbolic king of their assembly.

127. The date of Caitanya's birth and demise is disputed and there is no general consensus. Birth years are generally given as 1485 or 1486, and his demise as 1533 or 1534.

128. *Sajjanatoṣaṇī* 21, nos. 8–9 (1920): pp. 259–262. The list is also mentioned in *Sarasvatī Jayaśrī* (1935), pp. 43–44.

6. The devotional practice committee (*bhaktyānuṣṭhāna maṇḍalī*) was responsible for the maintenance of ancient sacred places, the building of new temples, and so on; it also arranged for the exploration of new areas in which to establish Gaudiya Math centers.

Bhaktisiddhānta confirmed his commitment to the aims of his father's association by not formally registering a new institution. In his letterheads and communications, he exclusively employed the name of the ancient *sabhā*. He regarded his movement as being rooted in Bhaktivinoda's, with himself only as its new president.

On June 23, 1920, six years after the demise of her husband, Bhaktisiddhānta's mother passed away. On September 6, 1920, Rādhā-Govinda deities were installed, and the center formerly known as Bhaktivinoda Āsana became "Sri Gaudiya Math." Bhaktisiddhānta's monastic centers eventually came to be known as the "Gaudiya Math," while the *Viśva Vaiṣṇava Rāja Sabhā* came to be known as the "Gaudiya Mission." The popular name "Gaudiya Math" was derived from the first Calcutta branch, as well as from the institution's weekly magazine, the *Gauḍīya*, which Bhaktisiddhānta launched in 1922.[129]

The 1920s witnessed a period of intense literary activity. In 1923, Bhaktisiddhānta published the *Bhāgavata Purāṇa*, a Sanskrit work printed in Bengali script that included his own commentary, as well as those of Madhva and Viśvanātha Cakravārtī Ṭhākura. He then edited and commented upon the *Caitanya Bhāgavata*, a popular biography of Sri Caitanya written in Bengali by Vṛndāvana dāsa Ṭhākura, which he published in Dacca in 1924. On December 16, 1924, he lectured at Benares Hindu University on "the Place of Vaiṣṇavism in World Religion." It was also during this period that he increasingly came to view his movement as being part of a greater, pan-Vaishnava community that encompassed both North and South India. In keeping with this view he began publishing the books of other Vaishnava lines, and encouraged devotional veneration to renowned Vaishnava teachers such as Madhva, Rāmānuja, Nimbārka, and Viṣṇusvāmī.

On January 29, 1925, Bhaktisiddhānta, accompanied by numerous followers and fellow pilgrims, began a one-month tour of various sacred places (*parikramā*) in the Nabadwip-Mayapur area, causing a new confrontation

129. Sambidananda Das, "History and Literature," ch. 13, p. 60.

with members of the orthodox *brāhmaṇa* community. Animosity had already been mounting toward him because of his 1911 speech against *brāhmaṇic* privileges and his efforts to promote Mayapur (as opposed to Nabadwip) as the authentic birthplace of Caitanya. On this day, as Bhaktisiddhānta and his rather large gathering of pilgrims walked through the streets of Nabadwip, they were suddenly attacked by an angry mob, and pelted with pieces of bricks and other dangerous projectiles. The incident is described in some detail in Swami Bhakti Vikāsa's biography. Because it is one of only a few available accounts, it is presented below in its entirety:

> The next morning 100 to 200 pilgrims, mostly males, returned to the place where they had been intimidated the previous evening. While Śrīmat Tīrtha Mahārāja was lecturing, a gang of ruffians suddenly appeared and pelted the elephant's trunk with brickbats. Parikramā attendees admonished the aggressors to desist from the offensive act of harassing the deities' mount, and to their surprise the rogues departed. But minutes later they returned wielding large sticks, which they had kept ready in nearby shops. The defenseless pilgrims quickly brought the deities of Sri Sri Rādhā-Govinda down into their midst, thinking that surely these felons would not continue their atrocities in the direct presence of the Lord. Then a well-known rich man of Navadvīpa [Nabadwip] drove up in a car and barked out an order, upon which ruthless blackguards lurking nearby, some perched on rooftops, let forth a volley of brickbats.
>
> The mahout quickly maneuvered the elephant away from trouble, but escape was not so easy for the pilgrims. Some found shelter in nearby homesteads, yet most doors remained shut. The few brave householders who dared offer refuge had their doors kicked and beaten on. Some devotees fled down adjacent alleys. Those who beseeched nearby coachmen to transport them were scornfully refused, and became further aghast to behold the horse carts loaded with stones as ammunition.
>
> The few devotees who tried to fight back were outnumbered and beleaguered.... A few devotees suffered severe gashes and fractures, one youth was knocked unconscious, *mṛdaṅgas* and banners were broken.... But although Navadvīpa's streets became stained by the blood of Vaishnavas... none were killed.
>
> Śrīla Sarasvatī Ṭhākura [Bhaktisiddhānta] had escaped due to the adroitness of Vinoda Bihārī Brahmacārī, who had entreated a

> reluctant house-owner to give them entry. Therein Vinoda Bihārī, being similar in size and appearance to his *gurudeva*, swapped his white clothing with the saffron of his guru-*mahārāja*. With great risk he then escorted Śrīla Sarasvatī Ṭhākura back to Mayapur.[130]

Although, in this case the procession party continued with its tour, in subsequent years it was accompanied by police escort.[131]

Orthodox sections of the Nabadwip community remained among Bhaktisiddhānta's strongest and most consistent opponents. This fact, however, did not deter him in his criticism of its views. In a 1927 letter to friend and supporter Madhusūdana Goswami, he noted that many caste Goswamis in pilgrimage sites such as Vrindavan cared for deities as a matter of business and gave mantras to disciples for the sake of earning a livelihood. He encouraged his friend to print local Hindi and Brajbuli leaflets about these issues, and thus earnestly attempt to regenerate genuine Caitanya bhakti.[132] Prior to this, in 1926, he had written an English work entitled *Vaiṣṇavism, Real and Apparent*, which denounced the perceived deficiencies of the Vaishnavas of his day.

In his crusade against hypocrisy and falsehood—born of his straightforwardness but also a modern trend—he acknowledged his debt to Bhaktivinoda. In an article published in the *Harmonist* in 1927 he wrote:

> Gaudamandal (the holy land of Gauda) had become an arena of the unholy contention of so called religious sects of every description.... Thakur Bhaktivinode appeared in this world out of divine pity for us with the object of remedying those disorders by the ministration of the healing balm of the loving instruction of Sree Caitanyachandra.[133]

In Bhaktisiddhānta's eyes, Bhaktivinoda had laid the groundwork for the restoration of Caitanya bhakti and its protection from the influence of corrupting elements such as the caste *brāhmaṇas* and the tantric *sahajiyā*

130. Vikāsa, *Śrī Bhaktisiddhānta Vaibhava*, vol. 1, pp. 87–88. There is no mention of the incident in Bhaktisiddhānta's diary.

131. Sambidananda Das, "History and Literature," ch. 13, p. 73.

132. Bhaktisiddhānta, *Prabhupādera Patrāvalī*, vol. 1 (January 15, 1927), pp. 33–34.

133. *Harmonist* 25, no. 1 (1927): p. 26.

movements. On the other hand, he thought, for a number of possible reasons, that Bhaktivinoda's approach had been too accommodating, if only out of necessity. Some of these reasons may have been that (1) although Bhaktivinoda disagreed with the orthodox caste Vaishnavas of Bengal about the location of Caitanya's birthplace, he nonetheless approached them in an attempt to maintain viable relations; (2) although Bipin Bihari Goswami's practice fell short of what Bhaktisiddhānta considered to be the highest standard, Bhaktivinoda nonetheless had taken initiation from him, accepting him as a guru; and, (3) some of Bhaktivinoda's early writings, such as his introduction to the *Kṛṣṇa Saṃhitā*, were self-consciously designed to attract the minds of the educated *bhadralok*, who were his main supporters. Moreover, Bhaktivinoda had adopted the esoteric path of *mañjarī* (young maiden) mysticism, which was practiced by the *bābājīs* and explicitly discussed it in his books. Bhaktisiddhānta, on the other hand, regarded this sort of practice as unsuitable for most of the religious practitioners of his time. In general, he considered many of Bhaktivinoda's followers to be incapable of elevating the practice of bhakti to the level of "purity" that Bhaktivinoda had originally envisioned. In 1927 he wrote:

> in the days of Thakur Bhaktivinod the number of devotees professing "Suddha bhakti" [pure bhakti] in Bengal were very few. His appeals had to be made to the class of "Misra bhaktas" (those that mix pure *bhakti* with either *jñana* or *karma*) and "Biddha bhaktas" (those that adulterate pure *bhakti* with their own speculative understandings), among whom he found supporters and sympathisers. The "Sajjana-toshani" of that period did not altogether escape the influence of the views of these supporters. Thakur Bhaktivinod, himself the Pioneer "Suddha bhakta," found it absolutely necessary to tolerate more or less this influence of "Misra bhaktas" and "Biddha bhaktas" within the movement.[134]

"Pure" (*śuddha*) bhakti meant bhakti that was free from the tendency to enjoy the fruits of knowledge (*jñāna*) or mundane action (*karma*). It meant service to God that was devoid of ulterior motives and actuated by love alone. The call of Bhaktivinoda to "expound to the whole world the teachings of Sri Mahaprabhu" was compelling, but Bhaktisiddhānta felt that

134. *Harmonist* 25, no. 1 (1927): p. 4.

this aspect of Bhaktivinoda's vision had been increasingly neglected.[135] Although he wished to build on Bhaktivinoda's legacy, he apparently had concluded that a bolder approach was in order:

> By the will of our Supreme Lord the Sajjana-toshani became subsequently strictly the organ of the Suddha-bhakti movement and it is a proof of the fact that Thakur Bhaktivinode's object is carried out that a large number of highly educated and sincere souls have been accepting the principle of "Suddha-bhakti."[136]

In a conversation from that period, Bhaktisiddhānta explained his approach as having come from his personal encounter with his guru Gaura Kiśora dāsa, who had exposed his pride in being an educated, accomplished scholar. As mentioned earlier, his own internal transformation had come about as a result of the profound feeling of being insignificant in comparison to the spiritual stature and character of his guru.[137] Because of this he had become convinced that only an encounter that forces persons to take a hard, honest look at themselves could create the basis for authentic religious insight and change. A "live and let live" approach was not enough. In general, however, the "highly educated" of Calcutta were difficult to court, and Bhaktisiddhānta's initial attempts were greeted with mixed feelings. Nonetheless, there were some notable exceptions.

In this regard, perhaps the earliest historical evidence of Bhaktisiddhānta's desire for a global movement can be found in an account of a 1922 meeting with Abhay Caran De, who at the time was the manager of a chemical factory owned by one Dr. Bose. De had been a strong sympathizer of Gandhi's and was politically involved with the Congress Party. He had been born in a Vaishnava family and his strong practice of Vaishnavism had then somewhat diminished, in his own words, "due to association with college friends." One of these friends, Narendranath Mallik, nonetheless persuaded him to attend one of Bhaktisiddhānta's lectures. As soon as De and his friend came into Bhaktisiddhānta's presence, he is reported to have remarked: "You are educated young boys. Why don't you take up Lord Caitanya's message and preach in the

135. *Harmonist* 25, no. 4 (1927): p. 84.

136. *Harmonist* 25, no. 1 (1927): p. 4.

137. Bhaktisiddhānta, *Prabhupadera Harikathāmṛta*, vol. 1, p. 34.

Western world?" In Abhay Caran De's account of this incident he notes his attempt to argue that as long as India remains dependent, no one will listen to her message. De also notes that this argument was soundly defeated by Bhaktisiddhānta. After this encounter, De apparently abandoned his nationalistic efforts and in 1933 accepted formal initiation from Bhaktisiddhānta. In 1966 he managed to fulfill the initial request of his guru by traveling to the United States and founding ISKCON under his *saṃnyāsa* name Abhay Caranaravinda Bhaktivedānta Swami.[138]

Bhadralok and Bhakti

Bhaktisiddhānta faced sections of the *bhadralok* that were more or less prone to assimilate European culture and were critical of traditional religions. The *bhadralok* had carefully staked out their cultural and social territory during the eighteenth and nineteenth centuries, but were situated in a liminal space between colonial and indigenous society, which produced, in the words of Dipesh Chakrabarty, a state of mental and cultural "homelessness."[139] This liminality had a parallel in the West, but for different reasons. In Europe, modernity rose with the industrial revolution to challenge those universalist narratives that provided meaning and a sense of direction in earlier societies, particularly with regard to religion.[140] In India, resentment of racial discrimination hindered cultural assimilation and integration, despite the *bhadralok's* fascination with the Enlightenment ideal of progress. While in their rhetoric the British advocated equality and intellectual freedom to claim possession of a higher moral ground, they nonetheless relied upon a policy of racial segregation to legitimize and maintain their rule. Put bluntly, the promise of equality and freedom was a self-conscious myth that was never intended to be fulfilled. In their struggle to resolve these ambiguities, significant sections of the *bhadralok* tied themselves to Western nationalistic ideologies. A notable exception

---

138. Swami Bhaktivedānta, lecture at Gorakhpur on February 15, 1971, *Bhaktivedānta Vedabase 2003* (Sandy Ridge, N.C.: Bhaktivedānta Archives, 2002).

139. Chakrabarty states that "middle-class Bengali Hindus of Calcutta often refer to the ancestral village in explaining where their *bari* [home] is even if their *basha* [temporary residence] bears a Calcutta address." Dipesh Chakrabarty, *Habitations of Modernity: Essays in the Wake of Subaltern Studies* (Chicago: University of Chicago Press, 2002), p. 120.

140. Peter L. Berger, Hansfried Kellner, and Brigitte Berger, *The Homeless Mind: Modernization and Consciousness* (New York: Vintage Books, 1974).

was Gandhi, who rejected both the European idea of the nation-state and the European model of progress, understood as unending industrial, technological, and economic development.[141] Using a term employed by Dipesh Chakrabarty, *bhadralok* aspirations for social and political *identity*, in which "differences were congealed or concealed," tended to be resolved by *proximity*, the state in which differences were "neither reified nor erased, but negotiated."[142] The affinity of the *bhadralok* for Western thought drew many to humanism and a more rational approach to the spiritual, both of which reduced their affinity for traditional religions. As a result, although many regarded Caitanya bhakti as regressive, or even harmful,[143] those involved in the national discourse regarded bhakti more positively as devotion to mythical ancestral males and "mother" India.[144] The following statement by Vijay Krishna Goswami, found in an *Amrita Bazar Patrika* article, nicely captures this mood:

> Can there be a matter of greater shame than this that we Indians, sons of the time old spirituality, have today, misled by the restless adolescence of the English, started repeating their materialistic shibboleths mumbling all the time that all *tapasya* and endeavours for the Supreme Spiritual Truth is but slothful stagnancy?[145]

For Bhaktisiddhānta, "homelessness" was not just a product of colonial displacement, but a primary existential condition of humanity, born of the tension between the forces of Nature (*prakṛti*) and its alleged metaphysical root (*aprakṛti*). Humans were in his view torn between the pursuit of impermanent worldly pleasures (culminating with death) and the cultivation of ever-enduring spiritual happiness on the metaphysical plane. Bhaktisiddhānta aimed to harmonize the two through the medium of bhakti, as understood after a laborious study (and internalization) of

141. See Mahatma Gandhi, *Hind Swaraj, or Indian Home Rule* (Navajivan Karyalaya: Ahmedabad, 1938).

142. Chakrabarty, *Habitations of Modernity*, p. 140.

143. Ramakanta Chakravarti, *Baṅge vaiṣṇava dharma: ekti aitihāsika ebaṃ samājatāttvika adhyāyana* (Kolkata: Ananda Publishers, 1996).

144. Dipesh Chakrabarty, *Provincializing Europe: Postcolonial Thought and Historical Difference* (Princeton, N.J.: Princeton University Press, 2000), p. 235.

145. "Sri Bijoykrishna and Spiritual Tradition" by Dilip Roy, *Amrita Bazar Patrika*, September 25, 1935.

Vaishnava texts. He came to reject modern Vedantic interpretations that had made work (*sevā*) for the material upliftment of the masses equivalent to direct worship of the Divine, as suggested on several occasions by Vivekānanda. This, in his view, would not solve humanity's basic existential problem, but only afford it temporary superficial relief. Bhaktisiddhānta also rejected the kind of Hindu activism that associated Krishna with the process of nation-building, because it openly attempted to project the aspirations of this world onto the metaphysical realm. Because of these standpoints, the *bhadralok* treated Bhaktisiddhānta sometimes with sympathy and sometimes with contempt.

In his attempts to reach mainstream culture, Bhaktisiddhānta did not hesitate to employ costly technical devices, from motorcars to automated presses (figure B.6). While some saw this as a progressive sign of modernity, others looked down upon it as incompatible with religious life, which for them was symbolized by renunciation and detachment from the world. Bhaktisiddhānta, on the other hand, viewed both the profane and the sacred as equally useful, so long as they were conducive to the cultivation of bhakti. For him everything was a manifestation of the potency of God, and thus "sacred" and "profane" were only relative categories. This approach was noticeable in his various "theistic exhibitions," in which the religious and the secular were showcased side by side. One such exhibit was held in 1935 in cooperation with the government of Bengal, and took place in Mayapur near the premises of the Gaudiya Math. It was divided into two sections, one secular and one religious. The secular section displayed medical, educational, and agricultural advances, child welfare activities and so forth. The religious section included a museum containing sacred items from various parts of India, books by various religious groups, rare manuscripts, photos of eminent saints, a large stone map displaying the pilgrimage route of Caitanya, and so forth. It featured over fifty stalls showcasing religious life in different parts of India. The ground was illuminated by electricity that had been drawn to Mayapur for the occasion. Prominent scientists and scholars were invited to lecture or to preside over scientific and cultural programs. While this exhibition created great amusement, an earlier one had produced turmoil and waves of dissent.

In September 1931, a flood caused a great humanitarian catastrophe in Bengal, and a famine arose among the poorer strata of society, particularly in the rural areas. At around the same time, Bhaktisiddhānta's third theistic exhibition took place in Calcutta, running from the sixth to the twenty-third of September and featuring eighty-five different stalls.[146] Although the *Harmonist* reports that the exhibition was visited by at least a million persons and was generally well received due to its novel admixture of mundane and religious material,[147] on the day of its inauguration the following negative piece appeared in the *Amrita Bazar Patrika*:

> To consider matters relating to the Gaudiya Math...an important public meeting will be held on Tuesday, September 8 at Sliyam Square at 5:30 PM. It is highly distressing to note that the Gaudiya Math is spending thousands in the name of a Theistic Exhibition when millions of our fellow brothers and sisters are pining for want of relief. All persons are earnestly requested to attend the meeting.[148]

Regardless of the protest that ensued, Bhaktisiddhānta would not bend to popular demands, and the exhibition continued on as planned, a decision that was decidedly against the grain of mainstream *bhadralok* sensibilities. Sometime later, during a lecture at the Krishnanagar Town Hall on June 16, 1933, he further explained his position as follows:

> We are approaching the intelligent section for expressing topics of ultimate value. One Mr. Roy was trying to uplift the slums here and wanted me to assist. But we don't support that. Let the world come up to whatever standard it may be able to. In any case it will bring misfortune, for altruism that is so narrowed, temporary, and time-serving, results only in no time to participate in spiritual things. One should not fill a hole with gold. Mr. MacDonald, a well-known Christian professor, gave a lecture at Calcutta University about how altruism is the unique property of Christianity. Yet this understanding should be enlarged and extended.... Twenty-four hours pass by, but what kind of help has been given? Those who can generate a lasting benefit and the method thus adopted should be appreciated...therefore we have no time for any other effort except glorifying Hari.[149]

146. A detailed description of the stalls is found in the *Harmonist* 29, no. 3 (September 1931): pp. 81–95, and 29, no. 4 (October 1931): pp. 108–126.

147. *Harmonist* 29, no. 5 (November 1931): p. 160.

148. *Amrita Bazar Patrika*, September 6, 1931.

149. Bhakti Bhūṣaṇa Bhāratī, ed., *Śrīla Prabhupādera Goloka-vaṇī*, vol. 1, pp. 49–50.

While maintaining this policy relative to his monastic Gaudiya Math ashrams, as far back as 1918 he had instructed his lay disciples to give charity and show compassion to the poor. He presented this as a prescribed duty, the neglect of which would create pride in wealth and a miserly heart—dangerous weaknesses for a *bhakta*.[150] Moreover, he himself always carried a supply of food on his travels, which he would make available to those in need.

It may be useful at this point to briefly compare Bhaktisiddhānta's ideas on humanitarianism and nationalism with those of a contemporary, the well-known Indian nationalist Bipin Chandra Pal (1858–1932). Like Bhaktisiddhānta, Pal had come from a *kāyastha* family and viewed himself a Caitanya *bhakta*. Along with Bal Gangadhar Tilak and Lala Lajpat Rai, he eventually became one of the leaders of the movement for self-rule or Swadeshi, and was also closely associated with the Brahmo Samaj, Keshub Chandra Sen, and the Brahmo Vaishnava missionary Vijay Krishna Goswami (his guru).[151]

A Comparison with Bipin Chandra Pal

In a number of early twentieth-century letters to a Christian friend, Pal explained what, in his view, the core of Vaishnavism was.[152] In a way that somewhat resembled Hegel's historical idealism, he wrote that the world in its relation to *brahman* undergoes a cosmic evolution, which is "the progressive revelation or realization of an Idea."[153] The Idea, understood as the divine consciousness of the absolute, was present in each stage of evolution, but was never fully realized. The world moves continuously, but its significance lies in the progression toward "some definite but unrealised though progressively realising state of perfection."[154] Pal also attempted to provide a detailed definition of the personal nature of the God of

150. Ananta Vāsudeva in *Sarasvatī Jayaśrī*, p. 26.

151. Alexander Lipski, "Bipincandra Pal and Reform Hinduism," *History of Religions* 11, no. 2 (1971): p. 229. See also Alexander Lipski, "Vijay Krsna Goswami: Reformer and Traditionalist," *Journal of Indian History* 52, no. 1 (1974).

152. Bipin Chandra Pal, *Europe Asks Who Is Shree Krishna: Letters Written to a Christian Friend* (Calcutta: Classic Publication, 2002).

153. Pal, *Europe Asks Who Is Shree Krishna*, p. 6.

154. Pal, *Europe Asks Who Is Shree Krishna*, p. 102.

Vaishnava theology (*bhagavān*), distinguishing between a personal and an impersonal aspect—*sagunam* and *nirgunam*. He stated that the world of Nature is *prakṛti*, and through it the Supreme Person (*puruṣa*) "operates for its own self-realisation and self-fulfilment."[155] Pal referred to the Italian freedom fighter Giuseppe Mazzini, who had stated that humanity was like a body made of limbs and organs, which represented its various nations and races. Taken together they formed the self-conscious universal Person. According to Pal, this self-conscious and self-active Person was equivalent to the Vaishnava concept of Nārāyaṇa. Nārāyaṇa, literally the "shelter of man," had three aspects: a transcendental aspect as the Supreme Person; a "Narottama" aspect as the best and ideal man; and, a "God in History" aspect as the force that "shapes the course of social evolution."[156] Pal considered the movements of society to be more important than (and as transcending) those of the individual, a view that he explained in his autobiography as follows:

> The life of an individual, however humble it may be, and howmuch-soever mean may be its value if taken in itself, is…found to have a worth far transcending its outer qualities, when studied as an expression and illustration of the general social movements about him.[157]

In his letters, Pal describes Krishna as the ideal role model for man, and the fullest revelation of God in man, since "God and man are really one."[158] While it is tempting to interpret this as a statement about the absolute oneness of Krishna with man, Pal conceived of God as possessing differentiated aspects, and it is plausible that he merely wished to underline the immanent nature of the divine. On the other hand, his view of Krishna was more mundane than the Vaishnava tradition generally allows, and Pal's "historical idealism" surfaces time and time again.

In contrast to Pal, Bhaktisiddhānta rejected the somewhat modern idea that God unfolded through humanity's material and social evolution,

---

155. Pal, *Europe Asks Who Is Shree Krishna*, p. 80.

156. Pal, *Europe Asks Who Is Shree Krishna*, p. 31.

157. Bipin Chandra Pal, *Memories of My Life and Times* (Calcutta: Bipinchandra Pal Institute, 1973), p. ix.

158. Pal, *Europe Asks Who Is Shree Krishna*, p. 32.

seeking instead to ground his thought in the philosophy of traditional Vaishnava texts.[159] According to him, the *jīva* was a metaphysical being, while the body and mind were products of nature (*prakṛti*). The latter was an external, separated energy of God that responded to individual and social actions (karma) through a series of short- and long-term reactions. Although, in the ultimate sense, the world is a manifestation of God's energy, since it originates from God, it is simultaneously different from God's inner metaphysical substance (*vastu*). Within Vaishnava circles, a simple metaphor is sometimes used to explain this point: a spider spins a web from its body and, in this sense, is one with the web; at the same time, however, the spider is in all respects independent and apart from the web, conceived as its generated energy. Although Bhaktisiddhānta recognized a resemblance between the form of Krishna and the form of man, conceiving man to be the product of God, he also recognized a difference in the sense that God's form is infinite, while man's is not.

This notwithstanding, Bhaktisiddhānta maintained a positive view regarding humanity's capacity to improve its own destiny. He was an advocate of *spiritual* evolution and *choice of action* in the world. On the other hand, his view of the world of matter was at odds with Pal's notion of a divine Idea progressively unfolding through humanity over time. In this regard, Bhaktisiddhānta maintained the classical Puranic view of the spiritual regression of human civilization during the age of *Kali*. Furthermore, to view Krishna, and subsequently bhakti, through the lens of a sociohistorical narrative was for him equivalent to subordinating bhakti to worldly motivated action. In his view, pure bhakti could never be motivated by anything other than itself—that is, by pure love (*prema*).

This brief example is intended to illustrate that few among the *bhadralok* considered Caitanya bhakti capable of standing on its own ideological and philosophical feet. Apart from Pal, there were other prominent *bhadralok* that attempted to combine Vaishnavism with other currents of thought (e.g., Bankim Chandra's well-known *Krishna Charitra*). Such persons tended to integrate Caitanya bhakti with humanistic or political ideas in a way that was in tune with prevalent intellectual trends, both in India and in the West. To present bhakti as a self-sufficient path, and Krishna as the metaphysical "Personality of Godhead," was the main objective of

---

159. See introduction to *Caitanya Bhāgavata* for the following presentation of Bhaktisiddhānta's thought: Bhaktisiddhānta Sarasvatī and Vṛndāvana dāsa Ṭhākura, *Caitanya Bhāgavata* (Calcutta: Śrī Gaudiya Math, 1984), pp. 5–10

Bhaktisiddhānta's effort, and the element that distinguished him from most of his Vaishnava and non-Vaishnava *bhadralok* contemporaries.

Institutional Practices and Challenges

During the 1920s Bhaktisiddhānta consolidated his institution. For purposes of conducting research and establishing new centers, he made a tour of India in November 1926. He founded new Maths, developed a new pan-Indian network, and helped to make Caitanya bhakti accessible to the middle and upper classes outside of Bengal. He also met with Vaishnavas from other communities, such as the Mahant of Nathdwara in Rajasthan, Gokulanātha Goswami in Bombay, and the head of the Vaishnava Math of Madhva in Udupi, Karnataka. It was during this period that he established the Paramahansa Math in Naimisaranya (Nimsar or Nimkhar, U.P.). Shortly thereafter, in a newly built temple in Mayapur, he installed the deities of Rādhā and Krishna (along with the images of India's four most prominent Vaishnava *ācāryas*). In doing so, he relied upon the mutual regard of the four *sampradāyas,* as well as their common philosophical stand relative to the nondualist Vedanta philosophy of Śaṅkara, which all four had resisted or modified in various ways. In a 1922 *Gauḍīya* article, Bhaktisiddhānta had already presented the four Vaishnava *sampradāyas* as being united with regard to the differentiation of a metaphysical individual self (*jīva*) from a personal God (*bhagavān*)—a conception that nondualism ultimately denied.[160] He had also written detailed articles in the *Gauḍīya* that provided biographical information, philosophical overviews, and a description of the disciplic lines of these *ācāryas.*[161] Bhaktisiddhānta found substantial parallels between the philosophies of Caitanya and Madhva Vaishnavism, particularly with respect to the theory of differentiation (*saviśeṣavāda*), which defined *viśeṣa* (difference) as being inherent in the individual properties of matter. This was a key argument in support of the notion that all manifestations of the world are essentially real, and not ultimately illusory, as nondualists tend to suggest. In *Harmonist* articles, however, he also pointed out the unique features of the philosophy of the Goswamis of Vrindavan as compared to that of the Mādhva tradition, particularly with regard to Madhva's concept of predestination, which the

---

160. *Gauḍīya* 1, no. 18 (1922): pp. 12–16, "Vaiṣṇava darśana" (Vaishnava philosophy).

161. The articles were written in the *Gauḍīya* from 1927, 2nd issue till 1928, 33rd issue.

Vaishnavas in Bengal rejected. Another point of difference was that the Madhvas only allowed caste *brāhmaṇas* to head their religious institutions and conduct private and public worship.[162] Nonetheless, following the example of Bhaktivinoda, Bhaktisiddhānta referred to his guru succession as the *Mādhva Gauḍīya Vaiṣṇava sampradāya*. Apparently he hoped that by making other Vaishnava *ācāryas* known in Bengal, and publishing their works, he could revitalize interest in the teachings of the Vaishnava schools, and in this way resist sectarian caste and regional consciousness, along with the mounting influence of nondualism.[163] Furthermore, the link to pan-Indian Vaishnavism provided a much broader perspective in terms of understanding the role of Caitanya and the Vaishnava guru within the frame of Hinduism. This appealed to many among the Indian middle class who were already familiar with various forms of Vaishnava thought and practice.

At the end of September 1927, he embarked upon an extensive tour in the north and west of the subcontinent, holding lectures and discourses in places such as Kasi, Lucknow, Jaipur, and Dwaraka.[164] In the following year, on September 28, 1928, he laid the ground stone for a large marble temple located in Baghbazar, North Calcutta; this temple was to become the administrative headquarter of his mission (figure B.8).

Certain events in 1929 indicated that the popularity of Bhaktisiddhānta and the Gaudiya Math was on the rise. On January 16, after establishing a Gaudiya Math in Delhi, he held discourses attended by the elite of the capital. In addition, the first postal outlet was opened in Mayapur on June 1, and on November 1 it was made into a permanent office. Mayapur itself had grown from a forsaken rural settlement to an increasingly popular pilgrimage site, and this was an unofficial acknowledgment of its growing importance. On October 5, 1929, Bhaktisiddhānta moved from Ultadingi Junction Road to the newly completed temple in Baghbazar, leading a large *kīrtana* procession through the streets of Calcutta. The installation of newly made deities of Caitanya, Krishna, and his consort took place along with an exhibition. A large religious festival was

162. *Harmonist* 31, no. 18 (May 1935): pp. 412–414, "A Word to Our Madhwa-Vaishnava Brethern."

163. See an article on Mādhva in the *Harmonist* 29, no. 7 (January 1932): pp. 215–218.

164. The biographical article in the *Gauḍīya* also mentions Kashi, Kanpur, Lucknow, Jaipur, Galta Parvat, Salimabad, Pushkar, Ajmeer, Dwaraka, Sudamapuri, Girnar hill, Prabhasa, Avanti, Mathura and Vrindavan, Delhi, Kurukshetra, and Naimisaranya.

organized, which included lectures, panel discussions, and mass distribution of sanctified food.

In terms of his movement, Bhaktisiddhānta clearly respected traditional *brāhmaṇic* standards of Sanskrit learning and ritual practice, which increased the reputation of his institution among Hindus all over India. Nonetheless he came to see advantages in new *bhadralok* institutional practices, particularly those related to the organization of missionary services and the coordination of his work with the laity. On one occasion, he objected to a complaint about plenary meetings and large assemblies, the backbone of modern voluntary organizations:

> there are some...who think assemblies, etc., to be useless as they were not prevalent in ancient times. We request the readers of the Sri Caitanya Charitāmrita to note that in the book there are mentions of *ista-gosthis* (meeting of devotees to talk about devotional topics), and also that the readers of the Shrimad Bhāgavatam are expected to know about the assemblies in which large audiences listened to the discourses on the Bhāgavatam.[165] Shri Caitanya Mahaprabhu and the followers of the teachings of the Shrimad Bhāgavatam have ever advised the people of the world that Shravana (audition or listening) and Kīrtana (recapitulation or chanting) are the surest means for the attainment of the highest blessedness.[166]

For Bhaktisiddhānta, the collective and social aspects of bhakti were as important as the individual ones. For that reason, he considered the practice of aural reception (*śravaṇa*) to include listening to others in open meetings for the discussion of service (*sevā*). He underlined cooperation with other *bhaktas* and the performance of *sevā* as the safest ways to avoid the influence of those that were inimical to bhakti.[167] Above all, however, Bhaktisiddhānta made it unequivocally clear that hearing the understandings of highly advanced *bhaktas* and reciting the sacred names of God were the most important means of gaining access to the metaphysical plane

165. Bhaktisiddhānta refers in the above to the setting of the *Śrimad Bhāgavatam*, where Parikṣit, a king doomed to die because of a curse, discoursed for seven days with the enlightened sage Śukadeva Gosvāmi.

166. Bhaktisiddhānta, *Shri Chaitanya's Teachings*, ed. Swami Bhakti Vilāsa Tīrtha (Madras: Shree Gaudiya Math, 1989), p. 248.

167. Letter dated October 20, 1928, in Bhaktisiddhānta, *Prabhupādera Patrāvalī*, vol. 1, p. 52.

and cultivating the inner core of bhakti. Recitation of the sacred names of Rādhā and Krishna (*harināma*) was the main spiritual practice of the members of the Gaudiya Math, and the recommended means of fostering an intimate loving relationship with the deity. Indeed Bhaktisiddhānta regarded absorption in the names of God as nondifferent from seeing God in person.[168] He encouraged disciples residing in his Maths to recite one hundred thousand names each day so as to maintain devotional consciousness while serving in the world, and he encouraged the laity to strive for this goal as well.[169] Bhaktisiddhānta viewed the aural recitation of *harināma* as being far superior to silent meditation, which was generally more difficult for an urban laity to execute. In this sense, he paralleled the reforms of middle-class Burmese Buddhists such as U Ba Khin, who developed a simpler, less taxing method of Vipāssana meditation for the urban laity.[170]

Harināma, the simple universal process that Bhaktisiddhānta envisioned for modern times, had been introduced by Sri Caitanya in the late Middle Ages. It was generally conducted in two basic forms: (1) a more individual and meditative form known as *japa*; and, (2) a more public form known as *kīrtana*, which consisted of either small or large groups of roaming singers accompanied by musical instruments. This latter, highly visible form is one of the things that made his movement easily recognizable by Hindus and non-Hindus alike. Indeed a good number of those that joined the Gaudiya Math had come from a non-Vaishnava background.

During the 1920s and 1930s, the majority of his supporters were laymen and laywomen, although the Math's outreach missionary efforts were conducted by a force of twenty *saṃnyāsins* whom Bhaktisiddhānta called the "living drums" of his mission.[171] When the Bhaktivinoda Āsana

---

168. Letter dated March 17, 1915, in Bhaktisiddhānta, *Prabhupādera Patrāvalī*, vol. 2, p. 3.

169. See, for example, a letter dated October 20, 1928, in Bhaktisiddhānta, *Prabhupādera Patrāvalī*, vol. 1, p. 53.

170. Gustaaf Houtmans, "The Biography of Modern Burmese Buddhist Meditation Master U Ba Khin: Life before the Cradle and Past the Grave," in *Sacred Biography in the Buddhist Traditions of South and Southeast Asia*, ed. Juliane Schober (Honolulu: University of Hawai'i Press, 1997).

171. In alphabetical order, they were Swami Bhakti Bhūdeva Śrauti, Swami Bhakti Gaurava Vaikhānasa, Swami Bhakti Hṛdaya Bon, Swami Bhakti Kevala Auḍulomi, Swami Bhakti Pradīpa Tīrtha, Swami Bhakti Prakāśa Araṇya, Swami Bhakti Prasuna Bodhāyana, Swami Bhakti Rakṣaka Śrīdhara, Swami Bhakti Sambala Bhāgavata, Swami Bhakti Sambandha

was first created, only laymen such as Kuñjabihārī Vidyābhūṣaṇa dāsa, a post office employee, came to live with him.[172] Apart from the *saṃnyāsins*, Bhaktisiddhānta relied heavily on such individuals for help in organizing all major aspects of his mission that related to the public—for example, fund-raising, popular programs, and the handling of the press.[173] This was necessary since his natural disposition was more reclusive and oriented toward philosophical study.[174] Bhaktisiddhānta particularly sought contact with the educated elite for discussions about Caitanya Vedanta, but required help in terms of organizing such meetings. Although Kuñjabihārī Vidyābhūṣaṇa never left his job as post officer, he nonetheless remained Bhaktisiddhānta's main assistant when it came to such practical affairs as management, finance, building contacts, and the like.

For Bhaktisiddhānta, married life among the laity meant creating a favorable environment for religious practice. Apart from the primary responsibility of caring for children and other dependents, this included service to God and guru as well as working for the spiritual upliftment of human society. He encouraged the laity to see family members not as objects of personal enjoyment, but as spiritual beings belonging to God. At the same time, Bhaktisiddhānta believed that the distracting influence of various worldly activities made married life less conducive to spiritual advancement than the more detached life of the Math.

Bhaktisiddhānta often visited the laity and held programs in their homes. In letters that he wrote to his lay disciples he encouraged them to donate a tangible portion of their income to support the work of the Math. He considered this to be one way of counteracting the tendency to indulge in the

---

Turyāśramī, Swami Bhakti Sarvāśva Giri, Swami Bhakti Sudhīra Yācaka, Swami Bhakti Śrīrūpa Purī, Swami Bhakti Svarūpa Parvata, Swami Bhakti Vaibhava Sāgara, Swami Bhakti Vicāra Yāyāvara, Swami Bhakti Vijñāna Āśrama, Swami Bhakti Vilāsa Gabhastinemi, Swami Bhakti Viveka Bhāratī. Biographical sketches of seventeen of them are found in Vikāsa, *Śrī Bhaktisiddhānta Vaibhava*, vol. 2, pp. 289–324.

172. Ananta Vāsudeva in *Sarasvatī Jayaśrī*, p. 34–35.

173. In general, Bhaktisiddhānta considered the practical and financial support of the laity to be as important and valuable as the more direct devotional service rendered by the renounced residents of the Math. An example in this regard is that of Bhaktirañjana dāsa, the main donor and constructor of the elaborate Gaudiya Math temple in Calcutta. During the opening ceremony of the Math, Bhaktisiddhānta made it a point to offer this individual his profuse thanks. Shortly after the opening Bhaktirañjana dāsa passed away, and each year thereafter Bhaktisiddhānta held a special ceremony of remembrance in his honor.

174. For biographical sketches of Kuñjabihārī Vidyābhūṣaṇa and Sundarānanda Vidyāvinoda see Vikāsa, *Śrī Bhaktisiddhānta Vaibhava*, vol. 2, pp. 332–339, 347–351.

comforts of family life. By making the laity spiritually dependent on the Math and the Math financially dependent on the laity, he effectively linked each to the other. The partnership with the laity was essential for the growth of the Gaudiya Math, and Bhaktisiddhānta's respect for Bhaktivinoda's example as a layman and *bhakta* constituted an important precedent in this regard. The Math delivered a number of key services to the laity in order to facilitate its cultivation of bhakti. It supplied personal guidance and training by senior *bhaktas*, regular temple programs, and a platform for fellowship and friendship with other practitioners. Leading *saṃnyāsins* were assigned the task of ministering to the laity, which often made association with competing religious institutions unnecessary. In its various publications, the Gaudiya Math would carefully scrutinize the differences between itself and other religious groups and institutions in Bengal. This served not only to educate the laity as to the complexity of religious theory and practice, but also to preserve its loyalty to the specific orientation of the Gaudiya Math.

Despite his openness to the development of relations between the laity and the Maths, Bhaktisiddhānta cautioned against the potential dangers of the modern institutionalization of religion.[175] In a 1932 article entitled "Putana," he wrote that

> the idea of an organized church in an intelligible form marks the close of the living spiritual movements. The great ecclesiastical establishments are the dikes and the dams to retain the current that cannot be held by any such contrivances. They indeed indicate a desire on the part of the masses to exploit a spiritual movement for their own purposes.[176]

A possible explanation for the wary tone of the article is that it was written at a time when tensions among his leading disciples had made him more skeptical. The collection of funds was a danger not only for the ascetic residents of the Math, but also for the leaders of the laity, since it often invited a desire for position and power—a fault that Bhaktisiddhānta had frequently pointed out while referring to other religious leaders and movements.[177] Institutional hierarchies also carried the potential of poisoning

---

175. See also Vikāsa, *Śrī Bhaktisiddhānta Vaibhava*, vol. 1, pp. 99–110.

176. *Harmonist* 29, no. 7 (January 1932): p. 208.

177. See, for example, his commentary on the *Caitanya Caritāmṛta*, Antya 9.69.

relationships among *bhaktas*, creating unwanted envy and engendering various struggles for power.

In a satirical article entitled "Gauḍīya Hospital," he likened the Gaudiya Math to a health clinic for curing such "worldly diseases" as pride, envy, and greed.[178] Although the article was generally addressed to the worldly minded, its message was relevant to the circumstances of the Gaudiya Math as well. The traps of self-indulgence and self-centeredness were constant challenges for an aspiring *bhakta*, and Bhaktisiddhānta kept a watchful eye on his disciples through his letters, articles, and personal instructions. He warned them against the pitfalls of perhaps the most dangerous enemy of any cooperative effort: pride.[179] To show how to live a simple life based on humility and service, he set an early example by refusing the pension of his former employer the Maharaja of Tripura, and by begging alms from the *bhadralok* in Calcutta.[180] Begging was for him a spiritual discipline, a way to nurture humility and inner dependency on God, but also an activity that made one accountable to the public for its support. Throughout the later part of his life, Bhaktisiddhānta stressed that proficiency in the art of bhakti required integrity, honesty, self-discipline, and self-sacrifice.

From the pages of the *Sarasvatī Jayaśrī* it is possible to extract a lively account of life in the Gaudiya Math from its earliest beginnings. Embracing the life of a resident in the ashram involved a rite of passage from a secular identity to one as a celibate student (*brahmacārī*). The candidate began his training by stepping into a new social and cultural territory chalked out in terms of Vaishnava philosophy, religious symbols, and rules of behavior. The novice was asked to relinquish previously acquired social codes and roles, and to internalize the identity of a Caitanya *bhakta* in dress, behavior, and values. He was also requested to cultivate obedience and to follow the instructions of the guru and senior members of the Math. After proving his commitment, the resident would receive *harināma* initiation and a new "spiritual" name from Bhaktisiddhānta. At this point, he could remain a celibate member of the ashram or join the laity (if that was his preference or he was deemed unfit for ashram life). If he chose to live in the ashram, he would continue the regulated

---

178. *Gauḍīya* 3, no. 3 (August 30, 1924): pp. 1–3, "*Gauḍīya Hāspātāla*."

179. *Harmonist* 32, no. 11 (February 1936): pp. 241–246, "'Big I' Versus 'Good I.'" This is a translation of an original Bengali article, published in the *Nadīya Prakāśa* on Janury 20, 1936.

180. Ananta Vāsudeva in *Sarasvatī Jayaśrī*, p. 75.

discipline (or *sādhana*) under the supervision of senior representatives of the guru. After a new round of screening, if the candidate was found fit he would receive initiation as a *brāhmaṇa* and be allowed to silently recite the *gāyatrī* mantra, consisting of prayers to the guru, Caitanya, and Krishna in his conjugal sports (*līlā*) (this initiation was also made available to the laity). He was then also authorized to wear a *brāhmaṇa* thread over the shoulder and across the chest, and personally worship the sacred images of the deities on the altar. As indicated by Bhaktisiddhānta, daily recitation of the sacred names and regular attendance at temple programs were the principal means of maintaining purity of body, mind, and soul. With the expansion of the movement beyond Bengal, and later India, the relationship between Bhaktisiddhānta and his disciples largely occurred via entrusted representatives (often the *saṃnyāsins*) and the publication of articles, letters, and speeches. The press created a virtual community that united the Gaudiya Math across regional and national borders.

The primary service of those living in the Math was missionary work, which required specialized skills such as writing, editing, proofreading, and operating a press. Other services included studying Vaishnava texts, marketing and selling various publications, organizing social and cultural events, raising funds, and ministering to the laity. During festivities and public programs, large-scale distribution of sanctified food (*prasāda*) was carried out. Many residents would travel long distances to lecture and meet with interested persons in various urban and rural areas.

Bhaktisiddhānta's writings and transcribed speeches indicate that he went to great pains to teach Vedanta philosophy to his students. In this regard, he would often use rational arguments, frequently referring to the classical literature of the tradition. In contrast to popular forms of Vaishnavism that discarded *brāhmaṇic* learning, he considered inquisitiveness and reason important for the healthy internalization of bhakti, and thus worked to revive the foundation of Vaishnava philosophy with the help of Madhva and Rāmānuja.

The 1930s witnessed the growth of the Gaudiya Math as one of the most dynamic religious movements in India. The institutional pillars of the Gaudiya Math were Bhaktisiddhānta himself as the initiating and instructing guru, the community of Math residents, and the laity. The presentation and diffusion of the mission took place through printed texts and public speeches. To these central aspects of Bhaktisiddhānta's work we will now briefly turn.

Guru and Sampradāya

The guru is one of the central institutions of Hinduism, and an essential element in all Indic religious systems.[181] Bhaktisiddhānta had strong faith in the transformative power of personal relationships, and the importance of personal example. The self-realized guru, in theological terms, was the transparent medium through which a sincere disciple could gain entry to the spiritual realm. In Bhaktisiddhānta's view, only service to a bona fide guru could reveal the metaphysical self in one of four relationships to God: (1) servitorship (*dāsya*); (2) friendship (*sakhya*); (3) parenthood (*vātsalya*); or (4) conjugal love (*mādhurya*).[182] Moreover, the role of the guru in Bhaktisiddhānta's organizational structure was crucial. The guru served as a focal point and unifying principle, provided a cohesive sense of direction and purpose, functioned as a compact authority in the resolution of tensions and conflicts, and afforded a visible profile to the outside world. As more and more persons embraced the Gaudiya Math, Bhaktisiddhānta's significance expanded.

The beginning student of the Gaudiya Math was called upon to test the qualifications of the guru by observing his actions, speech, and habits for an entire year. Bhaktisiddhānta considered this the length of time required to teach the candidate how to see the guru not as an object of personal enjoyment (*bhoga*), but as a subject of service.[183] Once established, the relationship between guru and disciple was intended to last for a lifetime on the basis of reciprocal loyalty and service. The disciple was expected to learn from his guru the exoteric and esoteric teachings of bhakti, as well as the appropriate attitude by which to cultivate his or her devotional life. The guru, for his part, was to be a living example (*ācārya*) of the teachings contained in texts such as *Caitanya Caritāmṛta* and *Śrīmad Bhāgavatam*.

Bhaktisiddhānta questioned the exclusive right of caste *brāhmaṇas* to be gurus for all classes and castes.[184] Although he did not directly oppose the rights of hereditary caste gurus, he undermined their legitimacy by acting as guru for all those who approached him, a *kāyastha* by birth. In

181. In reference to Caitanya *bhakti*, see Måns Broo, *As Good as God: The Guru in Gauḍīya Vaiṣṇavism* (Åbo: Åbo Academy University Press, 2003).

182. Bhaktisiddhānta, *Shri Chaitanya's Teachings*, pp. 587–591, "Krishna Prema."

183. *Gauḍīya* 1, no. 41 (1923): pp. 1–3, "Varṣa-parīkṣā" (one year test).

184. *Gauḍīya* 1, no. 10 (1922): pp. 1–2, "Varṇāśrama."

order to legitimize this stance, Bhaktisiddhānta presented the status of a Vaishnava as being higher than that of a *brāhmaṇa* (as noted above). He also revived a disciplic succession (*paramparā*) which included *śikṣā* (instructing) gurus from various castes that had won recognition in the Caitanya tradition as a result of their character, teachings, and high state of consciousness—an approach that was consistent with his emphasis on *bhāgavata vidhi*. While he also considered *dīkṣā* (formal ritual) initiation to be important, he nonetheless regarded character and quality of instructions to be more relevant.

Bhaktisiddhānta was aware that his understanding of the guru, as delineated above, was traditional and rather anachronistic in a modern secular environment. Thus in his own role as guru of the Gaudiya Math, he was often found to qualify his position by stating that the main qualification of a bona fide guru was humility—that is, the genuine capacity to regard oneself as the lowest of all and as a servant of disciples, well-wishers, and all mankind.[185] The worship of Bhaktisiddhānta as a guru of bhakti nonetheless remained a central aspect of the Gaudiya Math.

Sādhus and Varṇāśrama

Bhaktisiddhānta's earlier decision to initiate himself as a *saṃnyāsin*, the most revered *aśrama* of Hindu society, had important implications for the development of the Gaudiya Math. Through this move, Bhaktisiddhānta adopted a role that was not only consistent with the classical image of the Hindu sadhu, but also in keeping the sensibilities of modern India. In fact, turn-of-the-century Bengalis looked up to asceticism and self-sacrifice as a means of gaining inner strength for the struggle to emancipate India from colonial rule. As such, apart from its obvious spiritual dimension, the establishment of a *saṃnyāsa* order provided another basis for the Gaudiya Math to gain legitimacy in the eyes of mainstream Hindu society. Regarding Bhaktisiddhānta's self-initiation, it may have been actuated by three considerations: (1) Caitanya had not established a *saṃnyāsa* order in the Gaudiya tradition; (2) the orders in Bengal and Orissa were preeminently nondualist; and, (3) South Indian Vaishnava orders, such as those of Madhva, only accepted *brāhmaṇas*.

185. *Harmonist* 32, no. 14 (March 1936): pp. 313–320.

While the Gaudiya Math adopted the four ashrams more or less from the start, the emancipation of laity disciples from the caste system was not pursued with equal vigor, possibly because Bengali society was still deeply enmeshed in the traditional rules of Hindu culture. Although Bhaktisiddhānta's disciples acquired a new Vaishnava identity by ritual initiation, they were nonetheless forced to deal with orthodox (*smārta*) caste rules as soon as they left the ashram to marry. Intercaste marriages were looked down upon in Bengal, particularly in the rural areas, and Bhaktisiddhānta reluctantly decided not to press his views in this regard. In 1935 he wrote:

> I do not know what would be the situation if members of the devotional society (*bhāgavatas*) form a separate caste (*jāti*). In my opinion, their separate identity may be maintained while keeping their previous *varṇa*, or if they are genuine and courageous in their conviction, they may free themselves from the shackles of a misdirected caste society. All these opinions and their practical applications are entirely individual and should be made according to circumstance and need. Those who believe in *smārta* theories cannot properly relate to those who subscribe to the Vaishnava view.... Determination of what should be the *varṇa* of a particular individual is the essence of the divine (*daiva*) *varnāśrama*, and its aim is to not mix one's family identity with one's individual nature.[186]

In the same letter, he wrote that it was never his intention to start a social reform movement. His motive in criticizing other Vaishnava groups was to strengthen the Vaishnava community, but the *smārtas* had created such severe obstacles that he had been forced to actively resist them. While he agreed with the orthodoxy that *varṇāśrama* and its ritual practices (*saṃskāras*) were beneficial for spiritual well-being, he also understood that in its present form the institution was corrupt. In the *Gauḍīya* (1922), Bhaktisiddhānta wrote that

> today, at the distressing time of this *varṇāśrama dharma*, isn't it a duty of each intelligent person to make sure with utmost effort that the *varṇāśrama dharma* designated by *śāstra* is reestablished? The ghost that introduces itself as *varṇāśrama*, standing for many

186. Letter dated April 6, 1935, Bhaktisiddhānta, *Prabhupādera Patrāvalī*, vol. 3, p. 50.

> centuries on the skeleton of the [earlier] *varṇāśrama*, needs to be removed, and only after that can the skeleton be revived by pronouncing a mantra (*sañjīvanī*), restoring the dead to life.[187]

Bhaktisiddhānta considered the contemporary caste system to be a *secular* means of managing social relations. It had guaranteed continuity for Hindu culture and society in the face of foreign rule, but it was not adequate as a tool for the cultivation of bhakti. He thus viewed "Hinduism" and "caste" as inferior secular constructions compared to *sanātana dharma*, considered by him to be the perennial religion of the Vaishnavas. While objecting to the caste system, he resisted the *bhadralok* tendency to indiscriminately condemn the stratification of Hindu society. He regarded social stratification as a natural phenomenon in the sense that individual vocations were born of diverse personal qualities (*guṇa*) and diverse inclinations toward work (*karma*). His acknowledgment of the potential for a reformed *varṇāśrama* to rejuvenate Vaishnavism bore some similarity to the socioreligious vision of Gandhi and other progressive Vaishnavas of his time. In reality, however, there was significant difference between his and Gandhi's points of view, as can be seen from the following instance.

On December 23, 1932, during a meeting with the orthodox Hindu organization Shastri Parishad, Gandhi posed ten questions regarding both untouchability and its relation to sacred texts (*śāstras* or Shastras). A few days later, those questions were published in the *Hindustan Times* as follows:

> 1. Define untouchability according to Shastras. 2. Can the definition of untouchables given in the Shastras be applied to the so-called untouchables of the present day? 3. What are the restrictions imposed by Shastras on the untouchables? 4. Can an individual be free from untouchability in his own lifetime? 5. What are the injunctions of the Shastras regarding behavior of the touchables with the untouchables? 6. Under what circumstances will the Shastras permit temple entry by the untouchables? 7. What are Shastras? 8. How is authoritativeness of the Shastras proved? 9. How will the differences arising over the definitions or interpretations of Shastras be decided? 10. What are your conclusions?[188]

---

187. *Gauḍīya* 1, no. 10 (1922): pp. 1–2, "Varṇāśrama."

188. Mahatma Gandhi, *The Life and Works of Mahatma Gandhi* (New Delhi: Icon Softec, 1999), vol. 52, pp. 268–269.

In January 1933, Bhaktisiddhānta responded to these queries by writing a lengthy *Harmonist* piece entitled "Gandhiji's ten questions."[189] In this article, Bhaktisiddhānta characteristically defined untouchability not in terms of caste, but in terms of religious orientation: untouchables are those inimical to the concept of service to God. The temples of Vishnu were meant for all, he maintained, but more so for those that possessed a favorable attitude toward God, and were thus willing to undergo a process of personal transformation. This did not imply a rejection of those who were forgetful of their relationship with God, nor did it imply "that any person is to be looked down upon or disrespected."[190] It did, however, require those that were favorable to avoid the following forms of association with the unfavorable: giving and/or accepting gifts; offering and/or accepting foodstuffs; hearing and/or disclosing intimate matters. He stated that untouchability in terms of caste was a phenomenon that had developed in Hindu society for historical reasons.

In order to fight against untouchability, Bhaktisiddhānta suggested the ethics of "unconditional reverence for all entities by the realization and exclusive practice of the whole-time service of the Absolute."[191] The practice of divine love and service to the absolute implied moral responsibility toward all conscious beings—human and nonhuman alike. In his view, however, this responsibility did not primarily involve immediate concern for their material welfare; rather, it involved ultimate concern for their spiritual status and well-being.

For Bhaktisiddhānta, the problem of the untouchables as defined by Gandhi was a secular and/or a national issue, but not a truly religious one. He wrote that "Hinduism" itself was a secular idea created to accommodate social and political issues within a religious frame. He was skeptical of the uncritical identification of religious revival with humanitarian ideals, a tendency that was derived from the conditioning of liberal colonial education. According to Papia Chakravarty, this identification had greatly affected the shaping of Hindu nationalism and the assessment of the socioreligious condition of India.[192] Nonetheless, while Bhaktisiddhānta

---

189. *Harmonist* 30, no. 7 (January 1933): pp. 203–209.

190. *Harmonist* 30, no. 7 (January 1933): p. 203.

191. *Harmonist* 30, no. 7 (January 1933): p. 205.

192. Papia Chakravarty, *Hindu Response to Nationalist Ferment, Bengal, 1909–1935* (Calcutta: Subarnarekha, 1992), p. 226.

chalked a path that went beyond nationalist discourse, he also advocated a purification of the nation from within, and a recovery and reinstatement of its religious traditions. This indirectly contributed to a cohesive national identity, although it was not at all related to a particular political agenda.

Outreach: Language, Press, and Education

Bhaktisiddhānta possessed a style of writing and speaking that was at once concise and archaic—to a degree that appeared out of step with his time. His teachings were based on sacred texts that he had memorized through many years of study. Along the way he had developed the tendency to consider various philosophical issues in terms of dichotomous categories such as *bhajanānandī* and *ghoṣṭhānandī*, *saviśeṣa* and *nirviśeṣa*, *pāñcarātrika* and *bhāgavata*.[193] He believed that any positive statement becomes clearer if it is contrasted with a negative one, and he illustrated many of his ideas through the presentation of opposing views.[194] His mode of presentation was rational and straightforward, without any concession to poetic or literary aesthetics, almost as if it might have been influenced by his early involvement with mathematics and astronomy. His mastery of Vaishnava philosophy allowed him to refine his choice of words, and he explicitly aimed at bringing the tradition's key terms back to what he viewed as their pristine metaphysical meaning.[195] The intensity and concision of his thought, as well as his desire to present things without adulteration, may explain why he generally made no attempt to adjust his language to the audience. While on occasion he would go so far as to apologize for his

---

193. In an article in the *Gauḍīya*, Bhaktisiddhānta suggested that the Mādhva *sampradāya* is subdivided in *Dāsakūṭa* and *Vyāsakūṭa*. The former group is sometimes referred as *bhajanānandī*, and is more interested in ritual worship and meditation, while the latter is sometimes referred as *ghoṣṭhānandī*, and is more focused on learning and teaching the Sanskrit literature of the *sampradāya*. Bhaktisiddhānta adopted this distinction, particularly identifying with the *ghoṣṭhānandī*. *Gauḍīya* 6, no. 14 (1927): p. 13.

194. He wrote that "the truth (satya) is propagated in a two-fold way viz.—positively or by the method of direct support and negatively or the method of opposition . . . the truth cannot be made sufficiently known by the positive method alone," *Harmonist* 25, no. 1 (June 1927): pp. 5–6.

195. Bhaktisiddhānta Sarasvatī, *Vaiṣṇava-Mañjuṣā Samahṛti* (Calcutta: Śrī Gaudiya Math, 1922), vol. 1, pp. i–iv. See also the attempt in the *Harmonist* to create a specific English vocabulary for the translation of Vaishnava words like *līlā* and *rasa* that have no English equivalents. *Harmonist* 31, no. 1 (September 1934): pp. 22–23.

abstruse language, in most such cases his presentation was nonetheless considered impressive and thought provoking, if a bit unusual.[196] There were also times that he would request disciples to speak on his behalf.

Francis Yeats-Brown, the author of the well-known *Bengal Lancer* (1930), wrote of a personal encounter with Bhaktisiddhānta in *Lancer at Large* (1936). His recollection of that meeting, which occurred in the mid-1930s, is fully reproduced below:

> The cult of Kṛṣṇa is a pure and exalted doctrine; but I must confess that as explained by the publications of the Gaudiya math it is extremely complex: the most difficult that my poor brain has ever attempted to grasp. For instance, the President of the Math said in a lecture to his disciples: "The undesirable imperfection observed in the temporal relativity of Nature should not be carried to an unknown region where there is no such anthropomorphic ephemeral defective welcoming. The weight of such measuring temperament would prove too heavy to be carried by the feeble porter with mundane relative reasons. Moreover, there is the warranty of exact dovetailing in the Transcendental Vacuum." And again: "We need to explain that nescience is the cause of a deceptive idea of variety. Though our present mental cavity is ready to accommodate analogical exploitation, we must not anthropomorphise these frail ideas to the transcendence. Our comprehension will be plenary if we think that the transitory objective and subjective entities, transactions, and associations, are prevented from having an approach to the transcendence. This particular mentality can be counted as a particular phase of hallucination, apart from the real existence of the manifestive nature of the transcendence." A meaning there is. I think it can be put roughly thus: that the ordinary brain cannot distinguish between the various planes of existence, and that special methods are required to develop the special senses of the mystic. I give the extracts above in no rebellious spirit. Their writer is an athlete of the Undifferentiated Absolute who is preaching the old lesson that there are more things in Heaven and earth than are dreamt of in our mundane philosophies. Indeed, I find his

196. For example in a 1936 speech he stated that "the Bengali language, such as I command, is not easy... [I] do not know whether it will be intelligible to all." *Harmonist* 32, no. 14 (March 1936): p. 313.

> expositions stimulating, although I do not profess to understand them fully. Nowadays we are fed with too much pre-digested literary pap. Meaning is so minced-up and spiced that it can be assimilated while listening to the radio. This is a pity. For a change, it is a relief to bite on something hard.[197]

With his unorthodox language, Bhaktisiddhānta forced both readers and listeners to avoid predigested semantic associations. Ordinary words evoked habitual responses, but what was taken for granted could become fresh and vivid by means of uncommon metaphors and novel linguistic associations.

The production and distribution of various texts in Bengali, Sanskrit, Oriya, and other languages was a primary task for Bhaktisiddhānta. It is difficult to estimate how many pieces of literature were printed and sold by the Gaudiya Math, since no detailed account has thus far been discovered for either its periodicals or its other publications. However, the files of a legal case that began after Bhaktisiddhānta's passing provide some indication in this regard. According to those files, the yearly 1930s figure for periodicals was approximately 60,000 and the yearly 1930s figure for books was approximately 9,000.[198]

Like most of his *bhadralok* contemporaries, Bhaktisiddhānta understood the link between education and social and cultural empowerment, especially for the laity. In keeping with this understanding, he founded the Bhaktivinoda Institute in Mayapur on April 3, 1931—a school that attempted to combine secular with religious education. Although the school's teachers were affiliated with the Gaudiya Math, it received government support and was officially linked to Calcutta University, which administered the entrance examination to qualified students. At its peak the Bhaktivinoda Institute boasted an enrollment of 700 students, each of whom received instruction in both secular subjects and the philosophy and practice of Caitanya bhakti.[199]

---

197. Francis Yeats Brown, *Lancer at Large* (London: Victor Gollancz, 1936). I would like to thank Shaunaka Rishi for alerting me to this passage.

198. See "*Testamentary Suit no. 2 of 1938* in the High Court of Juricature at Fort William in Bengal." Kuñjabihārī Vidyābhūṣaṇa, who for many years was the head manager of the Gaudiya Math, testified that the sales figures for all four math presses amounted to 600 rupees per month for periodicals and 400 rupees per month for books. Bhaktisiddhānta's personal secretary Ananta Vāsudeva, on the other hand, testified as to a lower sales figure of 500 rupees per month for periodicals and 100 rupees per month for books.

199. Sambidananda Das, "History and Literature," ch. 13, p. 84.

Critical Voices

From a review of his articles and letters (at least those that are available), it is apparent that Bhaktisiddhānta spoke at considerable length about the decadence of most contemporary Vaishnava practitioners, and spared little ammunition in pointing out their alleged falsehoods and deviations.[200] In this regard, he self-consciously struggled to revive what he believed to be the lost religious core of his tradition—that is, the applicability of Krishna's personal devotional service to the ultimate satisfaction of every individual living being. Thus his writings and speeches often presented a strong challenge to those who stood in opposition to this core understanding.[201] Madhusūdana Sarasvatī, the prominent caste Goswami of Vrindavan mentioned earlier, was among those who supported him, but most of the *brāhmaṇa* clans in Bengal and Vrindavan severely criticized him for departing from hereditary *brāhmaṇism,* and for being a *kāyastha* who took it upon himself to initiate *brāhmaṇas.* Many attempted to invalidate his own initiation by pointing out that it may not have been formalized in the appropriate manner. Bhaktisiddhānta's presentation of a line of succession of gurus based on teachings (*śikṣā*) rather than formal initiation (*dīkṣā*) was in line with his position that *bhāgavata vidhi* was more important than *pāñcarātrika vidhi,* but it generated many protests. Some attempted to discredit his *saṃnyāsa* status, noting that he preferred to confer this upon himself rather than receive it from an established *sampradāya,* which was the traditional custom.[202] For this and other reasons, a lifelong breach was created between Bhaktisiddhānta and the religious orthodoxy of Vrindavan and Nabadwip (as well as other parts of India), despite the fact that he basically adhered to traditional forms of knowledge acquisition and practice.

---

200. See for example *Gauḍīya* 1, no. 12 (1922): pp. 1–2, "*Cyutagotra*" (the clan of the devious).

201. An example of apologetics is Bhaktisiddhānta Sarasvatī and Gauragovinda Vidyābhūṣaṇa, eds., *Pratīpa priyanāthera praśnera pratyuttara* (Calcutta: Bhaktivinoda Āsana, n.d). The booklet was a response to questions posed by Priyanātha Nandi, editor of the monthly periodical *Śrī Kṛṣṇacaitanyatattva Pracārika.* Priyanātha had questioned the legitimacy of a guru such as Bhaktisiddhānta, who was a non-*brāhmaṇa* and did not comply with orthodox (*smārta*) customs and rituals.

202. Stuart Mark Elkman and Jiva Gosvami, *Jiva Gosvamin's Tattvasandarbha: A Study on the Philosophical and Sectarian Development of the Gaudiya Vaisnava Movement* (Delhi: Motilal Banarsidass, 1986), p. 186. Elkman suggests that *saṃnyāsa* was an invention of Bhaktivinoda and Bhaktisiddhānta, but there is no evidence that Bhaktivinoda ever directly mentioned *saṃnyāsa* as a possibility for his developing movement, although he did advocate *varṇāśrama.*

Outside the Vaishnava fold, some among the *bhadralok* were critical of the fact that he used motorcars and printing presses, and constructed large temple complexes, all of which went against the traditional image of a renounced *saṃnyāsin*.[203] From a more humanist-secular vantage point, liberal modernists were disturbed by Bhaktisiddhānta's upfront textual literalism, preferring a historico-critical approach instead. Above all, few were open to the kind of transnational bhakti that he actively pursued.

In a somewhat humorous essay entitled "Real and Apparent," Bhaktisiddhānta sardonically reviewed the manner in which his movement was perceived by contemporaries. Vaishnavism was considered immoral, emasculating, and too feminine; it was also thought to be irrational and averse to the "most elementary needs of advanced material civilization."[204] He notes that most

> are not likely to accept a creed which may be suspected of a partiality for sexuality, passivism, childish ceremonial and credulity and which declares all secular effort whether moral, social, political, or philanthropic as utterly powerless for the amelioration of the lot of man nay which regards them as the root-cause of all the troubles that afflict this miserable world.[205]

Bhaktisiddhānta nonetheless proceeded to address these challenges with vigor. In his periodicals he responded to outside challenges through articles written by him or his disciples.

A new kind of mastery was required to deal with the complexities of modern society, but he cautioned that "mastery over Nature was attainable

---

203. One example is the article "Ascetism and Ascetics" by Umesa Candra Bhattacarya, who wrote in the *Prabasi*: "In the history of the world, everywhere we can see ascetics leaving the vices of women and gold. But many modern maths and hermitages do not leave women and are not averse to wealth. I know the owners of many hermitages who have kept a lot of money in the bank; one gets more than one thousand in interest from company papers. Apart from this, some have a large *zamindari* [land property]. And many own big buildings. I have protested that it is not according to the ideal of ascetism.... In reply one has let me remember that so many people live in buildings in the city, why should I not say anything about it? I have no objection if a rich man enjoys the property earned by himself or inherited, because there is no fakeness in it. But a saffron-wearing person will meditate on the *Pranava* (oṃ) before his disciples every morning and evening, and in private will count the cash with his treasurer; it is not simple living. It may harm the society. So I protest" (1936, p. 842).

204. Bhaktisiddhānta, *Shri Chaitanya's Teachings*, p. 444.

205. Bhaktisiddhānta, *Shri Chaitanya's Teachings*, p. 445.

only for the purpose of serving Godhead and not for selfish enjoyment."[206] He used automobiles (figure B.6) and telegraphs, broadcasted on the radio, and kept up with the news in the daily press. He also kept abreast of the latest developments in science and technology, in search of those that could be employed in the service of his mission.

The fine line that Bhaktisiddhānta trod between preservation and renewal involved the risk that the Gaudiya Math could be misunderstood and rejected by traditionalists and modernists alike. While this may superficially appear to have been the case—that is, that tradition and modernity, East and West, mixed freely in Bhaktisiddhānta's approach—such a conclusion does not, in my view, acknowledge the third space that he carved out for himself: that of being conceptually and theologically traditional on the one hand, and being practically and institutionally modern on the other. In this way, he carved an intermediate space for his movement within the ranks of the *bhadralok*, which ultimately attracted those who were looking for a way to practice Vaishnavism in modern times.[207]

The 1930s marked a new phase in Bhaktisiddhānta's life. India was still at the periphery of the empire, Britain at the center, and the time seemed ideal for the fulfillment of his long-standing desire to bridge the gap between Caitanya Vaishnavism and the West. The details of his attempt to do so, which ultimately boosted his mission in India, will be covered in the following chapter.

Final Days

On March 8, 1936, on the anniversary of Caitanya's birth, Bhaktisiddhānta was pleased to be informed that a Gaudiya Math center had been established in Rangoon, Burma, with the help of the minister of education.[208] On the morning of December 23, 1936, some of Bhaktisiddhānta's leading disciples traveled from Cuttack to enquire about their guru's health. At

206. Bhaktisiddhānta, *Shri Chaitanya's Teachings*, p. 452.

207. In this regard, it may be tempting to reduce Bhaktisiddhānta's approach to a sort of *hybridity*, to borrow a concept from Homi Bhabha, meaning in this case the pursuance of cultural authority by deforming colonial systems of knowledge through the medium of native ideas. However, as has been shown above, this was not the case. See Homi K. Bhabha, *The Location of Culture* (London: Routledge, 2004), p. 164.

208. *Gauḍīya*, 15, nos. 23–24 (January 16, 1937): p. 38.

that time, Bhaktisiddhānta instructed Kuñjabihārī Vidyābhūṣaṇa to function as the general manager of the Gaudiya Math for the remainder of his life, and requested his disciples give him full support, as well as respect his personal secretary Ananta Vāsudeva, who was one of the main editors of his publications. Moreover, he instructed that ten to twelve senior disciples should form a governing committee to manage all aspects of his movement. Finally, he reminded all the members of his mission not to quarrel with each other (figure C.1). Then, at 5:30 AM on January 1, 1937, Bhaktisiddhānta passed away. His demise was reported by a number of daily newspapers in India, giving some indication as to the level of significance he had achieved.[209]

The Will

The events immediately following Bhaktisiddhānta's demise led to a schism and had a pivotal impact in the future course of the Gaudiya Math. Because of this, and because they shed some light on the strength and weakness of Bhaktisiddhānta's movement, they are briefly summarized herein. Although devastating to Bhaktisiddhānta's cause both then and for a good bit of time thereafter, they indirectly paved the way for its expansion during the second half of the twentieth century.

One cause of the schism was the legal status of the Gaudiya Math. As has been noted earlier, Bhaktisiddhānta never registered his movement as a legal entity; thus it remained solely linked to his name and personal leadership, without the advantage of a formalized structure that could succeed him. This omission may have had its roots in Bhaktisiddhānta's own reservations about the institutionalization of bhakti. He was moreover convinced that a genuine spiritual leader is "self-effulgent," meaning that he naturally emerges as a result of his good qualities and exalted state of consciousness; thus he avoided appointing a successor, or calling upon his followers to do so by vote. This created a certain ambiguity, as many in the movement expected that a charismatic person would rise to replace Bhaktisiddhānta as the spiritual head of the institution.

209. See for example "Leader of Bengal Vaishnavism—A Tribute to the Memory of Late Bhakti Siddhant Saraswati," *Bombay Chronicle*, January 24, 1937.

Weeks after Bhaktisiddhānta passed away a crisis of succession ensued between two rival factions, each one headed by a leading disciple: one was centered on Ananta Vāsudeva, who had been elected by majority vote as the new successor (*ācārya*) at a general meeting in Mayapur; the other was led by Kuñjabihārī Vidyābhūṣaṇa, who initially went along with this vote, but contested it thereafter by filing a case with the Calcutta High Court. His aim was to divide the Gaudiya Math properties between the two groups. To this end he produced a signed 1923 testament in which Bhaktisiddhānta had appointed three fiduciaries to manage all his ancestral and acquired assets. Kuñjabihārī Vidyābhūṣaṇa was one of those fiduciaries, and in that capacity pleaded for a division of the institution. The files of this case are historically significant because they provide detailed documentation of the affairs of Bhaktisiddhānta's movement shortly after his demise, and put many of his ideas to the test.

Ananta Vāsudeva argued that as an ascetic *saṃnyāsin* Bhaktisiddhānta never conceived of himself as the owner of the Gaudiya Math, and that the institution thus belonged to his disciples, who had elected Ananta Vāsudeva successor by majority vote. For his part, Kuñjabihārī Vidyābhūṣaṇa argued that as the uncontested leader of the institution Bhaktisiddhānta did indeed own the properties and that his will should be considered the final word on the dispute. He then presented one that had been written by Bhaktisiddhānta on May 18, 1923, in connection with a hernia operation whose outcome had been uncertain (figure C.2).[210] The document contained detailed instructions about how to dispose of his paternal and acquired assets. In this will, Bhaktisiddhānta stated that as a *saṃnyāsin* he had used all his properties in the service of God and in the service of the Sri Caitanya Math images in Mayapur, and requested that his assets continue to be used in that way. The will stated that

> For the purpose that all the provisions of this my will may be carried into effect, I appoint my three *sishyas* [disciples] Sriyukta Paramananda Brahmachari, Sriyukta Kunjabehari Dasa adhikari Bidyabhusan (Rakshak—Protector—of Gaudiya Math), and Sriyukta Ananta Basudeb Brahmachari the executors. All of them jointly or

210. The will had been dictated and was handwritten in the Bengali language. Each page was signed by Bhaktisiddhānta as "Bimala Prasad Bhaktisiddhanta Sarasvati," as well as by a witness, Ram Gopal Dutt. It was translated and approved by the High Court, which regarded it as authentic; see appendix B.

> any one of them, after taking out the probate of this will, after my death shall carry into effect all the directions in this my will.... All my executors shall act in agreement with one another. In the event of any difference of opinion among them, the opinion of the majority of the executors shall prevail and acts shall be performed in accordance therewith.[211]

Regarding the possibility that the above may not be workable, the will stated that

> if none of the executors takes out the probate or if all of them die, then he who will be appointed the *sebait* or manager of my said Math by the consent of the majority of my *sishyas* meeting together shall be competent to preserve and look after as the *sebait*, the said Math, and the properties [to be] left by me according to the aforesaid provisions. But if that *sebait* be [found] unfit on any ground my *sishyas* shall be competent to discharge him and appoint another *sebait*, in the manner stated above.[212]

Significantly, the will made no mention of a specific guru-successor, recommending instead that affairs be managed by a board of executors. Among other things, this indicates that Bhaktisiddhānta was open to the idea of consensus on institutional matters and aware of the tentative nature of decision making—that is, that decisions could be amended and/or altered in the course of time. His will also included wording that addressed the possibility that some might change their role within the Math or choose to abandon present duties. It also hinted at a democratic system, in the sense that if the appointed executor was found lacking in any way, he could be removed by majority vote. The community of disciples, both the monastic *saṅga* and the laity, was to be the final authority. This reflected the acceptance of modern institutional structures and the importance of critical thinking in decision making.

Years of legal battling finally ended in 1942 when the court appointed three members of the Gaudiya Math to act as fiduciaries relative to

211. "Calcutta High Court Archive. *Testamentary Suit no. 2 of 1938*," doc. nr. 20: Draft nr. 32990 (554 Testy) of Will with Bengali handwritten text.

212. "Calcutta High Court Archive, *Testamentary Suit no. 2 of* 1938," doc. nr. 20.

Bhaktisiddhānta's properties. Prior to this, in 1940, Ananta Vāsudeva registered the Gaudiya Math as a nonprofit organization called the Gaudiya Mission so as to prevent any one individual from privately owning any part of the institution (figure C.3). The disputants divided the assets between these two institutions—that is, the Gaudiya Mission led by Ananta Vāsudeva and the Sri Caitanya Math led by Kuñjabihārī Vidyābhūṣaṇa. These assets comprised more than sixty Gaudiya Maths in India, one in London, and various properties in Bengal and Jagannath Puri.

The final legal division of the Gaudiya Math occurred in 1947. In the process, however, the momentum created by Bhaktisiddhānta during the 1920s and 1930s had been lost, and the reputation of the Gaudiya Math had suffered. Bhaktisiddhānta had been well aware of the tensions that existed among certain sections of his disciples, and in an almost prophetic 1935 interview with Shyamasundar Chakravarty was reported to have said:

> God is the shelter of all. He sends many obstacles and inconveniences to those who wish for shelter under Him, in order to test their ardour and steadiness.[213]

For insiders, the schism was a test of faith. Historically, it was a routinization of Bhaktisiddhānta's charisma, formalized through the division of the Gaudiya Math. Despite its deleterious effects, the schism indirectly and unexpectedly led to something new several decades later: the significant expansion of Bhaktisiddhānta's teachings throughout the world. This will be more thoroughly addressed in chapter 5.

Summary

This chapter has depicted the life and work of Bhaktisiddhānta Sarasvatī, as well as the development of his modern religious movement, the Gaudiya Math. From his father Bhaktivinoda, Bhaktisiddhānta learned the advantages of a strong literary background, an organized institutional effort, and making the *bhadralok* and the laity the financial backbone of his religious movement. He also inherited the universal vision of the Caitanya Vaishnava tradition, the doctrines of which he linked to the Vaishnava lines of South India. This was reflected in the literary output of the Gaudiya

213. Bhaktisiddhānta, *Shri Chaitanya's Teachings*, pp. 296–297.

Math, which, in addition to the works of Caitanya Vaishnavism, included the classical works of these traditions.

While maintaining strict adherence to the sacred medieval texts of Caitanya Vaishnavism, Bhaktisiddhānta simultaneously introduced important social, religious, and institutional innovations that placed him at loggerheads with the Vaishnava orthodoxy of his time. Bhaktisiddhānta worked to represent the understandings and practices of Caitanya Vaishnavism in a way that would make them interesting to the modern mind, and did so at a time when India's most popular social, political, and intellectual trends ran counter to the perspective he upheld.

The development of a multilingual press made Bhaktisiddhānta's ideas accessible to larger strata of the Hindu intelligentsia, both within and outside Bengal. He utilized modern means of publication, printing, transportation, and distribution, all of which were instrumental to the success of his movement. Bhaktisiddhānta's publication of Caitanya Vaishnavism's classic medieval texts is indicative of his intention to retain core elements of his tradition that went back to the time of Caitanya. Rather than choosing between the apparent opposites of Hindu "traditionalism" and "modernism," Bhaktisiddhānta chose to explore the capabilities and compatibilities of both, forging a new alternative path of his own. After spending fourteen years developing the Gaudiya Math in India, and opening centers in both the north and the south, Bhaktisiddhānta carried his message westward to Europe. The nature and scope of that venture will be discussed in the following chapter.

3

Bhakti Universalist

THIS CHAPTER EXPLORES what is arguably Bhaktisiddhānta's most enduring legacy: his conviction that Westerners could seriously embrace the teachings of Caitanya Vaishnavism, and his unprecedented attempt to spread those teachings beyond the shores of India. In this regard, the religio-philosophical and practical reasons for this venture will be examined, as will the Gaudiya Math's most significant encounters with the West.

Turmoil in Eurasia

Throughout the world, the period between 1874 and 1937 was a time of tremendous social, cultural, and technological achievement, but it was also a time of horrific political upheaval as well. At the beginning of this period the concept of "modernity" had captured the imagination of the British public, conveying a vast range of meanings, from a breaking with the past to the promise of endless progress.[1] It reflected an optimism born of the fact that the nineteenth century belonged to the industrial and technological superiority of Great Britain.[2] After all, by 1914 the British shipping industry had managed to established a line of commerce that spanned the entire globe and was fully backed by London's great financial and banking institutions; by this time, Great Britain controlled 40 percent of global shipping, while Germany, its closest competitor, controlled only 10 percent.

---

1. Martin J. Daunton and Bernhard Rieger, *Meanings of Modernity: Britain from the Late-Victorian Era to World War 2* (Oxford: Berg, 2001), p. 3.

2. Karl Polanyi, *The Great Transformation: The Political and Economic Origins of Our Time* (Boston: Beacon Press, 2001), p. 32.

Before this, in 1902, the laying of a transpacific communications cable that linked Vancouver, Queensland, and New Zealand marked the culmination of a project that began in the late nineteenth century with the laying of similar cables from London to Newfoundland on the Canadian coast, and from London to Wellington, Melbourne, and Bombay in the East. This important global network enabled merchants to be in direct contact with their sources of supply, allowing for the sale of commodities such as tea and cotton prior to their being shipped. By 1911 Britain also had established direct communications with Cyprus, Hong Kong, and Bombay through the medium of imperial wireless stations.[3]

In 1939 Britain's colonial domains encompassed 23.9 percent of the earth's surface (or 13,100,000 square miles), and comprised a total population of 470,000,000 persons.[4] Railways, agricultural production, shipping, and military might were the foundations of the empire; and among all of its vast and fabulous possessions, none could be compared, either in size, value, or quantity of riches, to India—the "jewel in the crown":

> At the turn of the century India had a territorial scope "Greater than the Roman Empire" of 1,802,629 square miles (a subcontinent equal in size to Europe minus Russia), and a population, according to official statistics, of 294,361,056 (India alone in 1900 had a population nearly five times that of the entire French colonial empire). India was administered by fewer than 1,000 covenanted members of the Indian Civil Service, almost exclusively British.... The Indian Army, with a core of 150,000 troops, made Britain the great military power in the East in the early years of the century. India bore the cost of an additional British garrison comprising 75,000 men, one-third of the British army. The Indian Army itself, supported by British sea power, could deploy troops throughout maritime Asia.... Indian revenues served as a guarantee for British investments in the subcontinent, especially in the immense Indian rail network, already the largest rail system in Asia.[5]

---

3. William Roger Louis, "Introduction," in *The Oxford History of the British Empire: The Twentieth Century*, ed. Judith M. Brown and William Roger Louis (Oxford: Oxford University Press, 2001), p. 5.

4. Mary Evelyn Townsend and Walter Consuelo Langsam, *European Colonial Expansion since 1871* (Chicago: J. B. Lippincott, 1941), p. 19.

5. Louis, "Introduction," pp. 5–7.

Indeed the Raj was considered so important to the empire that it was represented in the British Cabinet by its own secretary of state and governed by a specially appointed "viceroy" that managed its colonial affairs.

Then the "Great War" (1914–1918) came, shocking Britain, Germany, and their allies with the brutality of industrial warfare and marking the beginning of the decline of Europe's global hegemony. Both the Triple Entente and the Central Powers went to war with confidence and enthusiasm, believing their national causes to be just; but the war that was waged in the trenches of Belgium, northern Italy, and the eastern front ended with the loss of almost an entire generation of Europeans. In addition, a half million Indian soldiers had been drafted to fight alongside the British at different times throughout the conflict, and of these, approximately 60,000 lost their lives either on the western front or in the Middle East.[6] The participation of such a large number of Indian soldiers served to establish a profound connection between India and Europe, the scope of which had never been seen before. In 1919 a cessation of hostilities was finally achieved with the Treaty of Versailles, and life went back to a normality that was both deceptively calm and strikingly superficial; the peace, as is now well known, had not resolved a variety of issues, leaving the Central Powers bitter and dissatisfied, with wounds that would not heal. During the interwar years that followed, national romanticism gained strength in both Germany and Italy, combining imperialistic visions with a fascination for technology and machines.

In India, both during and after World War I, the impact of globalization was increasingly evident as the laying of railways and telegraphs across the subcontinent revolutionized communications. On the other hand, the financial repercussions of the war had been hard, and famine, disease, and economic depression created waves of unrest and dissatisfaction.[7] It was at this time that Indian nationalists began a sustained struggle for political emancipation through the *ahiṃsa* movement of Gandhi, the activism of both the Muslim League and the Congress Party, and the militantism of Subash Chandra Bose, who planned to ignite an armed war of independence. Prewar colonial policies had already spread discontent among the *bhadralok*, and in the interim years between the two wars the situation

---

6. Sugata Bose and Ayesha Jalal, *Modern South Asia: History, Culture, Political Economy* (London: Routledge, 1998), p. 127.

7. Bose and Jalal, *Modern South Asia*, p. 127.

continued to decline, as did relations between Hindus and Muslims. During this same period most regions of Eurasia were experiencing turmoil, upheaval, and transformations of their own. Imperialistic Japan had attacked China, Indochina had embarked upon a bitter campaign against French rule, and the Communists had begun to challenge capitalism on a global scale. In addition, the ideal of a modern egalitarian state had spread to the colonies through Western education, weakening colonial claims of European racial and political superiority.

While the climate in the United States during the second decade of the twentieth century was generally optimistic, Europe struggled to resolve a staggering crisis, brought about, for the most part, by the dissolution of the Ottoman Empire, Austria-Hungary, and the royal house of Germany. Unrest also increased in the East as Communist rule consolidated itself in Russia, the largest of the old Entente Powers. Amid all these difficulties Europe labored in vain to recover its economy and establish a working political and economic order. After an initial stage of apparent protectionism, the combined effects of Versailles's compensation demands and the Great Depression of 1929 created fertile soil for the rise of Nazism, soon to become the most formidable challenge to the status of Britain, her colonies, and her dependences in the global political scene. Meanwhile Great Britain had withdrawn into herself to assuage her grief and recover from the shock of the "war to end all wars." During this period, the adoption by the empire of a policy of economic protectionism and political laissez-faire led to the negotiation of new levels of self-government in India.

Crises in Bengal

At the end of the nineteenth century, the general optimism of the Bengali intelligentsia toward the project of the Raj was gradually replaced by a fresh wave of regionalism, nationalism, and anti-imperialism, and the spirit of religious innovation that had so infused certain sections of the *bhadralok* dampened in the face of increased political turmoil.[8] In 1911, the capital of the Raj was transferred from Calcutta to Delhi, and Bengal lost its paramount role in India's cultural and political life, having to share leadership with the north and the west. One outcome of this shift in power was the reduced migration of Bengali civil servants to other parts of India,

8. Raychaudhuri, *Perceptions, Emotions, Sensibilities*, p. 17.

something that in the nineteenth century had facilitated the spreading of movements like the Brahmo Samaj. Despite these setbacks, Bengal nonetheless remained "the center of the Hindu religious renaissance of the . . . early twentieth century" through the contributions of giants such as Tagore, Aurobindo, and Vivekānanda.[9] Several new religious movements emerged as well, but few had either the strength or the resources to establish themselves in other parts of India.[10]

Turbulence in Bengal, however, was linked not only to Indian dissatisfaction with colonial rule, but also to the cumulative impact of its religious and social history on Hindu-Muslim relations. In this regard, the religious divide between Hindus and Muslims was dangerously intertwined with a system of class stratification that left the Muslim peasant majority under the control of a minority of *bhadralok* landlords and administrators, which the peasants increasingly resented. The Cornwallis Code of 1793 inaugurated a series of extensive ownership laws that during the nineteenth and early twentieth century increased the revenues of these landlords, but also inadvertently created a set of circumstances that eventually caused upheaval and discontent among the Muslim peasant class. The resultant increase of tensions between the landowners and their Muslim workers led to a series of recurring uprisings that greatly destabilized the region. As Hindus and Muslims began looking upon each other with greater and greater enmity

9. Knut A. Jacobsen and P. Pratap Kumar, *South Asians in the Diaspora: Histories and Religious Traditions* (Leiden: Brill, 2004), p. 338.

10. Benoy Gopal Ray, *Religious Movements in Modern Bengal* (Santiniketan: Visva-Bharati Research Publications, 1965). Ray has examined a number of the religious movements and gurus that existed in Bengal during the nineteenth and first half of the twentieth century. He concludes that among these, only the Ramakrishna Mission and the Brahmo Samaj were genuine mass movements, in the sense that they directly or indirectly influenced most of the population of prepartition Bengal (p. 4). Ray also makes mention of the Gaudiya Math (pp. 64–65), the Bharat Sevashram Sangha of Praṇavānanda Swami (pp. 125–127), and the Hindu Mission (p. 131) as religious movements that managed to amass considerable followings and establish their presence in other parts of India. Ānandamayī Mā (1896–1982), or "Joy Permeated Mother," was one of a range of Bengali gurus that are said to have traversed India and attracted a significant number of followers; see also Lisa Lassell Hallstrom, *Mother of Bliss: Anandamayi Ma (1896–1982)* (New York: Oxford University Press, 1999). While Ray's overview is fairly comprehensive, it falls short of being complete (p. vi). It should be noted that among all the religious movements founded in Bengal during the colonial period, only the Ramakrishna Mission and the Gaudiya Math (in its various contemporary forms) continue to maintain a significant institutional presence outside of India. Two other Bengali-rooted religious organizations were globally active during the colonial period: (1) the Self-realization Fellowship, founded in North America in 1920 by Paramahaṃsa Yogānanda (1893–1952); and, (2) the Śrī Aurobindo Aśrama, founded in Pondicherry in 1926 by Śrī Aurobindo (1872–1950).

and distrust, the response of various Muslim organizations was to directly approach London to strike deals for separate electorates in Bengal and Punjab, where Muslims held a popular majority. In this way, religious and class divides combined with a political system that disenfranchised Muslim majority populations to create an extremely volatile situation that finally exploded in 1947—but that is getting a bit ahead of our story.[11]

The point of the above historical account is to provide a bit of international context, and more importantly to show that at the time that Bhaktisiddhānta was attempting to establish Caitanya Vaishnavism in Bengal, the societal milieu was extremely disturbed by nationalistic reactions to British rule on the one hand, and the challenges brought about by religious communalism, political unrest, and economic turmoil on the other.[12] Under these circumstances, the local population was first and foremost concerned with economic and sociopolitical upliftment, and gradually came to resent the God-centered teachings of the Gaudiya Math, considering them to be "too otherworldly" and "out of step" with the pressing material needs of the time. As mentioned earlier, in September 1931, after a devastating flood had left countless Bengalis homeless and starving, an article appeared in the *Amrita Bazar Patrika* that criticized the decision of the Gaudiya Math to expend thousands of rupees on a "theistic exhibition" at a time that "millions of... brothers and sisters" were "pining for want of relief."[13]

Clearly this and other unfavorable turns of events weighed in Bhaktisiddhānta's 1933 decision to send disciples to Britain and Germany—the primary subject of this chapter. A successful westward venture at this time held out the strong possibility of rekindling interest and respectability at home. Apart from this, the time was strategically ripe for another reason as well. Recent advancements in transportation and information technologies had served to bring Bengal and Europe closer together, thus paving the way for the Gaudiya Math's foray west.[14] In other words, the inauguration

---

11. Joya Chatterji, *The Spoils of Partition: Bengal and India, 1947–1967* (Cambridge: Cambridge University Press, 2007), p. 7.

12. The British attempted to quiet the unrest caused by the nationalist movement by allowing for self-government at the regional level; in this way they hoped to forestall a broader, pan-Indian, drive for sovereignty.

13. From the article entitled "A Protest Meeting" found in the *Amrita Bazar Patrika*, September 6, 1931.

14. Even a cursory reading of the Calcutta newspapers of that period, such as the *Bengalee*, shows that events in Europe were discussed in detail, as they directly affected India's economic and political situation.

of a mission to Europe in 1933 was a plausible way to gain a fresh start and invigorate the movement in Bengal during a period that was difficult in India and simultaneously advantageous for a mission to the West. Once made known, the European mission became a matter of considerable institutional pride, receiving wide coverage in all Gaudiya Math publications.

It is here important to note that these circumstantial, strategic, and more externally driven considerations remained ancillary to the fundamental philosophical and theological understandings that informed and ultimately actuated Bhaktisiddhānta's desire to spread the teachings of Caitanya Vaishnavism beyond the shores of India; these understandings had been embedded in the medieval teachings of Caitanya and his immediate followers, elaborately expressed in the visions and writings of Bhaktivinoda and held by Bhaktisiddhānta long before Indian nationalism had reached its peak, and long before Bengal's social, cultural, and political fabric had dangerously unraveled. The following sections consist of an exploration of these core notions, as will a good deal of the material found in chapter 4.

Turning to the West

As the crises in Europe deepened, Bhaktisiddhānta's mission to the West began to take shape. The crises in the world order had coincided with the growth of the Gaudiya Math in India, which Bhaktisiddhānta believed was a way to move beyond regional parochial concerns. His vision was that bhakti as devotion to the "Personality of Godhead" could flow from East to West in the shape of a universal theism, since "Sri Ramanuja and Sri Ananda Tirtha have strongly refuted Shankara's theory."[15] As he understood it, bhakti went beyond even claims to human exclusivism, and extended to animal and vegetal species as well. In 1927 he wrote:

> The Lord desires His word to be preached to all living beings. The Harmonist [a periodical of the Gaudiya Math in English] stands for this desire. She cherishes the faith that a day will come when His word will be preached everywhere all over the world through the medium of all the languages, including the language of animals and plants, when this will be practicable.[16]

---

15. *Gauḍīya* 16, no. 18 (1936): p. 299. Ānanda Tīrtha is another name of Mādhva.

16. *Harmonist* 25, no. 1 (June 1927): p. 5.

In other words, because Bhaktisiddhānta believed that consciousness is an inherent attribute of the atman, he considered that even nonhuman species could partake of divine association through exposure to the spiritual sound vibration of the names of Krishna. For him the writings of Bhaktivinoda contained the seed that could promote a change of consciousness on a global scale. In 1931 he wrote:

> That day is not far distant when the priceless volumes penned by Ṭhākura Bhaktivinoda will be reverently translated...into all the languages of the world. As soon as the sympathetic reader is in a position to appreciate the sterling quality of Ṭhākura Bhaktivinoda's philosophy the entire vista of the revealed literatures of the world will automatically open out to his reclaimed vision.[17]

Bhaktisiddhānta had carefully prepared the venture to the West by printing *Sree Krishna Chaitanya*, a lengthy book written by his disciple Niśi Kanta Sanyal, professor of history at Ravenshaw College, Cuttack. His goal was to introduce Caitanya instead of Krishna as the major focus of Vaishnava bhakti. The book also had the aim of providing a comparative view of theism. In the foreword Bhaktisiddhānta maintained that "Sree Krishna-Chaitanya's inculcations of the Personality of Godhead cannot be restricted to or accused of Idolatry."[18] It was meant to give a new perspective on the study of Hindu theism, critiquing a number of assumptions held by Western culture and its academic institutions.

Because Britain viewed India as a "dependency," which afforded it a lower status than "white" colonies like Canada and Australia, the prospect of establishing a religious mission in London appeared doubtful from the start. After all, with the exception of a few specialists and the employees of the Indian Civil Service, the British had little genuine knowledge of (or respect for) Indic philosophy and religion. On the other hand, the patronizing attitude of the British was an important gateway, and there were high levels of reciprocal intelligibility, since the Indian elite had a background in British language, literature, and thought. Regarding Germany, the prospect of a mission to this country seemed even more daunting because of the obvious language barrier. This, however, was offset by Germany's

17. *Harmonist* 29, no. 6 (December 1931): p. 167.

18. "Foreword" in Niśi Kanta Sanyal and Bhaktisiddhānta Sarasvatī, *Sree Krishna Chaitanya* (Madras: Sree Gaudiya Math, 1933), vol. 1, p. ii.

reputed academic traditions of Indology and Sanskrit, as well as Nazism's apparent fascination with its so-called Aryan past.[19] At this time, of course, Europe was in a deeply troubled and downward spiraling political situation, but there was also the possibility that this circumstance could engender a search for new spiritual directions.

Bhaktisiddhānta saw in Western secularization and material development the external causes of pride and moral degradation. He assessed the situation in May 1933, as Europe prepared for war:

> The West is proud of its civilization. It is anxious for conferring the boon of its advanced civilization on the nations of the world.... But is Western civilization itself a source of unmixed satisfaction for those who are its proud original possessors? They indeed possess superior material force. They are disposed to think that their superiority in brute force is evidence of their superior spiritual condition. The only answer to this terrible self-deception is being supplied by the recent never-ending crises of the affairs of the world that have been the outcome of their short-sighted handling by the self-conceited dominating temperament engendered in all modern peoples by their utter neglect of the spiritual issue.[20]

In Bhaktisiddhānta's view, the ultimate cause of all human conflict is forgetfulness of one's true spiritual identity and artificial identification with the domineering tendencies of the temporary body and mind. The rise of nationalism had brought about an exclusive focus on one such artificial identification, centered on the nation-state. This, however, had been accomplished at the cost of humanity's "fundamental" spiritual identity, which he considered paramount, being shared by all living beings:

> It is never possible to achieve internal harmony by an individual or a group in opposition to the nature of the entities themselves.

19. The term "Aryan" indicated the parent language of the Indo-European family of languages. It was later linked to the idea of a mythical Aryan race by racial theorists such as French Joseph Arthur de Gobineau (1816–1882). For the development of the concept of "Aryan" within Indo-European discourse see Stefan Arvidsson, *Aryan Idols: Indo-European Mythology as Ideology and Science* (Chicago: University of Chicago Press, 2006). For a historical study of the link between Aryan ideology and occultism, see Nicholas Goodrick-Clarke, *The Occult Roots of Nazism: Secret Aryan Cults and Their Influence on Nazi* (London: Tauris Parke, 2004).

20. *Harmonist* 30, no. 11 (May 1933): pp. 322–323, "Gaudiya Mission to the West."

> The hankering for domination that impels the conditioned soul on the course of his worldly activities is not conducive to the interests of the "*atman*" representing the principle of unhampered expansion. Such hankering is the perverted seeming substitute of the true instinct. The superimposition of this abnormal aptitude on the "*atman*" is effected by his incarceration in the double prison of the physical and mental bodies. These outer cases produce and keep up the delusion that they are a help and not the hindrances to the imprisoned soul's free and expanding activities. The wicked desire for domination over the entities of this world is the concomitance of this harmful subserviency of the soul to the dictates of his physical and mental envelopes.[21]

The possibility that a European could become a Krishna *bhakta* was theoretically formulated in the *Caitanya Caritāmṛta*, but seemed remote.[22] The first European to embrace Vaishnavism in India appears to have been Ronald Nixon in the late 1920s. A Cambridge graduate and pilot of the British Royal Air Force during the Great War, he worked as a professor of English at Lucknow University. He received initiation from a female Vaishnava guru that gave him the name Kṛṣṇaprema dāsa. Nixon was linked to the Vaishnava center of Vrindavan, but had no apparent link to Bengal.[23]

In the early twentieth century, some Bengalis had attempted to introduce Caitanya Vaishnavism in the United States, but with minimal and apparently short-lived success. The first attempt by a *bhadralok* appears to have taken place in the early 1910s, as tersely recounted by Farquhar:

> A Bengali, named Surendranath Mukerji, a nephew of Mr. Justice Anukul Chandra Mukerji of Calcutta, had rather a romantic history in America. He was a follower of Caitanya, and became a sannyāsī, taking the name Premānanda Bhārati. He was usually

21. *Harmonist* 30, no. 11 (May 1933): p. 322.

22. See, for example, the canonical text *Caitanya Caritāmṛta, Ādi līlā* 9.7, in which Kṛṣṇadāsa Kavirāja states *prabhu kahe, āmi "viśvambhara" nāma dhari, nāma sārthaka haya, yadi preme viśva bhari*: "Prabhu said: Let me assume the name Viśvambhara; the name is meaningful if I fill the universe with love of God (*prema*)."

23. David L. Haberman, "A Cross-Cultural Adventure: The Transformation of Ronald Nixon," *Religion* 23 (1993).

> called Bābā Bhāratī. He went to New York in 1902, and lectured on Krishna with great success not only in New York, but in Boston, Los Angeles (where he built a Hindu temple), and elsewhere. In 1907 he returned to India with a few American disciples, and opened a Mission in Calcutta. But funds failed, and he returned to America. He published two books, one on Krishna and one on Light on Life. He died in Calcutta in January 1914.[24]

Another Caitanyaite, Mahanambrata Brahmacārī, obtained a Ph.D. from the University of Chicago in the 1930s with a dissertation on the Vaishnava Vedānta of Jīva Goswami.[25] These few attempts had occurred in North America, but Britain and continental Europe had remained virtually untouched by Caitanya Vaishnavism up to the time of Bhaktisiddhānta.[26]

In his attempt to cross the European barrier Bhaktisiddhānta confronted at least five major challenges. The first was linguistic. Because most Caitanyaite texts had been originally written in Bengali and Sanskrit, there was an immediate need to find appropriate English terms for the philosophical and theological concepts found therein. During Bhaktisiddhānta time, however, only a handful of *bhadralok* were both proficient in all three languages *and* capable of adhering to the original text while making it intelligible to an English-speaking audience.

The second was hermeneutical. Colonial and Christian interpretations of Indian history and religion reflected a profound Eurocentric bias, and this would have to be understood and contested in the course of presenting any alternate perspective.

The third challenge pertained to the problem of cultural difference. By background, education, and training, most upper-caste Hindus looked down upon the British (and Europeans in general) as untouchable barbarians, and attempted to bar them from their inner ritual and socioreligious space. The British, on the other hand, tended to look down upon Hindus as

---

24. John Nicol Farquhar, *Modern Religious Movements in India* (London: Macmillan, 1929), p. 296.

25. Mahanambrata Brahmachari, *Vaiṣṇava Vedānta (the Philosophy of Śrī Jīva Gosvāmī)* (Calcutta: Das Gupta, 1974).

26. Premānanda Bhārati visited England once, and in 1936 Mahanambrata Brahmacārī gave lectures in London and traveled to various European countries, but their main field remained North America.

less civilized "heathens," and, for political reasons, attempted to bar them from full constitutional rights and agency as citizens. Moreover, there was a vast difference between the two cultures regarding such matters as dietary and hygienic standards, attitudes toward women, and the like. In this regard, *brāhmaṇic* clans tended to keep the British away from Hindu religious practices, fearing that they might be polluted by the Western habit of consuming meat and alcohol. Even dining with a Westerner was severely discouraged, particularly among upper-caste Vaishnavas who strictly abstained from meat eating, intoxication, and "illicit" sex, and one could lose social, religious, and intrafamilial status by doing so.[27] For these and similar reasons, it was apparent that a type of paradigm shift would have to take place before comfortable interaction could ensue.

The fourth challenge concerned the practicality of implementing *varṇāśrama*, the traditional Indic social system, on a broad scale—something that had been desired by Bhaktivinoda and begun by Bhaktisiddhānta through his own and his disciples' adoption of the *saṃnyāsa aśrama*. Could *varṇāśrama*, as a social system, work outside the Gaudiya Math? Was it possible to explain its rationale to a liberal Western audience?

The final challenge concerned the logistics of the trip itself. While the imperial center had opened up links with its periphery, only a small number of individuals had been able to travel from India to the coveted shores of the British Islands. The sheer cost of traveling and residing in the West meant that it was affordable only to the wealthiest of Hindu families. As for Indian religious figures, few among these had thus far made the trip abroad—for example, Rammohun Roy, Keshub Chandra Sen, and Vivekānanda. How would members of the Gaudiya Math, an institution that was wholly unknown outside India, attract the attention of the British and obtain permission to go?

As will be seen in the sections that follow, despite these various impediments, Bhaktisiddhānta's dream of introducing Caitanya Vaishnavism to the West was basically realized, but with limited results and a major German setback.

---

27. Gandhi, whose mother was a devout Vaishnavi, wrote in his autobiography of his guilt in having to conceal the fact that he occasionally ate meat prepared by a friend in school. Mahatma Gandhi and Mahadev Haribhal Dessai, *An Autobiography or the Story of My Experiments with Truth* (1927; Ahmedabad: Navajivan Publishing House, 1993), chs. 6, 7. When attending school in Calcutta, the revolutionary Bipin Chandra Pal hid his eating of meat from his strict Vaishnava family for fear that he would be reproached. Pal, *Memories of My Life*, pp. 160–161.

Departure for Europe

In April 1933 three of Bhaktisiddhānta's disciples departed overseas for Europe: senior *saṃnyāsin* Swami Bhakti Pradīpa Tīrtha, Swami Bhakti Hṛdaya Bon, and Saṃvidānanda dāsa, who had been admitted to the graduate program at the University of London. The degree to which Bhaktisiddhānta may have instructed these individuals about how to approach their mission is simply not known since there are no surviving records indicating that such discussions took place.[28] What we do have, however, is "My Advice," an article published in the *Harmonist* that presents excerpts from an address given by Bhaktisiddhānta a few weeks before the departure of his emissaries for London.[29] The article is of historical interest because it provides at least some sense of Bhaktisiddhānta's understanding of the mission, as well as his hopes, expectations, and concerns. As reported by the *Harmonist*, the address offers guidelines to his emissaries relative to the content and aim of their message, and also cautions them not to fall prey to certain potential pitfalls. The most relevant of the passages are presented below.

The first passage expresses Bhaktisiddhānta's conviction that a European audience will be receptive to the teachings of Sri Caitanya so long as matters are intelligently presented and logically supported with sound philosophical arguments:

> Those nations to whom you are going for the propagation of the chant of Hari are mounted on the summit of proficiency in all affairs of this world. They are practiced in the exercise of their rational judgment, are endowed with the quality of good manners and are superior and glorious in many respects. Therefore, we should maintain our hope unshaken that they will prove to be the worthiest recipients of the heard transcendental voice if we unlock to them the gates of the natural exhibition of abiding argument and enduring judgment.[30]

---

28. While there is no record of advisory conversations prior to the journey west, a small number of advisory letters remain that were sent by Bhaktisiddhānta to his disciples after their arrival in Europe. The content of some of these letters will be presented below.

29. *Harmonist* 30, no. 10 (April 1933): pp. 315–319, "My Advice." The address was delivered on March 18, 1933 at a "send-off ceremony" for his westward-bound disciples.

30. *Harmonist* 30, no. 10 (April 1933): pp. 317–318, "My Advice."

Although the preceding statement indicates Bhaktisiddhānta's appreciation for the many achievements of the West, the following remark qualifies this by noting that "mundane culture" will achieve "true significance" only if it embraces a higher sense of spiritual understanding—or as Bhaktisiddhānta metaphorically puts it, "the lotus feet of... Sree Guru":

> may we always remember that the experience of this world and all the highest excellences of mundane culture attain their true significance only if they are prepared to wait with utmost eagerness on the particle of dust of the lotus feet of my Sree Guru and that otherwise they are merely the mirage devised by the deluding potency for our ruin.[31]

In this regard, Bhaktisiddhānta exhorts his emissaries to

> proclaim to all the people that complete reliance on the Transcendental Absolute Truth is by far the highest form of freedom and one that is infinitely superior to the partial independent mastery over the distorted reflected entity in the shape of this mundane world.[32]

Apart from advising his disciples about the content of their message and encouraging them to present matters in a straightforward and logical way, Bhaktisiddhānta also makes a number of cautionary remarks relative to their work. These center upon the necessity of maintaining a high degree of spiritual inspiration, of avoiding the mentality of a "tourist," and of uprooting hidden desires for personal aggrandizement and reward:

> We must always bear in mind that we have been initiated in the vow of the peripatetic preacher for the sole purpose of promulgating the Heart's Desire of Sree Guru and Gauranga. If we are constantly inspired with the vow of discoursing the Truth under the guidance of the lotus feet of Sree Guru, no vain hankering for traveling, nor any veiled form of desire other than chanting of Hari will ever strike their terrors into our hearts.[33]

---

31. *Harmonist* 30, no. 10 (April 1933): pp. 317, "My Advice."

32. *Harmonist* 30, no. 10 (April 1933): pp. 319. "My Advice."

33. *Harmonist* 30, no. 10 (April 1933): pp. 318, "My Advice."

With regard to the collection of donations, Bhaktisiddhānta reminds his disciples that, according to the principles of Caitanya Vaishnava renunciation, contributions should be neither artificially rejected nor used for personal gain; rather they should be exclusively employed for the mission of the "Sree Chaitanya Math":

> The in-gathering of the smallest alms, even such as are gathered by the bees, is our only means for serving the manifestation of the Manifestive Divine Form of Sree Chaitanya Math all over the world. We are neither enjoyers nor abnegators of mundane entities. We recognize as our highest desideratum the desire for carrying the shoes of the transcendental order of the Paramahansas.[34]

He further advises them to sincerely and humbly convey Caitanya's teachings without compromise or pride:

> We should call at the door of each and every seeker of the Truth, conveying on our heads the baggage of the Real Truth. It is no business of ours to be elated or discouraged by the praise or neglect of any person. We must be constantly alive to the duty of enhancing the pleasure of our Master by serving Him with perfect sincerity.... We shall come across many persons in this world, possessing the endless variety of characters, disposed or hostile to the service of Krishna. But we should not slacken in our loving service to the Lord of our hearts by offering due honor to all persons.... It should be our only duty to constantly chant those words regarding the cleansing of the mirror of the heart of which He speaks in His Eight Precepts (shikshastakam), by following in His footsteps. We are only the bearers of the Transcendental Word. There is no scope for any arrogance or vanity of our own.[35]

This address was delivered on March 18, 1933. Three weeks later, on April 8, 1933, Swami Bon received the following communication from H. R. Gould, the private secretary to Sir Frederick Hugh Sykes (1877–1954), former governor of Bombay:

> My dear Swamiji, I am to say that His Excellency is writing about you to Mr. R. A. Butler, Under-Secretary of State for India. He

34. *Harmonist* 30, no. 10 (April 1933): pp. 319, "My Advice."

35. *Harmonist* 30, no. 10 (April 1933): pp. 316–318, "My Advice."

is sending off the letter by air mail, so that it will be received by Mr. Butler before you get to London.[36]

With this, and with all other arrangements having been made, Swami Bon and his two companions boarded the S. S. *Victoria* on April 10, 1933 and set sail for Naples, Italy—the first leg of their journey to London. On his person were additional letters from the governors of Madras and Bengal recommending him to the above-named Richard Austen Butler (1902–1982), parliamentary under-secretary of state for India, and Findlater Stewart (1879–1960), the permanent under-secretary in London.[37] Swami Bon expressed in his journal an eagerness to acquaint himself with the religious ideas of the British as well as the conviction that interreligious dialogue would generate mutual goodwill and "friendly understanding for the service of Godhead in which there is perfect harmony and eternal peace."[38]

According to Swami Bon's account, the three passed their time on the ship by discussing religion with two Christian missionaries. They reached Naples on March 20, where they first set foot on the land of the "all-whites."[39] The next day they traveled to Genoa and, as it chanced to be Italy's national holiday, "immensely enjoyed the military procession of an independent nation."[40] They then journeyed by rail to Paris, where they visited the Eiffel Tower and Napoleon's tomb, finally arriving at London's Victoria Station on April 22, 1933.

What follows are descriptions and analyses of Swami Bon's missions—first in Britain and then in Germany. During each of these tours

---

36. Swami Bon, *My First Year in England: Report of My Activities in the West from May 1933 to May 1934* (1934; Calcutta: N. K. Banerji, 1981), pp. 9–10. The 1934 edition is largely identical with the 1981 edition, the only difference being that the latter version contains additional chapters describing subsequent events up to the early 1940s. Swami Bon gives an account of the first two years of his venture to the West in two booklets. The first booklet focuses on the period between May 1933 and May 1934, and the second between June 1934 and August 1935. These two booklets constitute the primary source of information for this section.

37. Swami Bon received letters of recommendation from Madras governor George Frederick Stanley (1872–1938) on March 8, and from Bengal governor John Anderson (1882–1958) on March 11. He noted in his journal that during his meeting with Governor Anderson he was cautioned that it would be best to keep his mission strictly religious (i.e., nonpolitical) and gave assurances to the governor that this was indeed his intention (Bon, *My First Year in England*, p. 7). He also held several other letters of recommendation, one of which was from W. C. Wordsworth, the editor of the Calcutta daily *Statesman*.

38. Bon, *My First Year in England*, p. 11.

39. Bon, *My First Year in England*, p. 13.

40. Bon, *My First Year in England*, p. 13.

he participated in various events, held numerous lectures, and met with a variety of historically noteworthy individuals. However, more information is available about his time in England than his time in Germany, which largely consists of a listing of names, places, and events. Because of this, the following will describe only the highlights of Swami Bon's German tour. For scholars, researchers, and others that are interested in the details, a more thorough timeline can be found in appendix D.

Imperial London

At first the travelers were at a loss regarding where to go. After spending the night at the Indian Student Union, Swami Bon undertook to rent a flat, reporting that it was very difficult for an Indian to find a furnished house or flat in London. The "color question" was rather strong with the average men and women who let out houses and flats. He remarked that except the few officers who regularly went to India, most of the average people of England were almost entirely ignorant of India and India's people, about whom "they have very strange and crude ideas."[41]

Despite these barriers, the group successfully rented a flat at 39 Drayton Gardens in prestigious Kensington. They stayed at this address from May 10 to December 20, 1933, at which time they moved to Gloucester House at nearby Cornwall Gardens.

Swami Bon records with great optimism that on May 10 he

> interviewed Sir Findlater Steward at the India Office by appointment. I had a very lively talk, most freely, for forty minutes. I told him of the religious tolerance of the British Crown and explained how a loving relationship must be maintained between the Crown and the religious people. In India in early days, the king was to protect and support religious men, who in their turn were to pray for the safety of the throne. Sir Findlater was much satisfied. He questioned me about our mission's activities and lastly asked me what he could do for us. I asked for paying homage to Their Majesties on

---

41. Bon, *My First Year in England*, p. 14. After spending some time in Britain, however, Bon noted that "an Englishman in India is quite a different person from what he is in England...there he is always in his mask of keeping up an air of superiority while here he is exceptionally polite, obliging, amiable and friendly...once known one can breathe a free air in the company of an Englishman." Bon, *My First Year in England*, pp. 73–74.

> behalf of the mission, and to Parliament and the Prince of Wales, to deliver lectures in Parliament and in different universities. He said he would consult with Sir Samuel and help us in many ways.[42]

The letters of recommendation served them well and on June 7, 1933, the director of the London School of Oriental Studies, Sir Edward Denison Ross (1871–1940), organized a reception at his home to introduce the group to London's educated class. Seventy-eight guests turned out, including members of the British aristocracy, clergy, and press; a number of educated Indians were in attendance as well.

Edward Frederick Lindley Wood (1881–1959), a previous viceroy of India, Findlater Stewart, and R. A. Butler arranged an interview with King George V, and Swami Bon was introduced to the court by the high commissioner of India on July 20, 1933. Swami Bon remarked that the king appeared to be a patron and "defender" of the community of Vaishnavas. He concluded his account of the event by stating that a strong relationship between church and state was necessary "for the harmonious and progressive working of both."[43]

Lord Zetland (1876–1961) introduced Swami Bon to the archbishop of Canterbury, with whom he discussed various theological and interreligious issues. One such issue concerned the difference between confidential and reverential service to God in both Christianity and Vaishnavism, and another concerned the various possible conceptions of God, such as "Fatherhood, Friendship, Sonhood, and Consortship."[44] Swami Bon wrote in his diary that

> the Archbishop expressed sympathies for my activities in England and presented me his photo as a memento of my visit, which I accepted with great delight.[45]

The Marquess of Zetland became an important ally, assisting Swami Bon and Bhakti Tīrtha with many practical matters. Lord Zetland was born in London in 1876 under the name Lawrence John Lumley Dundas, Earl

---

42. *Harmonist* 30, no. 12 (June 1933): p. 383.

43. Bon, *My First Year in England*, p. 19.

44. Bon, *My First Year in England*, p. 19.

45. Bon, *My First Year in England*, pp. 19–20.

of Ronaldshay. He was known as Lord Dundas until 1892, and then as Earl of Ronaldshay until he succeeded his father as the Second Marquess of Zetland in 1929. He was a politician, educated at Harrow School and Trinity College in Cambridge. He functioned as governor of Bengal from 1917 to 1922, president of the Royal Geographical Society from 1922 to 1925, and president of the Royal Asiatic Society from 1928 to 1931. He was also a member of the Indian Round Table Conference in London (1931–32), which counted Mahatma Gandhi among its various participants. In June 1935 he became secretary of state for India and remained in that capacity until May 1940.[46]

Lord Zetland wrote to Swami Bon extending his support: "I need hardly assure you that you have my continual good wishes for your work in this country."[47] He had great sympathy for India and profound respect for its cultures and religions; throughout his career he worked toward and encouraged the revival of Indian education and religious life.[48] In a 1921 speech, delivered while functioning as chancellor of Calcutta University, he made the following statement:

> I desire to see the whole system [of education] given a more specifically Indian orientation. A system that produced not Indians, but imitations of Europeans, would stand self-condemned.... The system of higher education has undoubtedly been too greatly divorced from the peculiar genius, the ancient tradition, the modes of thought and the daily lives of those whom it has sought to educate. Why, otherwise, should we see on all sides of us an unconscious searching after a different educational atmosphere as, for example, in the case of the Gurukul at Hardwar, or of Shanti Niketan at Bolpur? This is an aspect of present education unrest which we must not and cannot ignore, for we cannot ignore to sacrifice the contribution which

46. Cameron Hazlehurst, Sally Whitehead, and Christine Woodland, *A Guide to the Papers of British Cabinet Ministers: 1900–1964*, Royal Historical Society Guides and Handbooks, 0080-4398, No. 19 (Cambridge: Cambridge University Press for the Royal Historical Society, 1996), pp. 126–127.

47. Bon, *My First Year in England*, p. 21.

48. Lord Zetland wrote several books about India and the Far East: e.g., *Sport and Politics under an Eastern Sky*, 1902; *India, A Bird's-eye View*, 1924; *The Heart of Aryavarth*, 1925; *Steps towards Indian Home Rule*, 1935. For a detailed biography of Lord Zetland, particularly of his political career, see John Gilbert Laithwaite, *The Marquess of Zetland, 1876–1961* (London: Oxford University Press, 1962).

India with its highly developed sense of religion and its glowing idealism, is capable of making to the moral and intellectual store house of mankind.[49]

During his time as governor of Bengal, Lord Zetland took the opportunity to visit Nabadwip and was impressed by devotional *kīrtana*. In his autobiography he wrote:

Two occasions that made the deepest impression on me were my visit to the ancient town of Nabadwipa (Nadia) to receive an address from the learned pandits, and one to Agartala, capital of Tripura State where I was fortunate enough to see a Vaishnavite Namkīrtana party. Both of these have been described in full in Chapter IV of my former book *The Heart of Aryavarta*. So I content myself with a brief allusion here. At the first after a strangely moving ceremony, recalling the old India of the sages, a Sanskrit title of great distinction was conferred on me, that of Nitibisarada (one well-versed in good government)...at the latter I witnessed the participants by

49. Lawrence, Second Marquess of Zetland, *Essayez: The Memoirs of Lawrence, Second Marquess of Zetland* (London: John Murray, 1956), p. 149. Zetland reports that this speech had been welcomed by the nationalist paper *Amrita Bazar Patrika*, which was often highly critical of his political stand against the noncooperation movement. Zetland proposed "evolution" toward home rule rather than "revolution," which he believed would only succeed in tearing down the present administrative system without providing a feasible alternative (pp. 148–152). Zetland had been aide-de-camp for Lord Curzon in 1900–1901, a role that had initially displeased the Bengalis. He commented that his election as governor of Bengal in 1917 had been received with mixed feelings: "The announcement of my appointment had not been well received in nationalist circles in Bengal. It was recalled that I had been a member of Lord Curzon's personal stuff during his Viceroyalty and Lord Carzon had grievously outraged Bengali sentiment on more than one occasion especially by his partition of the Province. Moreover, my attitude as a member of the Royal Commission on the Public Services was held to have tarred me with the brush of Conservative obscurantism, with the result that a vigorous press campaign had been directed against me. At the head of the assault were the two most influential Indian-owned newspapers in Calcutta: the *Bengalee*, the organ of Mr. Surendranath Banerjea, whose popularity with the nationalists of the Presidency had won for him the title of uncrowned 'King of Bengal,' and the *Amrita Bazar Patrika* controlled by Babu Moti Lal Ghose." Zetland, *Essayez*, p. 67. Upon the election of Lord Zetland as secretary of state for India in 1935, the *Amrita Bazar Patrika* published an article entitled "Lord Zetland and Patrika," June 8, 1935, p. 6. The article accused Lord Zetland of having being biased toward the Bengalis while serving as Lord Curzon's adjutant, although it also included an appreciation by the late editor Moti Lal Ghose for the sincere empathy that Lord Zetland had shown toward India and its population on various other occasions. Overall, the evidence appears to indicate that Lord Zetland was sincerely sympathetic towards India—and not merely for purposes of political gain.

> means of song and dance work themselves up into a state of religious ecstasy, which revealed to me a glimpse of a latent emotional reservoir beyond anything I had dreamt of.[50]

In London, he presided as chair to many of Swami Bon's public lectures and became president of the Gaudiya Mission that Swami Bon and Swami Bhakti Pradīpa Tīrtha had started shortly after their arrival. Lord Zetland also agreed to both edit and preface a compilation of Swami Bon's collected lectures.[51]

Like Lord Zetland, many of the British that had served in the Indian Civil Service came away with a close personal experience of India and continued to maintain a deep appreciation for Indic religion and culture long after their return to Great Britain. Another example is Sir Samuel Hoare (1880–1959), who preceded Lord Zetland as secretary of state for India (1931–1935) and was also favorably inclined toward Swami Bon, taking the time to introduce him to a number of religious organizations in England, including St. Mary's Convent at Wantage in Oxfordshire.[52] Viscount Halifax, viceroy for India, 1926–1929, also expressed appreciation for Swami Bon's mission:

> Dear Swami Bon, I am much interested and very pleased to hear that you are forming a branch of your mission in London. As you know, I am entirely sympathetic with your efforts to further the mutual understanding in spiritual matters between this country and India, and I wish you every success in your undertaking.[53]

In April 1934, the Gaudiya Mission Society was registered as an official institution at Caxton Hall in Westminster. Some of the members of the board that served at different times were Lord Zetland (who served as president), Lord Lamington, Sir Edward Denison Ross (who served as vice-chairman) and the Maharajas of Tripura, Darbhanga, and

---

50. Zetland, *Essayez*, p. 91.

51. Swami Bon, *My Lectures in England and Germany* (Vrindavan: Bhajan Kutir, 1984). The book was published much later and without the contribution of Lord Zetland.

52. As it so happened, Hoare's sister Annie Louisa, the sister superior of the convent, arranged for Swami Bon to visit on June 29, 1933.

53. Bon, *My First Year in England*, pp. 25–26.

FIGURE 3.1 The Council of the Gaudiya Mission Society, London. *Left to right, standing*: Swami B. P. Tīrtha, the Maharaja of Burdwan, Swami Bon; *sitting*: Lady Stanley Jackson, the Marquess of Zetland, and Lady Carmichael of Skirling.

Source: Swami Bhakti Hṛdaya Bon, *Second Year of the Gaudiya Mission in Europe* (London: Gaudiya Mission, 1935) p. 13.

Burdwan.[54] Significantly, the council included two prominent female members as well: Lady Stanley Jackson and Lady Carmichael of Skirling (figure 3.1).

The Gaudiya Mission Society functioned according to British rules, integrated both British and Indian individuals from the highest levels of political and cultural life, and had representatives from both genders. In many ways it was the embodiment of Bhaktisiddhānta's vision of a cooperative partnership between the (pragmatic) West and the (spiritual) East.[55] Miss Kathlee Shaw kindly placed her Sussex country house at the

54. At the time, the Maharaja of Tripura was Bir Bikram Kissore Manikya, the Maharaja of Darbhanga was Kamesvara Singh Bahadur, and the Maharaj of Burdwan was Bijay Chand Mahtab Bahadur.

55. Swami Bhakti Hṛdaya Bon, *Second Year of the Gaudiya Mission in Europe* (London: Gaudiya Mission, 1935), pp. 11ff. The office of the Society was at 3 Gloucester House, Cornwall Gardens, London, SW 7.

mission's disposal for the holding of programs and discussions; eventually it became a sub-branch of the center in London.

Although Bhaktisiddhānta planned a trip to Britain, the journey never materialized because of his declining health. His disciples had nonetheless broken new ground and plans were under way for the construction of Britain's first Hindu Temple, to be built in the heart of London. The cost of the temple building itself—about 300,000 rupees—was to be donated by Tripura's maharaja, Bir Bikram Kissore Manikya, while the cost of the residential quarters and the land, amounting to about three million rupees, was to be collected from wealthy sympathizers in India. The complex was to include a temple for worship, an ashram for residents, a hall for lectures, and a hostel for Indian students.[56] Unfortunately, the construction of the temple was delayed by the passing of Bhaktisiddhānta and the unexpected schism that ensued (see chapter 2), and was eventually halted altogether as a result of World War II.

Up to the end, Bhaktisiddhānta hoped to reach the entirety of the West. In one of his last articles, written in 1936, Bhaktisiddhānta acknowledged the positive response that his disciples had received in Britain and expressed his hope for a future mission in the United States:

> We request the devotees to be with us in praying for Śrī Gaurasūndara's [another name for Caitanya] grace (*karuṇāprārthī*) so that the Gauḍīya teachings will spread to America. By His grace discussion of Gauḍīya is already being done in Europe, and particularly in London. Why should America remain untouched?[57]

Bhaktisiddhānta rejected the notion that religion should be used for political purposes, and rejected fundamentalism as a means of effecting political change. This is exemplified by the fact that at the height of the struggle for Indian independence he received John Anderson, the acting governor of Bengal, as his special guest in Mayapur on January 15, 1935 (figure B.7).[58]

56. It is interesting to note that Śrī Śrī Lakṣmī Viṣṇu images were to be installed in the temple room for purposes of worship. Sri Vishnu and Sri Laxmi are of great antiquity, and were also the preferred images of puritan South Indian Vaishnavas. The decision to choose Sri Vishnu, as opposed to Sri Krishna, may have been made as a concession to certain British prejudices, suspicions, and misunderstandings, "Vishnu Temple in London," *Harmonist* 32, no. 19 (May 1936): pp. 454–455.

57. *Gauḍīya* 15, no. 1 (1936): p. 3.

58. *Harmonist* 31, no. 11 (January 1935): pp. 251–261.

This type of "consorting with the colonialist enemy" took a great deal of civil courage and made Bhaktisiddhānta a potential target of nationalist violence. Bhaktisiddhānta even went so far as to arrange for a large welcoming banner that read "God Bless the King," a deed that boldly confirmed his commitment to hospitality and governmental law and order.[59] None of this, however, was meant to imply that Bhaktisiddhānta was in support of either the Raj or British colonial interests in India. The act was a statement of the universal nature of reality and the fact that Indians and Britishers—indeed all living beings—shared a common spiritual identity that transcended all bodily, ethnic, religious, and geopolitical divides. In Bhaktisiddhānta's view, since God is the "Supreme Absolute Truth" and "the Cause of All Causes," there could be no fundamental difference between the God of the British and the God of the Vaishnavas; both could thus benefit from a shared religious language.

Analysis of the British Mission

While Swami Bon was clearly well-received in Britain, it is questionable whether this was due to the specific fact that he was a representative of the Caitanya Vaishnava tradition. A more likely alternative is that he was largely basking in the goodwill and sympathy that these leading Britishers had developed toward Indian culture and religion in general. This would have been especially so in the case of scholars, civil servants, and political leaders such as Lord Zetland who had spent significant portions of their lives on the subcontinent, and thus felt a profound love for all things Indian—perhaps mixed with a certain amount of justified colonial guilt. In other words, the honor, respect, and courtesy accorded Swami Bon by the king and other highly placed individuals was, above all, because he was viewed as a significant representative of Hinduism, an image that he might very well have cultivated regardless of how narrow or uninformed it was.

Moreover, despite Swami Bon's public relations triumphs and his ability to rub shoulders with the elite, he appears not to have succeeded in terms of deeply planting Caitanya Vaishnavism in British soil—that is, during his entire stay only a handful individuals became involved practitioners. One reason for this might have been that, at the time, English

59. See appendix B.

translations of Caitanya Vaishnava texts were few and far between, making it more difficult for the British to seriously comprehend the tradition. Perhaps more significant, however, was the fact that Swami Bon mostly focused on onetime public lectures without much follow-up, or on brief, largely casual conversations with scholars, religious leaders, and politicians. In other words, his approach seems to have been somewhat tentative, with only a slight penetration at the grassroots level: regular programs that straightforwardly presented the teachings of Sri Caitanya to the *general* British population and allowed for the gradual buildup of understanding and practice. During one lecture Swami Bon himself noted that he was sent to Europe "for exploring the chances of the acceptance of the teaching of Sri Krsna Caitanya by [those] who believe in the comparative study of religion."[60] This agenda appears to be confirmed by the fact that his lectures and presentations were mainly to societal associations, exclusive clubs, formal political receptions, universities, and the like; in other words, the institutions of the elite.[61]

Another reason for his mission's shallow penetration was likely the severe demands placed on serious adherents, many of which were difficult for Europeans to comprehend or follow, despite the fact that they were couched in Western dress. As presented by Swami Bon, the serious practice of bhakti required the adoption of a strict vegetarian diet and abstention from gambling, loose sexual conduct, and all types of intoxicants; it also required discipline, self-sacrifice, and obedience to the guru or spiritual master. Many of these requirements were (and still are) considered extremely difficult, or even unusual, from the general Western point of view.

When Swami Bon returned to India in 1935, he met with several members of the Gaudiya Math, including one of its most senior *saṃnyāsins*, a "godbrother" named Śrīdhara Swami. Recalling this meeting, Śrīdhara Swami wrote of his surprise in finding that Swami Bon had abandoned the traditional symbols, dress, and hairstyle of a Vaishnava, and had adopted a more European appearance in their stead. When questioned about this, Swami Bon reportedly answered that neither orthodox

60. Bon, *My Lectures in England and Germany*, p. 152.

61. Swami Bon reports that he sought to speak not only to the elite, the aristocracy, and the intelligentsia, but also to the poor and uneducated laborers of London, some of whom he found to be "fairly God-fearing—quite intelligent and polite." Bon, *My First Year in England*, p. 76. Nonetheless, these sorts of contacts appear to have been quite casual and only sporadic.

fashions nor orthodox modes of presentation would be accepted in the West—that Westerners could not be "pushed," since they had "their own reasoning or understanding, their own philosophy, etc."[62] If this represents an accurate account of Swami Bon's point of view, it offers a further possible explanation for his inability to attract few serious adherents: if one's mission to the West is guided by the conviction that Westerners are, for the most part, incapable of accepting Caitanya Vaishnavism in all of its philosophical, cultural, and practical aspects, this can become a self-fulfilling prophecy by attenuating one's approach to the point that it is no longer compelling or profound or distinctive enough to win genuine interest. Swami Bon was able to meet with influential figures and create favorable impressions, but the exploratory nature of his mission, the brevity and pace of his tour—and perhaps his own skepticism and hesitancy—as well as the restlessness of the political climate mentioned earlier, may have all conspired to limit the degree to which he factually penetrated his field.

The Mission in Nazi Germany

The Party of the National Socialist German Workers (Nationalsozialistische Deutsche Arbeiterpartei) had located its racial roots in India, linking Germany with a mythical Aryan race, and employing the Vedic swastika (at the time a popular sign of good luck) as the primary symbol of the Third Reich. Although the British Raj had also supported the notion of an Aryan invasion and Europe's so-called Indo-European ancestry, it had done so in a strictly colonial context. The alleged racial brotherhood between India and Britain had meant little in terms of genuine social equality, since the colonial British considered themselves superior and enacted policies that segregated Indians from Europeans, especially from 1857 onward.[63] In Germany, on the other hand, the concept of a racial Aryan brotherhood had implied increased recognition, a fact that Said fails to account

62. Sridhara Swami, http://bvml.org/audio/SBRSM/52_Prof_Schulze-Sadananda_and_Walter_Eidlitz-Vamana.mp3 (accessed on July 29, 2012).

63. Regarding Hindu perceptions of British discrimination see Tapan Raychaudhuri, *Europe Reconsidered: Perceptions of the West in Nineteenth Century Bengal* (Oxford: Oxford University Press, 1988), p. 180.

for in his critique of orientalism.[64] Despite the aggressive nationalism of the Nazis and their biased historical hermeneutics, Hindu India viewed Germany as a potential partner and praised its general hospitality and respect for Indian civilization, something that had not been found in the often humiliating attitudes and conduct of the Raj. This notwithstanding, Swami Bon's lectures on the teachings of Caitanya ultimately met with considerable resistance. In Hitler's Germany, religious ideas and the notion of an Aryan past were dangerously entwined with political rhetoric and racial ideology.[65]

In December 1933 Swami Bon traveled from London to Germany to deliver a series of arranged lectures. During this brief visit he had a fateful meeting with one Ernst Georg Schulze, a Ph.D. student of comparative religion at the University of Leipzig who eventually became the only serious Western student of bhakti that Swami Bon was able to bring back to India. After Bon's return to London, Schulze obtained a copy of the book *Shri Krishna Caitanya* by Niśi Kanta Sanyal and was deeply moved by the content. Writing to Swami Bon in 1934, he noted:

> It is since the year 1922 [he was born in 1908] that my life was engaged in the search for a deeper conception of Religion, Truth and Godhead—than the religion of my confession. I have never been interested in worldly learning. Studying all books on religious matters, the Comparative History of Religion, making the acquaintance of the devotees of the different religions—I longed for that religious devotee whose life is entirely given in the service

---

64. This view supports Richard King, who comments that "the examples of German Orientalists, on the one hand, and Japan, on the other, cast doubt upon Said's thesis that Orientalist discourse is always associated with an imperial agenda, since Germany had no Eastern empire to manipulate and control, and Japan was subjected to Orientalist discourses without ever being colonized by the West. Sheldon Pollock's discussion of German Orientalism suggests that the authoritative power of such discourses could be equally applied at home to create a powerful 'internal narrative,' in this case instrumental in the construction of a German national consciousness, and ultimately in the hands of the National Socialists in 'the colonization and domination of Europe itself.'" King, *Orientalism and Religion*, p. 85. For a discussion that contrasts the way the Aryan idea was used by the British and Bengalis to create a sense of kinship with the way it was used by the Germans (and other continental peoples) to create an exclusionist national identity based upon race, see Trautmann, *Aryans and British India*, p. 221.

65. For quite some time, all letters and journals pertaining to Swami Bon's German encounter appeared to have been lost. Recently, however, some portion of his original correspondence has resurfaced.

of Godhead—wishing nothing else but to hear something positive about the True Religion and the way thither.[66]

In March 1934 Schulze made his way to the Gaudiya Math in London to fully dedicate himself to spiritual practice and receive personal instruction from Swami Bon. While there he assisted Bon by translating his lectures into German and eventually accompanied him in the role of secretary on his extended German tour. With the London mission basically established it was quite natural that Swami Bon turned his attention to Germany, famous for its Indological scholarship. A detailed tour was prepared and Swami Bon spent hours a day corresponding with Nazi officials and academic institutions to firm up his plans.[67] On October 21, 1934, Swami Bon, along with his new German adherent and acting secretary, traveled from London to the Zoologischer Garten Station in Berlin. There they were met by *Regierungsrat* Hassenstein, his wife, and various other dignitaries, and conveyed to the Gaudiya Mission on Eisenacher Straße 29, which had been already procured before their arrival.[68]

From this Berlin address Swami Bon began holding regular public lectures and taking lessons in German. Most of his university lectures were prepared beforehand in English with the help of letters from Bhaktisiddhānta and Niśi Kanta Sanyal.[69] They were then translated into German by his secretary and read aloud by Swami Bon to his audience.[70] Apart from his meetings and lectures in Berlin, Swami Bon would spend much of the next seven months—until May 30, 1935—traveling throughout the Germanic lands: from Berlin to Leipzig, Dresden, Vienna, Bonn, Marburg, and many points in between. In the course of these travels he had

66. The letter is quoted with permission from Kid Samuelsson, private collection.

67. Bon reports that "about 4,500 letters left the Office of the Monastery within the last one year"—i.e., between May 1933 and May 1934; see *My First Year in England*, p. 84. These letters were addressed to many contacts in Europe and India, various universities, eminent scholars, the aristocracy and politicians.

68. At the time, the term *Regierungsrat* indicated a counselor to a government minister.

69. Bon acknowledged the contribution of Bhaktisiddhānta and Niśi Kanta Sanyal as follows: "Das Gedankengut meiner Vorlesungen wurde mir von meinem spirituellen Meister Paramahansa Sree Sreemad Bhakti Siddhānta Saraswati Goswāmi und meinem Gottbruder Herrn Prof. N. K. Sannyal, M.A., übergeben." Swami B. H. Bon, *Gedanken über den Hinduismus* (Berlin: Bon, 1935), pp. 7–8.

70. At around this time, *Regierungsrat* Martin Weigert became the first secretary of the Berlin Gaudiya Mission.

the opportunity to meet with such notables as Sanskrit scholar Helmuth von Glasenapp (1891–1963), historian Helmut Berve (1896–1979), Swiss Protestant theologian Karl Barth (1886–1968), and Peter Kahle (1875–1964), director of the Oriental Institute at Bonn University. He was also able to hold numerous lectures on such topics as "The Conception of Maya in the Indian Religious Philosophy," "The Aryan Indian Conception of God," and "The Way of the Aryan Indian to God" (see appendix D for a listing with details and notes). The remainder of this section consists of brief descriptions of four of Swami Bon's meetings, about which a little more is known.

While in Berlin, Swami Bon met regularly with Professor Eduard Spranger (1882–1963), an educator and philosopher who served as professor of philosophy in Leipzig (1911–20), Berlin (1920–45), and Tübingen (from 1946). Spranger was a student of Wilhelm Dilthey, and continued the research that his teacher had begun on the human sciences. His theories on adolescent education were influential in Germany during the 1920s. In the course of their meetings, Spranger had agreed to edit and introduce *Die Persönlichkeit und Bewegung Sri-Krishna-Chaitanyas,* intended to be Swami Bon's second book in the German language (his first book, *Gedanken über den Hinduismus,* had been published in 1935).[71] Unfortunately, the book was never published and the manuscript appears to have been lost. At Berlin University Swami Bon also met with mission professor Johannes Witte (1877–1945), one of the few lectors in Germany who was fluent in the Bengali language.[72] By his arrangement Swami Bon held two Berlin University lectures entitled "The Philosophy of Shri Krishna Chaitanya" and "India: Her Religion and Culture." According to the Swami's journal, these lectures were attended by over 500 students and scholars.

In Munich, Swami Bon met with Catholic missiology scholar Johannes Baptist Aufhauser (1891–1963). Aufhauser had earned a doctoral degree in theology in 1908, and one in philosophy in 1910. In 1918 he became assistant professor of missiology at Munich University, remaining in that post until the Nazis terminated the theology faculty in 1939.[73] In his journal

71. Bon, *Second Year,* p. 41.

72. Witte is credited with having published a collection of Bengali poetry that is considered to have been the first German book to appear with Bengali script alongside a German translation.

73. Gerald H. Anderson, *Biographical Dictionary of Christian Missions* (Wm. B. Eerdmans, 1999), p. 32.

Swami Bon records having had an interesting discussion with Aufhauser concerning the differences between Christianity and Hinduism, and the misunderstandings that can arise when the *philosophy* of religion is ignored.

Swami Bon also reports that in Tübingen he held a number of well-attended talks and spent two days discussing the *Vedas* and the Upanishads with Jakob Wilhelm Hauer (1881–1962), the noted Sanskrit scholar, Indologist, and leader of the German Faith Movement (*Deutsche Glaubensbewegung*). Hauer had been a missionary for the Basel Mission Society from 1900 until 1911 (the year he became a student at Oxford University), and had spent several years in India during that period of time. He eventually founded a movement that sought to direct Christian-dominated Germany toward a religion that could afford a direct experience of God (*Ergriffenheit*). According to Karla Poewe, Hauer's stated aim was to create a religion that embodied the essence of National Socialism and the new Germany, especially as shaped by the SS.[74] His movement attempted to amalgamate and employ notions from both German and Sanskrit literature, particularly the Bhagavad Gītā, which he viewed as describing the course of an unavoidable destiny (*Schicksal*). Hauer was apparently interested in exploring the ideas of the Gaudiya Math, believing that the Gītā could help Germans better understand the true nature of "the German soul." At its height, Hauer's Faith Movement consisted of approximately 200,000 followers and was extremely influential among the Nazis. It advocated the "blood and soil" ideology as well as the introduction of contemporary pagan rites.[75]

In her book *New Religions and the Nazis*, Karla Poewe describes the exchange of letters between Hauer and Swami Bon's German secretary that led to their meetings and the swami's subsequent talks.[76] On May 23, 1934, Ernst Schulze wrote a letter informing Hauer that Swami Bon represented the largest religious organization of orthodox *brāhmaṇas* (he may have referred to the Vaishnava communities) in India and

74. Karla O. Poewe, *New Religions and the Nazis* (London: Routledge, 2006), p. 18.

75. For a brief overview of the study of religion in German universities during the Nazi period, see Horst Junginger's article at http://homepages.uni-tuebingen.de/gerd.simon/religion_ns.htm (accessed on July 29, 2012).

76. Poewe, *New Religions and the Nazis*, pp. 81–82. Poewe reviewed three letters at the Bundesarkiv in Koblenz. The first two were written by Schulze on May 23, 1934 (N1131 61, Doc. 315) and June 21, 1934 (N1131 61, Doc. 316), and the third was written by Hauer on June 28, 1934 (N1131 61, Doc. 314); see p. 187.

considered the Germans to be "the most suited of all Western people for an understanding of the Indo-Aryan religions." Then in a June 21 letter Schulze sought Hauer's advice about the value of translating Swami Bon's English Bhagavad Gītā into German, claiming to have discovered the ancient primeval religion (*Urreligion*) that was common to both Indian and Western "Aryans." Hauer's interest had been stirred and on June 28, 1934, he replied that if Swami Bon could hold lectures in German, he would be interested in inviting him to speak.[77] Concerning Schulze's question about the Gītā, Hauer replied that since there was already a good Sanskrit-to-German version that directly conveyed the original meaning, an additional English-to-German version would not be much of a contribution. As a member of the *Indischen Ausschuss der Deutschen Akademie* (Indian Committee of the German Academy), Hauer was a figure of some importance in Nazi Germany; in this same letter he wrote:

> For years I have worked to further communication between Aryan India and Germany, and I am convinced that the new Germany, especially now through the German Faith Movement, whose goal it is to make the Aryan Faith in Germany effective again, will have much understanding for India and vice versa.[78]

Swami Bon remained in Germany until May 30, 1935, at which time he traveled back to London. Meanwhile his secretary, who had apparently remained in Germany, ran afoul of the Nazis and sought refuge in a Catholic monastery, where he met one Baron von Koeth, who also became interested in Bhaktisiddhānta's teachings. Schulze and von Koeth managed to escape from Germany together, reaching the Gaudiya Math in London sometime in July (figure 3.2). On August 21, 1935, they accompanied Swami Bon on his return trip to India.[79] Several weeks later, after

---

77. Hauer had been in touch with the Indian community in Germany and had recently invited a professor from Calcutta to lecture on Indian mysticism. Apparently, the talk had been well received.

78. Poewe, *New Religions and the Nazis*, p. 82.

79. Baron von Koeth discontinued his association with the Gaudiya Math after some time. Schulze remained in India and personally served Bhaktisiddhānta by lecturing and writing articles for the *Harmonist*. Eventually he became the only Westerner to receive formal initiation directly from Bhaktisiddhānta. Schulze received the name Sadānanda dāsā (eternal happiness).

FIGURE 3.2. *From the left*: Schulze, Swami Bon, and Baron von Koeth.

Source: Swami Bhakti Hṛdaya Bon, *Second Year of the Gaudiya Mission in Europe* (London: Gaudiya Mission, 1935) p. 27.

having spent two years and four months in Europe, Swami Bon once again set foot on Indian soil, arriving in Bombay on September 5, 1935.[80]

In his journal, Swami Bon noted that the reception he received in Germany rivaled that which he had experienced in London. His had been one of the first encounters of a representative of Vaishnavism with Europe, and it appeared to have gone fairly well. If nothing else, Swami Bon's time in Europe had shown that it was possible to meet with individuals at the highest levels of political, religious, and cultural life, and that the British and German elite had a serious interest in Indic religion. And yet, while the mission in Britain would remain fairly stable, its situation in Germany would deteriorate, despite the genuine goodwill of numerous well-wishers and friends.

80. Swami Bon was welcomed with a large reception when he later reached Calcutta.

Confrontation with Nazi Ideology: An Analysis

A critical article by the German scholar Theodor Steche appeared on January 8, 1936, in the book section of the official newspaper of the Nazi Party in Berlin, the *Völkischer Beobachter* (*The Popular Observer*). The article, entitled "From Asian Cultures" (*Aus Asiatischen Kulturen*), provides an interesting example of the Nazi reaction to Swami Bon during the early period of the Third Reich. The article consisted of a review of

> the printed booklet *Thoughts about Hinduism* (*Gedanken über den Hinduismus*) (printer H. Ban, Berlin, price 1 RM). It is a publication of lectures that the author, a leading missionary from the Indian Gaudiya Mission, gave at a number of German universities at the end of 1934. Here everything is viewed differently compared to ... [the views of] European scholars. He is of the opinion that the four Indian castes, whose original name means "color," relate to spiritual enlightenment. On the other hand, [he states that] all that is written in the Vedic texts about race comes from misinterpretation and pride. [He suggests that] the racial upper strata of the Indian people migrated out of India to the West and then migrated back, and much more. Everything has been presented as something spiritual and mystical. Here we have a very clever, but for Germans quite difficult to grasp, historical perspective by a wise man, but it comes from the emotions of a section of India, the non-Aryan Dravidian race. No one questions the right of the present people of India to create their worldview (*Weltanschauung*) in a way that matches the constitution of their blood. But it must be stressed that spreading Tridandi's religious teachings and thoughts contained in the book is out of question in today's Germany.[81]

The book contained chapters on many topics, but it was the initial one entitled "The Indo-Arian Message of the Gaudiya Mission" that had attracted the criticism. The point of view expressed in Steche's article was in sharp contrast to the favorable reactions of leading religious and Indological scholars, and marked the beginning of the end for the Gaudiya mission in

81. *Völkischer Beobachter*, August 1, 1936, p. 10.

Germany. Moreover, it demonstrated that the spiritual understandings of Bhaktisiddhānta and the racial ideology of Hitler and Nazi Germany were fundamentally antithetical and incompatible.[82]

As might be expected, Steche's brief critique did little justice to the complexity of the text in Swami Bon's compilation.[83] What follows is a more detailed summary of that text, which was taken from a speech given at the Lessing *Hochschule* in Berlin on September 8, 1934.

In his lecture Swami Bon noted that the word *Ārya* had been of little significance in India's religious and philosophical universe (*Begriffswelt*) and contained no clear correlation to race, as did the word *Han*, which was the name for the Aryans before they were divided into classes (*varṇa*).[84] He also noted that the rites and teachings of the Indic religions were meant for all human beings, without consideration of race. Concerning the notion of a so-called Aryan invasion, the Swami observed that there was no textual evidence indicating that the *brāhmaṇas* had migrated to India from Europe; instead he "radically" proposed that it had occurred in just the opposite direction—that is, from East to West: the Aryans originated from the Punjab and gradually migrated through Beluchistan, Afghanistan, and Persia, finally stopping at the shore of the Caspian Sea. There they divided themselves in two groups, one of which had traveled to central and northern Europe, and the other of which had returned to the shore of the river Sindhu in North India.[85]

Regarding the *varṇāśrama* system, Swami Bon confirmed that it had been the original social structure of the *brāhmaṇas*, and that those who fell outside this structure were considered impure (*mleccha*) and non-Aryan. However, he also noted that over the course of time the special qualities and customs of the *brāhmaṇas* had been transformed into a hereditary system, and that this development was responsible for the racial orientation

---

82. For a concise description of Nazi ideology as presented in the German media, see Adolf Hitler's speech on "Nationalsozialismus als Weltanshauung" at the Reichkulturtag, Nuremberg on September 1, 1933, reported in the *Völkischer Beobachter*, September 2, 1933. See also Adolf Hitler, *The Essential Hitler: Speeches and Commentary*, ed. Max Domarus and Patrick Romane (Wauconda, Ill.: Bolchazy-Carducci, 2007).

83. The copy consulted is located at the British Library in London. It was a gift signed by Saṃvīdānanda dāsa to the Indologist Lionel David Barnett, then professor of Oriental studies at the University of London, who supervised the former's doctoral thesis. The gift is dated February 5, 1935.

84. Bon, *Gedanken über den Hinduismus*, p. 11.

85. Bon, *Gedanken über den Hinduismus*, p. 15.

of the present caste system.[86] Many of the ideas in this lecture had been previously discussed by Bhaktisiddhānta, and represented an attempt to synthesize modern theories with indigenous historical accounts—without entirely compromising either side in the process.[87]

Finally Swami Bon suggested that the Aryan concept of a metaphysical self was distinct from the notion of self found in the three Semitic religions, as well as the writings of Aristotle, all of which defined "self" to various degrees in terms of the material mind and body. He also pointed out that the modern notion of being "Hindu" was merely a secular idea, and that the true nature of the self could be best understood by relying upon the teachings of *sanātana dharma*, the perennial religion of India.[88]

Swami Bon's booklet of German lectures also included talks on such subjects as "The Philosophy of Caitanya" (*Die Philosophie Śrī Kṛṣṇa Caitanyas*), "The Concept of *Māyā* in Indian Philosophy" (*Der Begriff der Māyā in der indischen Philosophie*), "The Concept of God and Soul" (*Der Begriff von Gott und der Seele*), "The Hindu Way to God" (*Der Weg der Hindus zu Gott*), "Hindu Theology" (*Die Hindu Theologie*), "The Worldview of Indian Philosophy and Religion" (*Die Weltanschauung in der indischen Philosophie und Religion*), and "The Mental Foundations of Caste" (*Die geistigen Grundlagen des Kastenwesens*). It was, however, his lecture on the Aryan past and the Aryan concept of race that naturally caught the attention of Nazi ideologists.

In a *Harmonist* article entitled "Soul and Mind as Subject Matter of the 13th Session of the German Philosophical Society," Schulze (now Sadānanda dāsa) attempted to clarify the position of Bhaktisiddhānta and the Gaudiya Math relative to Nazi ideology. The article, which was focused on the social and political implications of identity in relation to bhakti, objected to Steche's conclusion that

> the differentiations of the races developed during thousands of years have to do not only with the body but also with the mind and soul.[89]

---

86. Bon, *Gedanken über den Hinduismus*, pp. 13–14.

87. See chapter 5.

88. Bon, *Gedanken über den Hinduismus*, p. 15.

89. *Harmonist* 33, no. 1 (1936): p. 21.

In other words, Schulze objected to National Socialism's radical materialistic definition of the individual on the basis of race, which to some degree resembled attitudes on blood and heredity found in India's caste system—a system that Bhaktisiddhānta had long dismissed as being nonrepresentative of genuine *varṇāśrama dharma*. Schulze's critique went on to discuss an article written by one Dr. W. Steinbeck on the thirteenth session of the *Deutsche Philosophische Gesellschaft*, held in Berlin on September 21–23, 1936.[90] In this article, published in the *Völkischer Beobachter*, Steinbeck claimed that the concepts of mind (*Geist*) and soul (*Seele*) were foreign to Nazism; for Steinbeck, *Geist* was an abstract medium that accommodated the most contradictory ideas, and *Seele* was even worse because it implied that "man" was some sort of abstract entity. According to him, the concept of *Seele* could not account for the "community of nation" and was thus irrelevant:

> National-socialism does not require a philosophy of the relative realisation of life, but a joint cooperation on the plane of facts which are given by the historical existence of the nation and the race.[91]

In his critique, Schulze defended the idea of a conscious self that transcends bodily existence. He also noted that while one may belong to a particular race or nation, one's actions ultimately depend upon individual character. In other words, the fact of one's racial or national identity does not change the general fact that individual reason regulates the conscious and subconscious mind, and that human beings are not merely determined by social and hereditary structures.

In keeping with Bhaktisiddhānta's teachings and a Vedantic view of atman or self, Schulze maintained that the soul is the "regulative inner principle of body and mind," and that a precise analysis of the distinction between body, mind, and soul leads to the conclusion that ideas like race and nation concern the more external aspects of culture. For Schulze, both the body and the mind—in all of their various aspects—are mere coverings of the soul, which, in its conditioned state, mistakes itself for "the empirical psycho-mental ego." Although body and mind function within the sphere of the nation and the race, the societal regulations that govern

---

90. *Harmonist* 33, no. 1 (1936): pp. 19–23.

91. Quoted in *Harmonist* 33, no. 1 (1936): p. 20.

their functioning should be such that they do not interfere with the ultimate interests of the soul—that is, service to God. In Schulze's view, the real task is to grasp the difference between soul, mind, and body, and not merely to define their external functions. Regarding the core question of the existence of a transcendent self, he stated that

> we are far from encouraging the old metaphysical solutions which have been well refuted by Kant. We can have no knowledge of the *noumena*, of the things in themselves.[92]

However, although neither perception nor reason is capable of grasping the reality of the transcendental realm, the soul proper could do so through the full development of its contemplative devotional consciousness. To the natural objection that there *is* no "thing in itself," Schulze replied that it is irrational to suppose that this ontological category does not exist merely because, for the time being, one has no access to it. As one cultivates bhakti—that is, love for God through humility, devotion, and service—one moves beyond the limitations of sense and reason to a direct perception of the self and the supreme self through realization.

The above exchange clearly indicates that Bhaktisiddhānta's philosophical and theological understandings, as represented by his disciples, were incompatible with National Socialism's racial theory. In an entirely different context, but for similar reasons, Bhaktisiddhānta remained uninvolved in his country's nationalist struggle against British colonial rule. The concepts of nationality, race, caste, and the like were far too narrow to accommodate his spiritual vision for humankind. Rather his personal struggle was to establish, through dispassionate discourse, a vision of Caitanya Vaishnavism—of bhakti—that was capable of addressing the challenges and concerns of the collective global community.

Bhaktisiddhānta's Response to the European Missions

Several letters survive in which Bhaktisiddhānta comments on the mission to England and Germany and gives guidance and encouragement to his disciples. Swami Bhakti Pradīpa Tīrtha, one of the individuals that

92. Quoted in the *Harmonist* 33, no. 1 (1936): p. 22.

accompanied Swami Bon to Europe, includes excerpts from some of those letters in one chapter of the *Sarasvatī Jayaśrī*, the biographical work on the life of Bhaktisiddhānta:

> Your conversation with the cultured people of the West following the words of the Divine Lord will surely be appreciated by all sincere souls amid their busy life. I don't know anybody who is more delighted than myself to hear that at last the Gaudiya Math Office has been opened in the British Isles (April 21st, 1933).
>
> While delivering discourses about Harī [a name of Krishna] and speaking to many, maybe one or two good people may be attentive and listen to topics about the supreme person (*bhāgavatakathā*)—this is my close expectation (May 25th, 1933).
>
> The Esoteric representation need not be placed on the table at the sacrifice of the exoteric code and exposition, as the people are found to be very hasty to judge a person by his external appearance (June 27th, 1933).
>
> We are no meditators, but on the other hand solicitors of Congregational meetings. So shifting from the center of London is now out of question (July 26th, 1933).
>
> I have enjoyed much to learn that the senior Tridandi Swami has been honored and received by Her Majesty, the Queen of England. This unforeseen chance is really a very rare opportunity that hardly falls to the lot of a monk with his triple staff and bowl in his hand (August 21st, 1933).
>
> We take pride in that you are acting as our proxy in a distant land, where our crippled movements have not yet approached (August 21st, 1933).
>
> You should always be submissive and courteous to all whom you meet however unpleasant situation they create. You should know that you are after all poor Indians; you are always to crave sympathy from the people there right and left; specially as you are a true Vaishnava, you should endure all sorts of sufferings and should be proving fully submissive to all you meet in a foreign country (January 16th, 1934).
>
> May Śrī Kṛṣṇa bless you in your noblest endeavours in carrying the message of the Supreme Lord Śrī Caitanya to a land where such transcendental news had not reached before you graced the banks of the Thames (February 13th, 1934).

> Though we are distantly placed by the will of Providence, still the symbolical sounds in letters will not keep us at such a distance. No letters come from the God. His news come from the persons who are dear to him and our news also can be sent to Him through devotees. That communication can be made even before the Telegram or Air Mail or Wireless Radio. The Benign Hand of Śrī Kṛṣṇa is a better judge than our silly selves. We should ever be in the service of the Supreme Lord Kṛṣṇa, whatever troubles we meet in our journey of life (February 23rd, 1934).[93]

In another place, on May 27, 1934, he wrote:

> Work with extreme enthusiasm. Residents of England will slowly feel reverence for Indians and favour Bhagavat-sevā once images of Lord Jagannātha and Lord Caitanya are installed in the villages of England and *mahāprasāda* [sacred food] is distributed. . . . A competent person like * * * [*sic*] may go there and benefit them by upholding pure *sanātana dharma*. When will that day arrive when all residents of that country will chant the name of Gaurāṅga [Caitanya], honor the transcendental *mahāprasāda* of that temple with a spiritual frame of mind and understand and exercise genuine spirituality?[94]

Despite these encouraging words, Bhaktisiddhānta was keenly aware of the obstacles that confronted the mission. In an August 1933 letter he deplored the fact that various accomplished British scholars had been prejudiced by the negative depictions of Caitanya Vaishnavism found in the works of scholars such as Melville Kennedy.[95] Because of this, as well

93. *Sarasvatī Jayaśrī*, pp. 207–208.

94. Bhaktisiddhānta, *Prabhupādera Patrāvali*, vol. 2 (May 27, 1934), p. 72.

95. Bhaktisiddhānta referred to Melville T. Kennedy, *The Chaitanya Movement: A Study of Vaishnavism in Bengal* (1925; New Delhi: Munshiram Manoharlal Publishers, 1993). Some of the other scholars mentioned in this letter were Lionel D. Barnett (the director of Saṃvidānanda's thesis in London), Nicol MacNicol, Arthur Keith, Sylvain Lévi, and Moriz Winternitz. Nicol MacNicol among other works wrote *Indian Theism from the Vedic to the Muhammadan Period* (1915; Delhi: Munshiram Manoharlal, 1968). Arthur Berriedale Keith (1879–1944) was Regius Professor of Sanskrit and lecturer in constitutional history at the University of Edinburgh; Sylvain Lévi (1863–1935) was a well-known French orientalist (Bhaktisiddhānta seems to have been unaware of French intellectuals such as René Guénon that had a sympathetic view of Indian religious traditions); Moriz Winternitz (1863–1937) was an Austrian Indologist active at the University of Prague.

as what he perceived to be their own scholarly pride, he believed it would be difficult for them to comprehend the deeper philosophical nuances of Caitanyaite spirituality; once an opinion had been formed on the basis of elaborate research, it was very difficult to alter. Another challenge concerned the need to speak plainly and directly when contrasting the teachings of Caitanya Vaishnavism with those of Buddhist and other schools, without provoking irritation or annoyance. In this regard, Bhaktisiddhānta advised that although it was of little value to flatter an audience by compromising one's true point of view, each situation had to be handled with appropriate tact and sensitivity.[96]

While it would be fair to characterize Bhaktisiddhānta's missionary approach as containing a good tinge of zeal, it was nonetheless more reminiscent of Gandhi's renounced mood of service to humanity than the type of "muscular Christianity" that was popular among the British of that time. It should be noted, however, that Bhaktisiddhānta's apparent "loyalty" to the Raj and his willingness to engage the Nazis had nothing whatsoever to do with acceptance of British rule or approval of National Socialist ideology. From his vantage point, British or no British, Nazis or no Nazis, humanity would continue to suffer until it awakened to its true spiritual identity. His aim was to elevate mankind—whether in India, Germany, Great Britain, America, or anywhere else—by developing a favorable platform for the introduction and discussion of Caitanya Vaishnavism. The agency of a *bhakta* implied some measure of determined action, creative thinking, and the mood of a "spiritual warrior." The emphasis in Bhaktisiddhānta's approach did not lie in the use of force, but in the force of personal example and integrity of character. In the imperial context of the Raj, he (like Gandhi) opted for the employment of so-called feminine traits, such as humility and nonviolence, in an attempt to transform (or perhaps elevate) colonial consciousness. This, however, should not be taken to imply that Bhaktisiddhānta's approach was actuated by feelings of inferiority or servility relative to the West. What he sought for was philosophic and religious exchange among those he regarded as equals.

Christian God, and Vaishnava God

Although the mission to Europe was an important area of concern for Bhaktisiddhānta, he also kept his door open for religious dialogue at home.

96. Bhaktisiddhānta, *Prabhupādera Patrāvali*, vol. 2 (August 6, 1933), p. 70.

In January 1929, Albert Edward Suthers (1887–1984) visited Bengal and the Gaudiya Math as part of his research on Indian religions.[97] Suthers was an American Christian lecturer on the history of religion at Ohio Wesleyan University. He had taken a yearlong sabbatical in 1929 to conduct research in India.[98] The following is a summary of some of the points made during a conversation between Suthers and Bhaktisiddhānta that was transcribed and later published in the *Harmonist*.[99] It concerned the encounter between Vaishnavism and Christianity, and dealt with issues born of Europe's interaction with Indic religions throughout the colonial period.[100]

Suthers began his inquiry by asking about Vedantism. Bhaktisiddhānta replied that although Vedanta is generally viewed as being strictly nondualistic, almost all Vaishnava Vedantic schools conceive of *brahman* as a divine personality, and these far outstrip the nondualistic schools in terms of numbers of adherents. Bhaktisiddhānta suggested the *Bhāgavata Purāṇa* as the means to a more authentic understanding of Vedanta *sūtra*, because it enables one to resolve the apparent ambiguities of that text—nondualism versus dualism, immanence versus transcendence, and so on.[101]

---

97. Suthers was born in Queensland on June 25, 1887, and his ancestors were from either England or Scotland. He was baptized as a Methodist and immigrated to the United States in 1911. He graduated from Ohio Wesleyan in 1917. After graduation he received infantry training in Ontario and became a sergeant. He was transferred to field artillery and fought in France and Belgium. After the war he attended Edinburgh University, the Union Theological Seminary, and Columbia University, where he received a M.A. degree. He came to Ohio Wesleyan in the early 1920s and taught courses in the history of religion. From 1928 to 1929 he traveled to India, Australia, Malaya, Siam, and Arabia. In *School and Society* it is reported that "Dr. George Hollister, Hinghua, China, has been appointed professor of missions at Ohio Wesleyan University during the year's leave of absence of Professor Albert E. Suthers" (1929, p. 357). Suthers became professor of history of religion at Ohio Wesleyan University in 1931 and retired in 1954. A number of biographical sources are available at http://wc.rootsweb.ancestry.com/cgi-bin/igm.cgi?op=GET&db=wiseosmond&id=I82 (accessed on July 29, 2012).

98. In the same year, Suthers published an introduction to the book *Something about Sikhism* (1929).

99. Talks between Bhaktisiddhānta and his guests were often reproduced in English and Bengali in the *Gauḍīya* and the *Harmonist*, especially if the interlocutor was a foreigner.

100. Indians during the colonial period generally saw little difference between British and Americans; after all, both spoke the same language, were quite similar in appearance, and, in many cases, had close ancestral ties.

101. For Bhaktisiddhānta both immanence and transcendence were distinct from nature. The immanent aspect of God is known as *paramātma* (the minute personal form of God that exists even within the atom) and the transcendent aspect is known as *bhagavān* or the "Personality of Godhead." For him immanence and transcendence are two noncontradictory features of the Absolute, whose relation to the phenomenal world is likened to the relation of the substance to the shadow: "the shadow is not independent of the substance and yet it is not the substance"; *Harmonist* 32, no. 3 (October 1935): p. 72. Nature is remarkably similar to the Absolute because the divine substance is immanent in the shadow, without being of its essence.

He also pointed to the breadth and variety of readings of Hindu philosophy, making it difficult to reduce Hinduism to one single voice. He explained that what is generally understood as "tradition" within Indic culture is difficult to ascertain and thus requires careful study of the original Sanskrit sources, and particularly the Puranic literature, which is too often neglected. In his view, Caitanya Vaishnavism was Vedantic, nonsectarian, and compatible with the theistic understandings of the major Semitic religions—Judaism, Christianity, and Islam. Bhaktisiddhānta explained the more esoteric understandings of Vaishnava bhakti as a type of fulfillment of Christian aspirations rather than as their antithesis. If Christianity largely focused on the individual's relationship with God the father, Caitanya mysticism opened up the possibility of more intimate, spontaneous, and unconditional forms, up to and including the form of female love, considered the highest (and most complete) level of religious emotion between the *jīva* and God. Bhaktisiddhānta viewed Christianity not as an adversary but as a nonsectarian partner in the battle to forestall the godless tendencies of modern secular society and respiritualize the world.

In articles published by Suthers after he left India there was no explicit mention of either bhakti or Bhaktisiddhānta. While this omission may have been by conscious choice, it may as well have been the result of his inability to comprehend Bhaktisiddhānta's difficult style of English and the complexity of his thought. In "Arab and Hindu: A Study in Mentality," published in 1931, Suthers presented Hinduism as essentially nondualistic and mystical, a view that by then had become popular in Christian circles:

> The Aryan, brooding over the enigma of existence, took refuge from the mystery in a philosophy of denial. There is something elusive and equivocal about the First Cause, the nature of whose existence can only be affirmed, paradoxically enough, by negation. Is He this or is He that? "Neti, Neti"—not so, not so! Whatever He is, He is not that but something different.[102]

This description reflects many of the stereotypes that were commonly associated with Hinduism: otherworldly, nondualistic, and consisting of a

102. Albert Edward Suthers, "Arab and Hindu: A Study in Mentality," *Muslim World* 21, no. 2 (1931): p. 145.

negative theology. It is also interesting to note Suthers's linking of Aryan civilization with Indian religions, something that was quite in vogue at the time.[103]

In 1937 Bhaktisiddhānta passed away and shortly thereafter the leading members of his institution became embroiled in an internecine conflict that left his organization in ruins and threatened his legacy. The "Harmonist" principles of universal brotherhood and cooperation that he had so vigorously advocated had not survived their first real test (see chapter 2). Meanwhile, on the international front, World War II came to devastate Europe and turn most prewar visions on their head. Due to these grim internal and external circumstances, the missions in Britain and Germany gradually shrunk.[104]

Globalization of the Gaudiya Math

David Lehmann has argued that apart from capitalism and free market, religion contributes to globalization through the redrawing of borders.[105] Between the seventeenth and the twentieth centuries, the British Empire almost single-handedly redrew the political and economic map of Eurasia, and Christian missionaries from Scotland and England established powerful transnational networks based upon the notion of universal salvation.[106] Although Bhaktisiddhānta's mission began as a local "guru movement,"

---

103. Suthers, however, had a sympathetic view of Indian religions and the Orient. In "East and West: A Study of Irenics," he praised the fact that life in the East was not departmentalized as in the West because of the prominence of religious thought and practice, and he appreciated that religions such as Buddhism possessed a "consistent reverence towards life in every form" from which liberal Christians could possibly derive inspiration. Albert Edward Suthers, "East and West: A Study in Irenics," *Journal of Religion* 12, no. 2 (1932): p. 240.

104. After the schism, the plans for the Hindu temple in London were suspended, and Lord Zetland stepped down as the chair of the Gaudiya Mission in London. In 1939, Swami Bon left India in disappointment to travel in the United States and Japan, where he continued lecturing and meeting prominent personalities of the elite, this time without the support of the Gaudiya Math. He returned to India in 1941. Schulze remained in India, but because of his German nationality spent the war years in a British internment camp.

105. David Lehmann, "Religion and Globalization," in *Religions in the Modern World: Traditions and Transformations*, ed. Linda Woodhead, Paul Fletcher, Hiroko Kawanami, and David Smith (London: Routledge, 2002).

106. For a discussion of religious globalization see also Sander and Andersson, "Religion och religiositet i en pluralistisk och föränderlig värld—några teoretiska, metodologiska och begreppsliga kartor," in *Det mångreligiösa Sverige: ett landskap i förändring*, ed. Åke Sander and Daniel Andersson (Lund: Studentlitteratur, 2009), pp. 89–91.

his mature aspirations were for the teachings of Caitanya to expand to the entirety of the world. By utilizing modern forms of communication and institutionalization, the Gaudiya Mission took advantage of global networks that had been developed by the British Empire to bring its message to the shores of England, and from there to Germany. In this way it created a cultural counterflow from peripheral India to the center of European power while simultaneously maintaining the core of its own understanding of Vaishnava bhakti.

Karner and Aldridge have suggested that processes of globalization enhance the role of religion in the exploration of identity and in defining cultural and social belonging. They suggest that globalization stimulates an awareness of inherited cultural patterns and helps to transform them into well-articulated discourses. Religion thus becomes an instrument by which to resist the by-products of globalization—that is, enhanced individualism and the crises of local cultures.[107] Referring to Roland Robertson, Peter Beyer has further suggested that globalization establishes a connection between the local and the global. Local religions are transformed into global ones by the development of sophisticated missionary strategies that employ modern means of communication (such as the Internet); when these globalized forms return to their particular locality they transform it through newly acquired discourses. The local, in this case, is a product of how the global constitutes itself.[108] Thus globalization interactively involves a universalization of the particular and a particularization of the universal.[109]

Bhaktisiddhānta was heavily exposed to the process of globalization as introduced by the British Raj. Because of this he was able to identify and utilize modern means in an attempt to communicate Caitanya bhakti to a wider global audience. By operating on a transnational level, he hoped to make his voice heard outside of India and to strengthen his tradition at home. To better understand this process, it is useful to explore a definition of religious globalization offered by José Casanova.

Casanova has analyzed religious globalization as consisting of three elements: (1) confessional *deterritorialization,* meaning a disjunction of

---

107. Globalization entails "economic polarization, social atomization, as well as cultural crises that transform taken-for-granted, ascribed and inherited meaning into discourse." Christian Karner, Christian Karner, and Alan Aldridge "Theorizing Religion in a Globalizing World," *International Journal of Politics, Culture and Society* 18, nos. 1–2 (2004): p. 24.

108. Peter Beyer, *Religions in Global Society* (London: Routledge, 2006), p. 25.

109. Beyer, *Religions in Global Society*, p. 24.

the historical link between a local territory and a particular confessional religion; (2) *deprivatization*, meaning that religion is no longer regarded as an exclusively "private" affair, subjugated by policies of secularization; (3) and global *denominationalism*, meaning the expansion of transnational imagined communities.[110]

Bhaktisiddhānta promoted a *deterritorialization* of religion, taking advantage of modern opportunities to diffuse Vaishnavism beyond the geographical borders of India. By doing so, bhakti left its local "sacred space" and entered the foreign territory of the colonizing power. In England, Bhaktisiddhānta planned to create a new sacred space for the practice of bhakti by erecting the first Hindu temple in Europe, thus expanding the respectability and reputation of his tradition at home.

As the Gaudiya Math became a public institution, it entered a phase of *deprivatization* and gained political support from British and German government officers. One important prerequisite for that aid was the acceptance of the patronizing role of Britain, which was obtained by assuming a neutral political role. This implied further goodwill and support at the local level as well.

Global *denominationalism* implies that the Gaudiya Math attempted to generate transnational networks of practitioners through its missionaries and the press. This succeeded only to a small degree, and the leadership remained largely dominated by ethnic Bengalis. It was nonetheless an indigenous attempt to reach beyond the racial and religious divides of colonial society. The opening of the Gaudiya Math to all human beings held out the possibility that Westerners and other non-Indians could attain leadership roles, a diversification that enhanced its chances of survival, both locally and globally.

Summary

Bhaktisiddhānta's approach to the West was marked by a recognition and respect for the contrasts between European and Indian cultures and religions. His hope was not that the West would become the East, but rather that it would embrace the core of Caitanya's teachings from its own sociocultural standpoint. Those of the Gaudiya Math who ventured forth to

110. José Casanova, "Political Challenges from Religion in the 21st Century," paper presented to the conference "Religion in the 21st Century: Transformations, Significance and Challenges," University of Copenhagen, 2007.

Britain dressed and presented their message in ways that to a large degree were intelligible to European sensibilities. Their confrontation with the Nazis, however, set the limit for the process of dialogue, since National Socialist ideology compromised not merely the periphery, but the very core of Caitanyaite teachings regarding the equality of the *jīvas* and the spiritual brotherhood of all beings, beyond consideration of racial, ethnic, or national distinctions.

The Gaudiya Math's venture west marked the earliest attempt of a Vaishnava institution to establish itself in Europe. Its intellectual foundation rested in the production of English-language literatures that in some respects provided a more authentic understanding of Vaishnava bhakti than that which had been thus far presented in the writings of Christian scholars and Indologists. Bhaktisiddhānta also sought to provide a genuine alternative to the nondualistic understanding of Hinduism that had come to predominate, particularly within the Anglo-Saxon cultural sphere.

The fact that the Gaudiya Math was structured on the basis of modern organizational principles provided Bhaktisiddhānta's pan-Indian movement with an effectiveness that would have been otherwise unattainable. Bhaktisiddhānta employed Western methods in his effort to institutionalize Vaishnavism, but incorporated them in a way that was in keeping with his general spiritual aims. In his conception of the Vaishnavism that would spread "love of Godhead" throughout the world, there was no need for a sociopolitical uprising or some sort of revolt against modernity. For him, modernity would always be a useful tool, but its ideology of ever-expanding material progress held no sway and remained very much absent from his religio-cultural worldview. Bhaktisiddhānta considered that the fundamental problems of human society remain the same regardless of time, place, or circumstance and can only be permanently resolved through the reestablishment of mankind's eternal loving relationship with the "Supreme Person." This was the platform he had developed relative to Europe, and his disciples were trained to present Caitanya Vaishnavism in that way.

During his lifetime, the groundbreaking efforts of the Gaudiya Math relative to Britain, Germany, and the Christian world were not enough to create the type of mass movement that Bhaktisiddhānta had hoped for; nor were they able to precipitate a widespread shift of Western intellectual attitudes toward bhakti and theistic Vedanta. Nonetheless, Bhaktisiddhānta had shown that Caitanya Vaishnavism was, to some degree, viable outside of India. The Gaudiya Mission had attracted the attention of the elite of Britain and Germany, and had even managed to kindle serious interest among a handful of British and German citizens, one of whom was trained personally by Bhaktisiddhānta and remained a profoundly committed disciple and preceptor of bhakti throughout his life.[111] A precedent had been set, but for a number of reasons the timing appeared not to have been right.

Although Bhaktisiddhānta's mission west was by no means a crowning success, and he passed away with his universal religious vision ostensibly unfulfilled, as it turned out, the efforts of Swami Bon marked only the barest beginning of what was eventually to come about in the mid-1960s.

111. There were also two women in Great Britain that became Bhaktisiddhānta's disciples and remained faithful followers of his teachings throughout their lives.

4

Social Philosopher

THE ATTEMPT TO locate the religious core in Bhaktisiddhānta's writings poses a number of challenges. One is the complexity of his language; another is the sheer size of the literature that he published. Furthermore, Bhaktisiddhānta delineated his ideas mostly in periodical articles or in commentaries on traditional texts. An example is his *Anubhāṣya* commentary on *Caitanya Caritāmṛta* by Kṛṣṇadāsa Kavirāja, regarded by disciples as his magnum opus.[1] Like many thinkers that did not systematically present their thought in one or more volumes, his ideas are spread throughout various writings and texts.[2]

Personalism

During the later period of his life, Bhaktisiddhānta met with various Westerners to discuss religion and philosophy. Among these was Jan van der Stock of Batavia, whom he met on December 26, 1935.[3] In the course of this recorded conversation, Bhaktisiddhānta concisely stated

1. Bhaktisiddhānta's *Anubhāṣya* was completed in 1915. To gain some sense of it, English-language readers can turn to the translation and commentary of *Caitanya Caritāmṛta* by Swami A. C. Bhaktivedānta (2002). Bhaktivedānta's commentary is largely based on the commentary of Bhaktisiddhānta, and he directly refers to it 259 times: 95 in the *Ādī-līlā*, 113 in the *Madhya-līlā*, and 51 in the *Antya-līlā*.

2. Bhaktisiddhānta wrote commentaries on the following texts: *Caitanya Caritāmṛita*, *Bhāgavata Purāṇa*, *Upadeśāmṛta* by Rūpa Goswami, *Bhakti Sandarbha* by Jīva Goswami, *Caitanya Bhāgavata* by Vṛndāvana dāsa Ṭhākura, *Prameya Ratnāvalī* by Baladeva Vidyābhūṣaṇa, *Caitanya Candrāmṛta* and *Navadvīpa Śataka* by Prabhodhānanda Sarasvatī, and the *Brahma Saṃhitā*. See appendix E for a complete list of his works.

3. Batavia was the name of Jakarta during Dutch colonial rule in Indonesia. The original spelling given is Mr. Willion Henri Jan Vandor Stock, which appears to be wrong.

what can be regarded as the core conviction of a Caitanya Vaishnava: "We believe that there is a Personality of God-head and that we are persons."[4] These words refer to bhakti in the light of three classical paths (*mārga*): (1) the path of action (*karma*) for those who seek the fruits of work in this world; (2) the path of knowledge (*jñāna*) for those who seek to dissolve their personal identity and achieve freedom from bondage (*mokṣa*) by merging into *brahman*; and, (3) the path of bhakti for those who identify themselves as nonmaterial "infinitesimals" striving to develop a permanent relationship with the personal aspect of "Absolute Infinity."[5]

Bhaktisiddhānta sharpened the distinction between *jñāna* and bhakti in a way that is characteristic for the Caitanyaite philosophical school.[6] If personhood is the core and most important element of bhakti, then the path of *jñāna*, which proposes to dissolve personhood for the sake of liberation, is its antithesis—and this despite the fact that the *jñāna* of *advaita* never rejected bhakti, as is attested by centuries of vigorous *nirguṇa* bhakti in India. It was not the practice (*sādhana*) of *jñāna* that he resisted, but rather its ultimate goal. By generally pointing to Śaṅkara as the main representative of *jñāna*, Bhaktisiddhānta revived an ancient dialogue within Indian philosophy. He tended to treat modern Vedanta philosophies as variations on the theme of South Indian *advaita*. His goal, however, was not to explore *advaita* as such, but rather to contrast it with bhakti to highlight its specific features. The reason for reviving this debate lay in the fact that various nondualist orientations had gained remarkable ground during his time.

Bhaktisiddhānta also expressed his appreciation for Śaṅkara despite his philosophical resistance to nondualism. He regarded him as the cornerstone of the revival of Indic spirituality after the Buddhist period. In an article in the daily *Nadīyā Prakāśa*, he also pointed to a reconciliation between the personal and impersonal understanding of the divine. A true Vaishnava, he stated, is able to understand three complementary aspects of God: (1) *brahman*, the impersonal; (2) *paramātmā*, the personal

4. Bhaktisiddhānta, *Shri Chaitanya's Teachings*, p. 340.

5. Bhaktisiddhānta, *Shri Chaitanya's Teachings*, p. 342.

6. For a discussion of bhakti and *jñāna* see "Karma, Jnan and Bhakti," *Harmonist* 32, no. 7 (December 1935): pp. 148–153. See also Krishna Sharma, *Bhakti and the Bhakti Movement: A New Perspective. A Study in the History of Ideas* (New Delhi: Munshiram Manoharlal Publishers, 1987), pp. 268ff.

mediator; and (3) *bhagavān*, the personality of Godhead. Failure to do so was a symptom of ignorance of the truth of the real (*vastu tattva*). The three were nonexclusive and legitimate objects of contemplation, although a Caitanya *bhakta* would focus exclusively on the third personal aspect (*bhagavān*), considering the realization of both *brahman* and *paramātmā* to be incomplete.[7]

In order to further illuminate Bhaktisiddhānta's perspective, I will explore some of his earliest Bengali writings, which provide a rare, comprehensive account of his ideas about the society and religion of his time.

The Making of Society in Bengal

Between 1899 and 1900 Bhaktisiddhānta published his first monograph, *The Making of Society in Bengal: Varṇa and Dharmic Society* (*Baṅge Sāmājikatā: varṇa o dharmagata samāja*).[8] He had written it while working for the Maharaja of Tripura, who may have commissioned it and to whom it was dedicated. The maharaja's family was Vaishnava and supported Bhaktivinoda, so there is little reason to assume that Bhaktisiddhānta had to bend his ideas to suit the views of his employer. The booklet, which was meant for a broad audience, presented his views on colonial society, Hindu society, Hindu philosophy, and the theory and practice of bhakti. Although an early work, it contains Bhaktisiddhānta's most coherent and comprehensive statement of social analysis, incorporating several of the themes that were elaborated in his later thought, and it is thus a foundational text. The following provides a closer reading of this important work.

The *Baṅge Sāmājikatā* begins with a number of ontological statements based on classical Indian philosophy, above all Sāṅkhya, Vaiśeṣika, and

---

7. *Nadīyā Prakāśa*, *Janmāṣṭamī* issue (1934), p. 647.

8. I have consulted the original, whose full bibliographical entry is Bimala Prasad Siddhānta Sarasvatī, *Baṅge Sāmājikatā: varṇa o dharmagata samāja*, published from 181, Maniktala Street and printed by Gopalchandra Lahiri from "Purāṇa Press," Balaram Ghosher Street 21, Calcutta, Caitra, Śaka era 1821 (1899 CE). The front page is presented as figure B.3. The contents are author's introduction (pp. 1–9), "The Land of Bengal" (*Baṅgadeśa*, pp. 9–24), "*Varṇa*" (pp. 24–69), "*Dharma*" (pp. 69–128). Later editions have some variations in format and some topographic errors. The page number quoted in the following section refers to the edition published in 2002.

Vedanta. It states that (1) all categories of Nature (*prakṛti*) follow a set of common universal laws;[9] (2) the objects of Nature have specific differential qualities; (3) diversity is a trait of Nature; (4) Nature is a material potency and the consciousness of the living beings (*puruṣa*) is its substratum; (5) the conscious (*puruṣa*) and the unconscious (*prakṛti*) worlds are two fundamental categories of reality; (6) society is created by conscious beings; (7) society is defined by varieties of relationships; and (8) Bengali society appears to have lost its course.

The booklet begins by analyzing Nature and its categories:

> All events of Nature (*prakṛti*) follow certain common laws. All natural categories are distinguished by particular characteristics

---

9. The Sanskrit word *prakṛti* is a key concept of Saṅkhya philosophy and is difficult to translate. *Prakṛti* is the timeless essence of physicality and the primordial state of matter as well as an irreducible ontological category. It refers to the totality of physical and subtle objects linked together by a network of causal relationships. It also includes elements such as time and space. In Saṅkhya systems, *prakṛti* includes the five gross elements of earth, water, fire, air, and ether, the three psychic elements of mind, intelligence, and lower ego (*ahaṅkara*), as well as the three subtle qualities (*guṇa*) of purity (*sattva*), passion (*rajas*), and ignorance (*tamas*). These are in turn manifestations of more subtle states of unmanifested energy (*mahā-tattva*). *Prakṛti* is the original matrix of all material manifestations, and thus it means more than "matter," and will be translated here as "Nature" in the above sense. For a study of *prakṛti* see Knut A. Jacobsen, *Prakrti in Samkhya-Yoga: Material Principle, Religious Experience, Ethical Implications* (New York: Peter Lang, 1997). Classical Sāṅkhya divides reality into two broad categories: *prakṛti*, Nature, and *puruṣa*, nonmaterial beings. According to its view, Nature is unconscious but it awakens to life in contact with the *puruṣa*. *Puruṣa* is an atomic particle of spirit that *prakṛti* covers with a physical and subtle body consisting of mind, intelligence, and false sense of ego (*ahaṃkāra*). In classical Sāṅkhya, both body and mind are viewed as attributes of Nature, and the existence of God is denied. Consciousness is not a permanent attribute of *puruṣa*, but a temporary effect of its contact with *prakṛti*. However, there is a theistic tradition of Sāṅkhya that is presented in works such as the *Bhāgavata Purāṇa*. The theistic version argues that consciousness is a permanent attribute of the *puruṣa* and postulates the existence of God (*īśvara*). Surendranath Dasgupta provides an early reference to theistic Sāṅkhya in the Mahābhārata: "In the *Mahābhārata* XII.318 three schools of Sāṅkhya are mentioned, viz. those who admitted twenty-four categories…, those who admitted twenty-five (the well-known orthodox Sāṅkhya system) and those who admitted twenty-six categories. This last school admitted a supreme being in addition to *puruṣa* and this was the twenty-sixth principle." Surendranath Dasgupta, *A History of Indian Philosophy*, vol. 1 (Cambridge: Cambridge University Press, 1922), p. 217. See also John A. Grimes, "Darśana," in *The Hindu World*, ed. Sushil Mittal and G. R. Thursby (New York: Routledge, 2004), p. 545. Sāṅkhya constitutes the metaphysical foundation of the Yoga system, and a number of its conclusions are accepted by most Hindu philosophical schools, including those of Vedanta.

> (*viśeṣadharma*).[10] The difference between one substance and another is what constitutes that substance's *viśeṣadharma*. The particular property that distinguishes one substance (*dravya*) from another is constant.[11] *Viśeṣadharma* itself establishes the unique [*dvaitatā*, dual in the sense of distinct] identity of an object.[12]

Bhaktisiddhānta's presentation takes into account central elements of Sāṅkhya and Vaiśeṣika philosophy.[13] He first suggests the existence of Natural laws and then presents a differentiating principle (*viśeṣa*) that binds each object's inherent attributes to its specific substances within Nature. *Viśeṣa* in Indian philosophy refers to the individual qualitative particularity that makes each object distinctively unique. Here Bhaktisiddhānta implies that the distinctions found among attributes and objects of Nature

---

10. The word *viśeṣa* is important since it a philosophical concept developed by the school of Vaiśeṣika that was adopted by Vaishnavas to explain the reality of the plurality of forms. Mādhva believed that *viśeṣa* was the inherent link between objects and their attributes, and that "this capability is intrinsic to all objects and is not itself an attribute." Deepak Sarma, *An Introduction to Mādhva Vedānta* (Burlington, Vt.: Ashgate, 2003), pp. 72–73. For Mādhva there was an unbridgeable difference between *brahman* and *prakṛti* and therefore *viśeṣa*, Nature, and its attributes were not a transformation of divine potencies but eternally separated. Jīva Goswami—the prominent systematizer of the Caitanya tradition—apparently accepted Mādhva's explanation of *viśeṣa*, but not his view of potency. For Jīva, God (*bhagavān*) was simultaneously one with and different from Nature (*acintya-bhedābheda-vāda*). Nature was a transformation of God's potencies (*śakti-pariṇāma-vāda*). See Elkman and Gosvami, *Jiva Gosvamin's Tattvasandarbha*, pp. 39–42. In this text Bhaktisiddhānta likely uses the term *viśeṣa* in the sense given by Jīva Goswami, since he accepted the transformation theory.

11. According to Mohanty, "*dravya*—which perhaps it is more appropriate to translate as 'thing' than as 'substance'—is defined (1) as the locus of qualities (*guṇa-s*) and actions (*karma-s*), and (2) as the material cause (or 'inherence cause') of effects (i.e., that in which the effect inhere)." Jitendranath Mohanty, *Classical Indian Philosophy* (Lanham, Md.: Rowman & Littlefield, 2000), p. 48. While not entirely contradicting each other, the six orthodox Hindu philosophies, Nyāya, Vaiśeṣika, Sāṅkhya, Yoga, Karma Mīmāṃsā, and Vedanta, focus on different aspects of reality. The schools propose different taxonomies of substance, from the nine of Nyāya-Vaiśeṣika to the eleven of Mīmāṃsā. The exploration of the nature of material objects is the theme of the realist approach of the philosophy of Vaiśeṣika (particularity), which assumes that matter is made of particulars (atoms possessing inherent attributes) that are regarded as eternal (and different from the atoms of Western physics). The distinction between Nature (*prakṛti*) and a nontemporal self (*puruṣa*) is the intellectual achievement of Sāṅkhya. This and a number of other theories are further developed in the concise statements (*sūtras*) of Vedanta, which advocates a universal nonmaterial essence (*brahman*) as the ultimate basis of reality.

12. Bhaktisiddhānta, *Baṅge Sāmājikatā*, p. 1. I have tried to adhere to the original as far as possible in the translation while striving to clearly convey the meaning of the text.

13. Two classical texts of Caitanya Vaishnavism, the *Śrimad Bhāgavatam* and the Bhagavad Gītā, consistently refer to Sāṅkhya terminology and concepts.

are genuine and real, and not merely a product of ignorance. For Śaṅkara, on the other hand, attributes and particularity are ultimately a product of illusion (*vivarta*). Bhaktisiddhānta continues by stating that if two objects possess similar attributes, they can legitimately be classified as part of the same class or "society," at least in a general sense. He then proceeds to explore the relation between material objects and the internal processes of consciousness.

The *Baṅge Sāmājikatā* tells that there are various ways to understand the relation between Nature and conscious beings. Some view consciousness as one of the attributes of Nature, a view that Bhaktisiddhānta rejects. Others see two separated categories in the world, Nature and a substratum of conscious living beings (*puruṣa*).[14] The latter position implies that the conscious self is distinct from and superior to Nature, a view with which Bhaktisiddhanta agrees. Therefore, he notes,

> The world is the repository of... Nature and is one of the subordinate potencies of that conscious self.[15]

Bhaktisiddhānta contends that by making a close analytical study of reality it is possible to distinguish Nature as potency (*śakti*) from the conscious *puruṣa*, although the former is visible while the latter is regarded as nonmaterial and nonvisible. For him consciousness is inherent in the self as a defining element of its being, a view in keeping with the theistic Vedanta of the Vaishnava schools. The minute *puruṣa* is a nonmaterial conscious agent that acts in the world in an embodied form and tends to exploit the resources of Nature for its own purposes.

Bhaktisiddhānta rejects individualism and solipsism, and instead advocates the need for relationships, which he regards as a constitutive element of conscious experience. The plurality of conscious life is needed in order to provide rich varieties of relationships. In Bhaktisiddhānta's view, all animate and even inanimate forms—humans, plants, minerals, and so on—are ultimately part of the sphere of conscious life.

After positing that the conscious self is distinct from Nature, *Baṅge Sāmājikatā* proceeds to explore embodied life, suggesting that the conscious

---

14. It is relevant to note that in Vaishnava Vedanta the *puruṣa* possesses consciousness as an inherent attribute; in other words, consciousness is not a separate attribute to be disposed of in the stage of *mokṣa*, as in classical Sāṅkhya.

15. Bhaktisiddhānta, *Baṅge Sāmājikatā*, p. 1.

self is made of a substance that is distinct from Nature, as well as from the body/mind complex. Conscious beings are independent agents, but due to their desire to enjoy the objects of Nature they tend to become captivated by it, thereby losing their spiritual freedom. Spiritual knowledge, timeless existence, and pure bliss (*ānanda*) are the real attributes of the nonmaterial self, but in contact with Nature they are concealed.

The understanding of universal categories such as *prakṛti* and *puruṣa* and the concept of intransitive consciousness—that is, consciousness as the universal attribute of the nonmaterial self beyond the transitive permutations of Nature—led Bhaktisiddhānta to criticize materialism and human "species-ism." The latter refers to the human propensity to pay respect to fellow humans on the basis of their higher skills and rationality compared to animals and plants. Bhaktisiddhānta maintains that it is wrong to assume that humans are better simply because they possess more developed bodily and mental functions. Since body and mind are ultimately products of Nature, and the nonmaterial self is equally present in all life-forms, the former are ultimately external. Bhaktisiddhānta conceives the self as a nonmaterial person endowed with particular personal attributes such as a unique nonmaterial form, suprasensory perception, and distinctive emotions of love. The shared attribute of all living beings is not body and mind, but their possession of personal consciousness. Freedom and liberation imply not forfeiting transient personal attributes, but uncovering the permanent, inherent ones beyond the coverings of Nature. This is the core of Bhaktisiddhānta's universal vision.

After stressing personal individual attributes Bhaktisiddhānta explores a force that leads to interdependence and unity. A society (*samāja*) can only function in relation to *conscious beings* (*caitanyamaya*). Various life-forms generally tend to create unity among those possessing similar physical or mental attributes. Society then evolves into subcommunities on the basis of second-order attributes. When attributes are generic, the communities and subcommunities are large, but when they are specific, they are small. By increasing unity in a social system, differentiation from other societies and communities will naturally arise on the basis of attributes such as race and culture. Thus the concept of "Other" will gain prominence. In a social system, the border between insiders and outsiders is so important that "the purpose of unity is the intensification of difference."[16] While considering

---

16. Bhaktisiddhānta, *Baṅge Sāmājikatā*, p. 3.

the varieties of species, races, and societies to reflect Natural attributes born from the will and desire of the *puruṣa*, Bhaktisiddhānta resists on ethical and philosophical grounds any radical form of segregation within human societies, or discrimination against nonhuman species.

Bhaktisiddhānta notes that a tendency of modern society is to call for independence and individual rights in opposition to the restrictions posed by society. The idea of denying the constraints of society and embracing individualism in the name of liberalism or anarchism is a superficial solution, he maintains, because it overlooks the fact that social relations are necessary for survival and ultimate happiness. The question is not how to nullify social borders, but how to create a sense of higher unity that can counterbalance the destructive forces of differentiation. In his view, humanism, utilitarianism, and liberalism—popular among the *bhadralok* of his time—fail to provide a satisfactory foundation for a just society because of their prejudice against other species and other communities, despite their rhetoric. Materialism and naturalism fail because they only accept the reality of the body, or at best, the mind, denying the distinctive properties of consciousness. As he sees it, such ideologies are also used to justify discrimination among races or species on the basis of evolution, fostering a bewildering sense of pride and superiority. Society and social life, however, need to develop ethics and values that can point to something beyond the conflicts generated by material life. As he saw it, the need of the day was to inspire strong interpersonal bonds based on sincere affection, reciprocal respect, and fair dealings, and to foster a morally developed society that

> increasingly blooms by dint of principles rooted in conscience, and is honored as a unique storehouse of virtuous deeds.[17]

Bhaktisiddhānta criticized the impact that colonial society was having on the individual person. He found the control that it exercised to be hampering and artificial:

> The organization of [material] society has gradually grown stronger. Protective guards stand at its gates. Although it appears to be lacking in spiritual potency, it is nonetheless powerful in many respects

17. Bhaktisiddhānta, *Baṅge Sāmājikatā*, p. 3.

> and does not shrink when encountering obstacles. The energy of consciousness in the world, which [is meant for a spiritual purpose and] can be compared to a burning lamp, has surrendered much of its power to society at large. Having less strength, religions must attempt to survive by adapting themselves to the inner fabric of [mainstream] society.[18]

According to *Baṅge Sāmājikatā*, Hindu *dharma* had to a large degree lost its struggle to remain independent of modern social, economic, and political structures, and had been domesticated by colonial administration. It is nonetheless a principle of the natural world that more organized societies control weaker ones, and the standard of real power and prosperity is generally related to the level of social organization. As Bhaktisiddhānta saw it, weakness in social structures "is the cause of disaster for a group or society."[19] Social organization, even in matters of religion, had become a necessity, a position that Bhaktisiddhānta embraced with vigor later on.

He observes that history is increasingly understood in the modern world in a monetary utilitarian sense—that is, in terms of how successful humans are in accumulating wealth. Societies that lack a strong commitment to economic pursuits "are now considered barbarous or uncivilized by more socialized humans."[20] He notes that both colonial and indigenous societies in Bengal had lost sight of the inner unity of all conscious beings because they had been blinded by the accumulation of wealth and power.

In my opinion, Bhaktisiddhānta did not advocate the elimination of social differentiation. His support for *varṇāśrama dharma*, a traditionalist position, remained consistent all along. He suggested instead its improvement by enhancing the value of personal merit independent of caste.[21] Bhaktisiddhānta's initial exploration of universal ontological

---

18. Bhaktisiddhānta, *Baṅge Sāmājikatā*, p. 3.

19. Bhaktisiddhānta, *Baṅge Sāmājikatā*, p. 3.

20. Bhaktisiddhānta, *Baṅge Sāmājikatā*, p. 3.

21. Lorenzen makes the case that *saguṇīs* have traditionally supported the *varṇāśrama* system, while the minority of nirguṇis in North India have consistently rejected it. David N. Lorenzen, *Bhakti Religion in North India: Community, Identity and Political Action* (New Delhi: Manohar, 1996), p. 20. The Vaishnava mainstream in India has traditionally supported *varṇāśrama*, albeit not as synonymous with caste. Vaishnava bhakti contains unsettling elements that go against hereditary privileges, although in reality the caste system has played a decisive role in Vaishnava culture.

categories such as consciousness and Nature was in tune with the theistic Vedanta embraced by the school of Caitanya, but was so far mainly theoretical. He turned, therefore, to a more concrete analysis of the society of Bengal.

Indic Civilization

Bhaktisiddhānta starts the third section of *Baṅge Sāmājikatā* by addressing racial theories that played a powerful role in colonial ideology:

> Contemporary scholars that study human beings have established distinctions among humans around the earth in terms of their physical differences. It is unanimously acknowledged that there are differences within the entirety of the human race in regard to physical constitution, be it due to living in a particular place for a long period of time or due to some observed local factor.[22]

The theory of evolution explains the existence of races such as Caucasian, Mongolian, Malaysian, and Australian as the product of mutation from a common breed of ancestors. In contrast to colonial ideology, however, Bhaktisiddhānta notes that in the case of the Indo-European ancestors, society had been divided into Aryans and non-Aryans not according to race, but according to the ability to follow *varṇāśrama*. The term "Aryan" is, for Bhaktisiddhānta, related to character and behavior, not to blood or race. This view resurfaced later in relation to the encounter of his disciples with Nazi Germany (discussed in chapter 3).

Bhaktisiddhānta writes that

> some scholars have determined on the basis of detailed research that the prehistoric descendants of the Indian Aryans lived near the Caucasus mountains and gradually set up colonies while migrating from there to the Southeast. Nothing stands against the acceptance of these statements that arise from research, unless they are prompted by selfish interest.[23]

22. Bhaktisiddhānta, *Baṅge Sāmājikatā*, p. 13.

23. Bhaktisiddhānta, *Baṅge Sāmājikatā*, p. 13.

The question of the origins of the Indo-European Aryan civilization is still hotly debated in India and elsewhere.[24] Bhaktisiddhānta suggested that the evidence pointing toward an Aryan migration was weak. The theory of common Aryan ancestors linking the people of India with the British was carefully maintained by the establishment and was one of the arguments that legitimized the presence of the British in India. In their own eyes, the colonizers were light-skinned Aryans who had come to India in order to help their brownish Aryan cousins. However, neither the vast literature of the Puranas nor the older Vedic corpus mention an Aryan migration from the Caucasus. For this reason, Bhaktisiddhānta concluded that Western readings of Hindu texts had obscured, rather than illuminated, Indian history and compromised the search for alternative understandings:

> Contemporary Western scholars think that all histories in the Puranas are full of fantasy like Arabian and Persian fiction. They indulge in self-pride and state that histories like the Puranas are concoctions. They fear that their study will lead to the abandonment of ideas that they have already gained. In other words, with regard to the Vedic literature, they consider their sharp intellect to have reached the other shore in the river of scholarship. Now it is futile to try and bring that [intellect] back again; [it is like] moving against the current.[25]

Bhaktisiddhānta felt that the majority of Western scholars were more interested in mirroring themselves through an imagined Indian civilization than in understanding India as it is. For this reason, he regretted a general lack of knowledge about the Puranas.[26] He implied that the colonial machinery had enormous resources for producing knowledge about Hinduism and teaching it to the Indian middle class, but it did so with ulterior motivations.

---

24. For a history of the Aryan invasion debate, see Edwin Bryant, *The Quest for the Origins of Vedic Culture: The Indo-Aryan Migration Debate* (New York: Oxford University Press, 2001).

25. Bhaktisiddhānta, *Baṅge Sāmājikatā*, p. 14.

26. Ludo Rocher comes to a similar conclusion in his study of the way Western scholars during the colonial period approached the Puranas. Ludo Rocher, *The Purāṇas, A History of Indian Literature, Epics and Sanskrit Religious Literature*, vol. 2, fasc. 3 (Wiesbaden: Harrassowitz, 1986).

As a parenthesis it may be said that this opinion was not unusual at that time. Brian Pennington offers an account of a pandit in colonial Benares according to whom Hindu texts (*śāstras*) had been translated into English merely "to serve the interest of the king."[27] On this, as on other occasions, documents were falsified and the content of Hindu texts distorted to suit particular purposes. Bhaktisiddhānta echoed a feeling among traditional sections of Hinduism—plausible to some degree—that the British had studied only fragmental portions of the textual corpus of Indic religions without concern for gaining an accurate understanding of their complete worldview.

Despite his critique of colonial culture, Bhaktisiddhānta was not blind to the faults of his own indigenous society. He recognized that social mobility in Bengal was mostly restricted to the *bhadralok* to whom he belonged. A shift to another *jāti* or caste was hard to carry out:

> Nowadays, emerging sections of the middle class are attempting to obtain the designation *bhadra* and improve their own status.[28] There is no doubt that those among them who become both erudite in Sanskrit texts and expert in Western education will be honored and respected. Although there may or may not be an upliftment of the entire caste under the influence of such individual scholarship, it may be expected that an educated person will be held in esteem and worthy of the status of "gentle one." If the son of an illiterate *brāhmaṇa* compromises his education that is the basis of his standing, he will eventually produce offspring that are lower in the sense that they will also be lacking in education—this is most plausible and reasonable. Despite this fact, social relations will remain unchanged because they are based on one's birth in a particular caste [rather than on education]. Even now there has not been any tangible effect of social reform in terms of eradicating the predominant social [caste] system. It is extremely difficult to restore an object to its original state once it has been broken. [Similarly,] a society that has been divided in terms of tangible occupational categories cannot be expected to [automatically] unite simply because those occupations have ceased to exist.[29]

---

27. Pennington, *Was Hinduism Invented?* p. 144. This event took place during the crises that led to the suppression of *sati*.

28. "Bhadra" refers the *bhadralok*.

29. Bhaktisiddhānta, *Baṅge Sāmājikatā*, p. 30.

Bhaktisiddhānta agreed with Western and progressive Hindu critics that caste was an inadequate and degraded secular system because it no longer reflected the factual professions that it originally aimed to structure and facilitate. Caste in Hindu society had evolved on the basis of an ancient religious weltanschauung, but had long since forgotten the principles that motivated its existence. In Bhaktisiddhānta's view, the principle of *varṇāśrama* was universal, but required rearticulation and rethinking to make it viable for modern times.

Colonial Culture and Hindu Dharma

The last section of *Baṅge Sāmājikatā* deals with *dharma*, a word that can only be approximately translated as "religion."[30] For Bhaktisiddhānta, as for most Hindus, dharma was synonymous with life itself and the process of self-realization rather than with rituals or faith. He paints an idealized picture of India as the land of dharma and spirituality, since Indians had successfully resisted the unsettling rule of many foreign lords and uniquely maintained their allegiance to the religious traditions of their ancestors:

> Even today the Aryan way of life has been preserved with care.... There is no other race on the face of the earth that has maintained its own lineage (*jāti*) from ancient ages the way the Indians have.... [Their] lamp of knowledge was never fueled by utilitarian principles; while sustaining themselves by working in the world, they maximized their philosophical pursuits.[31]

According to *Baṅge Sāmājikatā*, following a tradition is a virtue, since religious and philosophical knowledge evolves slowly and in a cumulative way.[32] By following a tradition and applying established processes for the transmission of knowledge, a society can benefit from the accomplishments of

30. For a discussion about the use of the Western term "religion" in the early encounters between Europe and India, see S. N. Balagangadhara, *"The Heathen in His Blindness": Asia, the West and the Dynamic of Religion* (New York: Brill, 1994). Regarding the relation between the word "dharma" and "religion" in the colonial context, see Torkel Brekke, *Makers of Modern Indian Religion in the Late Nineteenth Century* (New York: Oxford University Press, 2002).

31. Bhaktisiddhānta, *Baṅge Sāmājikatā*, p. 40.

32. Here the term "evolves" is not used in the classical "history of religions" sense—i.e., a development from animism to monotheism.

previous generations.[33] Colonial society, on the other hand, lacked a proper spiritual foundation and a sense of continuity, representing a sudden break from the past. The tone of his observations now gain a peculiar wit.

Bhaktisiddhānta begins with the plain observation that the human body has senses for acquiring knowledge, as well as motor organs for accomplishing practical work. The former consists of eyes, nose, ears, mouth and skin, and the latter of legs, arms, voice, genitals, and the organ for evacuation.[34] He writes that Indic societies had prioritized the senses for acquiring knowledge and the cultivation of the mind, intellect, and spirituality. In colonial society, on the other hand,

> persons expert in driving the latest two-wheelers, having knowledge of applying screws to machines, expert in playing cricket, successful in riding horses and physical exercises, and capable of rowing boats, are considered to be honorable persons. Western education is drawing their attention to the assumption that practical results attained by means of the motor organs are more efficient than the results obtained by intellectual development.[35]

Bhaktisiddhānta adds that the subtle activities of mind and intellect had always been considered of higher value in Indian culture compared to manual work. This was reflected in the *varṇāśrama*, where specialists in knowledge, the *brāhmaṇas*, were regarded as the religious leaders of society. He observes that when the standard of civilization is measured by the efficacy of the working organs, civilizations that display better skills of action are regarded as more advanced. This led him to criticize the British emphasis on masculinity and vigor:

> for example an animal like a gorilla is much more active than a human being. To those who think that human beings are

33. P. T. Raju has suggested, in this regard, that this is a general characteristic of Hindu philosophy: "In Western philosophy, one school or system generally develops out of another, and each philosopher brands his thought with a new name. In India, on the contrary, every philosopher considers it an honour to belong to one or the other school, whatever differences he may have from his predecessors in the same school, and considers himself as an interpreter and elaborator of his teacher's thoughts." P. T. Raju, *The Philosophical Traditions of India* (Delhi: Motilal Banarsidass, 1998), pp. 37–38.

34. These are Sāṅkhya classifications.

35. Bhaktisiddhānta, *Baṅge Sāmājikatā*, p. 36.

> progressing when they become active like these animals and set the standard of progress in those terms, to them Indians will appear lazy, socially unempowered, impotent, and unfit to be regarded as humans. According to them the main cause of this impotence is intellectual pursuits.[36]

He then suggests that without the support of intellectual pursuits no human endeavor can last for long. In India, he writes, people know how to row, shoot arrows, craft clay objects, and prove their competence in practical skills. However, these activities are less significant than the gifts that India's sages have offered to the world.[37] For Bhaktisiddhānta, Indic civilization had consistently striven for understanding the nonmaterial self, understood as the root of action and knowledge:

> The aim of every conscious individual self (*jīva*) is to understand its own identity. Every conscious self has the attribute of perceiving its consciousness. The proper use of consciousness is to curtail the propensity of identifying oneself as the controller of the inanimate objects that one has acquired. Matter is weaker and unconscious and it is always dependent on the category of the conscious (*cetana padārtha*). One may be successful in attempting to exert control over it, but an undesirable consequence [of that] may be forgetfulness of the self (*ātmavismṛti*). . . . A sage from the West has stated that there is no need to be proud of one's possessions; rather, you should be proud of what you are (*tumi je vastu*).[38]

While worldly action is important to uphold life, knowledge of the self is even more so. Knowledge is prior to action since meaningful action cannot take place without some sort of knowledge. Apart from material knowledge, however, there is spiritual knowledge as well:

> for the spiritually inclined, knowledge or real knowledge can only be gained beyond the material world and without the help of the material senses.[39]

---

36. Bhaktisiddhānta, *Baṅge Sāmājikatā*, p. 36.

37. Bhaktisiddhānta, *Baṅge Sāmājikatā*, p. 37.

38. Bhaktisiddhānta, *Baṅge Sāmājikatā*, p. 37.

39. Bhaktisiddhānta, *Baṅge Sāmājikatā*, p. 37.

In Bhaktisiddhānta's view, colonial civilization had marked a shift in India from a search for the inner self to a search for material success. After addressing the importance of acquiring knowledge of the self, *Baṅge Sāmājikatā* provides an overview of various definitions of *dharma*:

> Some scholars say that the meaning of the verbal root *dhri* refers to "holding something." From the verbal root we derive one meaning of the word. There are other scholars who suggest that the true meaning of dharma should be taken from what it has acquired in various historical contexts and from real life at present. Other people say that the collective disposition of all human communities on earth is dharma. A fourth definition disagrees with the other three by suggesting that whatever one personally conceives and believes in is dharma, and whatever is opposed to this is nondharma.[40]

These definitions had been gathered from the *bhadralok* and represented a cross-section of popular opinions.[41] After acknowledging the plurality of views in modern times, the booklet provides a historical overview of dharma from a theistic perspective.

The early worship of the Aryans was based on awe and respect for the elements of nature, such as the heat of the sun or the power of the wind and fire. Gradually, however, Aryans began to worship the personified images of these energies, thus developing a more subtle form of worship that was later systematized in the karma section of the Vedas—the ritual backbone of Hinduism. After the Vedic period, a shift took place and the culture of the Upanishads emerged:

> With the end of the age of active work (*karma yuga*) an age of knowledge emerged, and various efforts were made for its development. [In keeping with this new phase,] the dharma of action was philosophically reassessed in the light of knowledge. Because of these intellectual pursuits, the self (*jīva*) was better understood; a subsequent phase brought about an analysis of pleasure and pain. In analyzing "whose pain," "what is pain," etc., the categories of enjoyer,

---

40. Bhaktisiddhānta, *Baṅge Sāmājikatā*, p. 38.

41. Regarding the construction of Hinduism and Hindu dharma during the colonial period, see, for example, Sugirtharajah, *Imagining Hinduism*.

> enjoyed, and enjoyment were revealed in the hearts of those who had knowledge of Natural objects. Currents of thought that previously were drawn toward external actions changed their course and joined this new orientation.[42]

This new period of introspection (*jñāna*) led to the realization of a nondual, nonmaterial essence beyond the realm of Nature (*prakṛti*)—that is, *brahman*. A more elaborate form of image worship also emerged from the development of religious thought. Finally, the bhakti tradition became more prominent, and worship of Krishna (the nonsectarian name for the universal supreme personality) grew in earnestness:

> The desire for liberation by self-centered *brahman* seekers and the desire of materialists to enjoy the fruits of their worldly actions decreased [in relation to the taste of personal relationship with Krishna]. . . . Prior to this, those that followed the paths of karma and *jñāna* had been unaware of the various loving relationships (*bhakti*) [with God].[43]

Baṅge Sāmājikatā presents bhakti as the final stage of an evolutionary process that begins with karma, passes through *jñāna*, and finally reaches the level of pure devotion, which in its highest manifestation is self-sufficient and free from the motives and aims of the earlier stages.[44] Bhakti in its purest form is oriented toward loving and being loved by a nonmaterial deity:

> Those who had studied the ultimate consequences of the path of karma and *jñāna* rejected even the path of knowledge (*jñāna*) mixed with action (*karma*) and took shelter of loving devotion (*bhakti*) instead. No matter how elevated is one's attachment toward karma or one's thirst of knowledge (*jñāna*), getting pleasure is one's most precious goal. In fact, attachment to action or thirst for knowledge is only oriented toward enjoyment. Even though the paths of karma and *jñāna* may be ends in themselves, they cannot be compared to a higher goal [i.e., that of bhakti].[45]

---

42. Bhaktisiddhānta, *Baṅge Sāmājikatā*, p. 41.

43. Bhaktisiddhānta, *Baṅge Sāmājikatā*, p. 44.

44. See *Bhakti-rasāmṛta-sindhu* (1.1.11) by Rūpa Goswami.

45. Bhaktisiddhānta, *Baṅge Sāmājikatā*, p. 42.

Bhaktisiddhānta maintains that the path of karma is ultimately a way for conscious beings to embrace the world and refine their capacity to control and exploit it. The path of *jñāna* rejects that approach, paving the way for the self to realize its ultimate independence from the world. The threefold path of action, knowledge, and bhakti gradually culminates in pure love (*prema*). *Prema* satisfies the ultimate search of the nonmaterial self for lasting fulfillment, since in its purest form it is uninterrupted and unmotivated. According to Bhaktisiddhānta, the schools of action and knowledge cannot fully grasp the ultimate goal of bhakti. From the active self of karma and the contemplative self of *jñāna*, Hindu seers had thus discovered bhakti and the idea of the spiritually interrelational self:

> The unblossomed and obscure philosophical texts (*darśana śāstras*) now soaked themselves in the nectar of spiritual emotions (*rasa*) that meditators experienced in their ultimate contemplation, and [these texts] abandoned their previous dryness. In the hearts of pure beings (*jīva*) and in pure sparks of consciousness emerged the pure and materially untinged personality of love (*prema vigraha*) imbued with spiritual emotions, that is, the form of Śyāmasundara [a form of Krishna]. With this, the selfish seekers of *brahman* devalued the desire of liberation [just as] they did with the minor temporary material enjoyment of people who enjoy the fruits of actions. Until then, the hidden form of the personality of love was far beyond the reach of *karmīs* or *jñānīs*.[46]

This understanding of bhakti was the fruit of Bhaktisiddhānta's laborious studies under the supervision of his father, Bhaktivinoda. It also provided the basis for a tentative dialogue between modern and traditional historical accounts. The idea of personhood that he presents in *Baṅge Sāmājikatā* has many philosophical implications for various Indic philosophies, among which he included Buddhism and Jainism. These will be addressed in the next section.

Personhood and Indian Philosophy

To clarify his view about the nonmaterial person and enhance the legitimacy of his position, Bhaktisiddhānta next critiques a number of well-known philosophies.

---

46. Bhaktisiddhānta, *Baṅge Sāmājikatā*, p. 44.

Baṅge Sāmājikatā describes empiricism as being flawed because sensory knowledge is prone to involve mistakes. Knowledge derived only from the senses provides a rather limited understanding of reality and ultimately leads to epistemological relativism. Nondualism attempts to avoid the problem of suffering by denying its primary cause (i.e., Nature) and postulating an ultimate impersonal state that lies beyond it. According to *Baṅge Sāmājikatā,* this approach does not take into account the possibility that there can be a nonmaterial level of reality that possesses personal form and attributes. Bhaktisiddhānta agrees with Śaṅkara that sensory knowledge leads to epistemological relativism because of the fallibility of sensory experience, and also agrees that it is important to maintain the authority of revealed texts such as the Vedanta and the Upanishads. At the same time he resists the assumption that spirituality must ultimately deny anything that even faintly resembles the perceivable world.[47]

Next *Baṅge Sāmājikatā* reviews four types of nonpersonal thought in Indic philosophy. The first regards sensory experience as an illusion; thus it devalues the importance of the world while refraining from making final statements about the nature of absolute reality. According to *Baṅge Sāmājikatā,* this perspective falls short because it cannot account for the enormous variety of objects found in the world. The second type is similar to the first in the sense that it refrains from drawing any conclusion about the nature of ultimate reality, but differs in the sense that it ascribes exclusive value to matter. As an example of this mode of thinking *Baṅge Sāmājikatā* offers Carvaka's radical materialism, which rejects any claim of an existence beyond the material world. The third type of nonpersonalism denies the eternal reality of consciousness and strives for a state of senselessness beyond personal awareness. It conceives of consciousness as a transitory and external attribute that ceases to exist when the state of ultimate liberation is achieved. *Baṅge Sāmājikatā* explains, in this regard, that unless one accepts the reality of conscious experience, neither the world nor knowledge itself can be proven to be real. The fourth type, represented by the philosophy of *advaita,* posits that ultimate reality consists of infinite nondual consciousness. In the liberated state, the seer is said to become one with this infinite consciousness after fully comprehending the falsity of projecting material attributes onto ultimate reality. The *advaita* perspective is viewed by Bhaktisiddhānta as a negating philosophy

47. Bhaktisiddhānta, *Baṅge Sāmājikatā,* p. 45.

that resists any attempt to explain *brahman* in terms of features that even vaguely resemble those of this world (*nirviśeṣa,* or "without" *viśeṣa,* i.e., the differentiating element).

In connection with the above discussion, it should be noted that most classical schools of philosophy traditionally favored nontheism and nonpersonalism. Only later manifestations of the schools of Yoga, Vedanta, Nyāya and Vaiśeṣika developed theistic orientations, having been inspired, it seems, by the increasing prominence of bhakti.

Bhaktisiddhānta concludes that Śaṅkara's epistemological method of extracting nonmaterial essence through the systematic negation of all sensory experience (*neti, neti*) is bound to be incomplete. The reason is that this method can only derive truths that pertain to the world of experience, and can say nothing about the nature of that which at least theoretically may lie beyond it. He also notes that because nondualism a priori denies the possibility of ultimate form and attributes, it closes itself off from ever comprehending the theory of nonmaterial personhood. Nondualism can only admit of embodied material personhood, which it dismisses as a transitory construction. This view of material form is in one sense held by Bhaktisiddhānta as well, although he regarded material form not as illusory, but merely impermanent. By pointing out some of the limitations of Śaṅkara's nondualism and the impersonalist theories of Indic philosophy, Bhaktisiddhānta hoped to present the full force of the personalist perspective. He concludes that

> *Brahman* [understood here as the supreme personality] exists by virtue of its own internal potency and transforms the entire universe (*brahmāṇḍa*) as well as Nature (*prakṛti*). By its shadow-like external potency it unfolds itself from the universes, and keeps them unmanifested (*avyakta*) by its internal potency. Wherever *brahman* and its self-situated potency do not manifest, the universes appear [instead] by its external potency . . . the dark inert potency (*māyā*) is a resultant shadow of the sunlike *brahman*. . . . There is not much difference between the transformations of the internal potency compared to those of the external potency. Whatever minor contradictory difference there is in the external potency that makes it incomplete, it is found in a complete manifestation eternally in the internal potency, in its [*brahman*'s] delightful infinite form replete with all potencies [i.e., Krishna].[48]

48. Bhaktisiddhānta, *Baṅge Sāmājikatā,* p. 48.

Nature is thus the product of the transformations of the external potency of the supreme personality, who is the ultimate aspect of *brahman* and thus entirely nonmaterial. The material and nonmaterial potencies resemble each other but are also distinct, just as a shadow is distinct from the original form that it mirrors. The world is a realm in which ignorance of spiritual reality causes pain and suffering, as well as rebirth. The contradictions that are experienced in the shadow-like external potency (*śakti*) of Nature are fully resolved in the complete *svarūpa*, or nonmaterial form of *brahman*—that is, Krishna.

The final section of the booklet provides an overview of a number of religious communities of Bengal, offering a critique of popular forms of Caitanya bhakti that in its view tended to blur the border between the material and the nonmaterial, watering down principles of ethics and moral conduct. At the end, Bhaktisiddhānta points to Caitanya as a possible solution to the challenges of modern societies. He suggests that only divine service can heal the human heart and remedy ignorance and social division. If human beings would simply set aside their caste-consciousness, he notes, the divine person would provide the knowledge for forming a truly universal community, inclusive of all beings: the all-embracing *jāti* or family of God. The last passage of the booklet consists of a verse attributed to Caitanya:

> I am neither a *brāhmaṇa* nor a king of men, neither a *vaiśya* nor a *śudra*, neither a *brahmāchārya* nor a *gṛhastha*, neither a *vānaprastha* nor a *saṃnyāsin*, but I am a lowly servant of a servant of the lotus feet of the lord of the *gopīs*, who is a sea of nectar filled with the pure and highest joy made manifest.[49]

According to Bhaktisiddhānta, while *varṇāśrama* is an important construction meant to ease the cultivation of bhakti by providing a socially stable environment, it is not foundational for religious identity, whereas divine service is.

In the *Baṅge Sāmājikatā* it appears that, despite his search for authenticity in indigenous traditions, Bhaktisiddhānta did not align himself with

49. Bhaktisiddhānta, *Baṅge Sāmājikatā*, p. 66. The quotation is from *Caitanya Caritāmṛta Madhya līlā* 13.75, translation by Dimock in Kṛṣṇadāsa *Caitanya Caritāmṛta of Kṛṣṇadāsa Kavirāja*, trans. Edward C. Dimock, Jr. (Cambridge, Mass.: Dept. of Sanskrit and Indian Studies, Harvard University, Distributed by Harvard University Press, 1999), p. 522.

what can be called the process of "inversion" carried out by certain strands of Hindu nationalism. This process has been explained by John Darwin as follows:

> In colonial Bengal, where the Hindu *bhadralok* resented exclusion from the government and the disparaging language of their colonial masters, nationalist rhetoric has turned the racial table. The "Hindu race" was much the more civilized. It shared its Aryan origins with the Europeans. It had a distinctive race mission—not political greatness or military power, but the exertion of "spiritual energy." By the deliberate emphasis upon cultural difference, the practice of strength and courage, and the rediscovery of a heroic past, Bengalis could acquire all the hallmarks of a "race," different from but as good as the one of the Europeans.[50]

I suggest that he also rejected nationalist attitudes such as

> the promotion of physical vigour and courage, the "manly" qualities to which Europeans abroad were inclined to attribute their military prowess and political dominance.[51]

Bhaktisiddhānta indirectly discouraged Indians from cultivating European "manliness," with its ideology of conquest and rule. To do so would have been tantamount to assimilating and duplicating European modernity, rather than producing an indigenous alternative. Instead he suggested a new path that would accommodate both modernity and Indic religious traditions:

> [N]owadays . . . some are not satisfied with Western ideas. It is, however, not unreasonable to accept these views, taking into account the specific time and circumstance. Change is a natural phenomenon like the stream of a river. Yet, those [who propose change] also face opposition from those who try to stick to the past. It is not unfair to bask in the memory of a golden past. But the approach is

50. Darwin, *After Tamerlane*, p. 348. He makes a concise summary of some of the points made by Chowdhury, *Frail Hero*, pp. 14, 17, 40, 44–45.

51. Darwin, *After Tamerlane*, p. 340.

> not always viable from the point of view of reality. At the same time it is not always desirable to uphold foreign (*vaideśika*) ideas and thoughts, forgetting entirely the ancient traditions of India and the land of one's birth by regarding them as error. Western thought is not without personal interest (*svārthaśūnya*). Too much emphasis on bygone traditions is also not without interests and motives. It is indeed always better to strike a balance between these two extremes.[52]

The *Baṅge Sāmājikatā* is a manifesto for this balanced vision. It was also his first systematic attempt to establish a dialogue with colonial culture and society. His purpose was to show that the idea of a nonmaterial person also relates to daily life in the world. According to Bhaktisiddhānta, the core problem of modern men and women was not primarily economic, social, or political. It was, above all, a crisis of consciousness, attitude, and understanding, fueled by the modern rise of impersonalist ideas and impersonal materialistic ideologies that disempowered the person's inner capacity to serve and love, as well as to seek emancipation from the bondage of worldly life. The *Baṅge Sāmājikatā* is not a conclusive work, but it reflects the social issues that Bhaktisiddhānta and sections of the *bhadralok* faced at the turn of the twentieth century. It also gives a sense of Bhaktisiddhānta's view on the role of religion in society, which he later applied through the medium of the Gaudiya Math.

Yukta Vairāgya

While the analysis of society that Bhaktisiddhānta embarked upon in the *Baṅge Sāmājikatā* enabled him to understand his own role within the religious and social context of his time, it was above all a theoretical study. What it lacked was a set of tools that could empower him to act within the frame of bhakti.

In the following years, Bhaktisiddhānta extracted from the teachings of Bhaktivinoda a key principle that pointed toward a philosophy of

52. Bhaktisiddhānta, *Baṅge Sāmājikatā*, p. 22.

devotional agency: *yukta vairāgya*[53] (roughly "engaging renunciation"), which meant to renounce the propensity to enjoy the objects of the world while actively engaging those objects in the service of God, to whom they ultimately belong. In the 1910s he emerged from a long period of semi-solitary contemplation and began to search for a perspective that would allow him to interact with society in a more direct way, crossing the borders that he had set for himself by the ascetic lifestyle that he practiced. A work by Bhaktivinoda, the *Caitanya Śikṣāmṛta* (*The Nectarean Teachings of Caitanya*), had exposed a youthful Bhaktisiddhānta to *yukta vairāgya*. Published in 1886, the work provides an account of Caitanya's teachings to Sanātana Goswami, as presented in the *Caitanya Caritāmṛta*.[54] There Bhaktivinoda commented that when the laity carry out household duties without attachment and steadily worship God, they become free from material bondage. Through bhakti the individual derives strength and establishes a close relationship with God. On the other hand, an ascetic who fails in his vows of renunciation can more easily become degraded, thus cheating himself and others. In other words, when a person engages material objects in the service of God, they do not bind that person to the material world; in the spirit of *yukta vairāgya*, one's material body and mind, one's home and material objects, are no longer spiritual impediments. The only necessary ingredient is the internal

53. These are precisely the words used by Bhaktisiddhānta. The word *yukta* is the past participial of the root verb *yuj*, from which the word *yoga* is derived. Apte translates *yukta* as "fastened, yoked, harnessed... [f]ixed, or intent on, absorbed or engaged in... [a]ctive, diligent." Vaman Shivaram Apte, *The Student's Sanskrit-English Dictionary* (Delhi: Motilal Banarsidass, 2000), p. 458. Monier Monier-Williams offers a similar translation of the word and adds to it "suitable, appropriate, proper," adding a sense of value to the word. Monier Monier-Williams, *A Sanskrit-English Dictionary* (Delhi: Motilal Barnasidass Publishers, 1999), p. 853. Thus the word broadly conveys the meaning of (1) joining, (2) a state of consciousness (intent on, engaged in) and (3) certain qualities of a person's actions (active, diligent). Apte translates *vairāgyaṃ* as "absence of worldly desires or passions" (p. 535). David Haberman in Rūpa Goswami's *Bhakti-rasāmṛta-sindhu* translates *yuktaṃ* as "balanced" and *vairāgyaṃ* as "detachment." He explains that it "is a state of balanced renunciation, where the devotee neither rejects the things of the world nor is ensnared by them, and thus is able to engage them freely in an enjoyable life of playful service." Rūpa Goswami and David L. Haberman, *The Bhaktirasāmṛtasindhu* (Delhi: Indira Gandhi National Centre for the Arts; Motilal Banarsidas, 2003), p. 93. Here Haberman emphasizes the act of engaging material objects rather than a passive "acceptance," where "there need not be wholesale or total rejection of everything of this world which may be useful for the services of the Lord, nor need there be any desire for earthly objects for one's own sense-enjoyments" (p. 259). The word "engaging" emphasizes the act of active participation.

54. Although Sanātana Goswami was born in a *brāhmaṇa* family, he served as minister to the late medieval ruler of Bengal, Hussain Shah.

determination and steadiness to serve God—and the strong desire to achieve success.[55]

Bhaktivinoda was a layman (*gṛhastha*), a *bhadralok*, and a colonial officer. From this position he asserted that the practice of bhakti at home was as legitimate as the one practiced by ascetic virtuosos, a development in laity status that Rammohun Roy had pioneered. This stance also legitimized the urban laity that regarded him as a leader. It was an important step forward relative to the functional modernization of Caitanya Vaishnavism, and a shift away from the otherworldliness that Vaishnavas were reputed to pursue.

While working on his commentary to the *Caitanya Caritāmṛta* in the 1910s, Bhaktisiddhānta once again encountered the conversation between Caitanya and Sanātana Goswami.[56] There, the concept of *yukta vairāgya* was presented by Caitanya in two key verses that also appear in an earlier work by Rūpa Goswami entitled *Bhakti-rasāmṛta-sindhu* (*The Ocean of the Nectarean Rasa of Bhakti*). They read as follows:

> When a person detached from ordinary worldly objects engages such objects in a proper fashion in a relationship with Krishna, that is called *yukta vairāgya*. But when those who crave for *mokṣa* renounce things that are connected with Hari, understanding them wrongly to be ordinary material objects, that is called *phalgu* (false) *vairāgya*.[57]

In a poem called *Duṣṭa-Mana*, Bhaktisiddhānta utilizes this principle to dissuade a *bhakta* from artificially practicing solitary meditation:

> Therefore, O cheating mind, you extol the glories of solitary meditation in the way that devious yogis cheaply display their powers. Please meditate with care on all that Prabhu Sanātana has taught.
>
> Never forget the two instructions and loudly recite the names of Hari [Krishna]. Never think that the concepts false renunciation (*phalgu*) and engaged renunciation (*yukta*), bound (*baddha*) and liberated (*mukta*), are one and the same.

---

55. Kedarnath Datta Bhaktivinoda, *Śrī Caitanya Śikṣāmṛta* (Mayapur: Śrī Caitanya Math, n.d.), pp. 72–74.

56. *Caitanya Caritāmṛta, Madhya līlā* 23.105.

57. *Bhakti-rasāmṛta-sindhu* (1.2.255–56).

> Wherever there is proper engagement and satisfaction, disease cannot be there. What more shall I say? In the absence of undue material attachment and with proper knowledge of relationships, everything is [seen as] Mādhava Himself [Krishna].
>
> That is *yukta vairāgya*, a most auspicious notion that reveals the grandeur of Hari within this world. Whenever the desire for fame stands at the heart of one's worship, wealth becomes a cause of duplicity.[58]

In his introduction to Bhaktivinoda's book *Sree Caitanya Mahaprabhu: His Life and Precepts,* completed on July 15, 1924, Bhaktisiddhānta looks upon the life of Bhaktivinoda in the light of this principle. He translates the word *bhakti* not merely as "devotion," but as "devotional service," conveying the idea of practical engagement rather than contemplation. Bhaktisiddhānta himself had intermittently practiced solitary esoteric meditation on the sacred names in the forests of Mayapur for more than ten years, but had apparently realized that this approach was suitable neither for himself nor for the laity. *Yukta vairāgya* became a key to his mission, so much so that Bhaktisiddhānta printed the above two verses next to the logo of the *Gauḍīya,* his weekly magazine. One practical application of this principle was the name that he gave to one of his presses: *bhagavāt yantra,* which literally means "God's machine." He came to regard his presses as worthy of worship because they sacralized *prakṛti* by printing bhakti literature.

Bhaktisiddhānta would defend the principle of *yukta vairāgya* against critics who viewed it as a pretext for materialism, or who objected to *saṃnyāsins* riding in cars or wearing leather shoes. In 1932, he once again explained the principle in *Relative Worlds,* a new English publication:

> *Prakṛti* and the *jīva* are relative to absolute reality, and share the characteristic of being energies or potencies of the Divine potent. The *jīva* is conscious and thus superior to *prakṛti,* but is also stranded in a marginal position between *prakṛti* itself and Divinity. It can come under the influence of either of them by personal choice. By engaging *prakṛti* in the workings of the Divine, however, the *jīva* attains gradual realization of the Divine presence in the world and generates a "spiritualization" of *prakṛti.* When engaged by the *jīva*

58. "*Nirjane Anartha,*" *Sajjanatoṣaṇī* (1920), pp. 9–13.

> for the purpose of *bhakti*, *prakṛti* transforms from an instrument of ignorance to a vehicle of spiritual knowledge.[59]

The rationale for this position is found in the idea that the "Supreme Personality" and his potencies are closely connected, which allowed for the possibility of a respiritualization of the world. This was also philosophically explained in the *Bhāgavata Purāṇa* (4.11.18):

> The supreme person (*bhagavān*) by his energy (*śakti*) of time causes the interaction of the qualities of nature (*guṇa*), and thus various potencies (*vīrya*) are divided. It appears that He acts, but He is not the actor, He kills, but He is not the killer. Thus it is all happening by His energy, which is difficult to be perceived or understood.[60]

The idea that God is one but also many, via a range of infinite potencies, had gradually gained prominence in the Vaishnava world. The concept of "potency" (*śakti*) had been clearly formulated by Jīva Goswami and Baladeva Vidyābhūṣaṇa, but it had received its earliest formulation with the master Viṣṇusvāmī. Bhaktisiddhānta understood *yukta vairāgya* as a practical form of religious service that facilitated the achievement of love for God (*prema*).

He particularly emphasized physical service to sacred sound—that is, the loud vocalization of the names of God, a form of meditation that would gradually elevate the consciousness of the performer to a nonmaterial (*aprākṛta*) domain beyond bodily and mental perception. In this sense, Bhaktisiddhānta resisted the Kantian theory that things-in-themselves were beyond the range of human perception. His epistemology distinguished sensory, mental, and intellectual perceptions from nonmaterial ones, which pertained to the nonmaterial self. The practical use of the material body and mind in terms of *yukta vairāgya* was the vehicle for accessing subtle states of consciousness. When used properly, he concluded, the body and mind were thus highly conducive for the progress of bhakti.

---

59. Bhaktisiddhānta Sarasvatī, *Relative Worlds: A Lecture delivered on the 26th of August 1932 at the Saraswata Assembly Hall of Shree Gauḍiya Math, Calcutta* (Calcutta: Shree Gaudiya Math, 1932).

60. *sa khalv idaṁ bhagavān kāla-śaktyā, guṇa-pravāheṇa vibhakta-vīryaḥ, karoty akartaiva nihanty ahantā, ceṣṭā vibhūmnaḥ khalu durvibhāvyā.*

Bhaktisiddhānta envisioned the propagation and practice of bhakti more in urban areas than in ascetic retreats. He spoke of the necessity of linking the consciousness of the *bhakta* to the community of fellow human beings, and to various objects of ordinary life, but in a mood of self-restraint and service. When properly understood and applied, *yukta vairāgya* was thought to protect the *bhakta* from self-indulgence and lapses. Ultimately, it made it possible for Bhaktisiddhānta to empower both the renounced celibates of the Gaudiya Math and the laity to act within society and promote Caitanya bhakti as a viable alternative for the Indian middle class and others.

Religion and Science

The idea of progress and the importance of science for improving society were important creeds of liberal sections of the *bhadralok*. Traditional religion was regarded by many as irrational, and it was under siege as much as religion was in Britain. Science was believed to produce theories that could be empirically proven and that led to new discoveries.[61] Religion or myths, on the other hand, were unverifiable because they rested on faith. The issue at stake was how to gain reliable and useful knowledge.

Bhaktisiddhānta believed religion and science to be complementary. Science provides only tentative explanations for various empirical problems because its theories are built on a limited amount of observations and are always open to revision as new information is gathered. Thus scientific theories can lead only to epistemological relativism. Empirical knowledge is useful on the level of the external reality, while religious knowledge is useful on the level of internal consciousness. Religious experiences, in his view, cannot be studied in an empirical way because they represent another "sort" of knowledge. Their "grammar" and "language" are different, but this does not imply a denial of reason. Bhaktisiddhānta envisioned a dialogue between religion and science, and in his "theistic exhibitions" he invited prominent scientists to lead interactive discussions.

Nonetheless, he expressed concern regarding the rise of materialistic ideologies and positivism in Bengal. In a letter dated April 25,

61. Nils Gilje, Sten Andersson, and Harald Grimen, *Samhällsvetenskapernas Förutsättningar* (Göteborg: Daidalos, 1993), pp. 16–20.

1934, addressed to his German disciple Sadānanda Das (Ernst Georg Schulze), he wrote:

> Empiric thinking breeds aversion to the service of the Absolute. There can be no relation of consistency between the conduct of the pure devotee and the empirical ideal. The intellect does not require to be driven along the old tracks of futility. The awakened spiritual faculty should not be prevented from having the sole initiative for regulating the perverted mental function.[62]

Bhaktisiddhānta sensed a turn toward radical empiricism in some sections of European culture—that is, the rise of the idea that the real was exclusively that which could be perceived by the physical and mental faculties. For Bhaktisiddhānta, worldly experience and the nonmaterial internal experience of bhakti were qualitatively different. Someone who wished to understand the nonmaterial sphere had to go through a process of relearning. Indeed, "to walk back is the first stage of walking in the path of spiritual living... the neophyte is required to offer his loyal unlearning submission."[63] This, however, should not be taken to imply that reason had no place in the service of bhakti. In fact, Bhaktisiddhānta believed that without a solid foundation in inquisitiveness and philosophy, bhakti would fall prey to sentimentalism and hedonism. For Bhaktisiddhānta, rationality is necessary in order to apply *yukta vairāgya* to an ever-changing cultural and social environment, and distinguish the core from the periphery. Reason, sharpened through the study of religious texts, the teachings of the guru, and those of the *sampradāya*, is ultimately able to take advantage of the inner "spiritual faculty." Failure to use reason brings stagnation to religious life, ultimately making the practice and theory of bhakti obsolete and out of step with the times. On the other hand, when reason acts independently of that "spiritual faculty," it ultimately leads to spiritual ignorance rather than enlightenment.

Translating Personhood

Bhaktisiddhānta's explorations of philosophy and science culminated in his desire to properly re-present and communicate the philosophy of

62. With permission from Kid Samuelsson, private collection.

63. Ibid.

Caitanya bhakti in a rational way. In order to do so, he frequently attempted to articulate what he meant by the concept of "person." He rejected the use of the terms *saguṇa* and *nirguṇa* to contrast the personalist and impersonalist approaches, since these terms reflected the nondualist view that form and personality were solely a product of the modalities (*guṇa*) of Nature. Bhaktisiddhānta pointed out that the personal aspect of God is *nirguṇa*, beyond the modalities of Nature, rendering the distinction meaningless. Instead he suggested the terms *saviśeṣa* and *nirviśeṣa* (with and without particularity or essential difference), which, in his view, better applied to the nonmaterial spheres and fulfilled the requirements of both dualists and nondualists.[64] He also searched for English terms that would do justice to the theological complexity involved in terms like *bhagavān* and *jīva*—terms that were essential for presenting the philosophy of personhood. In Jainism and Hinduism, the term *jīva* generally refers to an individual being that displays the symptoms of life, while *ātman* generally refers to the conscious self. In Bhaktisiddhānta's writings, however, they were used interchangeably, although he preferred the term *jīva* since, for him, individuality was the defining characteristic of the self.[65]

In 1871 Bhaktivinoda wrote an English essay entitled *The Personality of Godhead* that apparently provided an English rendering of the word *bhagavān*. Although Bhaktisiddhānta used this rendering in his writings and speeches, he used other renderings as well. The *Harmonist* became the vehicle through which tentative English formulations were presented (figure B.5). In the fourth issue of the *Harmonist* in 1927 there is an early translation of *bhagavān* as "the Personality of Transcendental Godhead."[66] Later on, the rendering "Supreme Personality of Godhead" emerged, but only rarely. The latter was the version consistently used by his disciple Swami A. C. Bhaktivedānta in his literature.[67]

The word "personality" conveys the understanding that God has qualities, emotions, and will; "transcendental godhead" conveys the idea that

64. *Gauḍīya* 1, no. 18 (1929), "Vaiṣṇava darśana," p. 13

65. See, for example, *Harmonist* 25, no. 4 (September 1927): p. 73: "The *jīva* is self-conscious and devoid of birth and death. The *jīva* takes different 'bodies' and 'minds' as the result of selfish enjoyment."

66. *Harmonist* 25, no. 4 (September 1927): p. 96. This statement was part of an appeal written by a number of disciples seeking support for public events in Benares, Vrindavan, Nimsar, and Kurukshetra.

67. The expression appears more than 7,000 times in the complete works of Swami Bhaktivedānta; see *Bhaktivedānta Vedabase 2003*.

God's personality is beyond the range of human sense perception; and "supreme" gives the sense that God is the origin and controller of all other beings, up to and including the "demigods" (*devas*). This understanding points toward a monotheistic view, although Bhaktisiddhānta accepted the thesis that "God" possesses other manifestations, of which the most central is Rādhā. Bhaktisiddhānta gave the words "person" and "personality" a primary role in his publications. He also often used their opposites—that is, "impersonal" and "impersonalists"—in order to illuminate their meaning, and developed criticisms of all schools of philosophy that subordinated the personal aspect to other categories. This became particularly evident in the most ambitious comparative study of religions undertaken by the Gaudiya Math, *Sree Krishna Chaitanya* (1933).

Well-established Christian theological terms such as "theism" and "monotheism" were sometimes used in Bhaktisiddhānta's writings to convey an English-language sense of the word *bhagavān* and the idea of a supreme divine person. It appears, however, that he preferred the more specific phrase "Personality of Godhead," since "God" and "theism" were susceptible to a number of hermeneutical ambiguities. As has been noted by Guy Beck, one such susceptibility concerns the fact that the Greek word *theos* has a wide variety of meanings and points to diffuse archaic perceptions of "divinity."[68] Hinduism tended to study the structure, substance, and nature of supreme reality, rather than that of a personal God in the Christian sense. Moreover, general terms such as "theism" and "God" can be used when referring to nondualist cosmologies as well.[69] There is, in fact, nothing that prevents nondualism from being regarded as a monotheistic philosophy. Another reason may have been that for Westerners the word "theism" was associated more with theology than philosophy, since the two disciplines had parted ways in the nineteenth century. In the words of Robert Jackson and Dermot Killingley:

> the difference between theology and philosophy is a Western one, and not part of the Indian tradition; many Hindus prefer to speak of philosophy rather than theology, feeling that "theology" implies uncritical acceptance of tradition.[70]

---

68. Guy L. Beck, *Sonic Theology: Hinduism and Sacred Sound* (Columbia: University of South Carolina Press, 1993), p. 12.

69. Beck, *Sonic Theology*, p. 12.

70. Robert Jackson, and Dermot Killingley, *Approaches to Hinduism* (London: John Murray, 1988), p. 168.

The choice of the term "Supreme Person" or "Personality" in combination with "Godhead," instead of simply "God," suggests that Bhaktisiddhānta may have preferred philosophical terms for presenting the Vedanta of the Caitanya school.

There is a contemporary school of philosophy in the West called "personalism."[71] It developed as a strand of Christian thought during the nineteenth and twentieth centuries, but its roots can be traced back to the eighteenth century. While mainstream Vaishnavism promoted the irreducible reality of the nonmaterial person as did this Western school, there is no evidence indicating that either Bhaktivinoda or Bhaktisiddhānta was aware of its existence. Moreover, the Vaishnava idea of *person* was markedly different from its Western counterpart. Unlike most Western personalists, who believed the body and mind to *be* the self, even in the afterlife, Vaishnava Vedanta considered them to be temporary coverings of a nonmaterial self, or *jīva*.

Although Bhaktisiddhānta displayed some familiarity with Christian doctrine, and occasionally used Christian terminology, he generally preferred to discuss issues that were linked either to Western philosophy and science or to Indian philosophy and religion, since these were of greater concern to the Hindu middle class of his time.

Personhood and the Place of Sexuality

The idea of "person" is indivisibly linked in Bhaktisiddhānta's thought to the personhood of God. However, in the Caitanya bhakti tradition, the idea that God is a person has implications that are not contained in the Abrahamitic

71. In Boston during the early twentieth century, Western personalism found a strong foundation in the school of the theistic personalist Bowne. Bowne defended personalism against what he described as the "impersonalism" of the "naturalistic obsession." Borden Parker Bowne, *Personalism* (Boston: Houghton Mifflin, 1908), p. 217. The school of personalism existed in a variety of forms, and tended to be linked to idealism and theism. Various theories of personalism shared the general notion that the person is foundational and basic and not emerging out of other entities or categories, and that the person, divine or human, plays the primary role in the structure of the universe. See R. T. Flewelling, "Personalism," in *Twentieth Century Philosophy: Living Schools of Thought*, ed. Dagobert D. Runes (New York: Philosophical library, 1943). There is no tangible proof that Bhaktisiddhānta ever read contemporary personalist works such as Albert Cornelius Knudson, *The Philosophy of Personalism: A Study in the Metaphysics of Religion* (New York: Abingdon Press, 1927). Nor is there evidence suggesting that he was aware of earlier personalist schools from Germany and Great Britain, such as those discussed by Jan Olof Bengtsson, *The Worldview of Personalism: Origins and Early Development* (New York: Oxford University Press, 2006).

religions, including, and especially, those that pertain to the expression of sexuality. According to Caitanya Vaishnavism, in order for there to be genuine loving exchange in the spiritual realm, the Absolute Truth must contain both a male and a female component. The male component, the supreme potent, is known as Krishna, and the female component, the supreme potency, is known as Rādhā. Around the relationship between these two aspects of the Absolute has evolved a highly sophisticated body of literature that presents an understanding of female love toward God the likes of which would be difficult to find in the history of religions.[72]

Following the tenets of this scholastic tradition, Bhaktisiddhānta conceived of two types of male-female love: the first is the ordinary garden-variety sexuality found in the transitory world; and the second is the spontaneous nonmaterial female love for God expressed by the fully realized *bhakta*. In this regard, the achievement of devotional service in an intimate female relationship with God is said to require the abandonment of one's temporary bodily designation of being either male or female, in the material sense. In Bhaktisiddhānta's view, however, the transformation to female love does not involve an external change of dressing habits and/or worldly interrelational conduct; rather it involves a change on the level of individual internal consciousness and experience. Moreover, it is not something sentimental, but requires the full use of human reason and will, as well as the close personal instruction and guidance of a qualified guru.

In a *Harmonist* article entitled "Sex" Bhaktisiddhānta indirectly criticized the masculinization of colonial society that set the white British male as the high point of an evolutionary process that legitimized colonial power.[73] According to him, the "suffragettes" of his time were fully justified in their protest against male domination. However, he saw them as still operating within the framework of a masculine mind-set. The solution was not to develop a muscular femininity—indeed he generally maintained a traditional view of the functional role of women—but to develop a spiritual psychology that exemplified the best of "feminine" traits and rejected the exploitative consciousness of both sexes. Such a psychology, he believed, would help to transform the self through acts of service. The crucial point for Bhaktisiddhānta was that on the material plane both

72. See Graham M. Schweig, *Dance of Divine Love: The Rasa Lila of Krishna from the Bhagavata Purana* (Princeton, N.J.: Princeton University Press, 2005).

73. *Harmonist* 32, no. 9 (January 1936): pp. 193–198.

sexes were ultimately interested in selfish enjoyment rather than the selfless service of God and others. For him, such a mentality was indicative of the living entity's tendency to lord it over material nature in imitation of God:

> Our perception of numerous units in the misguided world has given rise to a desire to lord it over others, but that act itself is the result of a wrong perspective.[74]

The challenge, in his view, was how to transform this potentially destructive propensity—this will to power—into a willingness to serve. In Bhaktisiddhānta's analysis, bhakti contains the important notion that we are all meant for giving loving service in reciprocation with God, and not for selfishly having that which is not ours to enjoy. In other words, the natural innate propensity of the self, according to Bhaktisiddhānta, is that of serving and giving loving pleasure to the "Personality of Godhead." And the highest and most complete expression of this pleasure-giving propensity is found in the love of Rādhā for Krishna. Indeed, Bhaktisiddhānta considered the theology of Rādhā to be the specific contribution of the Caitanya tradition to both Vaishnavism and world religion. However, given the cultural climate of the 1930s, he believed that it would take time before it would be properly understood. In a talk given in 1932 he stated that

> a Western savant might understand much of the narratives (*kathā*) of Lakṣmī and Sītādevī, but it will take him a long time before he can grasp the narrative of Rādhā.[75]

Understanding the subtle distinction between worldly and spiritual sexuality is fundamental to a comprehension of the Goswami literature on Caitanya mysticism. It is also necessary to an understanding of the loving affairs of Rādhā-Krishna and the service of their maidservants in Vrindavan. In this regard, Bhaktisiddhānta explains that the humble *bhakta*, feeling unqualified to serve Krishna directly, joyfully serves the servant of the servant of Rādhā and her companions instead—ever assisting them in their direct service to Krishna. This state of consciousness is

74. Bhaktisiddhānta, *Shri Chaitanya's Teachings*, p. 257.

75. *Gauḍīya* 13, no. 14 (November 10, 1934): p. 214.

achieved only by the most exalted Vaishnavas and is not to be imitated or approached by those that are not entirely free from material desire and ordinary sexual lust.[76]

This is why Bhaktisiddhānta objected so strenuously to the modern trend in Bengali literature of equating the loving exchanges of Rādhā-Krishna with ordinary worldly sexuality. He also resisted the kind of neohumanism that had reduced the spiritual narratives of Rādhā-Krishna to allegory and symbolism.[77] For Bhaktisiddhānta, devotional life implied, above all, active service and practical work. Rather than attempting to "see" the supreme personalities while still in an immature state, he suggested that one should first be recognized, or "seen," by means of one's sincere loving service, thus reversing the paradigm. The achievement of this state is said to require the cultivation of humility and patience, and its end result would be unalloyed service in separation (*vipralambha*). His view was inspired by the narratives concerning Caitanya found in the *Caitanya Caritāmṛta*.[78] In that text it is also explained that Caitanya is Krishna appearing in the mood and complexion of Rādhā; as such, serving Caitanya is equivalent to serving Rādhā.[79] Caitanya had promoted compassion for the suffering of the *jīvas*, which the school's theology

76. These arguments are further discussion in two pamphlets published in the 1930s. The first, *Rai Ramananda*, was written by Bhaktisiddhānta himself, and the second, *The Erotic Principle and Unalloyed Devotion*, was written by his disciple Niśi Kanta Sanyal. The account of Ramananda Raya, a retired minister of the Orissan king Pratāparudra and an intimate companion of Caitanya, has always been controversial. In the *Caitanya Caritāmṛta*, Kṛṣṇadāsa Kavirāja writes that Ramananda Rai bathed and dressed two female dancers (*deva-dāsīs*) of the Jagannātha temple in Puri, and also trained them to sing, dance, and perform his play *Jagannātha-vallabha-nāṭaka*. See *Caitanya Caritāmṛta, Antya līlā* 5.16–26. In the 1960s, Edward Dimock argued that Ramananda Rai was a *sahajiyā*. Edward C. Dimock, *The Place of the Hidden Moon: Erotic Mysticism in the Vaisnava-Sahajiya Cult of Bengal* (Chicago: University of Chicago Press, 1989), pp. 52–54. See the alternative view by Joseph O'Connell, "Were Caitanya's Vaiṣṇavas Really Sahajas? The Case of Ramananda Raya," in *Shaping Bengali Worlds*, ed. Tony Stewart (East Lansing: Asian Study Center, Michigan State University, 1989). Bhaktisiddhānta portrayed Ramananda Rai as a chaste and dispassionate Vaishnava.

77. See Satyavati Giri, *Baṅgla Sāhitye Kṛṣṇakathāra Kramavikāśa* (Kolkata: Ratnāvali, 1988), pp. 545–555. The author provides an extensive overview of the way the narratives (*kathā*) of Krishna and his consort have been variously dealt with in Bengali literature by authors such as Rammohun Roy, Bankim Chandra Chatterjee, Brahmabandhab Upadhyay, Sisir Kumar Ghosh, Rabindranath Tagore, and others.

78. Bhaktisiddhānta states that "Caitanya's play (*līlā*) is by nature in the mood of separation" (*gauralīlā svabhāvataḥ vipralambhamayī*). *Caitanya Bhāgavata*, ch. 15, verses 30–32, commentary, p. 318.

79. *Caitanya Caritāmṛta*, Ādi līlā 4.48–52, pp. 58–59.

FIGURE 4.1. The Logo of the Gauḍīya.

had equated with Rādha's compassionate mood.[80] In keeping with this understanding, Bhaktisiddhānta named his press *bṛhad mṛdanga* (the big drum), indicating that its purpose was to declare far and wide the importance of Krishna's sacred names.

Figure 4.1 is a later version of a logo that Bhaktisiddhānta designed for the *Gauḍīya* magazine, which attempts to portray this perspective. It appeared for the first time on the front page of the periodical on February 7, 1931.

On the logo's right side is a depiction of Rādhā-Krishna underscored by the word *rāga*, indicating the path of spontaneous loving service. Above and beneath Rādhā-Krishna, to the reader's left, is the book *Bhāgavata Purāṇa*, indicating spiritual instruction, and a drum, a press, and the word *kīrtana*, symbolizing the propagation of the sacred sound. On the logo's left side is a depiction of Lakṣmī-Nārāyaṇa seated on a throne and underscored by the word *vidhi*, indicating devotional service in awe and

80. Bhaktisiddhānta called this "kindness to the *jīva* (*jīve dayā*)," *Harmonist* 25, no. 4 (September 1927): p. 74.

veneration. Above and beneath Lakṣmī-Nārāyaṇa, to the reader's right, is the book *Pañcarātra*, indicating the rules of ritual worship, and a bell, a lamp, and the word "arcana," indicting the process of formal image worship. The logo shows that the path of spontaneous service to Rādhā and Krishna is performed through the propagation of literature and the recitation and singing of the names of the divine couple, while regulated practice and temple worship under the guidance of an accomplished guru is to be carried out simultaneously for the purpose of creating a strong basis for the growth of bhakti.

Summary

This chapter has explored Bhaktisiddhānta's core personalist philosophy. It has dealt with issues of definition, his critique of alternative views, the principle of constructive engagement with society, and the connection between social and gendered philosophy.

Bhaktisiddhānta proved in the *Baṅge Sāmājikatā* that he was informed and engaged early on in the society and culture of his time. He investigated differences and stratification in the religious and social fiber of Bengal, but also, more importantly, the indigenous and colonial production of these differences. He elaborated on current issues, from liberalism and utilitarianism to materialism and idealism, and the relation between Europe and India.

The *Baṅge Sāmājikatā* represents his first systematic attempt to establish a dialogue between colonial and indigenous Bengali culture. Bhaktisiddhānta spelled out the foundations for a dialogical encounter between apparent opposites such as object and subject, in-worldliness and otherworldliness, impersonalism and personalism, caste and *varṇāśrama*. He embarked on a broad assessment of personal subjectivity and agency, and refused to subordinate the person to impersonal philosophies. The perspective of nonmaterial personalism, and his definition of the relation between humans, God, and the world through a Vaishnava Vedantic lens, led him in the direction of an ethical rejection of racism, sexism, and species-ism.

Although Bhaktisiddhānta did not embrace humanism and rationalism, as did other Hindu reformers, his perspective allowed him to look at humanity as a product of divine potency, and thus rich with potential. He saw the role of reason as assisting the pursuit of transformation and reform of the self, and he advocated freedom of thought and choice as a natural attribute of the person. For him, the path of bhakti, the path of spiritual service, implied voluntary conscious action. Bhaktisiddhānta believed that Vaishnava society had to free itself from the constraints of caste to truly unleash its transformative power. He maintained that a *varṇāśrāma* system based on merit and personal qualities was a productive model for accommodating differences of quality as well as labor in an integrated social order that included asceticism as well. His copious printing and translation of religious literature allowed him to present the core of Caitanya bhakti to those who wished to read original texts and analyze the statements of the tradition in vernacular language. In this way, he resisted authoritarian and elitist approaches.

Bhaktisiddhānta carefully analyzed the workings of the religion and society of his time in order to find a balance between the values and principles of the personalist core that he embraced and the novelty and innovations of the modern world. His concept of the nonmaterial person was not disembodied or mystical, but immanent and active. This implied a struggle against the disempowerment of Hindu caste and the narrowing cultural boundaries of European colonialism, but it also implied an individual struggle against the constraints of body and mind through the principle of *yukta vairāgya*. These issues were vital during Bhaktisiddhānta's formative years and allowed important insights that drove him further toward new areas, which crystallized in his shaping of the Gaudiya Math and, at the end of his life, his venture to Europe.

5

Bhaktisiddhānta in Context

THUS FAR I have briefly reviewed the cultural, political, and religious history of India, focusing on the nineteenth and twentieth centuries, in an attempt to provide the tools by which to understand the religious social structures and ideas that were prevalent before and during the time of Bhaktisiddhānta Sarasvatī. I have also extensively explored Bhaktisiddhānta's life and writings in an attempt to uncover the personal agency and innovative thought that shaped his efforts to represent Caitanya Vaishnavism to the modern world. The aim has been to correlate social structures with personal agency so as to better understand the relation between the two, as well as to better grasp their respective significance. Theoretically, this approach should be applicable to the study of any past or present religious figure. Although personal agency depends on genius and creativity, the sociocultural context provides an indication of the medium—for example, the tools and modes of discourse—through which that agency expresses itself and meets its limitations. The basic assumption has been that when the sociocultural context undergoes transformation, various religious agents will respond by transforming established religious structures and orientations in an attempt to maintain their historical and social relevance. In late nineteenth-century colonial Bengal, the sociocultural context had changed to such a degree that Caitanya bhakti had become a less relevant tradition. In response, Bhaktisiddhānta reformulated and applied some of its core practices and understandings—based on bhakti personalism—so as to revive bhakti's relevance in a modern multiethnic, multireligious society.

The previous chapters have shown that the idea of "spiritual" or nonmaterial personhood informed the entirety of Bhaktisiddhānta's thought, religious vision, and understanding of agency. For him personhood—beginning with the personhood of the supreme absolute—implied a moral and spiritual dimension that structured human existence, giving it a fundamental sense of presence, responsibility, and meaning across time and space. The idea of being a nontemporal person was the foundation of his self-understanding and the basis of his concept of free will and individual choice, which had as its basis the understanding that bhakti is ultimately a voluntary "heart to heart" relation that cannot be imposed upon others. His religious understanding of personhood was not merely an abstract metaphysical principle, but had key implications relative to personal conduct, action, and moral choice. It motivated and inspired his struggle against caste restrictions and the religious dominance of the *brāhmaṇic* orthodoxy, as well as his desire to spiritually reform the modern world. It informed his basic understanding of religious practice, human relations, higher reality, and the ultimate goal of religious realization—that is, divine love.[1] It also somewhat enabled him to see the great theistic traditions of the world as personalist partners and inspired his philosophical struggle against those that stood in opposition to the personalist view: past and present nondualists, whose understanding of the absolute challenged the very core of his spiritual and philosophical conviction.[2]

This chapter will present, among other concluding reflections, a model that correlates religious ideas and social orientations within modern Hinduism, focusing especially on the Bengali Hindu middle class of the colonial period to which Bhaktisiddhānta belonged. It is hoped others may find a way to apply this model to Indic and non-Indic religious contexts as well. Its immediate aim, however, is to more precisely locate the place and significance of Bhaktisiddhānta within the social and religious context of his time.

To briefly summarize what has transpired thus far: chapter 1 has given an overview of the most influential religious ideas of the early and middle colonial period, chapter 2 has explored Bhaktisiddhānta's life and institution, chapter 3 has examined the bringing of his message to Europe, and chapter 4 has explored some of his key ideas. In this way, the book has attempted to answer to the question of how Bhaktisiddhānta Sarasvatī attempted to translate, establish, and convey the tradition of Caitanya bhakti in adaptation to the circumstances of modern colonial culture.

1. Bhaktisiddhānta defined Krishna—following Rūpa Goswami in *Bhakti-rasāmṛta-sindhu* 1.1.1.—as "Akhila—rasāmṛta mūrti," "Fountain-head of all relishing relationships or *rasas*." See Bhaktisiddhānta, *Shri Chaitanya's Teachings*, p. 78.

2. See also the discussion about Rammohun Roy in *Sarasvatī Jayaśrī, Śrī Parva*, p. 16

This final chapter addresses the question of how to place Bhaktisiddhānta's life and work within the framework of modern Hinduism in Bengal. In an attempt to identify its distinguishing features, his work will be contrasted with that of Swami Vivekānanda. The chapter will end with a final, brief analysis.

Reformer, Revivalist, or Both?

Before attempting to situate Bhaktisiddhānta within the larger context of modern Hinduism, it is necessary to examine whether Bhaktisiddhānta is best characterized as a modern reformer or as a religious revivalist.[3] The terms "reformer" and "revivalist" were in use at the time of Bhaktisiddhānta, and the question was addressed in his publications. Before exploring that response, it is important to be aware of ambiguities in this terminology when applied to a colonial context. In a modern democratic society, a reformer is considered to be improving a certain religious, cultural, or social system and is generally regarded as progressive or liberal, whereas a revivalist that aims at giving new life to an older system may be regarded as conservative or even reactionary. The former is generally seen in a more positive light than the latter. In a colonial setting, on the other hand, a reformer would often try to improve an indigenous system by introducing Western modes of thought and action, while a revivalist would attempt to be more in tune with indigenous values and be seen in a more positive light.[4] Another point is that the two types are not necessarily exclusive. In fact, a pure revivalist would likely be entirely out of step with his times, and a pure reformer would likely be a radical revolutionary; and neither of these extremes is generally the case. In other words, there are respects in which a revivalist is also a reformer and vice versa, and in this sense the terms can be considered two independent variables rather than two exclusive categories. While most scholars tend to think that "revivalist" and "reformer" are mutually exclusive categories, in my view, this is not necessarily the case. Bhaktisiddhānta, for example, was in various ways both a

---

3. Tapan Raychaudhuri has defined Hindu revivalism in the nineteenth century in Bengal as a small movement led by a rather contained group of traditionalist intellectuals. Raychaudhuri, *Europe Reconsidered*, p. xii. In the twentieth century revivalism acquired a far greater scope and became part of nationalist discourse.

4. See Amiya P. Sen, *Hindu Revivalism in Bengal, 1872–1905: Some Essays in Interpretation* (Delhi: Oxford University Press, 1993).

revivalist and a reformer, although he himself placed more emphasis on the revivalist aspect of his work.

The last years of Bhaktisiddhānta's life marked a phase of self-reflexivity, as he and his disciples felt the need to spell out more clearly their approach to action and the social world. An article in the *Harmonist* published in 1932 rejected the idea of reform:

> The world stands in no need of any reformer. The world has a very competent person for guiding its minutest happenings. The person who determines that there is scope for reform of the world, himself stands in need of reform. The world goes on in its own perfect way. No person can deflect it even the breadth of a hair from the course chalked out for it by providence. When we perceive any change being actually effected in the course of events of this world by the agency of any particular individual, we must know very well that the agent possesses no real power at any stage. The agent finds himself driven forward by a force belonging to a different category from himself. The course of the world does not require to be changed by the agency of any person. What is necessary is to change our outlook on this world.... The scriptures declare that it is only necessary to listen with an open mind to the name of Krishna from the lips of a bona fide devotee. As soon as Krishna enters the listening ear, he clears up the vision of the listener so that he no longer has any ambition of ever acting the part of a reformer of any other person, because he finds that nobody is left without the very highest guidance. It is therefore his own reform, by the grace of God, whose supreme necessity and nature he is increasingly able to realize, by the eternally continuing mercy of the Supreme Lord.[5]

This statement could be interpreted as a fatalistic outlook on the world, aimed at maintaining the status quo by regarding the world as helplessly controlled by the power of God and the law of karma. But it is important to remember that in the worldview of Caitanya Vaishnavism, the embodied self is regarded as largely controlled by the forces of Nature, and although humans appear to be agents, in the conditioned state actions are ultimately carried out by Nature and not by the self. In the conditioned state, the self

5. *Harmonist* 29, no. 11 (1932): p. 325.

is a mere passenger in a psycho-physical vehicle made of mind and body.[6] If the metaphysical self appears to be the agent under those circumstances it is only because of a false sense of identity with the workings of matter. Another point is that the arrangement of Nature was complete in itself, and replete with meaning and purpose emanating from the compassion and divine intelligence of a supremely conscious personality. Any attempt to reform the cosmic order through the mastery of machines or science carried the risk of disrupting the inner balance and harmony of the world. The text argues instead for a voluntary reform of the personal self, where true agency can take place at the level of desire and will. The text rejects the generic concept of reform—that is, the idea that through worldly agency alone it is possible to create a substantial and permanent improvement of the human condition. It proposes instead a revival of a mode of spiritual consciousness assumed as inherent in every living thing. In this view, that mode of consciousness is known as bhakti. Bhaktisiddhānta considered the process of bhakti to be transformative for the self, and since the self shared a social world of emotion, relationships, and consciousness that directly affected other human beings, bhakti had the potential to change the collective values and objectives that formed the basis of human society.[7] He believed that by changing the quality of human consciousness and overcoming the illusions posed by Nature it was possible to reach a state where the nonmaterial self could be free from its worldly constraints and realize the true potential of personhood.

Bhaktisiddhānta's reliance on the canonical texts of the tradition and his allegiance to the vision of a *sampradāya* of enlightened gurus support a revivalist understanding. Indeed the *Sarasvatī Jayāśrī* directly states that Bhaktisiddhānta viewed his work not as a reformation, but rather as a

---

6. See Bhagavad Gītā, 3.27, *prakṛteḥ kriyamāṇāni, guṇaiḥ karmāṇi sarvaśaḥ, ahaṅkāra-vimūḍhātmā, kartāham iti manyate*: "the self is illusioned by the ego and thinks 'I am the agent,' when in reality all actions are carried out by the qualities (*guṇa*) of Nature (*prakṛti*)."

7. For Ranajit Guha, on the other hand, bhakti is "an ideology of subordination *par excellence*" in terms of social, economic, and political structures. Ranajit Guha, "Dominance without Hegemony and Its Historiography," in *Subaltern Studies 6: Writings on South Asian History and Society*, ed. Ranajit Guha (New Delhi: Oxford University Press, 2005), p. 259. He does not explore enough, however, how loyalty to a deity interfered with loyalty to society and to colonial domination, nor how bhakti is a medium for social or ideological resistance. Much of Bhaktisiddhānta's work can be understood in terms of intellectual resistance to nondualism on the one hand and materialism/naturalism on the other, and it defied the status quo of his time.

reinstallation of an earlier personalist tradition.[8] He created a fracture with contemporary religious authority within the Vaishnava community not because he wished to improve the religious core as such, but because he believed that the Caitanya community had lost the ability to understand it, and was unable to apply the principles explained in the vast literary corpus of the tradition. He saw himself as performing a reestablishment of *sanātana dharma* to compensate for the deteriorating influence of the age of Kali. Along with this primary aim of revival came an institutional reform that sought to improve the practice and reputation of Caitanya Vaishnavism. Such reform, however, always remained secondary in Bhaktisiddhānta's eyes. A complete appreciation of Bhaktisiddhānta's understanding of revival, however, cannot be achieved unless one understands "tradition" as being something dynamic. Bhaktisiddhānta saw tradition as a continuous chain of transformations born of the dynamic interaction between the metaphysical core and the cultural context.

To deepen the understanding of Bhaktisiddhānta's concept of the revival of tradition it may be useful to refer to Catholic theologian Robert Schreiter, who has proposed that "tradition" contributes three things to the development of human communities: "resources for identity...[communal] cohesion and continuity...[and] resources for incorporating innovative aspects."[9] Schreiter suggests that a tradition sustains itself within a culture by nurturing *credibility* (cultural acceptance), *intelligibility* (the use of a sign system and codes that are close to the semiotic domain of the host culture), *authority* (the ability to speak and act on behalf of the tradition), and *affirmation* and *renewal* (the ability to incorporate innovations while confronting cultural change).[10] I suggest that Bhaktisiddhānta's revival of tradition can be understood more precisely by applying those analytical categories as follows:

1. He attempted to repair his tradition's *credibility* and temper cultural concerns regarding Caitanya Vaishnava morality by adopting the robes and asceticism of a renunciant; by so doing he aimed to elevate the reputation and standing of that tradition in the eyes of its native culture.

---

8. Sundarānanda Vidyāvinoda in *Sarasvatī Jayaśrī*, p. 215. See also *Sarasvatī Jayaśrī, Śrī Parva*, p. 18.

9. Robert J. Schreiter, *Constructing Local Theologies* (Maryknoll, N.Y.: Orbis Books, 1985), p. 105.

10. Schreiter, *Constructing Local Theologies*, pp. 107–108.

2. He helped to make Caitanya Vaishnavism accessible to the modern mind by producing numerous texts and periodicals that presented a personalist perspective on contemporary issues, thereby heightening his tradition's *intelligibility*.
3. He strove to revitalize his tradition's structure of *authority* by arguing for the merit of being a Vaishnava over and above either hereditary succession or ritual initiation, and proposing the enlightened guru as the foremost personal embodiment of Caitanya Vaishnavism.
4. He contributed to *affirmation and renewal* by taking advantage of the technical, scientific, and organizational innovations of the twentieth century so as to enhance the competitiveness and relevance of Caitanya Vaishnavism.

Bhaktisiddhānta's vision of a revival of the lost personal consciousness of bhakti within the self was neither utopian nor millenarian nor related to a golden age, but was firmly fixed in the present, since personal liberation from the chains of illusion was always a possibility at any point in time, and was not dependent on collective apocalyptic salvation. By viewing religious awakening as linked to the person rather than to society, the *Harmonist* article mentioned earlier resisted the dominant view that social or political reform was the means whereby real progress could be achieved. This set Bhaktisiddhānta apart from reformers like Rammohun Roy and Dayānanda Sarasvatī. At the same time Bhaktisiddhānta shared the kind of activism that characterized modernity, believing that personal action was the key to spiritual progress, even if only in terms of promoting open devotional practices and free religious education for the masses.

Bhaktisiddhānta's ultimate goal was to reach the masses, but apparently he thought that by first approaching the rich and powerful he would be able to influence the largest number of people with the least amount of effort—a conclusion that apparently led him to cooperate with the colonial establishment both in India and in the West. The question of how Bhaktisiddhānta's revival related to colonial society is of relevance and also needs to be assessed in greater detail.

Ashis Nandy has suggested that resistance to British culture and allegiance to indigenous traditions often occurred in indirect ways, one being through the use of language. He offers the example of Iswar Chandra Vidyasagar, who wrote strictly in Bengali, without ever once producing an English-language book. For Nandy this was an act of resistance that he contrasts, in a seemingly pejorative tone, with the efforts of so-called

"Neo-Hindus," who consistently compared India with Europe and "Indianized the West." Nandy calls Vidyasagar's approach "unheroic critical traditionalism."[11] He argues that this traditionalism found its most complete articulation in the life and work of Gandhi, since Gandhi not only rejected Western modernity, but actively searched for a more authentic way of life in the unheroic simplicity of the Indian village. Although Bhaktisiddhānta may have objected to Gandhi's politicization of Hinduism for reasons mentioned earlier, it can also be argued that he himself contributed indirectly to the development of a national traditionalist understanding. In his case it was carried out through an unheroic and pan-Indian attempt to strengthen personalist bhakti and champion Hindu modes of understanding the world through a large number of publications in vernacular languages (see appendix E). In this way, he challenged the mode of understanding of the missionaries and the colonial establishment, and at times his firmness and determination brought him closer to the role of a nonviolent, albeit heroic, "spiritual warrior."

Bhaktisiddhānta remained strongly committed to an emancipation of the self. For this reason, even while cooperating with the colonial establishment, he questioned the ultimate significance of categories such as race, nation, and gender. This approach increased his chances of international success because it was not bound to the social and political context at home. It could be applied on a global basis, although it largely failed to do so during his life. His institution, however, often appeared otherworldly to the *bhadralok* precisely because it was out of step with their understanding of religion as something that should be primarily involved in humanitarian works within their local environment.

Traditional and Modern Hinduism

The following four sections attempt to place Bhaktisiddhānta's work within the framework of "modern Hinduism" in Bengal by undertaking a general discussion and analysis of this concept. Although this analysis will by no means be exhaustive, it will include modern Hinduism's most well known trajectories. In order to sufficiently qualify the discussion I will begin with a brief analysis of the term "modern" (see appendix A for a discussion of the term "Hinduism").

---

11. Ashis Nandy, *The Intimate Enemy: Loss and Recovery of Self under Colonialism* (Delhi: Oxford, 1988), p. xvii.

"Modern" is a widely used term in academia and there is no consensus as to its precise meaning: it is defined differently in different scholarly contexts. In the social sciences it refers to the process whereby public domains are differentiated, as when the religious domain, for example, is separated from a secular or political domain. Shmuel Eisenstadt, on the other hand, has defined modernity as a distinct civilization, characterized by a new ontological vision and cultural program whose core is "an unprecedented 'openness' and uncertainty."[12] In this way he has challenged classic sociological analyses of such thinkers as Durkheim, Marx, and Weber, which predicted that the cultural program of modernity would be the model for all modern societies around the world. To this he has contrasted the idea of "multiple modernities," the idea that although all modern cultural forms are similar in some respects, they also differ according to diverse local or contextual social, cultural, political, and religious variables.[13] This is because various actors create unique modernities by reconstructing ideological and institutional patterns in interaction with those local variables.[14] Such a perspective may also be applied to processes of modernization that developed within narrower local contexts such as that of Bengal. According to Eisenstadt, modernity entails the possibility that human beings can forge their own future through autonomous acts. In the West, modernity was born of a budding sense of rational autonomy and civic independence, which led, in the formulation of Weber, to a sort of deconstruction of the idea that the world was God-ordained.[15] This entailed a move from predetermination to self-determination—that is, the possibility to choose between a religious or a secular approach to life that emphasizes the necessity of moral responsibility.

In colonial societies, on the other hand, the process of modernization tended to involve a tension between the Western model, viewed by many as foreign and intrusive, and one that was more indigenously grounded in local traditions. In colonial India, where the British effectively controlled the main institutional and economic structures, the process of modernization largely came from without, meaning that it was not a homegrown

12. S. N. Eisenstadt, *Comparative Civilizations and Multiple Modernities* (Leiden: Brill, 2003), vol. 2, p. 493.

13. Eisenstadt, *Comparative Civilizations*, vol. 2, p. 536.

14. Eisenstadt, *Comparative Civilizations*, vol. 2, p. 536.

15. Eisenstadt, *Comparative Civilizations*, vol. 2, p. 537.

phenomenon.[16] On the other hand, the symptoms of early modernity had been already present in the India of precolonial times. If in the West, society tended to become more homogeneous and secular, and major conflicts tended to center upon class, in India, society tended to remain more diverse and religious, and religion was the primary basis of Indian group identities.[17] Because of its different historical context, modernity in India was never influenced by secularization to the degree that it was in Europe, where, for example, radical currents of the Enlightenment, originating from anticlerical and antiroyalist ideas, created the basis for the French Revolution. Considering the above, if the terms "modernity" and "tradition" are juxtaposed, the difficulty becomes apparent. Is it meaningful to speak of tradition and modernity as opposed? Is modernity defined exclusively by secularism, or can a religious orientation be regarded as equally modern? Following Eisenstadt's analysis, the answer to this question is yes.

With these considerations in mind, it may be useful to look at a model of modern Hinduism—in the present study applied primarily to colonial Bengal and the *bhadralok*—proposed by Elizabeth De Michelis (figure 5.1). She has incorporated the work of John Nicol Farquhar (1928 [1914]), David Kopf (1969), Friedhelm Hardy (1984), Paul Hacker, and Wilhelm Halbfass (1988).[18]

This model has the advantage of recognizing the distinction between Classical Hinduism and Modern Hinduism (on the left). The use of the term "Classical" is somewhat ambiguous because it can be taken to mean that religions in precolonial times were static rather than dynamic. In this case the term simply refers to that which came before the colonial period, with no other connotation attached. De Michelis, following Kopf and Halbfass, further subdivides Modern Hinduism into Modern Hindu Traditionalism and Neo-Hinduism (lower right).[19] Although, like similar models, it contains obvious overlaps and blurred boundaries, it nonetheless serves the purpose of mapping—even if only tentatively—an extremely complex religious field. The model will be primarily used to explore and define key orientations of thought that allowed for a wealth of

16. Kaviraj, "Modernity and Politics in India."

17. Kaviraj, "Modernity and Politics in India," p. 144.

18. De Michelis, *A History of Modern Yoga: Patañjali and Western Esotericism*, p. 36.

19. De Michelis, *A History of Modern Yoga*, p. 38. The division between Neo-Hinduism and Modern Hindu Traditionalism is also discussed in similar terms by Halbfass, *India and Europe*, pp. 210–212, 219–222. See also Kopf, *British Orientalism*, pp. 192–213.

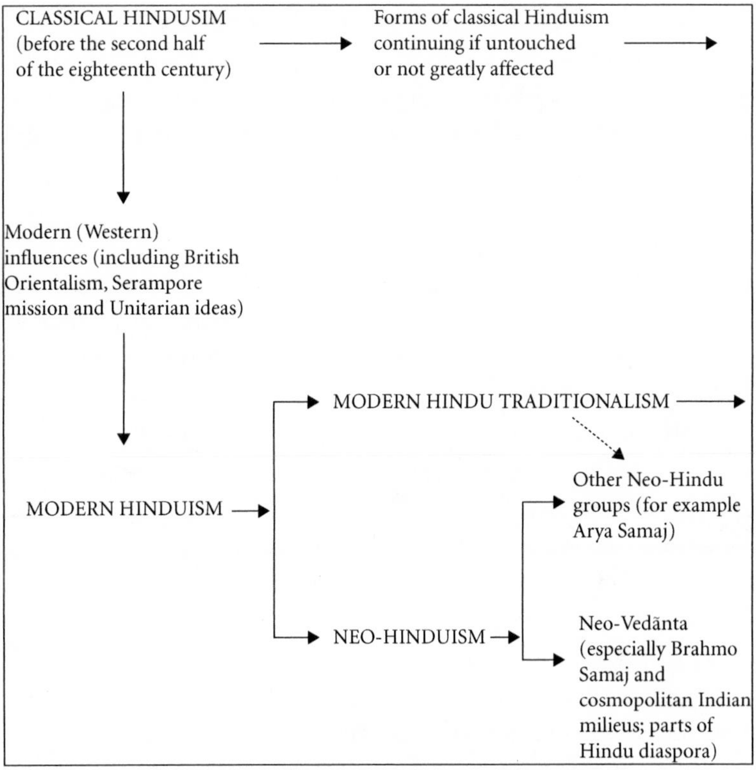

FIGURE 5.1 Development of Modern Hinduism according to De Michelis
Source: De Michelis, *A History of Modern Yoga*, p. 37

reciprocal pollination, as opposed to creating strictly separated categories of social, cultural and religious existences.

De Michelis' taxonomy of modern Hinduism reflects Halbfass's conclusion that

> Neo-Hinduism and Traditionalism are the two main trends in Modern Hindu thought, two ways of relating to the Hindu tradition while encountering the West.[20]

Halbfass's assessment was inspired by Hacker, who had recognized two categories within modern Hinduism: Neo-Hinduism and "surviving traditional Hinduism."[21]

20. Halbfass, *India and Europe*, p. 219.

21. Halbfass, *India and Europe*, p. 257.

De Michelis adds to the taxonomy of her predecessors by presenting two different orientations of traditional Hinduism: the first consists of "forms of classical Hinduism continuing [as] if untouched or not greatly affected"; the second consists of Modern Hindu Traditionalism, which she characterizes as having been affected by, and having creatively interacted with, the influences of the West.[22] I suggest that the first orientation was adopted by the Hindu religious elite—that is, those who upheld and applied traditional rules of law and conduct as defined by texts such as the *Manu smṛti*. It also encompassed orthodox *smārta brāhmaṇas*, who upheld social hierarchies and caste structures within Hinduism, and those who defended the infallibility of the Vedas. Included as well were Vaishnava communities that were culturally and religiously little touched by the presence of the British. For these elites, the reading and interpretation of texts was largely the privilege of the priestly class, the *brāhmaṇas*, according to well-preserved hereditary customs.

This orientation in its *ideal* form—since even the most orthodox groups naturally experienced *some* transformation and change—was characterized by fewer interpretations of the sacred texts, little or no interaction with the West, and limited social, political, or cultural change by the laity. Education was based on a foundation of traditional religious texts and covered logic, philosophy, legal principles, and codes of conduct that had been transmitted for centuries by recognized schools of learning. Besides the elite, another group can be included within this current: the mystics. Mystics such as ascetic *bābājīs*, Śaiva yogis, *sahajiyās*, and tantric Śaktas and many more individuals and groups tended to seclude themselves from society, which they perceived as a cause of disharmony for the self. Some of these individuals promoted community and social work, but only in as much as it served their mystical practice. The broad orientation mentioned above may also include popular folk religions found in villages outside the boundaries of the *brāhmaṇic* orthodoxy.

De Michelis marks the beginning of modern Hinduism with the British colonization of Bengal, a conscious but selective choice. This event nonetheless gave impetus to a variety of religious initiatives among the emerging *bhadralok*, some of which have been explored in the earlier chapters. According to her, Neo-Hinduism (with no pejorative connotations) emerged as a distinct religious current in Bengal with Rammohun

22. De Michelis, *A History of Modern Yoga*, p. 37.

Roy.[23] One important aspect of the development of modern, and more specifically Neo-, Hinduism was the gradual emphasis on nondualism, rationality, and the worship of an uniconic Deity. Halbfass notices that according to Rammohun Roy

> pure, monistically oriented monotheism—which is what he conceives at the true meaning of the "religious books"—is manifested particularly clearly in the "Veds" and in Śaṃkara's Vedānta...for all of the decisive texts ultimately teach the unity of God and the "rational worship of the God of nature."[24]

De Michelis suggests two orientations within Neo-Hinduism: Neo-Vedanta and Other Neo-Hindu groups; but here, also, she develops her taxonomy no further. I suggest that with particular reference to colonial Bengal the category of Neo-Hinduism includes, among others, at least two major and at times complementary orientations:

1. Vedantic nondualism (instead of neo-Vedanta in De Michelis's model, which is more vague)
2. Social and political activism

These orientations are far from exhaustive, but they will help to historically situate Bhaktisiddhānta's work with greater accuracy.[25] What follows is a brief explanation of each.

Neo-Hinduism

Vedantic nondualism may have been the most prominent and influential current of thought in Bengal during the period of the British Raj,

---

23. De Michelis, *A History of Modern Yoga*, p. 40.

24. Halbfass, *India and Europe*, p. 205.

25. I have been inspired by a taxonomy of modern Islam presented by Tariq Ramadan, which I have freely adapted. Ramadan, *Western Muslims*, pp. 24–30. Ramadan describes six tendencies within contemporary Islam: Scholastic Traditionalism, Salafi Literalism, Salafi Reformism, Political Literalist Salafism, 'Liberal' or 'Rationalist' Reformism, and Sufism. While I have adapted some of these categories to the present discussion, it is outside the scope of this book to embark upon a comparative analysis of the differences between modern Islam and modern Hinduism. However, the question of whether or not reason should be used for the making of independent interpretations of the Qur'an and the Sunnah—*ijtihad* (innovation) rather than *taqlid* (imitation)—appears to parallel Hindu concerns regarding the modern interpretation of religious texts.

and included intellectual movements that were represented by specific institutions and by individuals. It refers to those that introduced reforms within a particular context, applying reason to textual evidence found in the Vedas, the Upanishads, and, above all, Śaṅkara's *advaita* Vedanta. While stressing the validity of both approaches, it generally tended to subordinate iconic theism to a nondualist universalism as a means of creating unity among Hindus. As a result, it tended to blur the distinction between both dualism and nondualism and iconic and noniconic worship.[26] Vedantic nondualism bypassed the classical schools of Hindu law and more liberally incorporated ideas from the West, stressing rationalism, humanism, and a "reform from within." It tended to place less importance on *sampradāya,* and more on personal experience and the rational understanding of sacred texts. It thus represented a more autonomous approach than did traditionalist movements. This allowed for dynamic strategies of adaptation to the West, while keeping in view the goal of protecting Hindu identity variously understood through reformed religious practices. Because of its mostly nondualistic metaphysical perspective, it largely inspired egalitarianism and democracy. This orientation is exemplified in various degrees by Rammohun Roy, the Brahmo Samaj, and Swami Vivekānanda.[27] It is the current of Hinduism most well known outside Bengal.

Social and political activism was at times complementary to Vedantic nondualism and is an orientation that emerged as a result of direct contact with colonial culture, society, and administration. It tended to be based on a modern and critical reading of standard Hindu texts such as the Bhagavad Gītā, and it gave them a humanitarian/political interpretation in terms of ethics, authority, custom, and management of law. It strove to improve social and human conditions through political activism and nationalism. Examples of individuals that characterized this orientation are Bipin Chandra Pal (see chapter 2) and Aurobindo during his early years as a revolutionary.

---

26. See for example Brian A. Hatcher, *Bourgeois Hinduism, or the Faith of the Modern Vedantists: Rare Discourses from Early Colonial Bengal* (New York: Oxford University Press, 2008).

27. Rammohun Roy tended to blend nondualism with some theistic notions, as did the Brahmo Samaj in several of its religious and institutional developments, while Vivekānanda emphasized a more "straightforward" version of nondualism.

Modern Hindu Traditionalism

Regarding Modern Hindu Traditionalism, De Michelis, Hacker, and Halbfass do not elaborate on where it should be located. Halbfass offers the example of a modern pandit tradition represented by the Bengali Rādhākanta Deb, who composed a Sanskrit encyclopedia and corresponded with Western Indologists such as Emile Burnouf and Max Müller. In my view, the *Calcutta Dharma Sabha* stands as an early example of a modern Hindu traditionalist movement in Bengal. It was formed in 1831 as a response to the *Brahmo Sabha*, and may be considered an early manifestation of the tension between Neo-Hinduism and Modern Hindu Traditionalism. This modern movement is thought to have been the first traditionalist institution of the colonial period. It was formed by members of the Bengali intelligentsia whose ideas differed from those of the *Brahmo Sabha*, despite the fact that both groups emerged from the same equally modernizing, middle-class ranks. Indeed, it was this group that opposed the ideas of Rammohun Roy. Its main strategy was to formulate elaborate petitions for the colonial government, as Roy had done, but now for the purpose of defending the very Hindu traditions that Roy had so vigorously attacked.[28] According to John Zavos, this attempt led to the development of modern institutional forms similar to those of the *Brahmo Sabha*:

> These bodies were modern in the sense that they were governed by constitutions and aims and objectives, they had secretaries, executive boards and membership lists, and they employed techniques such as subscription campaigns, public meetings and petitions to authority. Within this framework, the Brahmo Samaj "represented" a reforming, modernizing constituency, and the Dharma Sabha "represented" a traditional, orthodox constituency.[29]

Both organizations gained members from the same group, that is, "the Calcutta *bhadralok*, a landowning, high-caste bloc, with vested interests in British rule, and after 1835, almost invariably English educated."[30]

---

28. Crawford, *Ram Mohan Roy*, pp. 145–156.

29. John Zavos, *The Emergence of Hindu Nationalism in India* (Delhi: Oxford University Press, 2000), pp. 44–45.

30. Zavos, *Emergence of Hindu Nationalism*, pp. 44–45.

Although the Neo-Hinduism of the *Brahmo Sabha* and the modern Hindu traditionalism of the *Dharma Sabha* emerged from the same social pool, what set them apart was their divergent approaches to modernity. In Halbfass's words:

> Traditionalism...has also taken in and assimilated new elements, and is by no means a mere continuation of that which existed before the encounter with the West. Similarly, it is *not* possible to describe Neo-Hinduism as a rigorous break with the past and its transmission. What distinguishes Neo-Hinduism and Traditionalism are the different ways on which they appeal to the tradition, the structures which they employ to interrelate to the indigenous and the foreign, and the degree of their receptivity vis-a-vis the West. Modern traditional Hinduism has preserved an essentially unbroken continuity with the tradition, and it builds upon this foundation, carries on what is already present in the tradition, even though additions are made and extrapolations occur. To be sure, Neo-Hinduism also invokes the tradition, tries to return to it, and hopes to find in it the power and context for its response to the West. Yet as Hacker emphasizes, this return is the result of a rupture and discontinuity. More important than the fact that foreign elements have been added to the tradition is that basic concepts and principles of this tradition have been reinterpreted and provided with new meanings as a result of the encounter with the West: "Neo-Hinduism...always implies reinterpretation." The link which the "Neo-Hindus" find to their tradition is, one may say, an afterthought; for they first adopt Western values and means of orientation and then attempt to find the foreign in the indigenous.[31]

While modern Hindu traditionalism tended to be open to the influence of modernity, it was less willing than its Neo-Hindu counterparts to surrender core understandings of sacred texts, indigenous religious values, and the worship of images. One way of characterizing this difference is to say that modern Hindu traditionalism made the tradition its point of departure rather than first assimilating modern ideas and then searching

31. Halbfass, *India and Europe*, pp. 219–220.

for traditional understandings that lent those ideas support. There were similarities nonetheless:

> the tenets of the essential unity and equality of religions and of a tolerance essentially intrinsic to Hinduism, both of which play such a major and obvious role in Neo-Hinduism, are by no means foreign to Traditionalism.[32]

These two polarities should be viewed as partially overlapping rather than fixed types, since

> orthodoxy and receptivity, openness and self-assertion, the new interpretation of indigenous concepts and a Hinduization of Western concepts, all these intermix in a variety of ways."[33]

Nonetheless, from this and other earlier discussions it becomes clear that what can be said to differentiate Neo-Hinduism from Modern Hindu Traditionalism is (1) a stronger breach with the past; (2) a tendency to give more weight to a new rational reading of the texts, bypassing traditional schools; (3) less allegiance to *sampradāyas* and gurus; (4) a tendency to regard God as abstract and uniconic; and (5) an emphasis on direct religious experience.

If we compare precolonial "classical" forms of Hinduism ("continuing [as] if untouched or not greatly affected") with Modern Hindu Traditionalism, some differences in emphasis emerge as well. The former, as described herein, may have tended to view modernity as something alien and dangerous, a product of European culture and a substantial shift from traditional Hindu values and ethics. Modernity would have tended to be represented as materialism, hedonistic consumerism, rationalization, and the replacement of the simple, austere, and spiritually conducive life of the village with alienating urbanization and "heartless" industrialism. This, it can be said, was the common early reaction to modern life of most of the world's religious traditions, including Christianity. Modern Hindu Traditionalism may be broadly understood as a middle path between classical Hinduism, which had little or no contact with Western modernity, and Neo-Hinduism, which did. It found itself intellectually engaged with

32. Halbfass, *India and Europe*, p. 221.

33. Halbfass, *India and Europe*, p. 220.

both, but also trying to define itself against them. It resisted the closer contact with the West of Neo-Hindu thought and practice, but also the views of classical Hinduism that were perceived to be outmoded. This book has elaborately shown that Bhaktisiddhānta's approach fits within the general category of Modern Hindu Traditionalism as described above. This category, however, is still too vague in terms of making a precise placement of his contribution. The following section redresses this shortcoming by proposing a novel orientation to specifically account for the unique representation of Caitanya Vaishnavism created by Bhaktisiddhanta's movement. The specificity of this trajectory should not be taken to preclude the possibility that other movements may also fit within its frame nor that other traditionalist orientations were found side by side. I have termed this orientation *Vedantic personalism.*

Bhaktisiddhānta, the Personalist

As hinted at above, apart from being descriptive of Bhaktisiddhānta, the trajectory of Vedantic personalism may include others such as Bhaktivinoda, the various Gaudiya Math institutions and Vaishnava personalities and groups among the *bhadralok* that had a clearly personalist orientation.[34]

Bhaktisiddhānta's emphasis on personhood in the context of the first half of the twentieth century was not only a clarification of the core of Vaishnava philosophy, but also a reaction to a turn toward impersonalism (or nondualism) in modern Hinduism. Within this particular context, the comprehensive formulation and presentation of an alternative philosophy of personalism can be regarded as Bhaktisiddhanta's most important statement and *the* distinguishing feature of his contribution.

According to Bhaktisiddhānta, pure bhakti could only develop relative to an object of devotion that is possessed of a supreme divine form and personality, with the full range of attributes that make intimate relationships of reciprocal loving service possible. In other words, an unequivocal requirement of Bhaktisiddhānta's religio-philosophic approach is that both the finite and the infinite aspects of the absolute are eternal loving personalities capable of active and emotional exchange. It is this understanding that is at the heart of the designation *Vedantic personalist* in the case of Bhaktisiddhānta.

---

34. There are also other currents of Modern Hindu Traditionalism, but these never became as prominent as their Neo-Hindu counterparts.

Bhaktisiddhānta shared with Vedantic nondualism the need to bypass the hereditary priestly orthodoxy in order to return to a pristine unmediated contact with the Vedas. For him, however, the Vedas were not limited to the earliest texts, but encompassed all later developments as well, including, most importantly, the theistic schools of Vedanta, and even the Puranas and the later bhakti literature—the literature he specifically attempted to revive. His approach was dualistic and iconic. He extracted dharma principles from a basically traditional reading of the sacred texts, but nonetheless managed to dynamically apply those principles in accordance with time, place, and circumstance. He spoke out against the rigid social structures of classical Hinduism, proposing instead a social fluidity based on personal merit, freedom of choice, and "transformation from within." He favored a relatively rational approach to religion, the democratization of knowledge through mass distribution of vernacular literature, and an end to the abuses of caste. On the other hand, he considered *varṇāśrama* to represent a natural division of labor and practice, but he mostly viewed it as relevant for Vaishnava and Hindu communities. He emphasized the individual study of sacred texts, the traditional role of the guru in religious life, and the secondary status of social and political work in comparison to the primary task of character development and self transformation. He criticized popular and folk religious practices such as erotic tantrism with as much fervor as the *bhadralok* of Vedantic nondualism, but objected to the nondualist conclusion that popular iconic bhakti was ultimately secondary, a type of "idol worship" or an obstacle to social, political, and national progress. He also acknowledged colonial institutional structures and was loyal to the empire for its promotion of religious freedom, which granted Hindus the right to practice dharma and live according to their own ethical and valuational standards, so long as these did not conflict with British law. Bhaktisiddhānta's lack of interest in actively resisting colonial rule or vigorously criticizing Western civilization also appears to have sprung, in part, from a desire for Indic-Western cooperation. This desire, which had characterized the generation of his father as well, was less in step with the sociopolitical sensibilities of his time, but was welcomed by figures such as Rabindranath Tagore.

Limitations and Strengths of the Model

The model that has been applied to colonial Bengal in the previous four sections, while helpful and relevant to a history of Hinduism at large, has its limitations, one of which is the danger of essentialism. In this regard, terms such as "Modern," "Classical," and "Hinduism" have their own conceptual limitations (see appendix A). Moreover, Bhaktisiddhānta was born a *bhakta* and "died" a *bhakta*, but this may be regarded as the exception rather than the rule. Persons pass through different stages in the course of their lives, as did his father, and their thinking, actions, and ideals transform accordingly, leading them in different directions at different points in time. For this reason, a taxonomy of fixed categories can never be accurate. Replacing these with notions like "trajectory" and "orientation" allows for more openness and fluidity within the model and for various levels of overlap and complementarity. Aurobindo, for example, first engaged in the struggle for political emancipation, and only later adopted the path of ascetic mysticism that led to the creation of "integral yoga."[35] At an early stage in his development, Vivekānanda was inspired by the spiritual mysticism of his teacher Ramakrishna, but as his thinking and experience evolved, he developed a Vedantic pathway that was increasingly involved in extroverted humanitarian work (*seva*).[36]

On the other hand, one of the strengths of this model is that it clearly indicates that modernization and Westernization are not necessarily synonymous, and that secularization does not necessarily follow from modernization. Eisenstadt's notion of "multiple modernities" allows for the inclusion of many more orientations within the frame of modernity, both religious and secular. Just as modernity developed differently in France, England, and the United States, the above analysis shows that it took various shapes in India as well.[37]

In this section I have attempted to highlight a largely overlooked chapter in the development of modern Hinduism in Bengal: the fact that a strong (and ultimately successful) personalist Vedanta current existed side by side with the more well known largely nondualist currents of its time. I have also attempted to distinguish the one from the other since each holds its own, often contradictory, view on such matters as Hindu iconic

35. Peter Heehs, *The Essential Writings of Aurobindo* (New Delhi: Oxford University Press, 2006), pp. xiv–xv.

36. Beckerlegge, *Swami Vivekananda's Legacy.*

37. Peter L. Berger, Grace Davie, and Effie Fokas, *Religious America, Secular Europe? A Theme and Variations* (Burlington, Vt.: Ashgate, 2008), p. 49. See also Gertrude Himmelfarb, *The Roads to Modernity: The British, French, and American Enlightenments* (New York: Knopf, 2004).

practice, the place and role of *varṇāśrama,* the relationship between reason and sacred texts, the ultimate nature of minute and infinite personhood, and the manner in which social and political life should be oriented, understood, and pursued.

The primary utility of the model presented herein is its attempt to link sociohistorical analysis with a taxonomy of philosophical orientations residing close to the core of religious identity and practice; because of this it can delve deeper than models that only account for institutional, political, or social variables.

The following section further clarifies Bhaktisiddhānta's Vedantic personalism by comparing it with Vivekānanda's Vedantic nondualism.

A Comparison with Swami Vivekānanda

Apart from the fact that Bhaktisiddhānta and Vivekānanda held very different understandings of Vedanta, there are a number of interesting parallels between these two personalities that bear mentioning. For one thing, they were contemporaries; for another, they both belonged to the educated *bhadralok,* as well as the same *kāyastha* "Datta" clan. Both chose ascetic gurus with a mystical orientation, both founded religious institutions in Calcutta that went on to become global movements, and both attempted to propagate their respective messages in accordance with a religious "universalism" that was grounded in Vedantic metaphysics. In addition, both were penetrating thinkers whose individual insights led each to conclude that humanity's existential ills could only be solved by a spiritual transformation that went beyond the shores of India, and that Vedanta should thus be made available to the English-speaking world. Finally, both were highly proficient when it came to employing modern technological, organizational and institutional means to achieve their respective goals. As indicated by the following passage, it was this sophistication that fascinated Dayānanda Sarasvatī upon paying a visit to Calcutta in the second half of the nineteenth century:

> the Bengalis steered Dayananda's mind out of the narrow ambit it had been moving on. They opened up new perspectives, and helped the Svāmī to think in broader social and national terms: to see education as the most important factor in the uplift of the people; to consider the wide social responsibilities of the state; to be aware

> of the different aspects of the plight of Hindu womanhood; and to think of Hinduism in a comparative framework. Dayananda saw at close quarters a superbly-organized effort at social and religious reform, and his eyes were opened to a new range of approaches. In Calcutta he discovered the great power of lectures and publications, the strength of organization and the receptivity of the urban middle-class to the call of reform.[38]

While the above similarities between Bhaktisiddhānta and Vivekānanda are clearly noteworthy, the nature of their differences is of greater relevance as far as the present discussion is concerned. The most significant of those differences are presented below.

To begin with, whereas Bhaktisiddhānta established his movement on the basis of the *brāhmaṇic* and Sanskritized Vaishnava lineages of India, Vivekānanda's movement was largely grounded upon the subjective mystical experiences of Ramakrishna—an approach that Bhaktisiddhānta considered less authentic. Moreover, Bhaktisiddhānta regarded Vivekānanda's idea of "poor Nārāyaṇa" (*daridra Nārāyaṇa*)—which implied a vision of man as God (Nārāyaṇa is a name of Vishnu)—as an imperfect understanding of the conclusions of Vedanta. For him, the centrality of the idea of a personal God and the potentiality of bhakti had been hinted at throughout history, but not fully realized.

Vivekānanda criticized bhakti for what he saw as its potential to give rise to exclusivism, but acknowledged that this danger was only present in the preliminary stages (*gauni*). When bhakti was "ripe," according to his definition of the term, there was no longer any danger of "hideous manifestations of fanaticism."[39] For Vivekānanda, bhakti was merely a means to an end, a tool to be jettisoned once one had attained complete enlightenment.[40] For Bhaktisiddhānta, on the other hand, bhakti was the be-all and end-all—the starting point, the means, and the end—of the

38. Jordens, *Dayananda Sarasvati*, p. 287.

39. Swami Vivekānanda, *Complete Works of Vivekananda*, vol. 3, pp. 32–33.

40. "We all have to begin as dualists in the religion of love. God is to us a separate Being, and we feel ourselves to be separate beings also...at last, however, comes the full blaze of Light, in which this little self is seen to have become one with the Infinite. Man himself is transfigured in the presence of this Light of Love, and he realises at last the beautiful and inspiring truth that Love, the Lover, and the Beloved are One." Swami Vivekānanda *Complete Works of Vivekananda*, vol. 3, p. 100.

quest for spiritual meaning, metaphysical engagement, and the attainment of unalloyed loving exchange with the "all-attractive ever blissful" supreme being.

Bhaktisiddhānta was among the small minority of Bengali intellectuals who openly resisted the general trend of the *bhadralok* toward nondualism, humanitarianism, and the struggle for national emancipation that Vivekānanda directly or indirectly inspired. In this sense, he was quite out of step with his times. For his part, Vivekānanda spoke for a moral and "muscular" reconstruction of India that inspired nationalistic feelings, but also warned against interpretations of his writings and speeches to that effect, pointing out that the root of the world's problem was spiritual, not material.[41] Vivekānanda's universalism was inclusive and formulated in terms of the ultimate spiritual oneness of all beings, an understanding of "liberation" (*mukti*) that necessarily entailed the dissolution of individual form and personality. Bhaktisiddhānta considered this a reductionist view of reality, particularly because it eliminated the possibility of intimate personal service to Krishna. Bhaktisiddhānta viewed love as the "highest subject of human poetry and the most powerful actor in all human activities."[42] However, he believed that the concept of love, which has higher spiritual dimensions, is often limited to the mundane sexuality of this world. In other words, the nontemporal self is potentially female, but female not in any kind of material sense:

> Our present objection to the female form is due to egotistic principle which for the same reason does not object or rather, readily enough adopts the male form as more properly representing the pure little soul. This repugnance to the female form prevents us from unprejudiced examination of the female sex.... Spiritual amour is

41. Swami Vivekānanda, *Complete Works of Vivekananda*, vol. 5, pp. 46, 217–18, vol. 6, p. 406. Beckerlegge suggests that "Vivekananda's concern about being branded 'political' went hand-in-hand with fear that being more outspoken might invite penalties from the British upon opponents of their rule in India and thus was in part at least a pragmatic response to a specific set of circumstances. The same can be said of the Ramakrishna movement's caution during the first two decades of the twentieth century when under suspicion of nurturing terrorism. The translation of this early policy of being apolitical appears to have taken place without reference to changing national and global conditions." Gwilym Beckerlegge, "Responding to Conflict: A Test of the Limits of Neo-Vedāntic Social Activism in the Ramakrishna Math and Mission?" *International Journal of Hindu Studies* 11, no. 1 (2007): p. 16.

42. Bhaktisiddhānta, *Shri Chaitanya's Teachings*, "Krishna-Prema," p. 449.

> the best mode of service of the Fullness of Divine Personality. In other words, the real Nature of Divine Personality can never be fully understood by those who are unable to appreciate the pre-eminent excellence of His service by amorous love.[43]

The goal of bhakti in the line of Rūpa and Ragunātha Goswami—two of Caitanya's primary disciples—had little to do with worldly sex and gender. All beings of this world carry the potential of participating in the spiritual dimension called Goloka Vrindavan. A special feature of the feminine mood—which was in keeping with the essential mood of Rādhā as manifested through the life of Caitanya and portrayed in the *Caitanya Caritāmṛta*—was the feeling of compassion and the desire to relieve suffering of other living beings, a mood that Bhaktisiddhānta had identified as one of his inner theological motives for propagating a new religious movement in India.[44] In this light, Bhaktisiddhānta had encouraged his disciples to "preach all over the world the teachings of Shri Rupa and Shri Raghunātha with all your might."[45]

Bhaktisiddhānta and Vivekānanda represent two different trajectories within modern Hinduism, born of the same cultural and religious domain. Here I have mainly emphasized Bhaktisiddhānta's role as a traditionalist, and the way he consistently referred to the premodern bhakti literature to identify the theological and philosophical core of Caitanya bhakti.

"Old Wine in New Bottle"

The interesting thing about Bhaktisiddhānta's place within modern Hinduism is that rather than attempting to adjust the core understandings of his tradition to suit the sensibilities of his times, he attempted to give those understandings a modern form of dress and expression—that is, to effect a change at the periphery—hence the reference in the above subheading to preserving the old wine while placing it in a new bottle. It is the fact that Bhaktisiddhānta worked and lived on the border between the urban Hindu bourgeoisie of Calcutta and a premodern Hindu world reaching back to antiquity that constitutes the subversive and challenging character of his life and work.

---

43. Bhaktisiddhānta, *Shri Chaitanya's Teachings*, "Krishna-Prema," p. 449.

44. Bhaktisiddhānta, *Shri Chaitanya's Teachings*, "Krishna-Prema," p. 471.

45. Bhaktisiddhānta, *Shri Chaitanya's Teachings*, "Krishna-Prema," p. 471.

The first step in gaining an accurate understanding of his place is therefore to grasp Bhaktisiddhānta's deep religious traditionalism. Here traditionalism is meant to indicate his specific commitment to the core teachings of Caitanya Vaishnavism, which included not only the works of such figures as Kṛṣṇadāsa Kavirāja Goswami, Rūpa Goswami, Sanātana Goswami, and Jīva Goswami, but also Vaishnava interpretations of earlier works such as the *Bhāgavata Purāṇa*, most of which he consistently studied, commented on, and published (see appendix E).[46] The second step in understanding Bhaktisiddhānta, however, is the view that he was also *more* than a Hindu traditionalist, as has been indicated repeatedly throughout this work. For the following reasons, he was also controversial, nonorthodox, modern/secular, and revival-/reform-oriented, but always in a specialized sense that was qualified by his traditionalism:

1. Like many religious transformers, Bhaktisiddhānta was a traditionalist who was far more concerned with universal principles than he was with the exact maintenance of sectarian, ethnical, or outmoded forms, formalities, and practices. This approach is what enabled him to effect apparently radical changes and to employ modern means with confidence. It can be seen in his championing of *śikṣā* over *dīkṣā* initiation, in the highly unorthodox manner in which he adopted *saṃnyāsa*, and in his frequent use of automobiles, printing presses, and the like. It can also be seen from the fact that while he vigorously strove for a recovery of the classic texts of his tradition (the hallmark of traditionalism), he just as vigorously strove against the hereditary privileges of the traditionalist Vaishnava *brāhmaṇas* of Bengal.

Bhaktisiddhānta opposed the exclusive right of the caste *brāhmaṇas* to interpret religious texts, and instead chose to *brāhmaṇize* all those that seriously accepted the process of Caitanya bhakti, regardless of class, race, or gender. He also argued that only those that were spiritually advanced on the path of bhakti—that is, genuinely qualified gurus in terms of character, behavior, and practice—could properly interpret and understand the texts of the tradition. In this way he reaffirmed the traditional requirement of competence (over and above mere rubber-stamping) relative to its highest authorities. Making these claims, the present study confirms

46. Bhaktisiddhānta mentioned in a conversation with Prof. P. Johans of St. Xavier's College that he philosophically particularly followed Jīva Goswami. See Bhaktisiddhānta Sarasvatī, *Śrī Śrī Sarasvatī Saṃlāpa* (Allahabad: Śrī Rūpa Gaudiya Math, n.d.) vol. 2, pp. 67–68.

and qualifies Kenneth Valpey's observation (further discussed in appendix A) that Bhaktisiddhānta reformed a number of traditional customs and practices.

2. Bhaktisiddhānta's views regarding caste, *brāhmaṇism*, egalitarianism, universalism, and so forth sprang from the teaching of his tradition, and less from the influences of colonial culture, Western values, and Western modes of thought. The resemblance of certain aspects of his perspective to modernism was to some degree coincidental. In other words, the inclusiveness and globalism that is evident in Bhaktisiddhānta's perspective sprang mainly from core understandings that were already embedded in the teachings of Caitanya and his immediate followers found in the Vaishnava literature. Moreover, his inclination toward rationalistic formulation stemmed not from his exposure to Western thinkers, but rather from his deep study of the rational arguments of Vedanta philosophy, which had developed over centuries of sophisticated discourse.

3. Along similar lines, Bhaktisiddhānta's pragmatic, utilitarian approach to modern means sprang not precisely from exposure to or fascination with the various products of science and technology, but rather from a modern interpretation of a core principle of Caitanya bhakti—that of *yukta vairāgya*. According to this principle, because everything emanates from God—making God the supreme controller and possessor of all manifestations and potencies in this world—all things (including those of modern human invention) are meant to be used in God's service. It was primarily this core traditional perspective that led him to conclude that when it comes to spreading the teachings of his tradition and building a national and international institution, "utility is the principle." On this basis, and as noted above, he had no qualms about using printing press, automobiles, radios, Western institutional structures, steamships, and other modern means to forward his purposes.

4. Unlike many of his *bhadralok* contemporaries, Bhaktisiddhānta's universalism, inclusiveness, and egalitarianism—that is, his worldview and world-approach—drew only a minor amount of inspiration from exposure to Western traditions of religion and scholarship. On the contrary, at the core of his desire to uplift humanity, break down the barriers of caste and race, emancipate the individual, and make Caitanya bhakti available to all was the understanding that "real identity" is not to be found in temporary bodily or mental designations, but rather in the understanding of oneself as an eternally conscious person, meant to serve

and love the "Personality of Godhead." According to this view, ignorance of one's spiritual identity is the ultimate cause of suffering, and the effort to remove this ignorance is the ultimate humanitarian work—that which can bring ultimate relief to the self. In other words, his egalitarianism was a spiritual egalitarianism and his humanitarianism had little to do with the upkeep of the temporary bodily dress. Here Bhaktisiddhānta raises the question of the ultimate satisfaction of the conscious self, conceived as a potent active principle that exists apart from the superfluous coverings of the gross body and subtle mind. Unless one comprehends and addresses the needs of this nonmaterial self, he argued, no amount of bodily and/or mental welfare will suffice. Put metaphorically, cleansing the cage cannot bring satisfaction to the bird; one must attend to the needs of the bird itself. As noted by Bhaktisiddhānta's disciple Bhaktivedānta Swami (briefly discussed below):

> There is a dormant affection for God within everyone; spiritual existence is manifested through the gross body and mind in the form of perverted affection for gross and subtle matter. Therefore we have to engage ourselves in occupational engagements that will evoke our divine consciousness.[47]

The view of Bhaktisiddhānta expressed in this fourth point is confirmed by Ramakanta Chakravarti (discussed in appendix A), who has noted that humanitarian work, in terms of such things as worldly education and health care, was not his primary aim (although he did promote material-cum-spiritual education in the Bhaktivinoda Institute; see chapter 2). For Bhaktisiddhānta, bhakti was the medicine that could heal the social and psychological ills of modern men and women, which he viewed as ultimately stemming from the selfish propensity to control and own the objects of Nature without understanding to whom they factually belong—a propensity that had been exacerbated by processes of cultural and technological rationalization championed by colonial modernity. This understanding of Bhaktisiddhānta's ethical, religious, and social approach makes it possible to characterize his contribution as a carefully framed universalism that went, at least to a fair degree, against the grain

47. Bhaktivedānta, commentary to *Śrīmad Bhāgavatam* [*Bhāgavata Purāṇa*] 1.2.8, in *Bhaktivedānta Vedabase 2003*.

of indigenous sectarianism, and beyond it as well. It appears, in other words, to cast Bhaktisiddhānta in a less sectarian light, while simultaneously acknowledging that, above all, Bhaktisiddhānta saw his task as the *recovery* of a lost spiritual tradition.

In summary, while a number of studies (reviewed in appendix A) tend to characterize Bhaktisiddhanta as a traditionalist, and others tend to characterize him as a modern reformer, in my view neither of these characterizations provides a complete picture. As this book has demonstrated, Bhaktisiddhānta's approach was multifaceted and capable of accommodating a wide range of highly contradictory currents. His responsiveness to modern times and the flexible manner in which he expressed and actualized his tradition enabled him to creatively reaffirm the global vision of Caitanya bhakti and present Vaishnava personalism in a way that to some degree also encompassed other theistic traditions.

Bhaktisiddhānta's Legacy

In the introduction of this work I made the following statement:

> After he passed away in 1937 [Bhaktisiddhānta's] movement largely disintegrated during a crisis of succession that ended in schism, and it seemed as if his life and work would remain a mere footnote in the annals of religious history. Some thirty years later, however, a watershed event would propel his movement to surprising heights and rapidly spread his perspective on the teachings of Caitanya throughout the world, making tens of thousands of non-Indian followers along the way.

It is now time to discuss this watershed event since it directly pertains to Bhaktisiddhānta's significance. On August 13, 1965, one of Bhaktisiddhānta's disciples, A. C. Bhaktivedānta Swami (1896–1977), set out by steamship for New York City to fulfill Bhaktisiddhānta's instruction to carry "the message of Caitanya" to the English-speaking world. Although Bhaktivedānta had been a lay businessman during the 1920s and 1930s, and thus had played only an indirect role in the development of the Gaudiya Math, throughout the years after Bhaktisiddhānta's demise this instruction had somehow remained in the forefront of his mind. When he arrived in New York Harbor some thirty-seven days after departing from India, Bhaktivedānta was more or less alone. He had come to America at the age of seventy without the backing of the Gaudiya Math, with only a handful of contacts, and with little means of visible support. After passing his first year without much tangible success, he settled into a small flat on New York's Lower East Side and from there founded the International Society for Krishna Consciousness (ISKCON), an institution that was largely modeled on the structure of the Gaudiya Math. Gradually, middle- and upper-middle-class Westerners—most of whom were part of the American counterculture—took an interest in his teaching and chose to become his disciples. Some twelve years later, on November 14, 1977, Bhaktivedānta passed away in Vrindavan, India at the age of eighty-one. However, in the years that transpired between his arrival and his demise he had managed to build ISKCON into an institution comprising thousands of dedicated members, establish Caitanya Vaishnava temples in most of the world's major cities, and publish numerous volumes of Caitanya Vaishnava texts (in twenty-eight languages), tens of millions of which were distributed throughout the world. In short, Bhaktivedānta had managed to achieve the level of social, cultural, and religious impact that Bhaktisiddhānta, and his father before him, had been working to achieve. This also included bringing dedicated Western Caitanya Vaishnavas back to India to teach the local peoples the Gaudiya Math understanding of their own tradition, and even to become accepted and admired spiritual leaders—gurus that have initiated thousands of members of India's indigenous population.

After Bhaktivedānta passed away, the global movement that he had inaugurated continued to grow, despite a number of significant setbacks, and inspired other of Bhaktisiddhānta's disciples and grand-disciples to also carry the message of Caitanya bhakti around the world. Today, besides ISKCON there are a number of international Caitanya Vaishnava institutions, all of which hark back to Bhaktisiddhānta's guruship, perspective, and mode of presentation.[48] Recently, there has been an attempt by the leadership of many of these organizations to develop closer interinstitutional cooperation. This attempt has resulted in the formation of the World Vaishnava Association, an alliance of like-minded

48. For an overview of these institutions, see B. A. Paramadvaiti Swami, *Our Family the Gaudiya Math: A Study of the Expansion of Gaudiya Vaisnavism and the Many Branches Developing around the Gaudiya Math* (Vrindavan: Vrindavan Institute for Vaisnava Culture and Studies, 1999).

organizations that hope to gradually coordinate their efforts under the common umbrella of the Viśva Vaishnava Rāja Sabhā earlier revived by Bhaktisiddhānta (see chapter 2).[49]

In comparison with his mentor and guru Bhaktisiddhānta, Bhaktivedānta—who as a youth had been Gandhian in his political orientation—was far more forceful in criticizing what he viewed as the growing materialism, impersonalism, and godlessness of the West. He also introduced Westerners to a form of Caitanya Vaishnavism that was far more authentically "Indian" in outward appearance, custom, and manner than Bhaktisiddhānta had apparently conceived, partially because of the eager reception that he received from the youth of the Western counterculture.[50] Nonetheless, these two personalities are inextricably linked—as guru and disciple—in sharing a vision of an international movement to make Caitanya bhakti widely available, particularly through an organized and institutionalized effort that welcomed proselytizing on a global scale. Following the example of Bhaktisiddhānta, Bhaktivedanta put a strong emphasis on commenting on, publishing, and distributing the Sanskrit and Bengali literature of the tradition, often quoting Bhaktisiddhānta's words in his translations in English. It is largely because of the connected efforts of these two figures, and the initial inspiration of Bhaktivinoda, that Vaishnavism has become, for the first time in its history, an established global religion with a visible presence throughout the world beyond the Hindu diaspora.

In closing this section, it is legitimate to inquire as to the future of the international movement that began with Bhaktisiddhānta and his father Bhaktivinoda. What future forms and trajectories will it take as it continues to reside in the ever-evolving cultural, social, political, and religious milieus of an ever-morphing world? Rādhānātha Swami, an American guru of ISKCON based in Chowpatti, Mumbai, writes:

> It is important to remain faithful to the siddhānta [philosophical conclusions] while being open to effective ways of reaching and sustaining people's hearts. The essential teachings should not be compromised in principle or practice. At the same time there

49. www.wva-vvrs.org (accessed on June 7, 2012).

50. For details, see volume two of the six-volume biographical account *Śrīla Prabhupāda-līlāmṛta*, by Satsvarūpa dāsa Goswami in Bhaktivedānta et al., *Bhaktivedānta Vedabase 2003*.

> needs to be a presentation in a way that will actually achieve the purpose of attracting people's hearts, nourishing faith, and sustaining devotion.[51]

The global future of the movement will depend on its ability to transform, adapt, and adjust in response to the progressive values, mores, and sensibilities that are characteristic of postmodern global cultures. The success of this program will require the tradition to explore its own textual sources and religious history for principles that enable innovation, adaptation, and change. This is a matter that various leaders of the movement have already begun to address. Put simply, the future of the movement may depend on whether or not it is able to creatively adapt its tradition to the times, as did Bhaktisiddhānta himself, while maintaining the integrity of its teachings and practices.

Future Pathways of Research

Despite the predictions of various late-twentieth-century secularist scholars, religion remains a markedly influential social, cultural, and political force. If anything, the matter of diverse religious beliefs (and the power of religious ideologies) has become an even more vital topic relative to the preservation of modern global societies.[52] In this regard, such phenomena as mass migration, 9/11, the Palestinian-Israeli conflict, and tensions between Pakistan and India clearly indicate that one of the great challenges of the twenty-first century will be to build solid bridges of understanding between the world's major religious traditions, and better comprehend their role in the present world. This is a task that calls upon scholars and others to develop projects that contribute reliable knowledge and new insights.

Following along these lines, this book has attempted to broaden and deepen the understanding of an important chapter of modern Hinduism, an effort that appears to be particularly relevant in light of the fact that India is currently on the rise in terms of economic power, political influence, and population growth. By providing an historical analysis of a

51. Personal communication, November 5, 2009.

52. Peter L. Berger, "The Desecularization of the World: A Global Overview," in *The Desecularization of the World: Resurgent Religion and World Politics*, ed. Peter L. Berger (Washington, D.C.: Eerdmans, Ethics and Public Policy Center, 1999).

sophisticated proponent of twentieth-century Hinduism, as well as the colonial context in which he functioned, I also hope to have shed some light on various points of commonality and difference between India and Europe in relation to religion and modernity. This opens up the possibility of exploring patterns of Indian modernity independent of those followed by the West. This is particularly relevant since Hindu middle-class modernity is socially, culturally, and symbolically more informed by religion than is European modernity. There is also a need to better understand the importance of modern traditionalist religions (and religious leaders such as Bhaktisiddhānta) to the overall history of Indian modernity as well as to the religious history of the world. As has been hinted at in this work, research on the history of modern Hinduism is in need of further detailed studies, and the one undertaken here may be regarded as a step in that direction.

This book can be seen as a contribution to the West's understanding of India in another sense. Bhaktisiddhānta's Vaishnava bhakti is a significant branch of one of the largest and most influential traditions in the religious life of India—and throughout the contemporary Hindu world. In all its various manifestations, Vaishnava bhakti is an immense source of religious inspiration within Hinduism on all levels, as is confirmed by the enthusiasm that greets the yearly celebration of holidays such as Krishna Janmāṣṭami, Rāmnavamī, and so on, and by recent political movements in India that have consistently adopted Vaishnava symbols. As such, it appears to warrant greater scholarly attention than it has thus far received in terms of understanding its history, its practices, its major religious figures (both past and present), and its philosophical rationale, particularly in relation to modernity and globalization.

Regarding the history, life and thought of Bhaktisiddhānta, many issues deserve greater attention. The writings of Bhaktisiddhānta have yet to be systematically presented, and translations of his Bengali works would make his thought accessible to a larger audience. Another area that awaits further investigation is the relationship between Bhaktisiddhānta's approach and that of premodern Vaishnavism in Bengal, as well as that of the disciples and institutions that have come after him. Finally, Bhaktisiddhānta's personalism and its place in the history of modern Indian philosophy have not been fully explored. A comparison between Indian and Western personalism also carries the potential of bridging cultural gaps and opening new venues of understanding between India and the West.

This book has managed to explore only a few of the themes that were central to Bhaktisiddhānta Sarasvatī's life and work. Rather than being *the* final word on this topic, its primary aim has been to open up a fresh area of study. To the degree that it has succeeded in doing so, I consider my task successful.

APPENDIX A

Theoretical and Methodological Notes

Hinduism and Bhakti

Any discussion about India from the point of view of Western scholarship must deal with the problem posed by the colonial past, and the ways in which India was colonized, interpreted, and constructed to fit into an imperialist agenda. The terms "Hinduism" and "religion," for example, are themselves quite problematic since they are born of Western and Christian thought and do not always reflect the complexity and diversity of Indic traditions. A translation of terms and concepts from one cultural domain to another is required, but it is bound to be only tentative and approximate since a comprehension of the full meaning of words related to Indic religions presupposes an extensive grounding in the rich religious thought of India. In some cases a translation may deal with concepts that have no equivalent in Western thought, and thus a rendition will be no more than an approximation. In the wake of the work on *Orientalism* by Edward Said, scholars such as S. N. Balagangadhara have called attention to the need to understand India's history and culture (and especially its religions) with fresh eyes, and to pay more attention to the ways in which Indians perceive and understand their own traditions.[1] Along similar lines, John Darwin has suggested that "European accounts of other cultures and peoples should no longer be treated as the 'authorized version,' however full or persuasive."[2]

Noel Salmond has highlighted a number of possible stereotypes regarding Indic religions: for example, that India is highly iconic whereas the West is uniconic, that Indian religions are mystical and metaphysically abstract whereas Western religion is

1. S. N. Balagangadhara, "How to Speak for the Indian Traditions: An Agenda for the Future," *Journal of the American Academy of Religion* 73, no. 4 (2005); Edward W. Said, *Orientalism: Western Conceptions of the Orient* (London: Penguin, 2003).

ethical and rational, and that India is otherworldly whereas the West is this-worldly, activistic, and based on in-worldly asceticism.[3] Such perceptions wrongly assume not only that Indic religions have one essence and are monolithic, but also that there is an unbridgeable dichotomy between "East" and "West"—almost ontological in nature—that makes it impossible for any real cohesion to exist between the two.

The use and definition of the terms "Hindu" and "Hinduism" are often debated. Both were created by outsiders and were not meant to reflect the self-perception of indigenous religious communities. The word "Hindu" has been used for a long time in relation to those belonging to a large variety of religious communities in the geographical area beyond the Indus River, loosely connected by a common cultural history. It came in vogue among Muslims during the Islamic period (ca. thirteenth to eighteenth century), and particularly during the Delhi Sultanate (1206–1526), but had earlier Persian roots. The term "Hinduism" was coined by eighteenth-century Christian missionaries in an attempt to define a world "religion" that could be easily distinguished from Christianity, Judaism and Islam: the one practiced by the "heathens" of South Asia.[4] There is scholarly consensus that the term is a questionable Western construct that was reinforced by both colonial administrators and Indologists such as Max Müller (1823–1900).[5] Since at least the sixteenth century, however, the term "Hindu" has been appropriated by South Asians (and later by the Indian diaspora) to distinguish their particular religious identity from that of other religious communities. It has thus acquired a certain degree of insider legitimacy, despite suspicions that it largely serves the purposes of Indian nationalism.[6] Will Sweetman has argued that the term "Hinduism" is useful when it refers not to one monothetic tradition, but rather to a *family* of religions that share a degree of affinity.[7] I have employed these terms in this extended religious sense, without reference to their possible political implications.

During the twentieth century the academic study of Hinduism became considerably more nuanced and sophisticated. Within this context there have been

2. Darwin, *After Tamerlane*, p. 14.

3. Salmond, *Hindu Iconoclasts*, pp. 3–4.

4. Heinrich von Stietencron, "Religious Configurations in Pre-Muslim India and the Modern Concept of Hinduism," in *Representing Hinduism: The Construction of Religious Traditions and National Identity*, ed. Vasudha Dalmia and Heinrich von Stietencron (New Delhi: Sage Publications, 1995), pp. 73–74.

5. See, for example, Günther-Dietz Sontheimer and Hermann Kulke, *Hinduism Reconsidered* (New Delhi: Manohar Publications, 1997).

6. For early indigenous uses of the word "Hindu" see Joseph O'Connell, "The Word 'Hindu' in Gaudiya Vaisnava Texts," *Journal of American Oriental Society* 93, no. 3 (1973).

7. Will Sweetman, "Unity and Plurality: Hinduism and the Religions of India in Early European Scholarship," *Religion* 31, no. 3 (2001): p. 219.

numerous studies on a variety of subjects. Some have focused on the attempt to define what Hinduism is, while others have concentrated on sacred Sanskrit and vernacular texts. Yet others have examined Indic philosophy and theology, Indic conceptions of self and identity, and/or Indic notions of the cosmic order. Apart from these, there have been a variety of studies on theistic movements, on nationalism, on the Indian diaspora, on caste, and on practices such as pilgrimage, worship and *rites de passage*. Despite the richness of this research, the study of bhakti (a central element of Hinduism) is, in the words of Gregory Price Grieve, "a supporting actor [at best]," and thus, "deserv[ing] [of] more attention."[8] According to Klaus Klostermaier, one reason for giving more attention to bhakti movements and their key personalities is that "the majority of Hindus today are followers of *bhaktimārga* [the path of bhakti]," particularly at the popular level.[9] David Lorenzen goes even further when he claims that

> today *bhakti* is the single most important element of both Hindu and Sikh religious traditions, so much so that both can be included within a more general category of *bhakti* traditions.[10]

Bhakti has been a central theme of this book. And yet, despite the term's widespread use, it is quite difficult to adequately translate into English, where it is commonly referred to as "devotion." The reason is that schools from tantra to yoga provide a large number of subcategories to qualify its generic meaning. Lorenzen, for example, suggests that the word can mean "to participate in" or "to share," in the sense of sharing in sacrificial offerings; he further suggests that it can be more generally defined as "personal devotion to a god or a saintly person."[11] Early orientalists such as Horace Hayman Wilson, Monier Monier-Williams, and George Abraham Grierson have identified bhakti as the monotheistic strand in Hinduism, and in this

---

8. Gregory Price Grieve, "Staking Out the Field: A Henotheistic Review of Supplemental Readers for the Study of Hinduism," *Journal of the American Academy of Religion* 76, no. 3 (2008): p. 735. After reviewing four North American and British readers for the study of Hinduism, Grieve concluded that in the North Atlantic region "the core of the academic study of Hinduism is still the study of scripture," that theistic bhakti has not received the attention it deserves relative to its size, that the study of philosophy and theology is considered important but is not yet a central element, and that identity and practice deserve more attention. Grieve, "Staking out the Field," p. 744. These observations may not always apply to continental Europe, where the situation is different than in North America and Britain.

9. Klaus K. Klostermaier, *A Survey of Hinduism* (Albany: State University of New York Press, 2007), p. 181.

10. David N. Lorenzen, "Bhakti," in *The Hindu World*, ed. Sushil Mittal and Gene R. Thursby (New York: Routledge, 2004), p. 185.

11. Lorenzen, "Bhakti," p. 185.

sense the word has been used to mean "devotion to a personal God."[12] However, the legitimacy of this translation has been questioned in recent years by scholars such as Krishna Sharma, who argues that bhakti historically includes nondualistic forms of religiosity, particularly among the Hindu poetic traditions of North India.[13] He also argues that the "narrow" theistic definition was adopted because the initial contact of Western scholars in Bengal was with Caitanya Vaishnavism, whose mainstream literature is more clearly personalist and theistic than that of other popular bhakti movements.[14] Within the framework of this study, bhakti has been understood as the development of a person's capacity to love through active and/or systematic participation in an intimate relationship with a supreme being.

The conceptual distinction between a "minor god" and a "supreme personal God" is of great importance for understanding the internal dynamics of bhakti within Hinduism. These notions can convey a variety of meanings, ranging from an all-pervading divine oneness (*brahman*) to a supreme personal deity (*bhagavān*) to lesser cosmic gods (*devas*) to village or folk deities worshipped outside the orthodox *brāhmaṇic* tradition. In discussing the philosophical basis of bhakti, a distinction is often made between *saguṇa* (with *guṇa* or attributes) and *nirguṇa* (without attributes), which indicates two different approaches to the divine.[15] *Saguṇa* bhakti is often applied in relation to the iconic worship of "high" personal deities such as Śiva and the members of his family, Vishnu, his *avatāras* and associates, or the goddess Devī in her multiple manifestations—such as the frightening Kālī or the lion-borne Durga. Although

---

12. Karen Pechilis Prentiss, *The Embodiment of Bhakti* (New York: Oxford University Press, 1999), p. 4. Graham Schweig has described bhakti particularly in reference to Krishna as "the loving dedication of the individual self (*bhakta*) to the supreme self (*bhagavat*) in which one becomes 'selfless,' in the sense that the heart of the individual self is wholly centered upon the divine (*bhakti*)"; this is carried out in one of five types of relationships, i.e. "(1) reverential love (*śānta*), (2) subservient love (*dāsya*), (3) mutual love (*sākhya*), (4) nurturing love (*vātsalya*), and (5) passionate love (*śṛṅgāra*)." Graham Schweig "Toward a Constructive and Comparative Theology of Krishna Bhakti for Contemporary Bengal Vaishnavism," *Journal of Vaishnava Studies* 18, no. 1 (2009): pp. 157–158.

13. Sharma, *Bhakti and the Bhakti Movement.*

14. Sharma suggests that "it is the bhakti tradition of Chaitanya and his Gauḍīya school of Vaishnavism which conforms most to the current academic definition of bhakti" and that "total dedication to a personal God as Krishna is the quintessence of Gauḍīya Vaishnavism." Sharma, *Bhakti and the Bhakti Movement*, p. 255. For a good synopsis of the earliest Caitanya Vaishnava literature see Sushil Kumar De, *Early History of the Vaisnava Faith and Movement in Bengal: From Sanskrit and Bengali Sources* (Calcutta: Mukhopadhyay, 1961). It is important to note that Caitanya Vaishnavism includes many orthodox, unorthodox, and syncretistic movements. A prudent estimate is that it today counts between 30 and 50 million adherents, mostly concentrated in the northeast areas of South Asia such as Orissa, Manipur, West Bengal, and Bangladesh.

15. *Guṇa* (rope) is a concept of Sāṅkhya philosophy and refers to three psychophysical "modes" that constitutes the foundational qualities of the world—i.e., purity or goodness (*sattva*), passion (*rajas*), and darkness or ignorance (*tamas*).

bhakti involves paying homage to an image or icon, there are a number of Hindu communities, such as the Kabīr *panthīs*, that worship an image as only a means of realizing an ultimate reality that is devoid of attributes. In such cases the worship of an image is conceived only as a transitory stage meant to ease meditation, and is forsaken when later phases of development are thought to have been reached. *Saguṇa bhaktas*, on the other hand, largely claim to worship a supreme being or person, who while devoid of material attributes is nonetheless endowed with *metaphysical* (nonmaterial or spiritual) attributes that include personality, form, spiritual senses, place, activities, associates, and paraphernalia. Thus they persist in defining theistic bhakti as *nirguṇa* despite the fact that they worship the deity or *form* of a supreme personal God. Recent studies of Hindi poets up to the seventeenth century have questioned the viability of the *saguṇa* and *nirguṇa* dichotomy, since for them these contradictory features appear to have coexisted.[16] In addition, studies of Hindus of the modern period such as Ramakrishna have shown that personal and impersonal bhakti have been often understood as two aspects or levels of the same mystical experience (although in most cases favoring a nondualistic perspective); in such cases it appears that a strict dichotomy is also hard to maintain.[17] These examples indicate that, for the most part, subtle doctrinal distinctions have been the product of debates among pandits rather than part of the factual experience of practicing mystics and/or *bhaktas*. The distinction between *nirguṇa* and *saguṇa brahman* is nonetheless clearly outlined in the philosophical schools of Vedanta, and it has been pointed out and discussed for centuries by nearly all Hindu gurus and teachers. As such, it has received appropriate attention in this study.

To avoid unnecessary ambiguities, and despite the fact that there are exceptions, I have chosen to tie the term *nirguṇa* to the concept of undifferentiated "nondualism" or *advaita*, and the term *saguṇa* to that of personalist "theism" or "dualism," since the ultimate meaning of these terms is understood differently by the different traditions. The choice of terms like "nondualism" and "theism" is also not entirely satisfying. Nondualism, for example, can be regarded as a theistic system if we move beyond the way "theism" is defined in the Abrahamitic religions, allowing *theos* to indicate not only a personal God, but also the impersonal *brahman*. In the philosophy of *advaita* there is also an understanding of God as *īśvara*. However, in that system *īśvara* is the external manifestation (*māyā*) of *brahman*, and not its fundamental nature. The word "nondualism" (*advaita*) indicates that the starting point of the original school is the *duality* between the world (*jagat*) and its personal aspects on the one side, and the metaphysical oneness of *brahman* on the other, which it attempts to overcome by assuming that the world and its personalities are ultimately a superimposition on the oneness of *brahman*. The word "monism" pays less justice to the subtlety of this point

16. Prentiss, *The Embodiment of Bhakti*, pp. 21–22.

17. Jeffrey John Kripal, *Kali's Child: The Mystical and the Erotic in the Life and Teachings of Ramakrishna* (Chicago: University of Chicago Press, 1995), p. 19.

of departure. Another of my practical choices has concerned the use of the term "theism" to refer primarily to those philosophical schools that conceive of a personal God possessing metaphysical (*aprākṛta*) rather than material (*prākṛta*) attributes (one reading of *saguṇa*, as indicated above), and specifically to those of theistic Vaishnavism. The primary goal of such schools is the development of bhakti in terms of divine love (*prema*) for Vishnu or, in the case of the Caitanya school, for Krishna and his beloved consort Rādhā. What legitimates this qualification is that bhakti to Śiva and Devī has tended to orbit around various strands of nondualism, in the sense that it has tended (albeit far from exclusively) to stress the ultimate oneness of the devotee with the deity.[18] Vaishnava movements, particularly those born from northern and southern *brāhmaṇic* schools (*sampradāya*), have tended to revolve around dualist approaches, and even more so in the case of the Caitanya school.[19] Within these schools *brahman* is basically understood as the impersonal potency (*śakti*) of a personal God (*bhagavān*). The life and work of Bhaktisiddhānta was framed as shown above within the religious context of the latter kind of theistic, personalist bhakti.

It has been noted earlier that the process of adaptation among the *bhadralok*, and the dynamic creativity that it generated in the nineteenth century, is generally known as the "Bengal Renaissance."[20] The use of the term "Renaissance" has been contested because the original phenomenon was more of a *new development* than a rediscovery of an ancient history, as the etymology of the word suggests.[21] The Renaissance in thirteenth-century Italy entailed, above all, the questioning of Christian civilization and the rediscovery of classical Greco-Roman philosophy and culture. Many among the *bhadralok* searched for their identity within ancient but relatively well-known Indic religions within a colonial context. In this qualified sense, it is perhaps legitimate to use the term Renaissance when referring to the *reassessment* of precolonial Hindu philosophy and practice pursued by persons such as Rammohun Roy, who aimed at the *creation* of new convergences and the domestication of foreign

18. In dualistic strands of Śaivism, such as South Indian Śaiva Siddhānta, the goal of the worshipper is to realize him- or herself as Śiva. This is very different from theistic strands of Vaishnava bhakti.

19. Lorenzen, "Bhakti," p. 208. See also Graham M. Schweig, "Krishna: The Intimate Deity," in *The Hare Krishna Movement: The Postcharismatic Fate of a Religious Transplant*, ed. Edwin F. Bryant and Maria Ekstrand (New York: Columbia University Press, 2004), pp. 15–16.

20. Here the term "Bengal Renaissance" roughly refers to the period between 1800 (the year in which Fort William College was founded) and 1947 (the year of India's independence). The period's precise length is debated, see Harder, *Bankimchandra Chattopadhyay's Śrīmadbhagabadgītā*, p. 2 n. 6. The "Hindu Renaissance" has been generally regarded as lasting for the same amount of time; see for example an early study by D. S. Sarma, *Studies in the Renaissance of Hinduism in the Nineteenth and Twentieth Centuries* (Benares: Benares Hindu University, 1944).

21. Kopf, *British Orientalism*, pp. 280–281. The word "Renaissance" is derived from the Latin *renasci*, meaning "to be born again."

elements in contact with British and European civilization. Any analysis of the Bengal Renaissance needs to account for both these elements.

Literature related to Bhaktisiddhānta

Bhaktisiddhānta Sarasvatī claimed to practice and represent a genuine form of Caitanya bhakti. This tradition has attracted the attention of various fields of research, from Indology to South Asian studies.[22] Attention has been paid to literature in Sanskrit and Bengali from the sixteenth century onward, as well as to extant *sahajiyā* traditions—popular movements that tended to assimilate the mysticism of Caitanya in terms of erotic tantra.[23] With the exception of what has been mentioned in certain Bengali texts, inaccessible to those who are unfamiliar with the language, not much is known about changes and developments in the tradition that occurred among the *bhadralok* during the colonial period.[24] And even these works have their limitations in the sense that they are scant and only accessible to those who read the language.

The specific study of Caitanya bhakti has grown in size due to the fact that it is the only Vaishnava tradition that has managed to sustain a significant missionary effort outside South Asia and the Hindu diaspora. Its cumulative printed output has been massive, with almost half a billion pieces of literature sold in over eighty languages since 1965.[25] This result can be almost exclusively traced to Bhaktisiddhānta's original movement, indirectly making it the largest producer and distributor of Hindu literature in the world. Despite its relatively small size in terms of members, the significance of the movement has rarely been questioned. For example, John Esposito and his colleagues have suggested that ISKCON[26] (the most well known of the institutions that have emerged in the wake of Bhaktisiddhānta's work) and Transcendental Meditation are the two Hindu movements that have most attracted European and American attention.[27] Klostermaier states that "the best known—but not the only—contemporary

22. For a bibliography of works in English and Bengali on Caitanya Vaishnavism, see Das, *Essays on Vaisnavism in Bengal*, pp. 39–103.

23. For information on the early Caitanya period, see, for example, De, *Early History*; Robert Sailley *Chaitanya et la dévotion a Krishna* (Paris: Dervy-livres, 1986); Harish Chandra Das, *Sri Chaitanya in the Religious Life of India* (Calcutta: Punthi Pustak, 1989); and Janardana Cakrabarty, *Bengal Vaisnavism and Sri Chaitanya* (Calcutta: Asiatic Society, 2000). For studies on *sahajiyā*, see Shashi Bhushan Dasgupta, *Obscure Religious Cults* (Calcutta: Firma K. L. Mukhopadhyay, 1976); and Dimock, *Place of the Hidden Moon*.

24. Hena Basu, ed., *Vaisnava Periodical in Bengal (1856–1983)* (Kolkata: Basu Research and Documentation Service, 2009), pp. 5–6.

25. www.sankirtananewsletter.com (accessed on August 28, 2011). The site provides a total figure of 483,188,569 pieces of literature sold worldwide.

26. ISKCON is popularly known as the Hare Krishna Movement.

27. John L. Esposito, Darrell J. Fasching, and Todd Vernon Lewis, *Religion & Globalization: World Religions in Historical Perspective* (New York: Oxford University Press, 2008), p. 289.

Hindu *bhakti*-movement in the West is ISKCON."[28] In the *Cambridge Encyclopedia of India* (1989) ISKCON is presented as the most important among the guru-disciple movements in the West, not the least because it has been fairly well received by Hindus in India compared to other movements such as Transcendental Meditation.[29] The novelty of guru movements such as ISKCON, and their struggle to adjust to the cultural and social contexts of the West, has caused Western societies a number of legitimate concerns. This, in turn, has stimulated the production of a sizable number of sociological studies, especially during the second half of the twentieth century.[30] For the most part, however, that body of material contains little information about the life and work of Bhaktisiddhānta, which has been largely overlooked by researchers in India as well. In the latter case, the reason likely concerns the fact that Indian scholars have tended to undervalue currents of thought not directly related to Hindu nationalism, political reform, and/or humanitarian issues.

Indeed the perception of this research gap was one of the factors that awakened my interest in Bhaktisiddhānta, especially since it appeared that he, and possibly others like him, had been basically marginalized by mainstream historiography, despite the fact that they have richly contributed to certain facets of modern Hinduism. The intention of the present work has been to recover and explore the details of this forgotten piece of history, which appears to indicate that Bhaktisiddhānta played a significant role in modern Hinduism's global development.[31]

---

28. Klostermaier, *A Survey of Hinduism*, p. 183.

29. Francis Robinson, ed., *The Cambridge Encyclopedia of India, Pakistan, Bangladesh, Sri Lanka, Nepal, Bhutan and the Maldives* (Cambridge: Cambridge University Press, 1989), p. 349.

30. Early studies were conducted by Judah J. Stillson, *Hare Krishna and the Counterculture* (New York: Viley, 1974 and E. Burke Rochford, *Hare Krishna in America* (New Brunswick, N.J.: Rutgers University Press, 1985). For later studies containing sociological analyses, see Finn Madsen, "Social Udvikling I Hare Krishnabevægelsen," Ph.D. diss., University of Copenhagen, 2001; Edwin F. Bryant and Maria Ekstrand, *The Hare Krishna Movement: The Postcharismatic Fate of a Religious Transplant* (New York: Columbia University Press, 2004); Graham Dwyer and Richard J. Cole, *The Hare Krishna Movement: Forty Years of Chant and Change* (London: I. B. Tauris, 2007, and E. Burke Rochford, *Hare Krishna Transformed* (New York: New York University Press, 2007).

31. Regarding historical marginalization see Wouter J. Hanegraaff, "On the Construction of 'Esoteric Traditions'," in *Western Esotericism and the Science of Religion*, ed. Antoine Faivre and Wouter J. Hanegraaff (Leuven: Peeters, 1998), p. 18. An early study of modern Hinduism is William Joseph Wilkins, *Modern Hinduism, Being an Account of the Religion and Life of the Hindus in Northern India* (T. Fisher Unwin: London, 1887). A seminal study was later written by Farquhar, *Modern Religious Movements in India*. For more recent studies see, for example, Glyn Richards, *A Source-Book of Modern Hinduism* (London: Curzon, 1985); Arvind Sharma, *The Concept of Universal Religion in Modern Hindu Thought* (Basingstoke: Macmillian, 1998), and *Modern Hindu Thought: The Essential Texts* (Oxford: Oxford University Press, 2002), Raychaudhuri, *Perceptions, Emotions, Sensibilities*; Brian A. Hatcher *Eclecticism and Modern Hindu Discourse* (New York: Oxford University Press, 1999); Peter Van der Veer, *Imperial Encounters: Religion and Modernity in India and Britain* (Princeton, N.J.: Princeton University Press, 2001; and David Smith, *Hinduism and Modernity* (Malden, Mass.: Blackwell, 2003).

The body of extant literature on Bhaktisiddhānta's life and work can be broadly characterized as "hagiographic" and "hermeneutical." Although the hagiographic literature contains a large amount of interesting detail, it rarely ventures to explore in depth the social and historical context, and thus lacks a comprehensive historical perspective. This literature may be further subdivided into "synchronic" and "diachronic." "Synchronic" hagiographies are those that have focused on Bhaktisiddhānta's life, presenting it in terms of "insider" hermeneutical parameters.[32] One prominent and well-researched example is a recent work by Bhakti Vikāsa Swami (2009).[33] The term "diachronic" refers to works that provide accounts of Caitanya Vaishnavism that stretch from the medieval period to the period after World War II, presenting Bhaktisiddhānta Sarasvatī as the fulfillment of centuries of religious development.[34] Hagiographic literature is essential in its own right because it enables the historian to comprehend the ways in which a religious community perceives itself, historically and otherwise. Its limitation is that it tends to portray religious personalities as normative and didactic, without a sufficiently detailed awareness of the social and cultural context—both of which are important to the historical and/or sociological study of religion.

Hermeneutical studies, on the other hand, are academic in nature and employ a large number of etic categories. Narasingha Sil, for example, has suggested that research on Ramakrishna and Swami Vivekānanda has been of roughly four types: (1) theological; (2) sociohistorical; (3) psychohistorical; or, (4) psychospiritual (relating to mysticism and religious experience).[35] While most academic studies containing references to Bhaktisiddhānta's life and work can be said to have fallen within the second of these categories, the present work has aimed to integrate a sociohistorical with a history of religious ideas approach, and to address theological, psychohistorical, and psycho-spiritual concerns whenever the need arose.

The earliest scholarly study on Bhaktisiddhānta was a 1935 University of London dissertation entitled "The History and Literature of the Gaudiya Vaisnavas and their Relation to Other Medieval Vaisnava Schools." It was authored by a disciple named

---

32. See Devamayī dāsī, "A Divine Life: Śrīla Bhaktisiddhānta Saraswatī Ṭhākura Prabhupāda," in *Prabhupada Saraswati Thakur: The Life and Precepts of Śrīla Bhaktisiddhānta Saraswatī* (Eugene, Ore.: Mandala Publishing Group, 1997); Swami Bhakti Śrīrūpā Bhāgavata, ed., *Advent Centenary Souvenir of Shri Shrila Prabhupad 1874–1974* (Calcutta: Gaudiya Mission, 1974); and Swami Bhakti Pradīpa Tīrtha, *Srila Sarasvati Thakura* (1940; Calcutta: Gaudiya Mission, 1998).

33. Bhakti Vikāsa Swami, *Śrī Bhaktisiddhānta Vaibhava: The Grandeur and Glory of Śrīla Bhaktisiddhānta Sarasvatī Ṭhākura* (Surat: Bhakti Vikas Trust, 2009).

34. Two examples are works by Swami Bhakti Vallabha Tīrtha, *Sri Caitanya*; and Swami Yati Bhakti Prajñāna, *Three Apostles of Gaudiya Vaishnava Movement* (Madras: Shree Gaudiya Math, 1994).

35. Narashingha P. Sil, "Ramakrishna-Vivekananda Research: Hagiography Versus Hermeneutics," *Religious Studies Review* 27, no. 4 (2001).

Saṃvidānanda dāsa,[36] and was commissioned by Bhaktisiddhānta himself. Although this work contains little discussion on the sociohistorical context, it does provide a brief biography of Bhaktisiddhānta as well as a history of the Gaudiya Math. In India, the literature published by Bhaktisiddhānta and the Gaudiya Math has been collected by at least two Calcutta libraries: the National Library and the Library of Bengali Literature, the *Baṅgīya Sāhitya Pariśat*. The fact that these references exist in library catalogues bears witness to his effort to reprint classical and traditional bhakti literature in Sanskrit and Bengali.[37]

Besides these somewhat sporadic references, from the 1960s onward Swami A. C. Bhaktivedānta, the founder of ISKCON, made his guru Bhaktisiddhānta Sarasvatī known in India and abroad through his own publications, which in various places cite Bhaktisiddhānta's devotional and institutional work.[38] A number of studies have highlighted aspects of their relationship, as well as the pivotal role played by Bhaktisiddhānta's father in providing the impetus for this emerging Caitanya movement. A few illustrative examples are provided below.

Arvind Sharma (1979) has suggested that Bhaktisiddhānta inspired Swami Bhaktivedānta to print books by comparing the press to a big drum that could reach an audience far beyond the aural range of a musical instrument.[39] Diana Eck (1979) has highlighted a key instruction that Bhaktisiddhānta gave to Swami Bhaktivedānta—that is, to "bring the message of Kṛṣṇa-*bhakti* to the English-speaking world."[40] In a study of ISKCON in India, Charles R. Brooks (1989) has suggested that Bhaktisiddhānta internalized the anticaste attitude of his father Bhaktivinoda Ṭhākura and "preached the paramount belief that status was not dependent on one's birth, but upon the quality of one's devotion to Kṛṣṇa."[41] Thomas J. Hopkins

36. Sometimes spelled "Sambidananda." The thesis deals with the history of Vaishnavism from the medieval to the modern period. The thirteenth chapter, titled "The Modern Movement," provides a critical study of the lives and works of both Kedarnath Datta Bhaktivinoda and Bhaktisiddhānta Sarasvatī, as well as a brief study of the history of the Gaudiya Math. The table of contents was published in the *Harmonist* 31, no. 21 (1935), pp. 496–498.

37. See, for example, National Library of India, *Catalogue of Sanskrit, Pali and Prakrit Books* (Calcutta, 1951), pp. 75, 159; B. S. Kesavan, Vinayak Yashvant Kulkarni, and Sahitya Akademi, *The National Bibliography of Indian Literature, 1901–1953* (New Delhi: Sahitya Akademi, 1962), p. 60.

38. For example, in a letter written to Acyutananda (August 14, 1971), Swami Bhaktivedānta refers to Bhaktisiddhānta as follows: "whatever success we have had in preaching Lord Caitanya's mission all over the world it is only due to his mercy." Swami Bhaktivedānta, *Bhaktivedānta Vedabase 2003*.

39. Arvind Sharma, *Thresholds in Hindu-Buddhist Studies* (Calcutta: Minerva, 1979).

40. Diana Eck, "Kṛṣṇa Consciousness in Historical Perspective," *Back to Godhead 14.10 (Bhaktivedanta Vedabase 2003)*, 1979.

41. Charles R. Brooks, *The Hare Krishnas in India* (Princeton, N.J.: Princeton University Press, 1989), pp. 86–87.

(1989) has explored the caste, class roots, and family backgrounds of the father Bhaktivinoda, the son Bhaktisiddhānta and the disciple Swami Bhaktivedānta, concluding that the original founder of the Krishna Consciousness movement may well have been Bhaktivinoda.[42] Guy Beck (1993) has argued that Bhaktisiddhānta emphasized sound meditation both as soft recitation (*japa*) and loud public singing (*saṅkīrtana*), following the example of his father.[43] Richard Young (1981) has quoted Bhaktisiddhānta's ethical critique of the theology of sin in Christianity.[44] Tony Stewart and Edward Dimock (1999) have acknowledged Bhaktisiddhānta's efforts to reprint the most widely read biography of Caitanya, the *Caitanya Caritāmṛta*.[45] Finn Madsen (1996; 2001) has analyzed the social structure of ISKCON and the role played by Bhaktisiddhānta in shaping its initial understanding of *varṇa* and ashram.[46]

Bhaktisiddhānta Sarasvatī has been sporadically referred to in various historical and sociological studies, but usually within the context of research related to the history of ISKCON and/or New Religious Movements. Although of value in and of themselves, these studies have their limitations in the sense that they tend to pay less attention to (1) historical roots; (2) religious ideas and worldviews (often a key to unlocking personal motivation); and (3) cultural biases (the viewing of Indic religions through the cultural lens of the West). Because there has been little treatment of Bhaktisiddhānta in terms of these important factors, they have been given particular consideration herein.

A handful of specialists outside the study of new religious movements have given hints of the life and work of Bhaktisiddhānta. Brian D. Marvin (1996), Jason Fuller (2004), and Varuni Bhatia (2008) have recently explored the life and thought of Bhaktisiddhānta's father, Kedarnath Datta Bhaktivinoda, a prominent *bhadralok*

42. Hopkins, "Social and Religious Background," p. 36.

43. Beck, *Sonic Theology*, p. 202.

44. Young quotes Swami Bhaktivedānta's a paraphrase of a section of Bhaktisiddhānta's commentary on the *Caitanya Caritāmṛta* (Madhya 15.163): "Lord Jesus Christ certainly finished the sinful reactions of his followers by his mercy, but that does not mean that he completely delivered them from the pangs of material existence. A person may be relieved from sins once, but it is a practice among Christians to confess sins and yet commit them again." Richard Fox Young, *Resistant Hinduism: Sanskrit Sources on Anti-Christian Apologetics* (Vienna: De Nobili Research Library, 1981), p. 116, n. 118.

45. Kṛṣṇadāsa Kavirāja, *Caitanya Caritāmṛta of Kṛṣṇadāsa Kavirāja*, pp. 66–68

46. The topic of *varṇāśrama* in the Gaudiya Math is dealt with in particular detail in Finn Madsen, "Tradition og fornyelse i Gaudiya Math," M.A. thesis, University of Copenhagen, 1996. A discussion of Bhaktisiddhānta's innovations in terms of negating hereditary *varṇa* and the guru's assessment of a disciple's *varṇa* is found in Madsen, "Social udvikling i Hare Krishnabevægelsen," pp. 164–178.

theologian in his own right.[47] They deserve attention relative to Bhaktisiddhānta because they explore the ground upon which his ideas were built. In his thesis, Jason Fuller has noted the importance of class for a proper contextual assessment of the work of Bhaktivinoda, as well as the Bengal Renaissance.[48] According to Fuller, Bhaktivinoda used his cultural capital as an influential *bhadralok* to rationalize the religious market in Bengal and contest the authority and power of representation of both the *brāhmaṇas* and the popular folk leaders; this he did by "branding" a new universal Vaishnavism that enabled him to "win the competition."[49] Fuller notes, however, that Bhaktivinoda proved to be a conservative traditionalist on social issues because even if he vehemently critiqued the injustice of caste—as in his work *Jaiva Dharma*—and suggested that everyone be treated equally according to ultimate principles of truth (*paramārthika*), he also encouraged a hierarchical social order for practical, everyday behavior (*vyavaharika*).[50] For Brian Marvin, Bhaktivinoda was more "a man of the status quo" than a social reformer, since he displayed a pronounced leaning toward otherworldly bhakti in the last part of his life. Marvin suggests that Bhaktivinoda's son, Bhaktisiddhānta, actively instituted "many of the reforms of Vaishnava society that his father had talked about"—particularly in terms of *varṇa* and *aśrama*—but elaborates no further on this matter.[51]

Varuni Bhatia provides a sociohistorical analysis of the ways in which Bhaktivinoda helped to transform the public image of Caitanya Vaishnavism from being seen as a popular religion that fostered licentious behavior to being seen as a respectable tradition that greatly contributed to Bengali history, literature, and society. Bhatia regards Bhaktivinoda's work as part of the program of "salvaging, institutionalizing, and authenticating Gaudiya Vaishnavism"—that is, as an attempt to *recover* that tradition in reaction to the *loss* of Bengali religion, life, and culture under colonial rule. In her analysis, she compares Bhaktivinoda's recasting of Vaishnavism as a

---

47. The social and cultural impact of the educated Bengali middle class or *bhadralok* has been described by Partha Chatterjee as follows: "this class... constructed through a modern vernacular the new forms of public discourse, laid down new criteria of social respectability, set new aesthetic and moral standards of judgment, and, suffused with its spirit of nationalism, fashioned the new forms of political mobilization that were to have such a decisive impact on the political history of the province in the twentieth century," Partha Chatterjee, *The Nation and Its Fragments: Colonial and Postcolonial Histories* (Princeton, N.J.: Princeton University Press, 1993), pp. 35–36.

48. Fuller has elsewhere invited a revision of the historiography of colonial India by drawing attention to class—and not only caste—as a key category for analyzing Hinduism in the context of colonial modernity. He has also suggested that both Hindu reformers and revivalists stemmed from the same class, and thus shared similar concerns for empowerment despite the fact that they used different methods. Jason D. Fuller, "Modern Hinduism and the Middle Class: Beyond Revival in the Historiography of Colonial India," *Journal of Hindu Studies* 2, no. 2 (2009).

49. Fuller, "Religion, Class, and Power," p. 331.

50. Fuller, "Religion, Class, and Power," pp. 193–194.

51. Marvin, "Life and Thought," pp. 306–307.

monotheistic and Sanskritic tradition with a strong theological foundation to the cultural and nationalistic approach of Sisir Kumar Ghosh (1840–1911). In conclusion she notes that the cultural and devotional recovery of Caitanya Vaishnavism by the *bhadralok* in the late nineteenth century was a concerted effort by key individuals rather than an institutionalized effort.[52] According to Bhatia, bhakti helped to forge India into a nation through its popular and cultural appeal (via key personalities such as Gandhi). However, she also notes that the kind of theological and specialized scholasticism that Bhaktivinoda introduced required an entirely different sort of institutional effort due to the metaphysical concerns that he aimed to fulfill.[53] According to Bhatia, Bhaktisiddhānta Sarasvatī inherited the theological orientation of his father, for whom Caitanya was above all a pedagogue and a theologian rather than a social reformer with egalitarian and antiauthoritarian ambitions. Bhaktivinoda, in her view, conceived bhakti as "a matter of dense contemplation and correct interpretation of a kind that required preceptorship within an institutional framework as a prerequisite of salvation," an indirect reference to the kind of institutionalization that Bhaktisiddhānta pursued later on.[54]

The above views tend to portray Bhaktivinoda as a social and religious traditionalist who was able to successfully *recover* the Sanskritic tradition of Caitanya bhakti and its ill-reputed mysticism, largely because of his influential position as a salaried *bhadralok* in the colonial administration. According to these views, this pioneer traditionalist work was later expanded and institutionalized by his son Bhaktisiddhānta Sarasvatī. Thus there is a certain consensus that Bhaktivinoda paid significant attention to theology and a textual tradition, and made use of his *bhadralok* competence in his religious life. Little, though, has been said in these studies about the ideas that moved Bhaktivinoda to envision a religious crossing of regional and national borders, de facto creating the theoretical basis for the global movement that we see today.

This issue has been addressed from the perspective of sociohistory and theology by Kenneth R. Valpey (2006). According to Valpey, Bhaktivinoda offered a universalist version of Caitanya bhakti. He did so by supporting both the universal application of *varṇa* and *āśrama*—understood as collective social obligations to create a stable social order conducive to the spiritual progress of the individual—and the emic category of self-surrender (*śaraṇāgati*). The latter "emphasizes the individual's ultimate obligation to surrender to divine will and is the process and modality for doing so."[55] Bhaktivinoda regarded bhakti as a universal principle that found

52. Bhatia, "Devotional Traditions," p. 2.

53. Bhatia, "Devotional Traditions," pp. 383–384.

54. Bhatia, "Devotional Traditions," pp. 371–372.

55. Kenneth Russell Valpey, *Attending Krishna's Image: Chaitanya Vaishnava Murti-Seva as Devotional Truth* (New York: Routledge, 2006), p. 87.

its most complete expression in the personalist worship of the form of Krishna, as defined in the *Bhāgavata Purāṇa*.[56] According to Valpey, Bhaktivinoda followed earlier Caitanya theologians by defining his perspective as providing a complete realization that encompasses all aspects of the Absolute, as opposed to *advaita*, which encompasses only a partial, if valid, realization.[57] Contrary to Roy, Bhaktivinoda considered Vaishnava image worship to be a material manifestation of the nonmaterial form of God, which is revealed to the heart of advanced devotees. Certain of these individuals then construct the physical *mūrti* via extrasensory states of perception. For those at the beginning stages of the practice of bhakti, image worship is considered essential; superior to this, however, is the worship of the deity within the heart, primarily through hearing (*śravaṇa*) and chanting (*kīrtana*)—the truly universal forms of bhakti.[58] Bhaktivinoda was one of the first Caitanya *bhaktas* among the *bhadralok* to clearly envision the spreading of the tradition outside of India, among persons of non-India background. By placing bhakti to Krishna above the system of *varṇāśrama* he also became one the first modern Vaishnava religionists in Bengal to make this system inclusive of all persons. With Bhaktivinoda, the traditional meaning of dharma gained three new purposes: (1) to maintain social stratification; (2) to renew bhakti in terms of individual practice; and (3) to reform it through a new universalization. For Valpey, the emphasis on individual bhakti is a particularly modern trait.

Valpey concludes that both Bhaktivinoda and Bhaktisiddhānta were open to the idea of the religious reform of the tradition so long as it made the "means of gaining spiritual qualification more accessible." At the same time, they apparently resisted the kind of "reform Hinduism" that consolidated ethnic and national boundaries.[59] Valpey explores the ideas of Bhaktivinoda and Bhaktisiddhānta primarily in relation to the development of Vaishnava image worship, largely leaving out Bhaktisiddhānta's employment of Caitanya bhakti to develop a *theory of empowerment* that directed his approach to contemporary religion and society. This matter has received particular attention in this book.

Jan Brzezinski, on the other hand, has suggested that Bhaktisiddhānta ultimately bypassed traditional structures by instituting the *śikṣa-guru-paramparā*, thus de facto shaping a new independent branch of Caitanya Vaishnavism.[60] Other scholars have highlighted Bhaktisiddhānta's more conservative traits. Hugh Urban has suggested that Bhaktisiddhānta was an orthodox in regard to left-hand tantric traditions,

56. Valpey, *Attending Krishna's Image*, p. 82.

57. Valpey, *Attending Krishna's Image*, pp. 90–91.

58. Valpey, *Attending Krishna's Image*, p. 96.

59. Valpey, *Attending Krishna's Image*, p. 103.

60. Jan Brzezinski, "The Paramparā Institution in Gauḍīya Vaiṣṇavism," *Journal of Vaishnava Studies* 5, no. 1 (1996–97).

which he firmly rejected.[61] Ramakanta Cakravarti (1985) has stated that the general orientation of Bhaktisiddhānta and his movement was eminently conservative and otherworldly:

> the Gaudiya Mission had ostensibly no social aims. It did not pretend that it was an organisation with a social mission. But it set up schools, libraries, research centers and free hospitals. These, however, had only secondary importance. Its primary object was to preach mysticism.[62]

Bhaktisiddhānta and his movement have been here portrayed as being primarily concerned with mysticism and the otherworldly. The assessment contains two assumptions: first, that Bhaktisiddhānta and his movement made a clear distinction between primary objectives such as mysticism and secondary ones such as social aims, and second that social aims were understood above all as humanitarian and educational. The first assumption may be justified, as we have seen earlier, but the second one leaves out the possibility that social aims referred to class relations, gender, polity, or personal well-being. While material upliftment and social empowerment may have been foreign concepts to traditional Vaishnavism, compassion, charity, and spiritual empowerment certainly have not.

Current research has thus reached a number of alternative conclusions regarding the life and thought of Bhaktisiddhānta Sarasvatī. These, however, have been largely based on a rather narrow selection of sources, and have relied upon either a theological or a social-historical perspective, without sufficiently combining the two. Bhaktisiddhānta's life and views have been studied here in terms of bhakti and its relation to society and culture; to do so I have placed Bhaktisiddhānta at the religious intersection of traditional and modern forms of Hinduism, as well as within the context of class and colonialism.

To summarize, the relevance of this book can be understood in terms of five considerations: First, studies of modern bhakti are still relatively marginal and less developed. As noted in the introduction, and elaborated upon in chapter 1, strong attention has been paid to modern Hindu movements with a nondualist orientation. In an almost canonical fashion, modern Hinduism is portrayed through the nondualist writings of Rammohun Ray, the Brahmo and Arya Samaj, Vivekānanda, Aurobindo, and Gandhi.[63] Although this perspective highlights a decisive development, which eventually led to key political, social, and cultural changes, it has the defect of excluding alternative voices, particularly those of a strongly dualistic and/or theistic nature. Second, while Caitanya Vaishnavism has been extensively studied in terms of its premodern and early-modern

61. Urban, *The Economics of Ecstasy*, p. 167.

62. Chakravarti, *Vaiṣṇavism in Bengal, 1486–1900*, p. 398.

63. See, for example, Sharma, *Modern Hindu Thought*.

history, little is known about its modern period. Third, in sociological studies of New Religious Movements that have emerged after World War II, considerable attention has been paid to ISKCON, which appears in almost all texts dealing with the subject; far less, however, has been said about the roots of this movement in Bengal. Fourth, this study fills a gap in the history of the early interaction between Hinduism and Europe. Last, while the life and works of Bhaktivinoda and Bhaktivedānta are relatively well known, Bhaktisiddhānta's life and works remain far more obscure.

Methodology

Although this book falls within the discipline of the history of religions, it has employed tools from related disciplines such as the sociology of religion. There are at least three research approaches in the humanities and social sciences: (1) research driven by a particular theory, such as Marxism or feminism; (2) research driven by a specific method, such as participant observation or hermeneutics; and (3) research driven by a problem.[64] In exploring and interpreting my sources, I have allowed the problem to direct my research, and have employed a number of theories and methodologies along the way.[65] The study is overall empirical—that is, I have used material that is in print and accessible to third parties. The primary methodology used herewith is therefore historical-critical and hermeneutical.[66]

Because of the colonial past, any historical study of South Asian religions that deals with the "modern" period—here understood as beginning with the British takeover of Bengal—must take into account not only national, but also transnational realities. This is the primary reason that I have chosen to discuss the history of India and, to a lesser degree, that of Britain and Europe. To do this properly required two things: (1) an awareness of the language and symbols of the tradition, as well as the history and aspirations of the Bengali middle class; and, (2) an awareness of how processes of globalization and transnational mobility, as well as the introduction of modern ideas, affected both local social structures and local perceptions. In this regard, Peter van der Veer has argued that "the study of South Asian religions...[must] combine historical awareness...and spatial mobility."[67] Gayatri

64. Regarding the social sciences, see Bo Rothstein, "Därför behövs annat akademiskt ledarskap," *Göteborgs Posten*, June 16, 2009.

65. See Richard King, for whom "good scholarship in whatever academic discipline has always been based upon the examination of a variety of perspectives." King, *Orientalism and Religion*, pp. 55–56.

66. For an introduction to historical critical theory and method, see John Tosh, *The Pursuit of History: Aims, Methods and New Directions in the Study of Modern History* (Harlow: Longman, 2002). Regarding hermeneutics see, for example, Paul Ricoeur, *Interpretation Theory: Discourse and the Surplus of Meaning* (Fort Worth: Texas Christian University Press, 1976).

67. Peter van der Veer, "Religion in South Asia," *Annual Review of Anthropology* 31 (2002).

Spivak has also pointed to the need for an awareness of mainstream colonial discourses that domesticated the colonized Other in terms that were in keeping with the dominating culture and its values. She, like many others, also encouraged the attempt to see the Other in terms of the Other's situation and perception.[68] Because of the sociohistorical setting of this inquiry, I have made use of postcolonial theories, as well as those of modernity and globalization, wherever appropriate.[69] In doing so I have pursued a nonreductionistic dialogical approach that attempts to take into account both Indian and Western perspectives.[70]

To explore the sociocultural, political, and colonial relationship between India and Britain (and/or India and Europe) can be a complex and often daunting task, especially because of the need to precisely define what "society" means within each of these highly diverse domains. In order to situate the study in a more precise sociological frame I have paid attention not only to colonialism, but also to the matter of caste and class, with the latter of these being the most significant, since it was from the *bhadralok* middle class that most of the responses to the West emerged.[71] The relationship between the perceptions, social standing, and culture of the *bhadralok* and the way they developed new convergences and Hindu vernacularizations relative to colonialism constitutes the more specific socioreligious frame of this study.

Emic and Etic

The field of religious studies is highly diversified, ranging from theology to secular religion, from Christianity to Islam, Judaism and folk religion. Religion—the definition of which is still a topic of controversy—may be studied as an ahistorical

---

68. Jonas Stier, *Kulturmöten: en introduktion till interkulturella studier* (Lund: Studentlitteraturen, 2004), pp. 139–149.

69. Postcolonial theory has proved useful in creating a critical frame to explore and analyze the colonial and postcolonial experience. It is a loose collection of perspectives rather than a fixed theoretical frame, based, however, on a solid body of research; see for example Robert J. C. Young, *Postcolonialism: An Historical Introduction* (Oxford: Blackwell, 2001). Postcolonial approaches that I have taken into account are those of Nandy, *The Intimate Enemy*; Gayatri Spivak, *The Spivak Reader: Selected Works of Gayatri Chakravorty Spivak*, ed. Donna Landry and Gerald M. MacLean (New York: Routledge, 1996); and Bhabha, *The Location of Culture*; as well as the foundational work of such scholars as Halbfass, *India and Europe*; Ronald B. Inden, *Imagining India* (Oxford: Basil Blackwell, 1990); and Raychaudhuri, *Europe Reconsidered*.

70. For an introduction to the dialogical approach, see Gavin Flood, *Beyond Phenomenology: Rethinking the Study of Religion* (London: Cassell, 1999), pp. 143–168. Referring to the work of Mikhail Bakhtin (1895–1975), Flood has suggested that rather than situated objectively, the scientific "observer is always situated and embodied, within a specific historical context, in a relationship of dialogue with the 'object'—in fact fellow 'subjects'—of inquiry." Flood, *Beyond Phenomenology*, p. 168.

71. For a discussion on the importance of class for the historiography of modern Hinduism, see Fuller, "Modern Hinduism."

independent variable (sui generis), or as a social, cultural, and/or psychological variable, entirely embedded in human experience. Historians of religion have for a long time practiced the *emic* perspective, which strives to achieve an accurate representation of its subject through close empathy. This methodology is particularly favored by those who are associated with the phenomenological school of Mircea Eliade.[72] A second possibility is to opt for a strictly *etic* perspective, which strives to achieve a neutral and/or objective view of a given phenomenon. This is a common approach in the social sciences.[73] My effort has been to provide a precise nonreductionistic understanding of the hermeneutical and epistemological categories used by Bhaktisiddhānta in his texts, while striving to view his ideas also from an outsider perspective.[74] In keeping with this aim, Bhaktisiddhānta's descriptions of mystical experiences and sacred ontology within the frame of bhakti are regarded as referring to a dimension of consciousness that transcends ordinary awareness. Thus, an assessment of the truth-value of these descriptions lies beyond the scope of this study. For similar reasons, I have also attempted to employ both emic and etic methodologies, and to explore the dialogical interaction between the two. This approach has been followed by such scholars as Wouter J. Hanegraaf, who explains it as follows:

> Emic denotes the "intersubjective patterns of thought and symbolic associations of the believers" or, expressed more simply, the "believer's point of view." An accurate presentation of the religion under study as expressed by the believers themselves must be the basis of the research. On the part of the researcher, the reconstruction of this emic perspective requires an attitude of empathy which excludes personal biases as far as possible. Scholarly discourse about religion, on the other hand, is not emic but etic. This means that it may involve types of language, distinctions, theories and interpretative models which are considered appropriate by scholars on their own terms. Scholars may introduce their own terminology and make theoretical distinctions which are different from those of the believers themselves. The final results of scholarly research should be expressed in etic language, and

72. See Mircea Eliade, *Patterns in Comparative Religion* (London: Sheed & Ward, 1958).

73. See Peter L. Berger and Thomas Luckmann, *The Social Construction of Reality: A Treatise in the Sociology of Knowledge* (New York: Anchor, 1967). For a good overview of various methodologies in religious studies, see for example Willi Braun and Russell T. McCutcheon, eds., *Guide to the Study of Religion* (New York: Cassell, 2000). For a discussion about the tension between various methodologies, as well as between religious studies and theology, see King, *Orientalism and Religion*, pp. 35–61.

74. Regarding the concepts of insider and outsider, see, for example, Elisabeth Arweck and Martin D. Stringer, *Theorizing Faith: The Insider/Outsider Problem in the Study of Ritual* (Birmingham: University of Birmingham Press, 2002).

> formulated in such a way as to permit criticism and falsification both by reference to the emic material and as regards their coherence and consistency in the context of the general etic discourse.[75]

The conclusions found in this work may not always represent the opinions of all the persons and institutions that are studied here. However, out of respect for those that have been helpful in affording their time, assistance, and access to rare documents and publications, I have chosen to use emic terminology when referring to the founders of the tradition or describing sensitive aspects of their philosophy and worldview.

Interviews and Participant Observation

Because so many years have passed since the demise of Bhaktisiddhānta, this study has made use of written texts, considering them to be the most reliable source. This notwithstanding, I conducted qualitative interviews with two surviving disciples—octogenarians who had only limited contact with their guru—as well as with approximately sixty members of the Gaudiya Math. The interviews with Bhaktisiddhānta's aged disciples helped to confirm and fill in a number of important historical details found in the written sources. While two other of his disciples were available during my fieldwork in India, their failing health did not allow for an interview. Most of my qualitative interviews did not involve the asking of a series of prearranged questions; rather they were guided by my research problem, which I explained to the subjects beforehand. I also completed interviews with representatives of other modern Hindu institutions in Bengal, an example being the Ramakrishna Mission in Kolkata. Although my fieldwork and interviews were not major sources for this project, they nonetheless familiarized me with a number of emic perspectives. To increase my understanding, I employed participant observation, which involved attendance at a variety of devotional rituals, lectures, and festivals. I spent a total of one year in West Bengal, which included stays in the major centers of Caitanya Vaishnavism in India—that is, Vrindavan near New Delhi and Jagannath Puri in Orissa, the birthplace of Bhaktisiddhānta. To further understand the global impact of Bhaktisiddhānta's movement, I also visited and/or resided in a number of Gaudiya Math and ISKCON centers in North America, Italy, Britain, Germany, and Sweden. The time in West Bengal was important not only for improving my language skills, but also for conducting the laborious collection of primary texts. It also allowed me to gain firsthand experience of the environment in which Bhaktisiddhānta's movement emerged and flourished.

---

75. Hanegraaff, *New Age Religion*, pp. 6–7.

Written Sources

Bhaktisiddhānta Sarasvatī is briefly discussed or mentioned in a number of academic studies (at least fifty in English alone), but in-depth research has remained surprisingly scanty in proportion to the role that he has played in shaping a global movement. One obvious reason is that his writings have never been published in a comprehensive way and are not easily available.[76] Gaudiya Math institutions have labored to keep several editions of Bhaktisiddhānta's Bengali titles in print, but most have never been translated into English. His literary output includes over 250 articles in various magazines, 144 published letters, nine traditional *Vaishnava* texts in Bengali and Sanskrit (with commentaries), two major biographies on Caitanya (with commentaries), books and articles on Indian astronomy, published conversations, lectures, and speeches, as well as a biography of his life (written by disciples and personally edited by him).[77] Despite this profusion, Swami Bhakti Tīrtha[78]—one of Bhaktisiddhānta's most important disciples during the formative years of the Gaudiya Math—stated in the 1960s that "no one has so far been able to collect all of Bhaktisiddhānta's writings."[79] As the movement fragmented shortly after Bhaktisiddhānta passed away, the bulk of his writings scattered as well; because of this, a major challenge of this project has been to locate the primary texts that were written and/or edited by Bhaktisiddhānta himself. In 2007, all issues of *The Harmonist or Shree Sajjanatoshani* (the Gaudiya Math's main English periodical) became available in India after a laborious fifteen-year effort to collect the series in original print. The compilation covers the period from June 1927 to June 1936 and comprises a total of 2,824 pages. The periodicals in Bengali from 1914 to 1936 have never been reprinted and were difficult to access, and many issues were not available in the public libraries of Kolkata. Through repeated attempts from October 2004 to October 2009, I was able to locate an almost complete collection of Bhaktisiddhānta's works in a number of public and private libraries, which brought me to various remote areas of

76. The most comprehensive collections of Bhaktisiddhānta's original works can be found in Kolkata at the Caitanya Institute (Rasbehari Avenue 72) and the Bhaktivedānta Research Centre (Motilal Nehru Road 110 A). His writings are also available in Gaudiya Math libraries across India, but only reprinted literature is easily accessible. A comprehensive collection of titles in Bengali, Sanskrit, and English are found in the National Library in Kolkata. Selected titles are also found in the British Library, in the library of the University of Chicago (twenty-four titles), and in major libraries of South Asian studies throughout the world.

77. See appendix E for a detailed bibliography of Bhaktisiddhānta's works.

78. Also known as Kuñjabihārī Vidyābhūṣaṇa.

79. Bhaktisiddhānta Sarasvatī, *Shri Chaitanya's Teachings*, p. iii. The book contains a collection of Bhaktisiddhānta's writings in English.

East India.[80] Articles written by Bhaktisiddhānta in the weekly *Gauḍīya*, the official Bengali mouthpiece of the Gaudiya Math, provided a close "insider" picture of his thought concerning Vaishnavism in Bengal. His personal letters illuminated his inner life as expressed in his mother tongue. And his commentaries on the canonical biographies of Caitanya—that is, the *Caitanya Caritāmṛta* and the *Caitanya Bhāgavata*—provided a systematic overview of his religious thought. For purposes of this book, I selected writings from all stages of his production so as to obtain a fair picture of his intellectual and religious development. In particular, *The Making of Society in Bengal (Baṅge Sāmājikatā)*, an early work completed at the turn of the twentieth century, shed light on some of Bhaktisiddhānta's earliest ideas about Hindu society, caste, European culture, modernity, and the role of religion in society. Prior to this study, this text had been largely ignored both by insiders and by outsiders.

During the intense years of missionary activity from 1920 to 1937, Bhaktisiddhānta rarely wrote by hand; rather he would dictate outlines of his texts or have disciples transcribe his words in shorthand. His lectures, dialogues, talks, and official addresses were jotted down as notes by disciples such as Praṇavānanda, Sundarānanda Vidyāvinoda, and Ananta Vāsudeva dāsa. These would be transcribed into drafts and restructured for greater intelligibility. Bhaktisiddhānta would then edit and refine the texts, and finally authorize their publication. Ananta Vāsudeva dāsa would then usually conduct a final editing before the text was sent to press. Many of the articles in the *Harmonist* that carry Bhaktisiddhānta's name, as well as those in the *Gauḍīya* and the *Nadīyā Prakāśa*, were apparently written in this fashion.[81] This accounts for the fact that the language and style of such writings is uneven. On the other hand, Bhaktisiddhānta paid close attention to the editorial process in order to ensure that whatever was published accurately reflected his thought. Because of this, these texts can be regarded as historically and biographically relevant.

From 1922 onward, most of the major events of Bhaktisiddhānta's life are minutely documented in the periodicals that he published. Beyond these, there are numerous hagiographic accounts, the earliest and perhaps the most reliable of which are the *Vaibhava Parva* and *Śrī Parva* of the *Sarasvatī Jayaśrī*

80. The author has been instrumental in the discovery of the private library of Sundarānanda Vidyāvinoda, a secretary of Bhaktisiddhānta. The library contains over two thousand volumes, including most of the original publications of Bhaktisiddhānta Sarasvatī as well as some of his unpublished works such as a typed English rendition of his diary and parts of an unpublished biography. The library also includes most of the original works of Kedarnath Datta Bhaktivinoda. It was first placed under the care of Swami Bodhayan at Mayapur's Gopinātha Gaudiya Math and has now been relocated to the Bhaktivedānta Research Centre in Kolkata. For a biographical sketch of Sundarānanda Vidyāvinoda see Vikāsa, *Śrī Bhaktisiddhānta Vaibhava*, vol. 2, p. 347–351.

81. See Vikāsa, *Śrī Bhaktisiddhānta Vaibhava*, vol. 1, p. 309.

(1934).[82] Additional biographical material came from the second unpublished volume of Saṃvidānanda dāsa's thesis (mentioned earlier). I considered this an important source because he drew from firsthand experience, and wrote his account in consultation with Bhaktisiddhānta himself.

Delimitations

A study of this kind cannot cover the entire field of modern Caitanya bhakti. I focused instead on selected individual (*micro*), institutional (*meso*), as well as global (*macro*) aspects of Bhaktisiddhānta's life and work. Individual and social structures have been regarded as interdependent based on the assumption that no individual can create religious change without the support of favorable social conditions, and that no social structure can generate religious change without the creative agency and genius of empowered individuals. The timeline of this study began with Bhaktisiddhānta's birth in 1874, and has ended with his passing away in 1937. The events that occurred both before and after this period have provided a bit of historical context for the primary events that were narrated herein. However, with the exception of the life of Bhaktisiddhānta's father, these have been considered secondary and supportive elements. Another delimitation is that the study have explored Bhaktisiddhānta's life and thought primarily in connection with the *bhadralok* and British colonial times. While important, the relation between Bhaktisiddhānta and Bengal's more traditional groups of Caitanya Vaishnavism have only been briefly discussed herein. Generic terms such as "West," "Europe," and "European culture" are geographically contained. The term "West" has referred to the North Atlantic region, and "Europe" has indicated primarily Britain and Germany, who were protagonists in the events narrated herein. Sweden played a later role by providing a home to the first European teacher of Caitanya bhakti in Scandinavia, the Austrian Jew Walther Eidlitz (1892–1976), who arrived in Sweden in 1946.[83] His German teacher, Ernst Georg Schulze (1908–1977), was the only Westerner to be personally trained by Bhaktisiddhānta, receiving the name Sadānanda dāsa.[84] Together with other sympathizers they formed a group that introduced bhakti to Germany and

---

82. The *Vaibhava Parva* consists of a collection of memories written by Bhaktisiddhānta's disciples and covers the period from 1911 to 1925. Although it has some inconsistencies, it is based on firsthand accounts, and was reviewed by Bhaktisiddhānta himself. It was offered to him in 1934 as a token of appreciation for his sixtieth birthday.

83. Eidlitz was initiated by Swami Bon, who had been sent by Bhaktisiddhānta to London and Germany to establish Gaudiya Math branches (see chapter 3). For a biography of Swami Bon see Måns Broo, "Bhakti Hriday Bon Maharaja (1901–1982)," M.A. thesis, Åbo Akademi, 2002.

84. The meeting between Eidlitz and Sadānanda is narrated in Walther Eidlitz, *Bhakta: Eine indische Odyssee* (Hamburg: Claassen, 1951), ch. 16.

Sweden independent of the Gaudiya Math, and primarily through the pen of Walther Eidlitz.[85] In 1973, ISKCON, under the leadership of Swami Bhaktivedānta, established its first Swedish center in Stockholm. The present study of Bhaktisiddhānta's life thus serves as a background for several historical trajectories that carry on into the present, but that have fallen outside the scope of this work.

Bhakti in the Precolonial Period

For reasons explained earlier, it has been important to point out the difference between nondualist and theistic views of Indic philosophy and bhakti. Within mainstream currents of modern Hinduism such theoretical or philosophical distinctions are not emphasized, but they are rather important for a proper understanding of traditionalist forms of Hinduism, as well as classical and medieval religions as a whole. These differences found their most powerful philosophical formulation in the Hindu schools of Vedanta, by far the most influential within Hinduism since the time of Śaṅkara (ca. 700 CE). They were a significant area of concern for Bhaktisiddhānta and were frequently discussed by contemporaries such as Vivekānanda. The relevance of exploring Vedantic theism and nondualism, and the religious currents associated with them, also lies in the fact that each tends to define itself in terms of the position of the other.[86] The concept of *brahman* has been incorporated in all theistic philosophies, including that of Caitanya Vaishnavism. The theoretical and practical differences between nondualism and theism are so distinctive that they form alternative notions of identity and practice, and point to entirely different religious aims. Bhaktisiddhānta claimed on several occasions to represent a theistic strand of Vedanta that he believed to be the core of his religious identity as a Krishna *bhakta*. To grasp the meaning of this claim, it is necessary to provide a brief account of the historical development of the school of Vedanta.

Arguments in favor of the fundamental theory of Vedanta were formulated by Bādarāyaṇa in the *Vedānta Sūtra*, a work that gained further prominence as a result of Śaṅkara's commentary, the *Śārīraka-bhāṣya*,[87] which has remained a key

---

85. See Walther Eidlitz, *Krsna-Caitanya: Sein Leben und seine Lehre* (Stockholm: Almqvist & Wiksell, 1968). In Swedish see, for example, Walther Eidlitz, *Den glömda världen: om hinduism och meditation* (Stockholm: Askild & Kärnekull, 1972).

86. For an example of a confrontation between *saguṇa* Vaishnavas and *nirguṇa* Śaivas—in this case among pundits in 1860s Rajasthan—see Catherine Clémentin-Ojha, "A Mid-Nineteenth-Century Controversy over Religious Authority," in *Charisma and Canon: Essays on the Religious History of the Indian Subcontinent*, ed. Vasudha Dalmia, Angelika Malinar, and Martin Christof (Oxford: Oxford University Press, 2001).

87. For a comparative analysis of Śaṅkara's *Śārīraka-bhāṣya* with the commentary of Rāmānuja, see *The Vedānta-Sūtras: with the Commentary by Sankarācārya and Rāmānūja*, ed. Max Müller, trans. George Thibaut, vols. 34, 38, 48, The Sacred Books of the East (Oxford: Clarendon Press, 1890).

contribution to Hindu thought up to the twenty-first century. Śaṅkara read the *Vedānta Sūtra* as a presentation of nondualism (*advaita*). He considered the words of the Vedas to be literally true, proposing that the ultimate basis of reality was an eternal divine consciousness referred to as *brahman*. This notion ran counter to mainstream Buddhist doctrines that wholly denied the existence of a perennial reality. Realization of the eternal *brahman* was natural, although Śaṅkara presented *brahman* as being ultimately devoid of attributes such as personality.[88] In his commentary, Śaṅkara undermined theistic bhakti in terms of its ultimate claims by erasing the ultimate distinction between the devotee or *bhakta* and the object of bhakti—that is, a personal God. According to Śaṅkara, the self experiences a false sense of individual personal identity and the plurality of the world so long as it is covered by *māyā*, the external power of *brahman*. When the self becomes aware that its very experience of rebirth is an illusion and that its only identity is the singular, objectless consciousness that constitutes pure being, it is liberated from the cycle of birth and death. For Śaṅkara only *brahman* was real in the ultimate sense, whereas the world of form and personality (including the form and personality of a personal God) was a mere superimposition, the nature of which was ultimately indescribable. In other words, the plurality of the world was simultaneously a factual emanation of *brahman* and an illusion.

Five mainstream Vaishnava schools founded respectively by Rāmānuja (ca. 1017–1137), Madhva (1238–1317), Nimbārka (n.d.), Vallabha (1479–1531), and Caitanya offered critiques of Śaṅkara's nondualism, and in this way paid homage to his genius. The earliest Vaishnava response came from Rāmānuja, who called his philosophy *viśiṣṭādvaita* (qualified nondualism) because it linked the ultimate oneness of reality (or God) with the existence of the variety of differentiative attributes (*viśeṣa*) within this world. While Rāmānuja agreed that nothing existed beyond the metaphysical *brahman*, he viewed *brahman* as possessing personal attributes. For him, the world was real because it constituted the body of *brahman*. The most seminal Vaishnava critique of Śaṅkara was arguably provided by the South Indian dualistic (*dvaita*) school of Madhva, to which the Caitanya school later claimed linkage. Madhva's *dvaita* Vedanta suggested that there was an irreducible difference between the metaphysical self (atman) and the metaphysical personality of God. Although, originally, Śaṅkara's *advaita* was an effort to present a well-designed response to the hegemony of Buddhism, it soon created a dialogue within Hinduism that has continued to this day:

> ever since Śaṅkara put forth his system of *advaita*, Hindu philosophical and theological discussion has been a dialectical controversy within the Vedānta school of philosophy between his non-dualism on the one hand and various

88. Śaṅkara adopted in a parallel way Buddhist elements such as the concept of *māyā* and monastic institutions; see Sharma, *Bhakti and the Bhakti Movement*, p. 135.

> shades of "qualified" non-dualism (*viśiṣṭa-advaita*) or dualism (*dvaita*) on the other. On the practical religious level the two sides of this discussion have been identified with *jñāna yoga* and *bhakti yoga* respectively.[89]

On the level of practice, *jñāna mārga* became associated with philosophical analysis (*manana*) and meditation in pursuit of the gradual achievement of a direct and immediate experience of universal Selfhood (*brahman*). *Jñāna* yoga strove to transform the consciousness of the subject through knowledge of identity (*aham brahmāsmi*—I am *brahman*), while bhakti emphasized the active *relationship* between a subject and an object of love, as well as participation in devotional acts. Although *jñāna* yoga became identified with the path leading to nondualist realization, it generally included elements of iconic worship and bhakti, since Śaṅkara considered it useful for those at the mundane initial stages of realization. For the Vaishnava schools, however, bhakti was not merely a means to an end that lied beyond it—as Śaṅkara contended—but rather the means as well as the end in and of itself. Although Vaishnava theists asserted the distinction between the subject and object of bhakti, their dualism rarely contradicted the ultimate oneness of reality. They perceived the world as a manifestation of one supreme God possessing a variety of mundane (*prakṛta*) and metaphysical (*aprakṛta*) energies. Bhakti gradually grew to become far more popular compared to *jñāna* because it was open to all *varṇas* and ashrams of the Hindu social system, while *jñāna* remained traditionally restricted to the *saṃnyāsins*. The responses of Madhva and Rāmānuja were institutionalized—following the example of Śaṅkara—in chains of gurus (*sampradāya*) and monastic communities (*maṭh*), which to some degree reproduced the institutional structures of Buddhists and Jains. Most Hindu schools acknowledged bhakti as an important ingredient in all the various paths (*mārga*) of yoga.

For one thousand years after the time of Śaṅkara—who had set the agenda—the dialogue between *jñāna mārga* and *bhakti mārga* remained a key issue. The Caitanya school kept refining theism through an intricate exploration of religious emotions (*rasa*), and produced significant texts on the theory and practice of bhakti up to the middle of the eighteenth century. The last precolonial critique of Śaṅkara's Vedanta was formulated by a Caitanya *bhakta*:

> the Vaishṇava bhakti movement, which started with Rāmānuja, may be said to have exhausted its possibilities as a philosophical system by the time Baladeva Vidyābhūshaṇa wrote his commentary on the Brahmasūtra from the standpoint of the Gauḍīya Vaishṇavas, that is Caitanya's sect. Baladeva's date is not known with certainty, but one of his works is dated 1764, so that it may be presumed that his commentary was written about the same time,

89. W. G. Neevel, "The Transformations of Śrī Rāmakrishna," in *Hinduism: New Essays in the History of Religion*, ed. B. L. Smith (Leiden: Brill, 1976), p. 85.

> that is about 10 to 15 years before the birth of Rāmmohan Roy. In a sense Baladeva brings to a close the intellectual age that began with Śaṅkara, for his was the last commentary on the Brahmasūtra. With Rāmmohan begins a new age.[90]

It is arguable whether the Vaishnava bhakti movement exhausted its philosophical arsenal by then, but it is not as controversial to suggest that the eighteenth century brought to a close one of the most productive periods of Hindu philosophy. The seed of a new era was sown in 1757 with the battle of Plassey. The British gradually acquired control over Bengal, and Europe came closer to the Hindu world than ever before. The next period would be dominated by the intense attempt by *bhadralok* such as Bhaktisiddhānta to reflect in various ways on British culture and its implications, and to explore new ways of relating to it. Traditional Indian pandits engaged far more sporadically in philosophical exchanges with Western Indologists and missionaries.[91] Śaṅkara's nondualism gradually acquired a new significant role in the period after the British conquest of Bengal, but it was transformed and adapted by the *bhadralok*, at times in radical ways, which earned it the epithet of "Neo-Vedānta" (see chapter 5).

---

90. A. K. Majumdar, *Bhakti Renaissance* (Bombay: Bharatiya Vidya Bhavan, 1979), p. 92.

91. According to Richard Fox Young, Christian doctrine was not studied and debated as a philosophical system by Hindu pundits in the same way as Buddhism had been. Apparently orthodox Hindu pundits rarely considered Christian theology as a serious object of systematic study, except in cases where Christianity was formulated in Sanskrit; see Young, *Resistant Hinduism*, pp. 13ff.

APPENDIX B

Images

FIGURE B.1 Bimala Prasad Datta

Source: Prabhupada Saraswati Thakur: The Life and Precepts of Śrīla Bhaktisiddhānta Saraswatī (Eugene, Ore.: Mandala Publishing Group, 1997), p. 17. This and the following images from this source are published with permission from Mandala Publishing.

FIGURE B.2 Kedarnath Datta Bhaktivinoda

Source: Srigouranga Smaranamangala or Chaitanya Mahaprabhu: His Life and Precepts (Calcutta: K. Dutt, 1896). Published with permission from the Bhaktivedanta Research Centre, Kolkata.

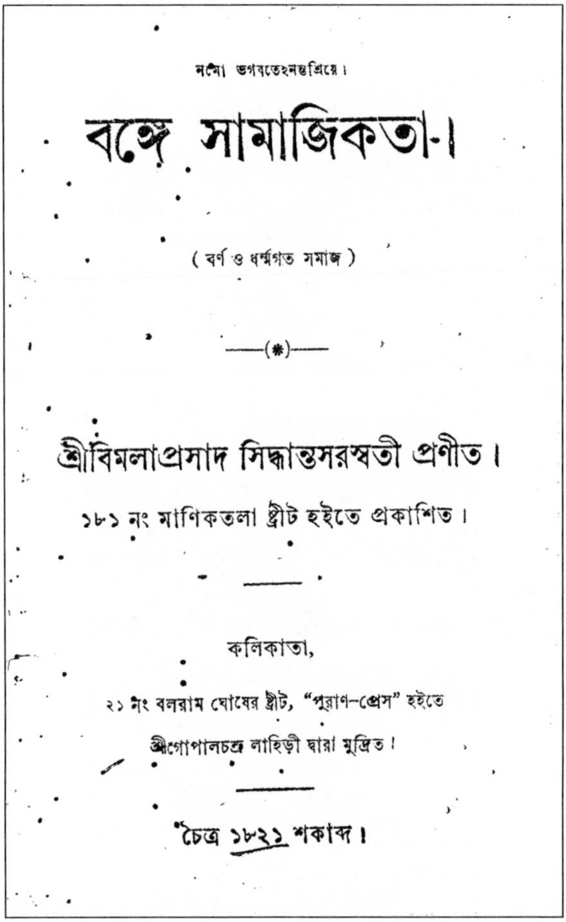

নমো ভগবতেঽনন্তপ্রিয়ে।

বঙ্গে সামাজিকতা।

(বর্ণ ও ধর্ম্মগত সমাজ)

—(*)—

শ্রীবিমলাপ্রসাদ সিদ্ধান্তসরস্বতী প্রণীত।

১৮১ নং মাণিকতলা ষ্ট্রীট হইতে প্রকাশিত।

কলিকাতা,

২১ নং বলরাম ঘোষের ষ্ট্রীট, "পুরাণ-প্রেস" হইতে

শ্রীগোপালচন্দ্র লাহিড়ী দ্বারা মুদ্রিত।

চৈত্র ১৮২১ শকাব্দ।

FIGURE B.3 The front page of the *Baṅge Sāmājikatā: varṇa o dharmagata samāja* published by Bhaktisiddhānta in 1899.

Published with permission from the Bhaktivedanta Research Centre.

FIGURE B.4 Bhaktisiddhānta two days after *saṃnyāsa*, March 29, 1918

Source: Prabhupada Saraswati Thakur: The Life and Precepts of Śrīla Bhaktisiddhānta Saraswatī, p. 22.

ALL GLORY TO THE DIVINE MASTER
AND
THE SUPREME LORD SREE KRISHNA-CHAITANYA

SREE

SAJJANA-TOSHANI,
THE HARMONIST

VOL. XXV. JUNE 1927, 441 Chaitanya-Era. NO. 1.

Obeisance

I do obeisance to the Divinely beautiful lotus Feet of Sree Gurudeva, to all the revered Gurus and the devotees of Vishnu ;

Obeisance to Sree Rupa himself with his elder brother (Sanatan) attended by Raghunath in the company of his associates and followers, and with Jiva (Goswamin).

Obeisance to Krishna-Chaitanyadeva with His own, with Advaita and with the Abadhuta (super-ascetic) Nityananda.

Obeisance to the Feet of Sree Radha and Krishna attended by Lalita and Sree Bishakha with their mates.

Manifold obeisance to Thee who is by Name Krishna-Chaitanya, Whose Beauty is of the yellow colour,

Who by Quality is exceedingly merciful, Whose Function is bestowing the Love of Krishna and Who is Krishna Himself.

Obeisance to Thee, Thakur Bhaktivinode, by name Sachchidananda,

The greatest of the followers of Sree Rupa, an Embodiment of Gaur's Love.

FIGURE B.5 The cover of the first issue of *The Harmonist,* the English-language periodical that continued the legacy of the Sajjana-Toshani.

Published with permission from the Bhaktivedanta Research Centre.

FIGURE B.6 Riding a car near Naimisaranya

Source: Prabhupada Saraswati Thakur: The Life and Precepts of Śrīla Bhaktisiddhānta Saraswatī, p. 129.

FIGURE B.7 Reception for governor John Anderson, Mayapur, January 15, 1935. John Anderson was at the time the governor of Bengal.

Source: Prabhupada Saraswati Thakur: The Life and Precepts of Śrīla Bhaktisiddhānta Saraswatī, p. 82.

FIGURE B.8 The Gaudiya Math at Bagbazar.

Published with permission from the Gaudiya Mission, Bagbazar, Kolkata.

MAP B.1 Map of Bengal in the 1930s.

APPENDIX C

Documents

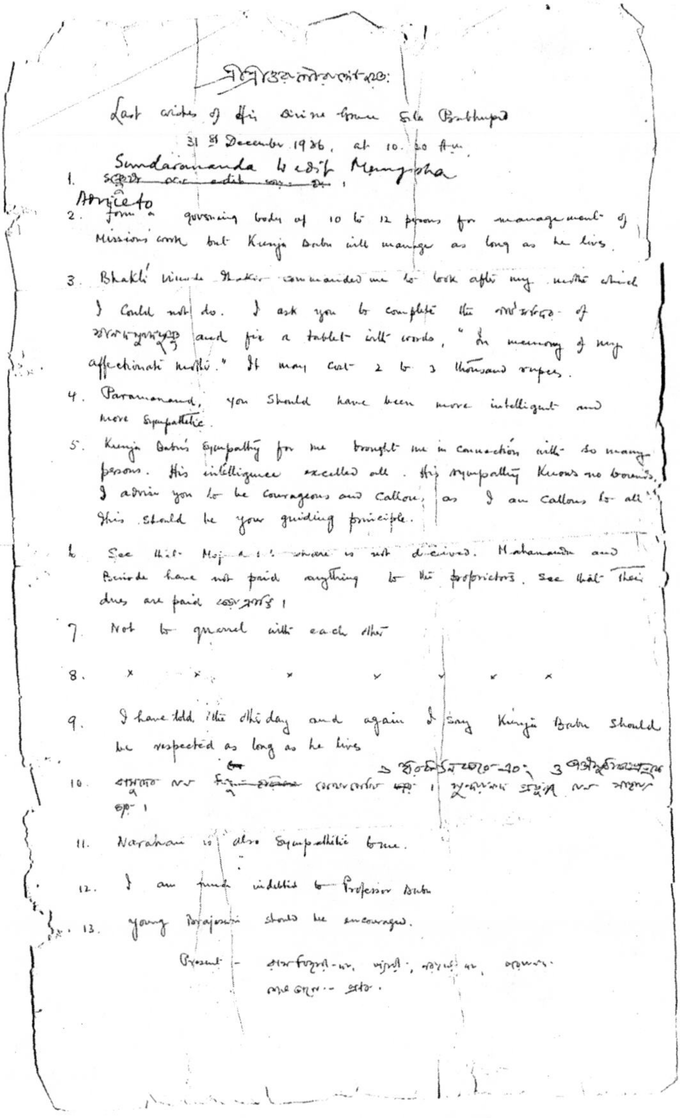

[illegible]

Last wishes of His Divine Grace Srila Prabhupad

31st December 1936, at 10.30 A.m.

1. Sundarananda to edit Harmonist [illegible]

2. Advice to form a governing body of 10 to 12 persons for management of Missions work but Kunja Babu will manage as long as he lives.

3. Bhakti Vinode Thakur commanded me to look after my mother which I could not do. I ask you to complete the [illegible] of [illegible] and fix a tablet with words, "In memory of my affectionate mother." It may cost 2 to 3 thousand rupees.

4. Paramanand, you should have been more intelligent and more sympathetic.

5. Kunja Babu's sympathy for me brought me in connection with so many persons. His intelligence excelled all. His sympathy knows no bounds. I advise you to be courageous and callous, as I am callous to all. This should be your guiding principle.

6. See that Mojumdar's share is not deceived. Mahananda and Benode have not paid anything to the proprietors. See that their dues are paid [illegible]

7. Not to quarrel with each other

8. × × × × × × ×

9. I have told the other day and again I say Kunja Babu should be respected as long as he lives

10. [illegible]

11. Narahari is also sympathetic to me.

12. I am much indebted to Professor Babu

13. Young Brajeswari should be encouraged.

Present :- [illegible]

FIGURE C.1 Minutes of the last wishes of Bhaktisiddhānta

Published with permission from the Bhaktivedanta Research Centre, Kolkata.

All glories to Śrī Śrī Guru and Gaurāṅga

Last wishes of His Divine Grace Srila Prabhupada

December 31, 1936, at 10.30 AM

1. Sundarananda [Vidyāvinoda] to edit Manjusha [*Vaiṣṇava-Mañjuṣā Samahṛti*]
2. Advice to form a governing body of 10 to 12 persons for management of Mission's work, but Kunja Babu [Kuñjabihārī Vidyābhūṣaṇa] will manage as long as he lives.
3. Bhaktivinode Thakur commanded me to look after my mother, which I could not do. I ask you to complete the *nāṭamandira* [a hall within or in front of a temple] of Sānandasukhadakuñja and fix a tablet with words, "In the memory of my affectionate mother". It may cost about 2 to 3 thousand rupees.
4. Paramanand, you should have been more intelligent and more sympathetic.
5. Kunja Babu's sympathy for me brought me in connection with so many persons. His intelligence excelled all. His sympathy knows no bounds. I advise you to be courageous and callous as I am callous to all. This should be your guiding principle.
6. See that Mejo Babu's share is not deceived. Mahananda and Binode have not paid anything to the proprietors. See that these dues are paid to the last coin.
7. Not to quarrel with each other.
8. xxxxxxx
9. I have told the other day and again I say Kunja Babu should be respected as long as he lives.
10. [Ananta] Vāsudeva should write, execute *bhājana* and *kīrtana*, and help Bhaktisudhākara Prabhu [Niśi Kanta Sanyal] and Sundarānanda Prabhu.
11. Narahari is also sympathetic to me.
12. I am much indebted to Professor Babu [Niśi Kanta Sanyal].
13. Young Brajaswami should be encouraged.

Present—Raybihārī dāsa, Pyāri, Narahari dāsa, Paramānanda

Signed—Praṇava

FIGURE C.2 The will of Bhaktisiddhānta, May 18, 1923

Published with permission from the Bhaktivedanta Research Centre, Kolkata.

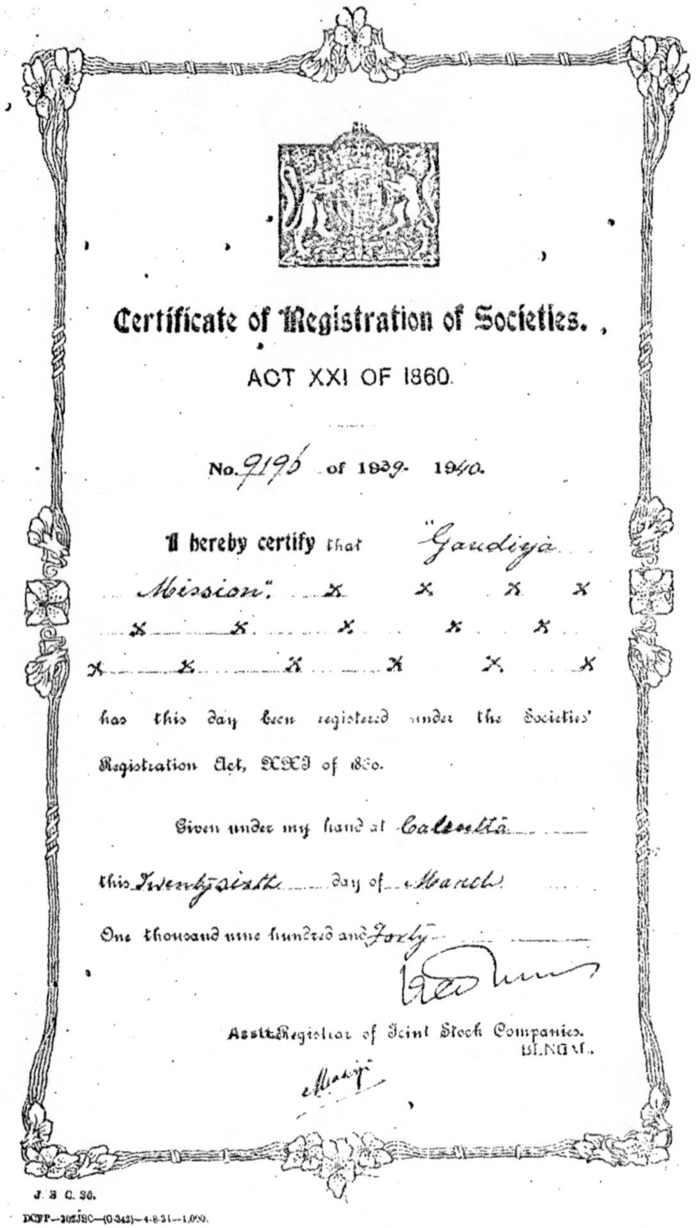

Certificate of Registration of Societies.

ACT XXI OF 1860.

No. 9196 of 1939-1940.

I hereby certify that "Gaudiya Mission".

has this day been registered under the Societies' Registration Act, XXI of 1860.

Given under my hand at Calcutta

this Twenty sixth day of March

One thousand nine hundred and Forty.

Asstt. Registrar of Joint Stock Companies.
BENGAL.

J. S. C. 36.

DCPP—105JSC—(G-343)—4-8-31—1,050.

FIGURE C.3 Registration of the Gaudiya Mission, March 26, 1940
Published with permission from the Gaudiya Mission, Bagbazar, Kolkata.

APPENDIX D

Tour to Central Europe

Timeline of significant events and encounters in Swami Bon's tour of Germany and other countries of central Europe (with notes and available details):

1. Arrival Berlin on October 21, 1934. Meeting with Joseph Goebbels (1897–1945), minister of propaganda, by the arrangement of Sir Eric Clare Edmund Phipps (1875–1945), the British ambassador to Berlin. At the meeting, Goebbels was presented with several Gaudiya Mission publications and extended his support for the mission's religious activities in Germany. Goebbels was also invited to be the guest of honor at the Gaudiya Mission's celebration of Sri Caitanya's birthday, although there is no evidence that he actually attended this event.[1]
2. Berlin: regular meetings with professor of philosophy Eduard Spranger (1882–1963) (see chapter 3 for details); meeting at the Lessing-*Hochschule* with Richard Heinrich Grützmacher (1876–1959), theologian and head of the department for *Religionswissenschaft*, who invited Swami Bon to give a series of lectures; meeting with Johannes Witte (1877–1945), mission professor at Berlin University (see chapter 3 for details); visit to the Grunewald-Gymnasium, a high school where he spoke "to teacher and pupils about the function of the human soul."[2]

1. The event was the 449th anniversary of Caitanya's birthday, which occurred on March 20, 1935, at the Gaudiya Mission in Eisenacher Straße. Bon wrote a letter to Dr. Seifert, secretary at the Propaganda Ministerium abt. VII, Wilhelplatz 8–9, Berlin W. 8, on March 2, 1935 (I wish to thank Dr. Måns Broo for sharing this letter). In that letter, Bon invited Mr. and Mrs. Goebbels to attend the function and requested commercial cooperation on behalf of the laity and business community of the Gaudiya Math in India. The cooperation concerned, among other matters, the purchase of a printing press and perfumes. Although a meeting with Hitler also appears to have been discussed, its occurrence is nowhere mentioned in Swami Bon's report, suggesting that it never took place.

2. Swami Bon, *Second Year*, p. 44.

3. Berlin: meeting with Reverend Birger Forell (1893–1958) of the Church of Sweden, who is described as "an erudite scholar and a sincere friend of spiritual India"[3]; visits to the bishop of the Russian Orthodox Church as well as Prince and Princess Massalsky.
4. Berlin: meeting with the Sanskrit scholar Helmuth von Glasenapp, who arranged for Swami Bon to lecture at Königsberg University. Departure for Leipzig on November 12, 1934.
5. Leipzig: meeting with historian Helmut Berve (1896–1979), who arranged for Swami Bon to lecture on "The Conception of Maya in the Indian Religious Philosophy"; Swami Bon notes in his journal that approximately 700 persons attended the event. Departure for Dresden on November 15, 1934.
6. Dresden: lecture on "The Aryan Indian Conception of God," arranged by the leader of the Academic Nazi Organization; Swami Bon notes in his journal that about 800 representatives of the army, government, and local intelligentsia were in attendance; lessons in Sanskrit to students at the local *Hochschule*; visit to the Opera House, where the minister of interior, Dr. Woelker, conveyed official greetings from the Saxon government. Departure for Prague on November 17, 1934.
7. Prague: meeting with Moritz Winternitz (1863–1937), the renowned Austrian professor of Sanskrit literature at Prague University; Swami Bon also gave a Prag University lecture on "The Way of the Aryan Indian to God."
8. Vienna: lecture on "India, her Culture and Religion" arranged by the *Kulturbund* (cultural association) and presided over by the geographer Eugen Oberhummer (1859–1944); Swami Bon notes in his journal that the lecture was well received and that afterward he was invited to dinner parties and small receptions by a number of the attendees. Departure from Vienna to Munich on November 26.
9. Munich: meeting with a young German scholar who had taught at Vishva Bharati, Rabindranath Tagore's University in Santiniketan, Bengal; lecture titled "Bhakti" arranged by the Indian Section of the German Academy; Swami Bon notes in his diary that it was well attended; meeting with Johannes Baptist Aufhauser (1891–1963), catholic scholar of missiology (see chapter 3 for details).
10. Tübingen: meeting with Jakob Wilhelm Hauer (1881–1962), Indologist and leader of the German Faith Movement (*Deutsche Glaubensbewegung*) (see chapter 3 for details).
11. Beuron: visit to the largest Benedectine Monastery in Germany located in the Donau valley to lecture on "Hindu Theology," attended by 300 monks; the lecture had been arranged by Pater Daniel Feuling and was chaired by Archabbot Dr. Raphael Walzer.
12. Bonn: meeting, on December 13, 1934, with Peter Kahle (1875–1964), director of the Oriental Institute at Bonn University; meeting with noted Swiss Protestant

---

3. Swami Bon, *Second Year*, p. 44.

theologian Karl Barth (1886–1968); Swami Bon notes in his journal that they discussed the many points of similarity and difference between Christianity and Hinduism, and the importance of dialectics in systematic theology.

13. Marburg: meeting with Rudolf Otto (1869–1937), Lutheran theologian and professor of comparative history of religion, about whom Swami Bon wrote, "Prof. Otto took all care to arrange everything in the best possible way. Prof. Otto, whose humility is in contrast to his erudite knowledge of the Hindu Scriptures and the history of Religious India, discussed many hours . . . the different aspects of Hinduism and the 'hermeneutic' principles as to how to understand them correctly."[4] Departed Berlin for London on May 30, 1935.

Returned to Germany on August 12, 1935, and departed for India nine days later on August 21, 1935

4. Swami Bon, *Second Year*, p. 63.

APPENDIX E

Works by Bhaktisiddhānta Sarasvatī

A comprehensive but not full list of Bhaktisiddhānta's works appeared in the *Gauḍīya*, vol. 15, issues 23–24 (January 16, 1937), pp. 41–44. I have added missing titles and unpublished works. Two titles that I discovered are marked as "*recently recovered.*" A number of Bhaktisiddhānta's lectures, speeches, poetry, letters, and conversations with guests were first published in the periodicals of the Gaudiya Math and later in separate volumes.

Original Works by Bhaktisiddhānta

Prahlāda-caritra (*The Life and Deeds of Prahlāda*) five chapters in Bengali verse, 1886 (it is most probably lost)

Baṅge Sāmājikatā: varṇa o dharmagata samāja (*Sociality in Bengal: Varṇa and Dharmic Society*), 1899

Brāhmaṇa o vaiṣṇavera tāratamya-viṣayaka siddhānta (*Comparative Conclusions Concerning Brāhmaṇas and Vaishnavas*), 1911, revised and enlarged in 1934

Bhaktibhāvana-pañjikā, Navadvīpa-pañjikā (1914) (*The Bhaktibhavana Almanac, The Navadvīpa Almanac*) with dates for religious festivals and for ritually important events

Vaiṣṇava-mañjuṣā-samāhṛti (*A basket of collected definitions about Vaishnavism*), Vaishnava encyclopedia in four volumes, 1922–1925

A Few Words on Vedanta, 1932

Rai Ramananda, 1932 (English)

Relative Worlds, 1932

The Vedanta: Its Morphology and Ontology, 1932

Books on Astronomy (jyotiṣa) *Published between 1896 and 1914*

Ārya-siddhānta by Āryabhaṭa (sixth century), co-edited by K. Dutt
Bhauma-siddhānta, mathematical calculations compared to those of Western astronomy, co-edited by K. Dutt
Jyotiṣa-tattvam by Raghunandana Bhaṭṭācārya
Ravicandrasāyanaspaṣṭha, annotations by Bhaṭṭotpala; mathematical calculations compared to those of Western astronomy
Sūrya-siddhānta, Purva and *Uttara* sections; translation from Sanskrit to Bengali and annotations by Bhaktisiddhānta

Published in the Magazines *Bṛhaspati* and *Jyotirvida*

Bhaṭa-dīpikā-ṭīkā by Paramadīśvara, co-edited by K. Dutt
Camatkāra-cintāmaṇi by Paramadīśvara, co-edited by K. Dutt, translation by Kunjavihāri Jyotirbhuṣaṇa
Dina-kaumudī by Paramadīśvara, co-edited by K. Dutt
Laghu-jātaka, annotations by Bhaṭṭotpala (tenth century)
Laghuparāśarīya or *Uḍūdaya-pradīpa,* annotations by Bhairava Datta, co-edited by K. Dutt
Siddhānta-śiromaṇi, Golādhyāya (in *Bṛhaspati*) and *Grahaganitādhyaya* (in *Jotirvida*) with *Vāsanā* commentary by Bhāskarācārya (twelfth century); translation in Bengali and annotations by Bhaktisiddhānta

Canonical Works Published with a Commentary by Bhaktisiddhānta

Upadeśāmṛta, by Rūpa Goswami, with translation and a commentary called *Anuvṛtti,* 1914
Śrī Caitanya-caritāmṛta, by Kṛṣṇadāsa Kavirāja Goswami, with a commentary called *Anubhāṣya,* 1915
Śrīmad-bhāgavatam, with commentary, 1923–1935
Bhakti-sandarbha, by Jīva Goswami, with Bengali translation and a commentary called *Gauḍīya-bhāṣya,* only the initial portion, 1924–1933
Prameya-ratnāvalī, by Baladeva Vidyābhūṣaṇa, with a commentary called *Gauḍīya-bhāṣya* 1924
Śrī Caitanya-bhāgavata, by Vṛndāvana dāsa Ṭhākura, first edition 1924; second edition with a commentary called *Gauḍīya-bhāṣya,* 1932

Śrī Caitanya-candrāmṛta and *Śrī Navadvīpa-śataka*, both by Prabodhānanda Sarasvatī, with translation and a commentary called *Gauḍīya-bhāṣya*, 1926

Śrī Brahma-saṁhitā, chapter 5 with commentary by Jīva Goswami; translation and paraphrase of that commentary in English by Bhaktisiddhānta, 1932

Īśopaniṣad

Unpublished Works

The commentary (*Anubhāṣyam*) on the *Vedānta-sūtra* by Madhva

Sarasvatī-jayaśrī, a volume called *Śrī-parva*, recently recovered

Diary 1904–1936, recently recovered

Books Written or Edited by Bhaktivinoda and Published by Bhaktisiddhānta

Amṛta-pravāha-bhāṣya (*The Flow of Nectarine Commentaries*), a commentary on the *Caitanya-caritāmṛta*

Arcana-kaṇa (*A Drop of Image Worship*)

Arcana-paddhati (*The Ritual Manual for Image Worship*)

Bhagavad-gītā, with translation and commentary (*Rasika-rañjana*)

Bhajana-rahasya (*The Secret of Bhajana*)

Gītā-mālā (*A Garland of Songs*)

Gītāvalī (*A Series of Songs*)

Hari-nāma-cintāmaṇi (*The Touchstone of the Names of Hari*)

Kalyāṇa-kalpataru, (*The Auspicious Wish-Fulfilling Tree*)

Jaiva Dharma (*The Dharma of Jīvas*)

Life and Precepts of Sree Chaitanya Mahaprabhu

Sanmodana-bhāṣya (*Ecstatic Commentaries*) a commentary on the *Śikṣāṣṭaka* by Sri Caitanya

Śaraṇāgati (*Surrender*) (Bengali, English, Tamil)

Śrī Caitanya-śikṣāmṛta (*The Nectarian Teachings of Sri Caitanya*) (Bengali, English, Telegu)

Śrī Caitanyopaniṣad

Śrī Navadvīpa-dhāma-māhātmya (*The Glory of the Sacred Place of Navadvīpa*)

Śrī Navadvīpa-dhāma-granthamāla (*A Garland of Texts about the Sacred Place of Navadvīpa*)

Tattva-muktāvalī (*A Pearl Necklace of Truths*)

Tattva-sūtra (*Sūtras about the Truth*) (in Devanāgarī script)

Tattva-viveka (*Investigation about the Truth*)

The Bhagavat: Its Philosophy and Theology

Canonical Works by Other Authors Published by Bhaktisiddhānta

Gaura-kṛṣṇodaya (*The Advent of Gaura Kṛṣṇa*) by Govinda dāsa, 1914
Maṇi-mañjarī (*The Buds of Gems*) by Madhva with translation, 1926
Vedānta-tattva-sāra (*The Essential Truths of the Vedanta*) by Rāmānujācārya with translation, 1926
Prema-bhakti-candrikā (*The Soothing Moonlight of Pure Devotional Love*) by Narottama dāsa, 1927
Sadācāra-smṛti (*The Smṛti Text of Proper Conduct*) by Madhva with translation, 1927
Hari-nāmāmṛta-vyākaraṇa (*The Grammar of the Nectarean Names of Hari*) by Jīva Goswami, 1928
Hari-bhakti-kalpa-latikā (*The Wish-Fulfilling Creepers of Devotion to Hari*) with translation (author unknown), second edition with Bengali translation, 1931
Prema-vivarta (*The Transformation of Pure Love*) by Jagadānanda Paṇḍita
Sat-kriyā-sāra-dīpikā (*A Commentary about the Essence of Auspicious Rituals*) by Gopala Bhaṭṭa Goswami
Saṁskāra-dīpikā (*A Commentary about the Rituals of Purification*)
Śrī Caitanya-maṅgala by Locana dāsa Ṭhākura

Articles in the Sajjanatoṣaṇī

1897

Sanskrit bhaktamāla, a review of the Sanskrit text *Bhaktamāla*

1899

Śrīman Nāthamuni (Nāthamuni)
Yāmunācārya (Yāmunācārya)
Śrī Rāmānujācārya (Rāmānuja)

1915–16

Pūrva bhāṣā (Introductory Words)
Prāṇīra prati dayā (Compassion toward Living Beings)
Śrī Madhvamuni-carita (The Life and Works of Madhva Muni)
Ṭhākurera smṛti-samiti (The Memorial Assembly for Bhaktivinoda Ṭhākura)
Divyasūri vā Ālvāra (Divyasūri or Ālvāra, saint in Rāmānuja's *sampradāya*)
Jayatīrtha (Jayatīrtha)
Godādevī (Godādevī)
Pāñcarātrika adhikāra (Rights According to the *Pāñcarātrika* System)
Prāpti svīkāra (Letter of Acknowledgment of Receipt)
Vaiṣṇava smṛti (The *Smṛti* Texts of the Vaishnavas)

Śrī patrikāra kathā (The Message of the Magazine)
Bhaktāṅghri-reṇu (The Dust of the Feet of the *Bhaktas*)
Kulaśekhara (Kulaśekhara)
Sāmayik prasaṅga (Concerning Current Events)
Śrī Gaurāṅga, philosophical topics concerning Sri Gaurāṅga (Caitanya)
Abhakti-mārga (The Path of Nonbhakti)
Viṣṇu citta (Consciousness of Vishnu)
Pratikūla matavāda (Opposing Theories)
Mahātmā śrīla Kṛṣṇadāsa, (The Great Soul Kṛṣṇadāsa Kavirāja)
Toṣaṇīra kathā (The Message of *Sajjanatoṣaṇī*)
Śrī guru svarūpa (The Real Identity of the Guru)
Prabodhānanda (Prabodhānanda)
Śrī bhakti-mārga (The Path of Bhakti)
Samālocanā (Critical Review)
Toṣaṇī-prasaṅga (Regarding the *Sajjanatoṣaṇī*)
Artha o anartha (The Substantial and the Worthless)
Baddha, taṭastha o mukta (The Bound, the Marginal, and the Liberated)
Gohite pūrvādeśa (Previous Instructions about the Welfare of the Cows)
Prākṛta o aprākṛta (Material and Nonmaterial)
Antardvīpa (an article about the island of Antardvīpa in Nabadwip)
Prakaṭa-pūrṇimā (The Full-Moon Appearance)
Caitanyābda (The Era Beginning with Caitanya)
Upakurvāṇa (Time-Limited Celibate Student)
Varṣa-śeṣa (The End of the Year)

1916–17

Nava-varṣa (New Year)
Āsaner kathā (The Message of the Āsana)
Ācārya-santāna (Descendants of the *Ācāryas*)
Videśe gaura-kathā (The Message of Gaura Abroad)
Samālocanā (Critical Review)
Āmāra prabhura kathā (Topics about My Master), about Gaura Kiśora dāsa Bābājī
Vaiṣṇavera viṣaya (The Material Possessions of a Vaishnava)
Guru-svarūpe punaḥ praśna (Another Question about the True Identity of a Guru)
Vaiṣṇava-vaṁśa (The Lineage of the Vaishnavas)
Viraha-mahotsava (The Great Festival of Separation)
Śrī patrikāra ukti (Statements of the Magazine)
Prākṛta-rasa-śata-dūṣaṇī (The Hundred Flaws of Materialistic *Rasa*)
Duiṭi ullekha (Two Mentionable Things)

Gānera adhikārī ke? (Who Has the Right to Sing?)
Sadācāra (Proper Conduct)
Amāyā (Nonillusion)
Prārthanā-rasa-vivṛti (An Account of the Various Tastes of Prayers)
Pratibandhaka (Obstacles)
Bhāi sahajiyā (My Brother Sahajiyā)
Varṣa-śeṣa (Year's End)

1917–18
Nava-varṣa (New Year)
Samālocanā (Critical Review)
Sajjana—kṛpālu (A Devotee Is Merciful)
Śakti-pariṇata jagat (The World as Transformed Potency)
Sajjana—akṛta-droha (A Devotee Has no Enmity)
Sajjana—satya-sāra (A Devotee Is thoroughly Truthful)
Prākṛta śūdra vaiṣṇava nahe (A Materialistic *Śūdra* is not a Vaishnava)
Nāgarī-māṅgalya (Auspiciousness for Town Women)
Sajjana—sama (A Devotee Is Equipoised)
Sajjana—nirdoṣa (A Devotee Is Faultless)
Sajjana—vadānya (A Devotee Is Munificent)
Bhāḍaṭiyā bhakta nahe (A Hired Person Is not a Devotee)
Sajjana—mṛdu (A Devotee Is Mild)
Sajjana—akiñcana (A Devotee Is without Possessions)
Sajjana—śuci (A Devotee Is Clean)
Vaiṣṇava darśana (Vaishnava Philosophy)
Varṣa-śeṣa (Year's End)

1918–19
Nava-varṣa (New Year)
Sajjana—sarvopakāraka (A Devotee Is Beneficial to All)
Sajjana—śānta (A Devotee Is Peaceful)
Gaura ki vastu? (What Is Gaura?)
Sajjana—Kṛṣṇaika-śaraṇa (A Devotee Is Exclusively Surrendered to Krishna)
Sajjana—akāma (A Devotee Is without Passion)
Sajjana—nirīha (A Devotee Is Harmless)
Sajjana—sthira (A Devotee Is Firm)
Sajjana—vijita-ṣaḍ-guṇa (A Devotee Has Conquered the Virtues)
Śrī-mūrti o māyāvāda (The Image and the Doctrine of Māyāvāda)
Śrī Viśva-Vaiṣṇava-rāja-sabhā (The Royal World Vaishnava Association)
Sajjana—mita-bhuk (A Devotee Accepts Sense Objects in Moderation)
Bhaktisiddhānta (The Philosophical Conclusion of Bhakti)
Sajjana—apramatta (A Devotee Is Not Insane)

1919–20

Varṣodghāṭa (Ushering in the New Year)
Sajjana—mānada (A Devotee Honors Others)
Sajjana—amānī (A Devotee Is Undesirous of Respect)
Sajjana—gambhīra (A Devotee Is Solemn)
Sajjana—karuṇa (A Devotee Is Compassionate)
Sajjana—maitra (A Devotee Is Friendly)
Kāla-saṁjñāya nāma (The Sacred Names according to the Divisions of Time)
Śaukra o vṛttagata varṇa-bheda (Social Divisions according to One's Own Nature and Birth)
Karmīra kanakādi (Gold and Other Assets of a Materialistic Worker)
Guru-dāsa (The Servant of the Guru)
Dīkṣita (The Initiated)

1920–21

Hāyanodghāta (Ushering in the New Year)
Aikāntika o vyabhicāra (Single-Mindedness and Deviation)
Nirjane anartha (Obstacles in Solitary Worship) (the poem *duṣṭa mana! tumi kiser vaiṣṇava?*)
Sajjana—kavi (A Devotee Is a Poet)
Cāturmāsya, (The Four Months)
Pañcopāsanā (The System of Worshiping Five Images)
Vaiṣṇavera smṛti (The *Smṛti* Texts of the Vaishnavas)
Saṁskāra-sandarbha (A Treatise on Purification Rituals)
Sajjana—dakṣa (A Devotee Is Skilled)
Vaiṣṇava-maryādā (Appreciating Vaishnavas)
Sajjana—Maunī (A Devotee Is Silent)
Yogapīṭhe śrī-mūrti-sevā (Serving the Image at Yogapīṭha)
Aprākṛta (Nonmaterial)

1921–22

Nava-varṣa (New Year)
Saviśeṣa o nirviśeṣa (With and Without Particularity)
Meki o āsal (False and Real)
Smārta Raghunandana, article about the *smārta* Raghunandana
Hari-nāma mahā-mantra (The Great Chant of the Names of Hari)
Mantropāsanā (Worship by Mantra)
Niṣiddhācāra (Forbidden Conduct)
Śikṣāṣṭakera-laghu-vivaraṇa (A Short Description of the Eight Instructions [by Caitanya])

Articles in the Gauḍīya

First Year (1922–23)

Śrī-kṛṣṇa-janma (The Birth of Sri Krishna)
Madhura lipi (Sweet Writing)
Loka-vicāra (Public Opinion)
Paramārtha (The Highest Aim)
Purāṇa-saṁvāda (The Message of the Puranas)
Nīti-bheda (Ethical Differences)
Ruci-bheda (Differences in Taste)
Śrī Jīva goswami (Jīva Goswami)
Gauḍīye prīti (Affection for the *Gauḍīya*)
Durgā-pūjā (Worship of Durgā)
Śāradīyā avāhana (Welcoming the Autumn)
Je dike bātās (Whichever Direction the Wind Blows)
Marūte secana (To Sprinkle Water in the Desert)
Smārtera kāṇḍa (The Vedic Literature Sections of the *Smārtas*)
Vicāra-ādālata (Court of Judgment)
Sevāpara nāma (A Positive Service Attitude to the Sacred Name)
Tridaṇḍi bhikṣu gīti (The Song of a Monk Holding the Triple Staff)
Śrī Madhva-janma-tithi (The Birthday of Sri Madhva)
Varṇāśrama (*Varṇa* and Ashram)
Aprakaṭa-tithi (Disappearance Day)
Vraje vānara (Monkeys in Vraja)
Cyuta-gotra (A Deviated Lineage)
Nṛmātrādhikāra (The Right of Every Human Being)
Bhṛtaka-śrotā (A Hired Audience)
Vaiṣṇavao abhṛtaka (A Vaishnava Is Never Hired)
Dīkṣā-vidhāna (The Rules of Initiation)
Āsurika pravṛtti (Demonic Propensities)
Śrī Baladeva Vidyābhūṣaṇa, a brief biography of Baladeva Vidyābhuṣaṇa
Sadācāra-smṛti (The *Smṛti* Text for Proper Conduct), a discussion of *Sadācāra-smṛti* by Madhva
Pañcarātra (The Rituals Called *Pañcarātra*)
Nigama o āgama (The Vedas and Related Sacred Texts)
Śrī Viśvanātha Cakravartī (Viśvanātha Cakravartī)
Vaiṣṇava darśana (Vaishnava Philosophy)
Varṇāntara (Changing *Varṇa*)
Paricaye praśna (A Question about Identity)
Asatye ādara (Fondness for Untruth)
Ayogya santāna (Unworthy Son)

Aśūdra dīkṣā (Initiation for Non-*śūdras*)
Pūjādhikāra (The Qualification to Perform *Pūjā*)
Anātma-jñāna (Knowledge of the Nonself)
Nija-paricaya (One's Own Identity)
Vaṁśa-praṇālī (The System of Hereditary Lineages)
Gaura-bhajana (Worship of Gaura)
Dhānyā o śyāmā (Grains and Weeds)
Tṛtīya janma (Third Birth)
Avaidha sādhana (Illegitimate Practice)
Baija-brāhmaṇa (Hereditary *Brāhmaṇa*)
Pracāre bhrānti (Mistakes in Preaching)
Bhāgavata-śravaṇa (Hearing the *Bhāgavata*)
Maṭha ki? (What Is a Math?)
Āche adhikāra (There Is Qualification)
Śrīdhara Svāmī (Śrīdhara Swami)
Vyavahāra (Conduct)
Kamīnā (Scoundrel)
Śakti-sañcāra (Saving Potency)
Varṣa-parīkṣā (Yearly Examination)
Eka jāti (One *Jāti*)
Ihaloka paraloka (This World and the World Beyond)

Second Year (1923–24)

Varṣa-praveśa (Entering the New Year)
Brahmaṇya-deva (The God of the *Brāhmaṇas*)
Guru-bruva (Imitation Gurus)
Kīrtane vijñāna (Realized Knowledge in *Kīrtana*)
Āvirbhāva-tithi (Appearance Day)
Maṭhera utsava (Festivals of the Math)
Gosvāmi-pāda (The Respected *Goswami*)
Kṛṣṇe bhoga-buddhi (The Psychology of Enjoying Krishna)
Dīkṣita (The Initiated)
Gauḍīya bhajana-praṇālī (the Process of *Gauḍīya* Worship)
Śrī-vigraha (The Image)
Jābāla-kathā (The Story of Jābāla)
Smārta o vaiṣṇava (*Smārtas* and Vaishnavas)
Sāmājika ahita (What Is Unbeneficial for Society)
Prākṛta bhoktā ke? (Who Is the Real Enjoyer?)
Gauḍīyera veṣa (The Dress of the *Gauḍīyas*)
Pratisambhāṣana (Speech in Response)
Sūtra-vidveṣa (Enmity against the Sutras)

Third Year (1924–25)

Gauḍīya hāspātāla (Gaudiya Hospital)
Bhāgavata-vivṛti (Explanation of *Śrīmad-Bhāgavatam*)
Śrī Kulaśekhara (Kulaśekhara)
Meyeli hinduwānī (Effeminate Hinduism)

Fourth Year (1925–26)

Madhura lipi (A Sweet Letter)
Aśrauta-darśana (Non-Vedic Philosophy)
Vedānta-tattva-sārer upodghāta (Introduction to the *Vedānta-tattva-sāra*)

Fifth Year (1926–27)

Darśane bhrānti (Error in Philosophy)
Vaiṣṇava-śrāddha (Vaishnava Funeral Rites)
Ālocakera ālocanā (A Critique of Critics)
Nyākābokāra svarūpa (The Real Nature of a Foolishly Credulous Person)

Sixth Year (1927–28)

Māna-dāna o hāni (Offering Respect and Losing It)
Gauḍapura (The City of Gauḍa)
Āsala o nakala (Real and Fake)
Ahaituka dhāma-sevaka (An Unmotivated Servant of the Holy Places)
Sarva-pradhāna vivecanāra viṣaya (The Most Important Thing to Consider)
Bhāi kutārkika (Brother Quibbler)
Kṛṣṇa-bhakta nirbodha nahen (A *Bhakta* of Krishna Is Not a Fool)
Prācīna Kuliyāy sahara Navadvīpa (The Town of Nabadwip Is Old Kuliya)
Kapaṭatā daridratāra mūla (The Cause of Poverty Is Deceit)
Ekaścandra (One Moon)
Puṇyāraṇya (A Sacred Forest)
Goḍāy galad (An Error in the Fundamentals)
Nīlācale śrīmat Saccidānanda Bhaktivinoda (Bhaktivinoda in Jagannath Puri)

Seventh Year (1928–29)

Virakta jaghanya nahe (A Renunciant Is Not Contemptible)
Āmi ei nai, āmi sei (I Am Not This, I Am That)
Vyavasādārera kapaṭatā (The Merchants' Cheating)
Haṁsajātira itihāsa (The History of the Descendens of the Swanlike)
Mantra-saṁskāra (The Purification of Mantra)
Bhoga o bhakti (Enjoyment and Bhakti)
Sunīti o durnīti (Good and Evil Policies)
Kṛṣṇa-tattva (The Truth about Krishna)
Śrīdhāma-vicāra (Examining a Sacred Pilgrimage)

Ekāyana-śruti o tad-vidhāna (The *Ekāyana-Śruti* and Its Regulations)
Pratīcye kārṣṇa sampradāya (The Disciplic Order of Krishna in the West)
Pañcarātra
Nīlācale śrīmad Bhaktivinoda (Bhaktivinoda in Jagannath Puri)
Tīrtha Pāṇḍarapura (The Holy Site of Pandarpur)
Manikya bhāskara (The Effulgent Manikyas), a praise of the Maharaja of Tripura
Vaiṣṇava-smṛti (Scriptures Giving Rules of Vaishnava Behavior)
Mahānta guru-tattva (The Truth about a Great Guru)
Boṣṭam pārlāmeṇṭ (Vaishnava Parliament)
Alaukika bhakta-caritra (The Unworldly Life and Deeds of a *Bhakta*)
Sumedhā-tithi (An Auspicious Day for the Intelligent), about the anniversary of Bhaktivinoda

Eighth Year (1929–30)

Śrīdhāma Māyāpura kothāya? (Where Is the Sacred Site of Mayapur?)
Gauḍācale śrī Bhaktivinoda (Bhaktivinoda in Bengal)
Sātvata o asātvata (Devotees and Nondevotees)
Bhārata o paramārtha (India and the Highest Aim)
Paramārthera svarūpa (The Real Nature of the Highest Aim)
Prācīna Kuliyāya dvārabhet (Entrance Fees in Old Kuliyā [Nabadwip])
Śikṣaka o śikṣita (The Teacher and the Taught)
Viṣayīra Kṛṣṇa-prema (The Materialists's Love for Krishna)
Āśramera veṣa (Appropriate Dress for the Ashram)

Ninth Year (1930–31)

Śrī-bhakti-mārga (The Path of Bhakti)
Bhava-rogīra hāsapātāla (A Hospital for the Materially Diseased)
Jagabhandhura Kṛṣṇānuśīlana (The Practice of Krishna-Bhakti of Jagabandhu)

Tenth Year (1931–32)

Gauḍīya mahimā (The Excellence of the *Gauḍīya*)
Sat-śikṣārthir vivecya (What a Student of the Truth Ought to Analyze)
Nimba-bhāskara (Nimbarka)
Ajña o vijñera narma-kathā (Playful Talks between an Ignorant and a Wise Man)
Vaiṣṇava-vaṁśa (The Vaishnava Clan)
Kanphucor vicāra (The Deliberations of Confucius)

Eleventh Year (1932–33)

Ekādaśa prārambhikā (Beginning the Eleventh Year)
Vaiṣṇave jāti-buddhi (Considering a Vaishnava to Belong to a Particular *Jāti*)
Mādhukara bhaikṣya (What Should Be Begged from Door to Door)
Duṣṭi-vaiklavya (Distress from Corruption)

Āmāra kathā (My Message)
Sat-śikṣā pradarśanī (The Exhibition of Religious Education)
Kṛṣṇa bhakti-i śoka-kāma-jāḍyāpahā (Devotion to Krishna is the Exclusive Way to Transcend Grief, Desire, and Inertia)
Kṛṣṇe matirastu (May Your Resolution Be Toward Krishna)

Twelfth Year (1933–34)
Kṛpāśīrvāda (Merciful Blessings)

Thirteenth Year (1934–1935)
Sva-para-maṅgala (Auspiciousness for Oneself and Others)
Vaikuṇṭha o guṇa-jāta jagat (Vaikuṇṭha and the World Born of Three Guṇas)
Bhogavāda o bhakti (The Philosophy of Hedonism and Bhakti)

Fourteenth Year (1935–36)
Nava-varṣa (New Year)
'Baḍa āmi' o 'Bhālo āmi' (I Who Is Great and I Who Is Good)
Tadvana (That Forest)
Vāstava-vastu (The Real Essence)

Fifteenth Year (1936–37)
Hāyanodghāta (Ushering in the New Year)

Bibliography

PRIMARY SOURCES

Periodicals

Bengalee, daily, Calcutta (English)
Bombay Chronicle, Bombay (English)
Gauḍīya, weekly, 1922–1937, Calcutta (Bengali)
Nadīya Prakāśa, daily, Mayapur (Bengali)
Prabasi (Bengali)
Sajjanatoṣaṇī, monthly, published from April 1879 by Bhaktivinoda, edited from 1914 by Bhaktisiddhānta (Bengali)
Sree Sajjana-toshani, the Harmonist, monthly and fortnightly, 1927–1936, Calcutta (English, Sanskrit)
Amrita Bazar Patrika, daily, 1931–1935, Calcutta (English)
Völkischer Beobachter, daily, September 1933, October 19, 1935—January 31, 1936, Berlin (German)

Official Documents

Calcutta High Court Archive. *Testamentary Suit no. 2 of 1938* in the High Court of Juricature at Fort William in Bengal.

Works in Bengali and Sanskrit (including translations)

Bādarāyaṇa and Rai Bahadur Śrīśa Chandra Vasu. *The Vedānta-Sūtras of Bādarāyaṇa, with the Commentary of Baladeva*. Allahabad: Pāṇiṇi Office, Bhuvaneśwarī āśrama, 1912. (Sanskrit and English)
Bhaktisiddhānta Sarasvatī, Bimala Prasad Datta. *Almanac for the year 1917*. Calcutta: Saraswat Chatuspathi, n.d. (English and Bengali)

———. *Baṅge Sāmājikatā: varṇa o dharmagata samāja*. Calcutta, 1899. (Bengali) This title is authored by Śrī Bimalā Prasāda Siddhānta Sarasvatī. Bhaktisiddhānta often signed his correspondence as "Siddhānta Sarasvatī." The following titles most often carry the name Bhaktisiddhānta Sarasvatī.

———. *Baṅge Sāmājikatā: varṇa o dharmagata samāja*. Mayapur: Śrī Caitanya Maṭh, 2002. (Bengali)

———. *Brāhmaṇa o Vaiṣṇava: tāratamya-viṣayaka siddhānta*. Mayapur: Śrī Caitanya Math, 1934. (Bengali, Sanskrit)

———. *Brāhmaṇa o Vaiṣṇava: tāratamya-viṣayaka siddhānta*. Mayapur: Śrī Caitanya Math, 2000. (English, Sanskrit)

———. *Diary 1904–1936*. Unpublished. (Bengali, English)

———. *Prabhupādera Harikathāmṛta* [collection of speeches]. Vols. 1–3. Mayapur: Śrī Caitanya Math, 2002.

———. *Prabhupādera Patrāvalī* [collection of letters]. Vols. 1–3. Prayag: Śrī Rupa Gaudiya Mission, 1984. (Bengali)

———. *Śrī Śrī Sarasvatī Saṃlāpa* [collection of conversations]. Vol. 2. Allahabad: Śrī Rūpa Gaudiya Math, n.d.

———. *Vaiṣṇava-mañjuṣā Samahṛti* [A Casket of Collected Entries about Vaishnavism]. 4 vols. Calcutta: Śrī Gaudiya Math, 1922–25. (Bengali)

Bhaktisiddhānta Sarasvatī and Vṛndāvana dāsa Ṭhākura. *Caitanya Bhāgavata*. Calcutta: Śrī Gaudiya Math, 1984. (Bengali)

Bhaktisiddhānta Sarasvatī and Kṛṣṇadāsa Kavirāja. *Caitanya Caritāmṛta*. Calcutta: Śrī Gaudiya Math, 1990. (Bengali)

Bhaktisiddhānta Sarasvatī and Vyāsadeva. *Śrīmad Bhāgavatam*. Calcutta: Śrī Gaudiya Math, 1995. (Sanskrit, Bengali)

Bhaktisiddhānta Sarasvatī, Danavir Goswami, et al. *The Sūrya-Siddhānta and Siddhānta-Śiromaṇi*. Kansas City: Rupanuga Vedic College, 2007. (Sanskrit, Bengali, and English)

Bhaktivinoda, Kedarnath Datta Ṭhākura. *Dattakaustubham*. Calcutta: Kedarnath Datta, 1886. (English and Sanskrit)

———. *Jaiva Dharma*. Bimala Prasad Siddhānta Sarasvatī, 1917. (Bengali)

———. *Jaiva Dharma*. Madras: Sree Gaudiya Math, 1975. (English)

———. *Shri Chaitanya Shikshamritam*. Madras: Sree Gaudiya Math, 1983. (English)

———. *Śrī Caitanya Śikṣamṛta*. Mayapur: Śrī Caitanya Math, n.d. (Bengali)

———. *Śrī Godruma Kalpataru: Shri Shri Nama Hatta*. Edited by Swami Jayapataka. 1891; Mayapur: Sri Sri Hare Krishna Nama Hatta, 1989. (English)

———. *Srigouranga Smaranamangala or Chaitanya Mahaprabhu: His Life and Precepts*. Calcutta: K. Dutt, 1896. (English and Sanskrit)

———. *Śrī Kṛṣṇa Saṃhitā*. Calcutta: Īśvaracandra Vasu Company, 1880. (Bengali, Sanskrit)

———. *Svalikhita-Jīvanī*. Edited by Lalita Prasad Datta. Calcutta: Lalita Prasad Datta, 1916. (Bengali)

Bhāratī, Bhakti Bhūṣaṇa, ed. *Śrīla Prabhupādera Goloka-vaṇī*. 2 vols. Nabadwip Bhakti-kevala Auḍulomi Śrī Kṛṣṇa-Caitanya Sevāśrama, 1997. (Bengali)

Goswami Jīvā and Satya Narayana das. *Bhakti Sandarbha*. Vrindavan: Vrindavan Research Institute, 2005. (Sanskrit and English)

Goswami Rūpa and David L. Haberman. *Bhakti Rasāmṛta Sindhu*. Delhi: Indira Gandhi National Center for the Arts; Motilal Banarsidass, 2003. (Sanskrit and English)

Kavirāja Kṛṣṇadāsa. *Caitanya Caritāmṛta of Kṛṣṇadāsa Kavirāja*. Translated by Edward C. Dimock. Co-editor, Tony Stewart. Cambridge, Mass.: Dept. of Sanskrit and Indian Studies, Harvard University, distributed by Harvard University Press, 1999. (English)

Vidyāvinoda, Sundarānanda, ed. *Sarasvatī Jayaśrī: Vaibhava Parva*. Calcutta: Śrī Gaudiya Math, 1934. (Bengali)

———. *Sarasvatī Jayaśrī: Śrī Parva*. Unpublished. (Bengali)

The Vedānta-Sūtras: With the Commentary by Sankarācārya and Rāmānūja. Translated by George Thibaut. Edited by Max Müller. Vols. 34, 38, 48, The Sacred Books of the East. Oxford: Clarendon Press, 1890.

Works in English and German

Bhakti Hṛdaya Bon Swami. *Gedanken über den Hinduismus*. Berlin: Gaudiya Mission, 1935.

———. *My First Year in England. Report of my activities in the West from May 1933 to May 1934*. London: Gaudiya Mission, 1934. Second edition, Calcutta: N. K. Banerji, 1981.

———. *My Lectures in England and Germany*. Vrindavan: Bhajan Kutir, 1984.

———. *Second year of the Gaudiya Mission in Europe*. London: Gaudiya Mission, 1935.

Bhaktikusum Sramana Swami. *Prabhupāda: Srila Sarasvati Thākura*. Mayapur: Sri Caitanya Math, 1983.

Bhakti Pradīpa Tīrtha Swami. *Srila Sarasvati Thakura*. 1940; Calcutta: Gaudiya Mission, 1998.

Bhaktisiddhānta Sarasvatī. *A Few Words on Vedanta*. Madras: Shree Gaudiya Math, 1932.

———. *Rai Ramananda*. Madras: Shree Gaudiya Math, 1932.

———. *Relative Worlds: A Lecture delivered on the 26th of August 1932 at the Saraswata Assembly Hall of Shree Gauḍiya Math, Calcutta*. Calcutta: Shree Gaudiya Math, 1932.

———. *Shri Chaitanya's Teachings*. Parts I and II. Edited by Swami Bhakti Vilāsa Tīrtha. Madras: Shree Gaudiya Math, 1989.

———. *The Vedanta: Its Morphology and Ontology. A Lecture delivered on the 27th of August 1933 at the Saraswata Assembly Hall of Shree Gauḍiya Math, Calcutta*. Calcutta: Shree Gaudiya Math, 1933.

Bhakti Śrīrūpā Bhāgavata Swami, ed. *Advent Centenary Souvenir of Shri Shrila Prabhupad, 1874–1974*. Calcutta: Gaudiya Mission, 1974.

Bhakti Vallabha Tīrtha Swami. *Sri Caitanya: His Life & Associates*. San Rafael, Calif.: Mandala Publishing, 2001.

Bhaktivedānta Swami, A. C. et al.. *Bhaktivedānta Vedabase 2003*. The Bhaktivedānta Archives, 2002. Complete works in DVD format.

Bhakti Vikāsa Swami. *Śrī Bhaktisiddhānta Vaibhava: The Grandeur and Glory of Śrīla Bhaktisiddhānta Sarasvatī Ṭhākura*. Surat: Bhakti Vikas Trust, 2009.

Bhaktivinoda, Kedarnath Datta Ṭhākura. *The Poriade, or Adventures of Porus*. Calcutta: G. P. Roy & Co., 1857.

———. *The Bhagavat: Its Philosophy, Its Ethics and Its Theology (A Lecture Delivered at Dinajpore in 1869)*. Edited by Bhaktisiddhānta Sarasvatī. Calcutta: Sri Gaudiya Math, Ultadingi Junction Road, (n.d.).

———. *The Hindu Idols: An Answer to "'Prof. Max Muller on Durga."* Calcutta: Tract Society, January 1899.

Dāsī, Devamayī. "A Divine Life: Śrīla Bhaktisiddhānta Saraswatī Ṭhākura Prabhupāda." In *Prabhupada Saraswati Thakur: The Life and Precepts of Śrīla Bhaktisiddhānta Saraswatī*, 13–49. Eugene, Ore.: Mandala Publishing Group, 1997.

Gandhi, Mahatma. "The Life and Works of Mahatma Gandhi." New Delhi: Icon Softec, 1999. (Electronic resource with complete works)

Narasingha Swami, B. G. *The Authorized Sri Caitanya-Saraswata Parampara*. Bangalore: Gosai Publishers, 1998.

Paramadvaiti Swami, B. A. *Our Family the Gaudiya Math: A Study of the Expansion of Gaudiya Vaisnavism and the Many Branches Developing around the Gaudiya Math*. Vrindavan: Vrindavan Institute for Vaisnava Culture and Studies, 1999.

Sanyal, Niśi Kanta, and Bhaktisiddhānta Sarasvatī. *Sree Krishna Chaitanya*. Vol. 1. Madras: Shree Gaudiya Math, 1933.

Sanyal, Niśi Kanta. *Sree Krishna Chaitanya*. Vol. 2. Kolkata: Gaudiya Mission, 2004.

———. *The Erotic Principle and Unalloyed Devotion*. Calcutta: Gaudiya Math, n.d.

Vivekānanda Swami. *The Complete Works of Swami Vivekananda*. 8 vols. Kolkata: Advaita Ashrama, 2006.

Yati Bhakti Prajñāna Swami. *Three Apostles of Gaudiya Vaishnava Movement*. Madras: Shree Gaudiya Math, 1994.

SECONDARY SOURCES

Abbott, Elizabeth. *A History of Celibacy*. Cambridge: Lutterworth Press, 2001.

Abhik Banerjee, Subhankar Ghosh, Srabani Pal, and Kalyan Mitra. "Some Distinguished Former Students: Scottish Church College." *Scottish Church College Souvenir*. Kolkata: Scottish College, 1999.

Agrawal, Madan Mohan. *Six Systems of Indian Philosophy: The Sutras of Six Systems of Indian Philosophy with English Translation, Transliteration, and Indices.* Delhi: Chaukhamba Sanskrit Pratishthan, 2001.

Ahmad, Aziz. *An Intellectual History of Islam in India.* Edinburgh: Edinburgh University Press, 1969.

Anquetil-Duperron, Abraham Hyacinthe. *Oupnek'hat (Id Est, Secretum Tegendum): Opus Ipsa in India Rarissimum, Continens Antiquam Et Arcanam Doctrinam, Quatuor Sacris Indorum Libris, Rak Beid, Djedjr Beid, Sam Beid, Athrban Beid, Excerptam...* Argentorati, 1801–1802.

Anquetil-Duperron, Abraham Hyacinthe, and Thaddeus Anselm Rixner. *Versuch Einer Neuen Darstellung Der Uralten Indischen All-Eins-Lehre, Oder Der Berühmten Sammlung... Erstes Stück Oupnek'hat Tschehandouk Genannt.* Nuremberg: Steinischen Buchhandlung, 1808.

Apte, Vaman Shivaram. *The Student's Sanskrit-English Dictionary.* Delhi: Motilal Banarsidass, 2000.

Arvidsson, Stefan. *Aryan Idols: Indo-European Mythology as Ideology and Science.* Chicago: University of Chicago Press, 2006.

Arweck, Elisabeth, and Martin D. Stringer. *Theorizing Faith: The Insider/Outsider Problem in the Study of Ritual.* Birmingham: University of Birmingham Press, 2002.

Balagangadhara, S. N. *"The Heathen in His Blindness": Asia, the West and the Dynamic of Religion.* New York: Brill, 1994.

———. "How to Speak for the Indian Traditions: An Agenda for the Future." *Journal of the American Academy of Religion* 73, no. 4 (2005): 987–1013.

Bandyopadhyaya, Sekhara. *Caste, Culture, and Hegemony: Social Domination in Colonial Bengal.* Thousand Oaks, Calif.: Sage Publications, 2004.

Basham, A. L. *The Wonder That Was India: A Survey of the Culture of the Indian Sub-Continent before the Coming of the Muslims.* New York: Grove Press, 1954.

Basu, Hena, ed. *Vaisnava Periodical in Bengal (1856–1983).* Kolkata: Basu Research and Documentation Service, 2009.

Basu, Shamita. *Religious Revivalism as Nationalist Discourse: Swami Vivekananda and New Hinduism in Nineteenth-Century Bengal.* Delhi: Oxford University Press, 2002.

Bayly, Christopher Alan. *Empire and Information: Intelligence Gathering and Social Communication in India, 1780–1870.* Cambridge: Cambridge University Press, 1997.

Beck, Guy L. *Sonic Theology: Hinduism and Sacred Sound.* Columbia: University of South Carolina Press, 1993.

Beckerlegge, Gwilym. "The Hindu Renaissance and Notions of Universal Religion." In *Religion in History: Conflict, Conversion and Coexistence,* edited by John Wolffe, 129–160. Manchester: Manchester University Press and the Open University, 2001.

———. “Responding to Conflict: A Test of the Limits of Neo-Vedāntic Social Activism in the Ramakrishna Math and Mission.” *International Journal of Hindu Studies* 11, no. 1 (2007): 1–25.

———. *Swami Vivekananda’s Legacy of Service: A Study of the Ramakrishna Math and Mission*. Oxford: Oxford University Press, 2006.

Bengtsson, Jan Olof. *The Worldview of Personalism: Origins and Early Development*. New York: Oxford University Press, 2006.

Berger, Peter L. “The Desecularization of the World: A Global Overview.” In *The Desecularization of the World: Resurgent Religion and World Politics*, edited by Peter L. Berger, 1–18. Washington, D.C.: Eerdmans, Ethics and Public Policy Center, 1999.

Berger, Peter L., Grace Davie, and Effie Fokas. *Religious America, Secular Europe? A Theme and Variations*. Burlington, Vt.: Ashgate, 2008.

Berger, Peter L., Hansfried Kellner, and Brigitte Berger. *The Homeless Mind: Modernization and Consciousness*. New York: Vintage Books, 1974.

Berger, Peter L., and Thomas Luckmann. *The Social Construction of Reality: A Treatise in the Sociology of Knowledge*. New York: Anchor, 1967.

Beyer, Peter. *Religions in Global Society*. London: Routledge, 2006.

Bhabha, Homi K. *The Location of Culture*. London: Routledge, 2004.

Bhatia, Varuni. “Devotional Traditions and National Culture: Recovering Gaudiya Vaishnavism in Colonial Bengal.” Ph.D. diss., Columbia University, 2008.

Bhattacharya, Jogendra Nath. *Hindu Castes and Sects: An Exposition of the Origin of the Hindu Caste System and the Bearing of the Sects Towards Each Other and Towards Other Religious Systems*. 1896; Calcutta: Editions Indian, 1973.

Bhattacharya, Tithi. *The Sentinels of Culture: Class, Education, and the Colonial Intellectual in Bengal (1848–85)*. Oxford: Oxford University Press, 2005.

Bogdan, Henrik. *Western Esotericism and Rituals of Initiation*. Albany: State University of New York Press, 2007.

Bose, Subhas Chandra, Sisir Kumar Bose, and Sugata Bose. *An Indian Pilgrim: An Unfinished Autobiography*. Calcutta and Delhi: Netaji Research Bureau and Oxford University Press, 1997.

Bose, Sugata, and Ayesha Jalal. *Modern South Asia: History, Culture, Political Economy*. London: Routledge, 1998.

Bowne, Borden Parker. *Personalism*. Boston: Houghton Mifflin, 1908.

Brahmachari, Mahanambrata. *Vaiṣṇava Vedānta (the Philosophy of Śrī Jīva Gosvāmī)*. Calcutta: Das Gupta & Co., 1974.

Braun, Willi, and Russell T. McCutcheon, eds. *Guide to the Study of Religion*. New York: Cassell, 2000.

Brekke, Torkel. *Makers of Modern Indian Religion in the Late Nineteenth Century*. New York: Oxford University Press, 2002.

Broo, Måns. *As Good as God: The Guru in Gauḍīya Vaiṣṇavism*. Åbo: Åbo Academy University Press, 2003.

———. "Bhakti Hriday Bon Maharaja (1901–1982)." M.A. thesis, Åbo Akademi, 2002.

Brooks, Charles R. *The Hare Krishnas in India*. Princeton, N.J.: Princeton University Press, 1989.

Brown, Francis Yeats. *Lancer at Large*. London: Victor Gollancz, 1936.

Bryant, Edwin. *The Quest for the Origins of Vedic Culture: The Indo-Aryan Migration Debate*. New York: Oxford University Press, 2001.

Bryant, Edwin F., and Maria Ekstrand. *The Hare Krishna Movement: The Postcharismatic Fate of a Religious Transplant*. New York: Columbia University Press, 2004.

Brzezinski, Jan. "The Paramparā Institution in Gauḍīya Vaiṣṇavism." *Journal of Vaishnava Studies* 5, no. 1 (1996–97): 151–182.

Burke, Edmund. *Articles of Charge of High Crimes and Misdemeanors, against Warren Hastings, Esq. Late Governor General of Bengal*. London: J. Debrett, 1786.

Cakrabarty, Janardana. *Bengal Vaisnavism and Sri Chaitanya*. Calcutta: Asiatic Society, 2000.

Casanova, José. "Political Challenges from Religion in the 21st Century." Paper delivered at the conference "Religion in the 21st Century: Transformations, Significance and Challenges." University of Copenhagen, 2007.

Chakrabarty, Dipesh. *Habitations of Modernity: Essays in the Wake of Subaltern Studies*. Chicago: University of Chicago Press, 2002.

———. *Provincializing Europe: Postcolonial Thought and Historical Difference*. Princeton, N.J.: Princeton University Press, 2000.

Chakrabarty, Sudhir. *Gabhīra Nirjana Pathe*. Kolkata: Ananda Publishers, 1989.

Chakravarti, Ramakanta. *Baṅge vaiṣṇava dharma: ekti aitihāsika ebaṃ samājatāttvika adhyāyana*. Kolkata: Ananda Publishers, 1996.

———. *Vaiṣṇavism in Bengal, 1486–1900*. Calcutta: Sanskrit Pustak Bhandar, 1985.

Chakravarty, Papia. *Hindu Response to Nationalist Ferment, Bengal, 1909–1935*. Calcutta: Subarnarekha, 1992.

Chanda, Mrinal Kanti. *History of the English Press in Bengal, 1780 to 1857*. Calcutta: KP Bagchi, 1987.

Chatterjee, Partha. *The Nation and Its Fragments: Colonial and Postcolonial Histories*. Princeton, N.J.: Princeton University Press, 1993.

Chatterjee, Satischandra, and Dhirendramohan Datta. *An Introduction to Indian Philosophy*. Calcutta: University of Calcutta, 1950.

Chatterji, Joya. *Bengal Divided: Hindu Communalism and Partition, 1932–1947*. Cambridge: Cambridge University Press, 1994.

———. *The Spoils of Partition: Bengal and India, 1947–1967*. Cambridge: Cambridge University Press, 2007.

Chowdhury, Indira. *The Frail Hero and Virile History: Gender and the Politics of Culture in Colonial Bengal*. Oxford: Oxford University Press, 1998.

Clémentin-Ojha, Catherine. "A Mid-Nineteenth-Century Controversy over Religious Authority." In *Charisma and Canon: Essays on the Religious History of the Indian*

Subcontinent, edited by Vasudha Dalmia, Angelika Malinar, and Martin Christof, 183–201. Oxford: Oxford University Press, 2001.

Cox, Jeffrey. *Imperial Fault Lines: Christianity and Colonial Power in India, 1818–1940*. Stanford: Stanford University Press, 2002.

Crawford, S. Cromwell. *Ram Mohan Roy: Social, Political, and Religious Reform in 19th Century India*. New York: Paragon House, 1987.

Darwin, John. *After Tamerlane: The Global History of Empire since 1405*. London: Allen Lane, 2007.

Das, Ajit. *Jātavaiṣṇava kathā*. Kolkata: Charuvaka, 1993.

Das, Harish Chandra. *Sri Chaitanya in the Religious Life of India*. Calcutta: Punthi Pustak, 1989.

Das, Rahul Peter. *Essays on Vaisnavism in Bengal*. Calcutta: Firma KLM, 1997.

———. "Review: Dušan Zbavitel, 'Bengali Literature'" *Indo-Iranian Journal* 27, no. 1 (1984): 51–69.

Das, Sisir Kumar. *Early Bengali Prose, Carey to Vidyasagar*. Calcutta: Bookland, 1966.

Dāsa, Śrī Haridāsa. *Śrī śrī gauḍīya vaiṣṇava jīvana*. Nabadwip: Śrī Haribol Kuṭir, 1975.

Dasgupta, Shashi Bhushan. *Obscure Religious Cults*. Calcutta: Firma K. L. Mukhopadhyay, 1976.

Dasgupta, Surendranath. *A History of Indian Philosophy*. Vol. 1. Cambridge: Cambridge University Press, 1922.

Daunton, Martin J., and Bernhard Rieger. *Meanings of Modernity: Britain from the Late-Victorian Era to World War II*. Oxford: Berg, 2001.

De, Sushil Kumar. *Bengali Literature in the Nineteenth Century, 1757–1857*. Calcutta: Firma K. L. Mukhopadhyay, 1962.

———. *Early History of the Vaisnava Faith and Movement in Bengal: From Sanskrit and Bengali Sources*. Calcutta: Mukhopadhyay, 1961.

De Michelis, Elizabeth. *A History of Modern Yoga: Patañjali and Western Esotericism*. London: Continuum, 2004.

Dhar, Niranjan. *Vedanta and Bengal Renaissance*. Calcutta: Minerva Associates, 1977.

Dimock, Edward C. *The Place of the Hidden Moon: Erotic Mysticism in the Vaisnava-Sahajiya Cult of Bengal*. Chicago: University of Chicago Press, 1989.

Dirks, Nicholas B. *The Scandal of Empire: India and the Creation of Imperial Britain*. Cambridge, Mass.: Belknap Press of Harvard University Press, 2006.

Dwyer, Graham, and Richard J. Cole. *The Hare Krishna Movement: Forty Years of Chant and Change*. London: I.B. Tauris, 2007.

Eck, Diana. "Kṛṣṇa Consciousness in Historical Perspective." *Back to Godhead 14.10 (Bhaktivedanta Vedabase 2003)*, 1979.

Eidlitz, Walther. *Bhakta: Eine indische Odyssee*. Hamburg: Claassen, 1951.

———. *Den glömda världen: om hinduism och meditation*. Stockholm: Askild & Kärnekull, 1972.

———. *Krsna-Caitanya: Sein Leben und seine Lehre.* Stockholm: Almqvist & Wiksell, 1968.

Eisenstadt, S. N. *Comparative Civilizations and Multiple Modernities.* Leiden: Brill, 2003.

———. "Multiple Modernities." *Daedalus* 129, no. 1 (2000): 1–30.

Eliade, Mircea. *Patterns in Comparative Religion.* London: Sheed & Ward, 1958.

Elkman, Stuart Mark, and Jiva Gosvami. *Jiva Gosvamin's Tattvasandarbha: A Study on the Philosophical and Sectarian Development of the Gaudiya Vaisnava Movement.* Delhi: Motilal Banarsidass, 1986.

Embree, Ainslie T. *The Hindu Tradition.* New York: Random House, 1972.

Esposito, John L. *The Oxford History of Islam.* New York: Oxford University Press, 1999.

Esposito, John L., Darrell J. Fasching, and Todd Vernon Lewis. *Religion & Globalization: World Religions in Historical Perspective.* New York: Oxford University Press, 2008.

Faivre, Antoine. *Access to Western Esotericism.* Albany: State University of New York Press, 1994.

Farquhar, John Nicol. *Modern Religious Movements in India.* London: Macmillan, 1929.

Flewelling, R. T. "Personalism." In *Twentieth Century Philosophy: Living Schools of Thought,* edited by Dagobert D. Runes, 321–342. New York: Philosophical Library, 1943.

Flood, Gavin. *Beyond Phenomenology: Rethinking the Study of Religion.* London: Cassell, 1999.

Frykenberg, Robert E. "India to 1858." In *The Oxford History of the British Empire,* vol. 5, *Historiography,* edited by Robin W. Winks and Alaine M. Low, 194–213. Oxford: Oxford University Press, 2001.

Fuller, Jason D. "Modern Hinduism and the Middle Class: Beyond Revival in the Historiography of Colonial India." *Journal of Hindu Studies* 2, no. 2 (2009): 160–178.

———. "Religion, Class, and Power: Bhaktivinoda Thakur and the Transformation of Religious Authority among the Gauḍīya Vaiṣṇavas in Nineteenth-Century Bengal." Ph.D. diss., University of Pennsylvania, 2004.

Gandhi, Mahatma. *Hind Swaraj, or Indian Home Rule*: Navajivan Karyalaya: Ahmedabad, 1938.

Gandhi, Mahatma, and Mahadev Haribhal Dessai. *An Autobiography, or the Story of My Experiments with Truth.* 1927; Ahmedabad: Navajivan Publishing House, 1993.

Gandhi, Mahatma, and Bharatan Kumarappa. *Hindu Dharma.* Ahmedabad: Navajivan Publishing House, 1950.

Ganguly, Debjani. *Caste, Colonialism and Counter-Modernity: Notes on a Postcolonial Hermeneutics of Caste.* New York: Routledge, 2005.

Gilje, Nils, Sten Andersson, and Harald Grimen. *Samhällsvetenskapernas förutsättningar.* Göteborg: Daidalos, 1993.

Giri, Satyavati. *Baṅgla sāhitye kṛṣṇakathāra kramavikāśa*. Kolkata: Ratnāvali, 1988.

Goodrick-Clarke, Nicholas. *The Occult Roots of Nazism: Secret Aryan Cults and Their Influence on Nazi*. London: Tauris Parke, 2004.

Grieve, Gregory Price. "Staking out the Field: A Henotheistic Review of Supplemental Readers for the Study of Hinduism." *Journal of the American Academy of Religion* 76, no. 3 (2008): 716–747.

Griffin, Zebina Flavius. *India and Daily Life in Bengal*. Philadelphia: American Baptist Publication Society, 1896.

Grimes, John A. "Darśana." In *The Hindu World*, edited by Sushil Mittal and G. R. Thursby, 531–552. New York: Routledge, 2004.

Guha, Ranajit. "Dominance without Hegemony and Its Historiography." In *Subaltern Studies 6: Writings on South Asian History and Society*, edited by Ranajit Guha, 210–309. New Delhi: Oxford University Press, 2005.

Haberman, David L. "A Cross-Cultural Adventure: The Transformation of Ronald Nixon." *Religion* 23 (1993): 217–227.

———. "Divine Betrayal: Krishna-Gopal of Braj in the Eyes of the Outsiders." *Journal of Vaishnava Studies* 3, no. 1 (1994): 83–111.

Halbfass, Wilhelm. *India and Europe: An Essay in Understanding*. Albany: State University of New York Press, 1988.

Hallstrom, Lisa Lassell. *Mother of Bliss: Anandamayi Ma (1896–1982)*. New York: Oxford University Press, 1999.

Hanegraaff, Wouter J. *New Age Religion and Western Culture: Esotericism in the Mirror of Secular Thought*. Albany: State University of New York Press, 1998.

———. "On the Construction of 'Esoteric Traditions.'" In *Western Esotericism and the Science of Religion*, edited by Antoine Faivre and Wouter J. Hanegraaff, 11–62. Leuven: Peeters, 1998.

Harder, Hans. *Bankimchandra Chattopadhyay's Śrīmadbhagabadgītā: Translation and Analysis*. New Delhi: Manohar Publishers & Distributors, 2001.

Hartshone, Charles. "Pantheism and Panentheism." In *The Encyclopedia of Religion*, edited by Mircea Eliade and Charles J. Adams, 11:165–169. New York: Macmillan, 1987.

Hatcher, Brian A. *Bourgeois Hinduism, or the Faith of the Modern Vedantists: Rare Discourses from Early Colonial Bengal*. New York: Oxford University Press, 2008.

———. "Bourgeois Vedanta: The Colonial Roots of Middle-Class Hinduism." *Journal of the American Academy of Religion* 75, no. 2 (2007): 298–323.

———. *Eclecticism and Modern Hindu Discourse*. New York: Oxford University Press, 1999.

Hazlehurst, Cameron, Sally Whitehead, and Christine Woodland. *A Guide to the Papers of British Cabinet Ministers: 1900–1964*. Royal Historical Society Guides and Handbooks, 0080–4398, No. 19. Cambridge: Cambridge University Press for the Royal Historical Society, 1996.

Heehs, Peter. *The Essential Writings of Aurobindo*. New Delhi: Oxford University Press, 2006.

Herder, Johann Gottfried von. *Johann Gottfried von Herder's Sämmtliche Werke*. Ed. Johann von Müller. Stuttgart, 1829.

"Hill Tipperah or Tripura." In *The Encyclopaedia Britannica*. Cambridge: Cambridge University Press, 1911.

Himmelfarb, Gertrude. *The Roads to Modernity: The British, French, and American Enlightenments*. New York: Knopf, 2004.

Hitler, Adolf. *The Essential Hitler: Speeches and Commentary*. Edited by Max Domarus and Patrick Romane. Wauconda, Ill.: Bolchazy-Carducci, 2007.

Hopkins, Thomas J. "The Social and Religious Background for Transmission of Gaudiya Vaisnavism to the West." In *Krishna Consciousness in the West*, edited by David G. Bromley and Larry D. Shinn, 35–54. Lewisburg, Pa.: Bucknell University Press; London: Associated University Presses, 1989.

Houtmans, Gustaaf. "The Biography of Modern Burmese Buddhist Meditation Master U Ba Khin: Life before the Cradle and Past the Grave." In *Sacred Biography in the Buddhist Traditions of South and Southeast Asia*, edited by Juliane Schober, 310–344. Honolulu: University of Hawai'i Press, 1997.

Hunter, William Wilson. *A History of British India*. Vol. 1. London: Longmans, 1899.

Inden, Ronald B. *Imagining India*. Oxford: Basil Blackwell, 1990.

Jackson, Robert, and Dermot Killingley. *Approaches to Hinduism*. London: John Murray, 1988.

Jacobsen, Knut A. *Prakrti in Samkhya-Yoga: Material Principle, Religious Experience, Ethical Implications*. New York: Peter Lang, 1997.

Jacobsen, Knut A., and P. Pratap Kumar. *South Asians in the Diaspora: Histories and Religious Traditions*. Leiden: Brill, 2004.

Johnson, Gordon, and Peter James Marshall. *Bengal: The British Bridgehead: Eastern India, 1740–1828*. Vol. 2, *The New Cambridge History of India*. Cambridge: Cambridge University Press, 1987.

Jordens, J. T. F. *Dayananda Sarasvati: His Life and Ideas*. Delhi: Oxford University Press, 1978.

Karner, Christian, and Alan Aldridge. "Theorizing Religion in a Globalizing World." *International Journal of Politics, Culture and Society* 18, nos. 1–2 (2004): 5–32.

Kaviraj, Studipta. "Modernity and Politics in India." *Daedalus* 129, no. 1 (2000): 137–162.

Kennedy, Melville T. *The Chaitanya Movement: A Study of Vaishnavism in Bengal*. 1925; New Delhi: Munshiram Manoharlal Publishers, 1993.

Kesavan, B. S., Vinayak Yashvant Kulkarni, and Sahitya Akademi. *The National Bibliography of Indian Literature, 1901–1953*. New Delhi: Sahitya Akademi, 1962.

Killingley, Dermot. "Rammohun Roy's Interpretation of the Vedānta." In *Perspectives on Indian Religion: Papers in Honour of Karel Werner*, edited by Karel Werner and Peter Connolly. Delhi: Sri Satguru Publications, 1986.

King, Richard. *Orientalism and Religion Post-Colonial Theory: India and "the Mystic East."* London: Routledge, 1999.

———. "Orientalism and the Modern Myth of 'Hinduism' (Western Christian Notions of Indian Religion at the Interface between Post-Colonial Theories of Religions)." *Numen* 46, no. 2 (1999): 146–185.

Kipling, Rudyard. *Departmental Ditties, Barrack-Room Ballads and Other Verses.* New York: United States Book Co., 1890.

Klostermaier, Klaus K. *A Survey of Hinduism.* Albany: State University of New York Press, 2007.

Knudson, Albert Cornelius. *The Philosophy of Personalism: A Study in the Metaphysics of Religion.* New York: Abingdon Press, 1927.

Kopf, David. *The Brahmo Samaj and the Shaping of the Modern Indian Mind.* Princeton, N.J.: Princeton University Press, 1979.

———. *British Orientalism and the Bengal Renaissance: The Dynamics of Indian Modernization, 1773–1835.* Berkeley: University of California Press, 1969.

Kripal, Jeffrey John. *Kali's Child: The Mystical and the Erotic in the Life and Teachings of Ramakrishna.* Chicago: University of Chicago Press, 1995.

Laird, M. A. *Missionaries and Education in Bengal, 1793–1837.* Oxford: Oxford University Press, 1972.

Laithwaite, John Gilbert. *The Marquess of Zetland, 1876–1961.* London: Oxford University Press, 1962.

Lanjuinais, Jean-Denis. "Analyse de l'Oupnek'hat." *Journal asiatique* April 1823, 213–236.

Larson, Gerald James. *India's Agony over Religion.* Albany: State University of New York Press, 1995.

Leonowens, Anna Harriette. *Life and Travel in India: Being Recollections of a Journey before the Days of Railroads.* Philadelphia: Porter & Coates, 1884.

Lethbridge, Roper. *The Golden Book of India: A Genealogical and Biographical Dictionary of the Ruling Princes, Chiefs, Nobles, and Other Personages, Titled or Decorated of the Indian Empire.* Delhi: Aakar Books, 2005.

Lipner, Julius J. *Brahmabandhab Upadhyay: The Life and Thought of a Revolutionary.* Delhi: Oxford University Press, 2001.

Lipski, Alexander. "Bipincandra Pal and Reform Hinduism." *History of Religions* 11, no. 2 (1971): 220–235.

———. "Vijay Krsna Goswami: Reformer and Traditionalist." *Journal of Indian History* 52, no. 1 (1974).

Lorenzen, David N. "Bhakti." In *The Hindu World,* edited by Sushil Mittal and Gene R. Thursby, 185–209. New York: Routledge, 2004.

———. *Bhakti Religion in North India: Community, Identity and Political Action.* New Delhi: Manohar, 1996.

Louis, William Roger. "Introduction." In *The Oxford History of the British Empire: The Twentieth Century*, edited by Judith M. Brown and William Roger Louis, 1–46. Oxford: Oxford University Press, 2001.

Macaulay, Thomas Babington. "Minute of Indian Education." 1835. *Macmillan's Magazine*, May–October 1864, 3–6.

———. *Critical and Historical Essays: Contributed to the Edinburgh Review*. London: Longmans Green and Co., 1866.

———. *Critical, Historical, and Miscellaneous Essays and Poems*. Vols. 5–6. New York: A.C. Armstrong & Son, 1860.

MacNicol, Nicol. *Indian Theism from the Vedic to the Muhammadan Period*. 1915; Delhi: Munshiram Manoharlal Publishers, 1968.

Madsen, Finn. "Social udvikling i Hare Krishnabevægelsen." Ph.D. diss., University of Copenhagen, 2001.

———. "Tradition og fornyelse i Gaudiya Math." M.A. thesis, University of Copenhagen, 1996.

Majumdar, A. K. *Bhakti Renaissance*. Bombay: Bharatiya Vidya Bhavan, 1979.

Marvin, Brian D. "The Life and Thought of Kedarnath Datta Bhaktivinode: A Hindu Encounter with Modernity." Ph.D. diss., University of Toronto, 1996.

———. (Shukavak Dasa). *Hindu Encounter with Modernity: Kedarnath Datta Bhaktivinoda, Vaishnava Theologian*. Riverside, Calif.: Sanskrit Religions Institute, 1999.

McDaniel, June. *The Madness of the Saints: Ecstatic Religion in Bengal*. Chicago: University of Chicago Press, 1989.

Michaels, Axel. *Hinduism: Past and Present*. Princeton. N.J.: Princeton University Press, 2004.

Michel, Suzanne M. "Golden Eagles and the Environmental Politics of Care." In *Animal Geographies: Place, Politics, and Identity in the Nature-Culture Borderlands*, edited by J. Wolch and J. Emel, 162–183. London: Verso, 1998.

Mohanty, Jitendranath. *Classical Indian Philosophy*. Lanham, Md.: Rowman & Littlefield, 2000.

Monier-Williams, Monier. *A Sanskrit-English Dictionary*. Delhi: Motilal Barnasidass Publishers, 1999.

Munshi, K. M., ed. *British Paramountcy and Indian Renaissance*. Vol. 9.1, *The History and Culture of the Indian People*. Bombay: Bharatiya Vidya Bhavan, 1963.

Müller, Max, trans. *The Upanishads*. Sacred Books of the East. Oxford: Clarendon Press, 1879.

Nandy, Ashis. *The Intimate Enemy: Loss and Recovery of Self under Colonialism*. Delhi: Oxford, 1988.

National Library of India. *Catalogue of Sanskrit, Pali and Prakrit Books*. Calcutta: National Library, 1951.

Neevel, W. G. "The Transformations of Śrī Rāmakrishna." In *Hinduism: New Essays in the History of Religion*, edited by B. L. Smith, 51–97. Leiden: Brill, 1976.

O'Connell, Joseph. "Jati Vaiṣṇavas of Bengal: 'Subcaste' (Jati) without 'Caste' (Varna)." *Journal of Asian and African Studies* 17, nos. 3–4 (1981): 13–28.

———. "Were Caitanya's Vaiṣṇavas Really Sahajas? The Case of Ramananda Raya." In *Shaping Bengali Worlds*, edited by Tony Stewart, 11–22. East Lansing: Asian Study Center, Michigan State University, 1989.

———. "The Word 'Hindu' in Gaudiya Vaisnava Texts." *Journal of the American Oriental Society* 93, no. 3 (1973): 340–344.

Oddie, Geoffrey A. *Imagined Hinduism: British Protestant Missionary Constructions of Hinduism, 1793–1900*. New Delhi: Sage Publications, 2006.

Otto, Rudolf. *India's Religion of Grace and Christianity Compared and Contrasted*. London: Student Christian Movement Press, 1930.

Pal, Bipin Chandra. *Europe Asks Who Is Shree Krishna: Letters Written to a Christian Friend*. Calcutta: Classic Publication, 2002

———. *Memories of My Life and Times*. Calcutta: Bipinchandra Pal Institute, 1973.

Panikkar, K. M. *Asia and Western Dominance: A Survey of the Vasco Da Gama Epoch of Asian History, 1498–1945*. London: Allen & Unwin, 1953.

Pearson, M. N. *The Portuguese in India*. Cambridge: Cambridge University Press, 1987.

Pennington, Brian K. *Was Hinduism Invented? Britons, Indians, and the Colonial Construction of Religion*. Oxford: Oxford University Press, 2005.

Poewe, Karla O. *New Religions and the Nazis*. London: Routledge, 2006.

Polanyi, Karl. *The Great Transformation: The Political and Economic Origins of Our Time*. Boston: Beacon Press, 2001.

Porter, A. E. *Census of India 1931: Bengal and Sikkim, Imperial and Provincial Tables*. Vol. 5, part 2. Calcutta: Central Publications Branch, 1932.

Prakash, Gyan. "Science between the Lines." In *Subaltern Studies 9: Writings on South Asian History and Society*, edited by Shahid Amin and Dipesh Chakrabarty, 59–82. Delhi: Oxford University Press, 2005.

Prentiss, Karen Pechilis. *The Embodiment of Bhakti*. New York: Oxford University Press, 1999.

Radhakrishnan, Sarvepalli. *Hindu View of Life*. Oxford: George Allen and Unwin, 1927.

———. *An Idealist View of Life*. 1932; London: G. Allen & Unwin, 1947.

———. *Our Heritage*. Delhi: Hind Pocket Books, 1973.

Raju, P. T. *The Philosophical Traditions of India*. Delhi: Motilal Banarsidass, 1998.

Ramadan, Tariq. "Europeanization of Islam or Islamization of Europe?" In *Islam, Europe's Second Religion: The New Social, Cultural, and Political Landscape*, edited by Shireen T. Hunter, 207–218. Westport, Conn.: Praeger, 2002.

———. *Western Muslims and the Future of Islam*. New York: Oxford University Press, 2004.

Ray, Benoy Gopal. *Religious Movements in Modern Bengal*. Santiniketan: Visva-Bharati Research Publications, 1965.

Ray, Ratnalekha. "Change in Bengal Agrarian Society ca. 1760–1850: A Study in Selected Districts." Ph.D. diss., University of Cambridge, 1973.

Raychaudhuri, Tapan. *Europe Reconsidered: Perceptions of the West in Nineteenth Century Bengal*. Oxford: Oxford University Press, 1988.

———. *Perceptions, Emotions, Sensibilities: Essays on India's Colonial and Post-Colonial Experiences*. Oxford: Oxford University Press, 1999.

Richards, Glyn. *A Source-Book of Modern Hinduism*. London: Curzon, 1985.

Ricoeur, Paul. *Interpretation Theory: Discourse and the Surplus of Meaning*. Fort Worth: Texas Christian University Press, 1976.

Robertson, Bruce Carlisle. *Raja Rammohan Ray: The Father of Modern India*. Oxford: Oxford University Press, 1999.

Robinson, Francis, ed. *The Cambridge Encyclopedia of India, Pakistan, Bangladesh, Sri Lanka, Nepal, Bhutan and the Maldives*. Cambridge: Cambridge University Press, 1989.

Rocher, Ludo. *The Purāṇas. A History of Indian Literature, Epics and Sanskrit Religious Literature*, vol. 2, fasc. 3. Wiesbaden: Harrassowitz, 1986.

Rochford, E. Burke. *Hare Krishna in America*. New Brunswick, N.J.: Rutgers University Press, 1985.

———. *Hare Krishna Transformed*. New and Alternative Religions Series. New York: New York University Press, 2007.

Roy, Rammohun. *The Precepts of Jesus: The Guide to Peace and Happiness, Extracted from the Books of the New Testament Ascribed to the Four Evangelists*. Calcutta: Baptist Mission Press, 1820.

———. *Translation of Several Principal Books, Passages, and Texts of the Veds, and of Some Controversial Works of Brahmunical Theology*. London: Parbury, Allen & Co., 1832.

———. *The Precepts of Jesus the Guide to Peace and Happiness, Extracted from the Books of the New Testament Ascribed to the Four Evangelists. To Which Are Added, the First, Second, and Final Appeal to the Christian Public in Reply to the Observations of Dr. Marshman of Serampore*. London: John Mardon, 1834.Said, Edward W. *Orientalism: Western Conceptions of the Orient*. London: Penguin, 2003.

Sailley, Robert. *Chaitanya et la dévotion a Krishna*. Paris: Dervy-livres, 1986.

Salmond, Noel A. *Hindu Iconoclasts: Rammohun Roy, Dayananda Sarasvati, and Nineteenth-Century Polemics against Idolatry*. Waterloo, Ont.: Wilfrid Laurier University Press, 2004.

Sambidananda Das. "The History and Literature of the Gaudiya Vaisnavas and Their Relation to Other Medieval Vaisnava Schools." Ph.D. diss., University of London, 1935.

Sander, Åke, and Daniel Andersson. "Religion och religiositet i en pluralistisk och föränderlig värld—några teoretiska, metodologiska och begreppsliga kartor."

In *Det mångreligiösa Sverige: ett landskap i förändring*, edited by Åke Sander and Daniel Andersson, 37–284. Lund: Studentlitteratur, 2009.

Sardella, Ferdinando. "The Two Birthplaces of Śrī Caitanya Mahāprabhu: Gauḍīya Vaiṣṇava Groups in Navadvīpa and Māyāpura During the Gaura Pūrṇimā Festival 2002." M.A. thesis, University of Gothenburg, 2002.

Sarkar, Sumit. *The Swadeshi Movement in Bengal, 1903–1908*. New Delhi: People's Publishing House, 1973.

Sarkar, Susobhan Chandra. *On the Bengal Renaissance*. Calcutta: Papyrus, 1979.

Sarkar, Tanika. *Rebels, Wives, Saints: Designing Selves and Nations in Colonial Times*. Ranikhet: Permanent Black, 2009.

Sarma, D. S. *Studies in the Renaissance of Hinduism in the Nineteenth and Twentieth Centuries*. Benares: Benares Hindu University, 1944.

Sarma, Deepak. *An Introduction to Mādhva Vedānta*. Burlington, Vt.: Ashgate, 2003.

Schreiter, Robert J. *Constructing Local Theologies*. Maryknoll, N.Y.: Orbis Books, 1985.

Schweig, Graham M. *Dance of Divine Love: The Rasa Lila of Krishna from the Bhagavata Purana*. Princeton, N.J.: Princeton University Press, 2005.

———. "Krishna: The Intimate Deity." In *The Hare Krishna Movement the Postcharismatic Fate of a Religious Transplant*, edited by Edwin F. Bryant and Maria Ekstrand, 13–30. New York: Columbia University Press, 2004.

———. "Toward a Constructive and Comparative Theology of Krishna Bhakti for Contemporary Bengal Vaishnavism." *Journal of Vaishnava Studies* 18, no. 1 (2009): 151–173.

Sen, Amiya P. *Hindu Revivalism in Bengal, 1872–1905: Some Essays in Interpretation*. Delhi: Oxford University Press, 1993.

Sengupta, Nitish K. *History of the Bengali-Speaking People*. Orpington: Grantha Neer, 2001.

Sharma, Arvind. *The Concept of Universal Religion in Modern Hindu Thought*. Basingstoke: Macmillian, 1998.

———. *Modern Hindu Thought: An Introduction*. Oxford: Oxford University Press, 2005.

———. *Modern Hindu Thought: The Essential Texts*. Oxford: Oxford University Press, 2002.

———. *Thresholds in Hindu-Buddhist Studies*. Calcutta: Minerva, 1979.

Sharma, Krishna. *Bhakti and the Bhakti Movement: A New Perspective. A Study in the History of Ideas*. New Delhi: Munshiram Manoharlal Publishers, 1987.

Sil, Narashingha P. "Ramakrishna-Vivekananda Research: Hagiography versus Hermeneutics." *Religious Studies Review* 27, no. 4 (2001): 355–362.

———. *Swami Vivekananda: A Reassessment*. Selinsgrove, Pa.: Susquehanna University Press, 1997.

Smith, A. Christopher. "The Legacy of William Ward and Joshua and Hannah Marshman." *International Bulletin of Missionary Research* 23, no. 3 (1999): 120–129.

Smith, David. *Hinduism and Modernity*. Religion in the Modern World. Malden, Mass.: Blackwell, 2003.

Sontheimer, Günther-Dietz, and Hermann Kulke. *Hinduism Reconsidered*. New Delhi: Manohar Publications, 1997.

Spivak, Gayatri Chakravorty. *The Spivak Reader: Selected Works of Gayatri Chakravorty Spivak*. Edited by Donna Landry and Gerald M. MacLean. New York: Routledge, 1996.

Stier, Jonas. *Kulturmöten: en introduktion till interkulturella studier*. Lund: Studentlitteraturen, 2004.

Stietencron, Heinrich von. "Religious Configurations in Pre-Muslim India and the Modern Concept of Hinduism." In *Representing Hinduism: The Construction of Religious Traditions and National Identity*, edited by Vasudha Dalmia and Heinrich von Stietencron, 249–290. New Delhi: Sage Publications, 1995.

Stillson, Judah J. *Hare Krishna and the Counterculture*. New York: Viley, 1974.

Sugirtharajah, Sharada. *Imagining Hinduism: A Postcolonial Perspective*. London: Routledge, 2003.

Suthers, Albert Edward. "Arab and Hindu: A Study in Mentality." *Muslim World* 21, no. 2 (1931): 143–150.

———. "East and West: A Study in Irenics." *Journal of Religion* 12, no. 2 (1932): 230–241.

Sweetman, Will. "Unity and Plurality: Hinduism and the Religions of India in Early European Scholarship." *Religion* 31, no. 3 (2001): 209–224.

Tagore, Rabindranath. *Towards Universal Man*. New York: Asia Publishing House, 1961.

Thomas, Frederic C. *Calcutta Poor: Elegies on Urban Poverty*. Armonk, N.Y.: M. E. Sharpe, 1997.

Tosh, John. *The Pursuit of History: Aims, Methods and New Directions in the Study of Modern History*. Harlow: Longman, 2002.

Townsend, Mary Evelyn, and Walter Consuelo Langsam. *European Colonial Expansion since 1871*. Chicago: J. B. Lippincott, 1941.

Trautmann, Thomas R. *Aryans and British India*. Berkeley: University of California Press, 1997.

Urban, Hugh B. *The Economics of Ecstasy: Tantra, Secrecy, and Power in Colonial Bengal*. New York: Oxford University Press, 2001.

———. "Songs of Ecstasy: Mystics, Minstrels, and Merchants in Colonial Bengal." *Journal of the American Oriental Society* 123, no. 3 (2003): 493–519.

Urquhart, W. S. *Pantheism and the Value of Life, with Special Reference to Indian Philosophy*. London: Epworth Press, 1919.

———. *The Vedānta and Modern Thought*. London: Humphrey Milford, 1928.

Valpey, Kenneth Russell. *Attending Krishna's Image: Chaitanya Vaishnava Murti-Seva as Devotional Truth*. New York: Routledge, 2006.

van der Veer, Peter. *Imperial Encounters: Religion and Modernity in India and Britain.* Princeton, N.J.: Princeton University Press, 2001.

———. "Religion in South Asia." *Annual Review of Anthropology* 31 (2002): 173–187.

Vijay, Pinch. "Bhakti and the British Empire." *Past and Present* 179, no. 1 (2003): 159–196.

Waardenburg, Jean Jacques. *Muslim Perceptions of Other Religions: A Historical Survey.* New York: Oxford University Press, 1999.

Ward, William. *A View of the History, Literature, and Religion of the Hindoos; Including Translations from Their Principal Works.* 2 vols. London: Committee of the Baptist Missionary Society, 1817.

———. *A View of the History, Literature and Mythology of the Hindoos: Including a Minute Description of Their Manners and Customs, and Translations from Their Principal Works.* 2 vols. Serampore: Mission Press, 1818.

———. *A View of the History, Literature, and Religion of the Hindoos and Translations of Their Principal Works.* 2 vols. London: Kingsbury, Parbury, and Allen, 1822.

Wilkins, William Joseph. *Modern Hinduism, Being an Account of the Religion and Life of the Hindus in Northern India*: T. Fisher Unwin: London, 1887; rpt. New Delhi: Book Faith India, 1999.

Wink, Andre. *Al-Hind: The Making of the Indo-Islamic World.* Vol. 2. Boston: Brill Academic Publishers, 2002.

Woodhead, Linda, Paul Fletcher, Hiroko Kawanami, and David Smith, eds. *Religions in the Modern World: Traditions and Transformations.* London: Routledge, 2002.

Young, Katherine K. "Women in Hinduism." In *Today's Woman in World Religions*, edited by Arvind Sharma, 77–136. Albany: State University of New York Press, 1994.

Young, Richard Fox. *Resistant Hinduism: Sanskrit Sources on Anti-Christian Apologetics.* Vienna: De Nobili Research Library, 1981.

Young, Robert J. C. *Postcolonialism: An Historical Introduction.* Oxford: Blackwell, 2001.

Zavos, John. *The Emergence of Hindu Nationalism in India.* Delhi: Oxford University Press, 2000.

Zetland, Lawrence, Second Marquess of. *Essayez: The Memoirs of Lawrence, Second Marquess of Zetland.* London: John Murray, 1956.

Index

Note: Material in figures is indicated by italic page numbers.